Management

Theory and Practice

Edited by **Gerard Griffin**
Monash University, Australia

Management

"Theory and

Practice

Moving to a New Era

First published 1998 by
MACMILLAN EDUCATION AUSTRALIA PTY LTD
627 Chapel Street, South Yarra 3141

Associated companies and representatives
throughout the world

National Library of Australia
cataloguing in publication data

Management theory and practice : moving to a new era.

Bibliography.
ISBN 0 7329 5045 7.

1. Management – Congresses. 2. Management – Research –
Congresses. I. Griffin, Gerard. II. Australian and New
Zealand Academy of Management. III ANZAM '97 (1997 :
Melbourne, Vic.).

658

Typeset in Adobe Garamond by
Witchcraft Colour, South Melbourne

Printed in Hong Kong

Contents

v

List of contributors

Bruce Acutt, Faculty of Business, Central Queensland University

Alexander J. Alexopoulos, Department of Management, Monash University

Bruce J. Avolio, Centre for Leadership Studies, State University of New York, Binghamton

Kyle Bruce, Department of Economics, University of Wollongong

John Chapman, Queensland Horticulture Institute, Department of Primary Industry, Queensland

Max Coulthard, Department of Management, Monash University

Kevin Daniels, Sheffield University Management School

Cathy Fisher, Department of Management, University of Tasmania

G. Richard Gates, Department of Marketing and Management, University of New England

Fiona Graetz, Bowater School of Management and Marketing, Deakin University

Gerard Griffin, Department of Management, Monash University

Dallas Hanson, Department of Management, University of Tasmania

James D. Hunter, Department of Marketing and Management, University of New England

Kevin Jarvie, Melbourne Business School, University of Melbourne

Boris Kabanoff, Department of Management, Queensland University of Technology

David Lamond, Macquarie Graduate School of Management, Macquarie University

Helen Lange, Macquarie Graduate School of Management, Macquarie University

Ann Lawrence, Bowater School of Management and Marketing, Deakin University

Geoffrey Lewis, Melbourne Business School, University of Melbourne

Johanna Macneil, Bowater School of Management and Marketing, Deakin University

John McWilliam, Bowater School of Management and Marketing, Deakin University

Stephanie Miller, Department of Management, Victoria University of Technology

Lindsay Nelson, Department of Management, University of Tasmania

Paul L. Nesbit, Department of Management, University of Wollongong

Peter O'Neill, Department of Management, Monash University

Ken W. Parry, Department of Human Resource Management, University of Southern Queensland

Ian Ramsay, Faculty of Law, University of Melbourne

Amrik S. Sohal, Department of Management, Monash University

Peter Standen, Department of Management, Edith Cowan University

Milé Terziovski, Department of Management, Monash University

Phyllis Tharenou, Department of Management, Monash University

Edward Vaughan, Department of Management, Monash University

Rhett H. Walker, Department of Management, University of Tasmania

Li-Anne Woo, School of Banking and Finance, University of New South Wales

Introduction

Gerard Griffin

This book brings together a selection of the contributions to the 11th International Conference of the Australian and New Zealand Academy of Management (ANZAM), held at Monash University, Melbourne, Australia from 3 to 6 December 1997. The papers in this book were selected both for their excellence and for their relevance to the theme of the Conference, which was "Management Theory and Practice: Moving to a New Era".

Management practices do indeed appear to have moved to a 'New Era'. Intensifying global competitive pressures and rapid technological changes, especially in information technology and communications, are just two of the influences combining to produce radical changes in the nature and structure of business, and indeed in the meaning and process of work itself. Management practices, and the theories upon which such practices are based, must respond rapidly to these changes so that the possibilities offered by this new era may be best grasped, and the challenges which it presents may be most appropriately met.

The 11th ANZAM Conference presented an ideal opportunity for over 300 management academics to discuss, debate and analyse the implications of these new practices. A wide range of papers were presented in the six conference streams: Strategic Management; Workplace Management; Organisational Behaviour and Culture; General Management; Social Issues in Management; and Management History, Theory and Education. The nineteen papers are drawn from these streams. The contributions in Section A focus on theory and education. Lamond's paper, Back to the Future: Lessons from the Past for a New Management Era, seeks guidance for the future from Henri Fayol's ideas about managerial work. While acknowledging that Fayol's work has been described by one prominent theorist as "folklore", Lamond seeks to rekindle interest in this work by focusing on what he perceives as insights in Fayol's ideas that are relevant to the new era of management.

Bruce's paper is titled Economists' Evolving Conceptualisation of Management: Opening the Black Box. He argues that a journey through the history of economic thought reveals that economists across the spectrum of thought and ideology have considered the coordinating role of management as crucial to the processes of generating and sustaining competitive advantages and to the creation of wealth. The paper concludes that the recent contribution of evolutionary economists and their 'conversation' with strategic management scholars owe a great debt to earlier economic thinkers.

In *Towards a More Integrative Cross-Functional Approach to Management Education,* Walker and his colleagues argue that management education that develops a deep understanding of one or more discipline areas, but does not encourage students to see connections between the courses that they study, may not meet current organisational needs. They hold that the present organisational trend towards agility and flexibility demands not only that employees be equipped with necessary technical knowledge, but that they must be able to integrate and use that knowledge in a creative manner. This is supported by findings of the recent Karpin Report. They suggest that a possible remedy for a too-specialised approach lies in integrated assessment patterns, with an emphasis on attitude change and integrative ability rather than a revolutionary alteration of the knowledge base.

The four papers in Section B offer perspectives on leadership and teams. In *Examining a Full Range Leadership Development System* Avolio reviews the conceptualisation and measurement of a "full range" of leadership styles. He outlines and analyses multiple dimensions of leadership at three distinct levels of analysis: individual, group and organisational culture. He concludes his overviewof recent research in leadership by highlighting promising areas for future research.

Parry argues, in *How to Use the Grounded Theory Method to Research Leadership,* that this theory method has not characterised the study of leadership to date. He contends that there is a strong argument that, because leadership can be viewed as a process of social influence, the grounded theory method is suitable for analysing leadership. He postulates that this theory is underutilised because the relevant literature is not strong on detailing how it may be used to research the social influence processes of leadership. This article goes some way toward redressing that perceived shortfall by proposing some procedures and considerations by which the grounded theory analysis of leadership can be undertaken validly and reliably.

The need for better practices in recruitment and team formation is evident in both the private and public sector, as both sectors become more competitive. To maximise employee productivity, the selection of individuals for specific job types and the placement of these individuals with other employees, demands careful consideration. In *The Relevance of the Team Management IndexÆ for Recruitment and Teams in an R&D Environment* Chapman and Acutt examine the use of a behaviour based personality test, the Team Management Index (TMI) which identifies preferred work styles in individuals. They apply the Index to three generic positions in a public research and development organisation and conclude that, if used correctly, the TMI can be a useful tool for team building.

Miller's paper, *The Management of Teams and Technology in Small Organisations: Moving to a New Era?* examines the use of communication and information technologies to support teamwork within small to medium sized organisations in the western metropolitan region of Melbourne. The results of a survey of 156 organisations are presented. Computer-based technologies are regarded as essential contributors to efficiency but, she argues, the benefits of collaborative work offered by these technologies are not being extensively exploited within her survey population. She finds that responses to attitudinal statements indicate that teamworking is associated with improved organisational performance and that organisations using electronic mail report greater satisfaction with their teams than those which do not use electronic mail.

Section C contains a selection of papers focusing on work forms and practices. The contribution from Hunter and Gates, *Outsourcing: 'Functional', 'Fashionable' or 'Foolish'?* analyses the outsourcing phenomenon and questions the rationale for its adoption. Is it a 'blinkered' decision made by managers looking for a 'quick fix' solution in order to meet performance objectives set by their masters; or a decision reached through critical analysis of all the dimensions encompassed by the outsourcing process? They contend that an examination of current management practice and research suggests that managers are ill prepared to undertake the critical assessment required to fully comprehend the dimensions of outsourcing. Their paper discusses these issues and their implications, urging caution in the unquestioning adoption of management fads that are short on critical thought and long on ideological rhetoric.

Lamond et al examine *Contexts, Cultures and Forms of Teleworking*. They note that the fusion of information and communication technologies is creating a radical change in the ways we do business, and even in the way we understand the concept of work. Teleworking is one of a suite of so-called flexible work practices now gaining widespread acceptance, but it appears to be favoured more as an idea rather than as a practice. This paper proposes a conceptual model for understanding the differential incidence of teleworking between companies and between countries, and for understanding the various forms that telework can take.

In *Individual - Organisational Value Congruence in Human Resource Practitioners* Lawrence examines the extent to which the individual values of Australian human resource practitioners are perceived to be congruent with those of their employing organisations. Findings indicate that this occupational group place high importance on the individual Clan and Adhocracy values ('developmental humanism') and Market values and low importance on Hierarchy values ('utilitarian instrumentalism'). By contrast, human resource practitioners in Australia perceive organisational values in practice to be more consistent with Hierarchy and Market values than Clan and Adhocracy values. Consequently, human resource practitioners experienced low levels of individual - organisational value congruence. The implications of these findings for organisational strategy and the roles of human resource practitioners are briefly discussed.

The final paper in this Section, O'Neill and Sohal's *Business Process Reengineering: Application And Success In Australia* presents the results of a study investigating the extent of Australian thinking and experience with Business Process Reengineering (BPR). The data for the study was gathered through a postal questionnaire survey which was mailed to 535 of Australia's top businesses. The findings of the survey are compared with earlier studies on BPR conducted in the United States and the United Kingdom/Europe. The paper also provides recommendations for mangers which are seen as important for successfully implementation of BPR projects.

Section D contains a selection of papers dealing with strategy and performance. The ability to 'think strategically' depends on the interaction between situational factors in the organisational setting and the characteristics of the individuals involved. The paper by Graetz and her colleagues, *Encouraging Strategic Thinking at 'Communications Co.': Linking Behavioural Styles to Creativity,* considers two questions. Does the decision style of middle managers at Communications Co. relate to their ability to think strategically? What is the effect of group dynamics as an intervening variable in the quality of scenario planning? While the results do not indicate a clear link between decision styles and level of creativity, group dynamics clearly acted as an intervening variable. The study also found that behavioural styles are strongly influenced by the prevailing workplace culture.

Moving to a New Era in International Strategic Management: Identifying Export Success Factors of Australian Entrepreneurial Record Companies by Alexopoulos and Coulthard uses five dimensions (innovativeness, proactiveness, competitive aggressiveness, risk taking, and autonomy) to develop an entrepreneurship profile of 20 Victorian-based record companies. The study found those record companies who had an 'entrepreneurial orientation' were higher export performers than conservative-orientated companies. Various 'best practice' firms were identified and a profile of key export success factors developed. Overall, this study provides a useful starting point for business practitioners exploring strategic opportunities overseas.

The pressure to increase the value created for shareholders has led many Australian companies to review their diversification strategies. In their paper *The Relationship Between Diversification and Economic Performance: The Australian Experience* Lewis and Jarvie, covering the period 1985 to 1994, examine the history and types of diversification of 63 of Australia's largest listed companies and analyse whether, in an Australian context, there is a relationship between the type of diversification and performance. Performance is measured using market, economic and accounting measures. The major conclusion of the study is that there was no consistent relationship between the degree of diversification and performance for the companies studied.

Terziovsky's *Best Predictors of High Performance Quality Organisations: Evidence From Australia and New Zealand* analyses a large data base of questionnaire responses from Australian and New Zealand manufacturing firms. Multiple discriminant analysis was used to explore the differences between firms grouped according to their level of organisational peformance. The study concludes that high peforming organisations focus on the 'softer' quality practices, such as breaking down barriers between departments and continuous improvement, while low performing organisations tended to focus on the 'harder' quality practices, such as ISO 9000 certification and benchmarking.

The growing importance of China as a world economic power, and a trading partner to Australia and New Zealand, has been one of the more highly visible changes of recent years. Vaughan's paper, *Going Against Custom: On the Management of Joint Ventures in China,* examines the problems for management of particpation in Sino-Western joint ventures. He argues that explanations based on cultural differences are only partially correct, and that it is necessary to take into account the tensions between Western managements' desire for economic efficiency and Chinese managements' need to accommodate socialist goals such as minimising unemployment.

Section E contains three papers examining ownership, power and advancement. *Takeover Defence Decisions: A Study of the Impact of Management and Large Shareholder Ownership* by Lange and her colleagues seeks to establish what form of management and ownership structure are exhibited by firms that propose and subsequently adopt anti-takeover amendments in a firm's article of associations. They conclude that the collective proportion of shareholdings of directors is of greater significance than the actual structure of the board itself. They also suggest that external monitoring by large shareholders is useful to ensure fair and proper decisions on the part of the board.

Nesbit and Kabanoff's paper is titled *An investigation of the relationship of power and cognition of organisational elites, using computer-aided content analysis of annual reports.* They apply the metamorphic theory of power to the study of organisational elites, specifically the CEO and the board of directors. Two CEO power factors and three board power factors were developed as measures of CEO and board power. Using computer-aided content analysis of annual reports a range of hypothesised relationships of elite power and cognition are explored

The final paper, *Tharenou's Predictors of Advancing in Management: Advancers Versus Nonadvancers,* explores career progression in management. Using longitudinal samples of three cohort pairs, consisting of those who had advanced versus those who had not advanced in management, predictors of advancement are examined at three increasingly higher transition points. Entry to management was explained by career tournament wins, individuals' managerial traits, and gender-linked social factors. Advancement from initial to middle management continued to be explained by traits and gender-linked social factors, and also by promotion opportunities and investments in human capital. Advancement from mid to upper levels was explained by returns on earlier challenging work assignments, but also by gender-linked effects in relation to promotion and job moves, and male managerial hierarchies.

Overall, these papers contributed to significant debates, discussions and disagreements at ANZAM '97. Hopefully, they will engender similar responses from the broader management community.

Section A
Theory
and education

Back to the future: Lessons from the past for a new management era

David Lamond

Abstract

Henri Fayol's (1949) ideas about managerial work have been dismissed as 'folklore' (Mintzberg, 1973/1980; 1975/1989). At the same time, despite ongoing criticism by Mintzberg (1973/1980; 1975/1989) and others, it has been argued that Fayol's management functions 'still represent the most useful way of conceptualising the manager's job' (Carroll and Gillen, 1987: 38). This paper is designed to rekindle interest in Fayol's work, by way of more balanced and considered reflection on his ideas. In doing so, the paper re-presents the key concepts of Fayol's (1949) work with a focus on the insights it provides for the 'new era of management'.

> ... that is what learning is. You suddenly understand something you've understood all your life, but in a new way.
> 'Doris Lessing, The Four-Gated City, 1969'

Introduction

Fayol's (1949) treatise on General and Industrial Management is a rather thin work in terms of its size but not in terms of the impact that it has had on managers and the practice of management around the world, either directly or indirectly. Indeed, Fayol has been described as 'the greatest of the European pioneers of management' Urwick (1949: v). Fayol's work has also been described as 'folklore' (Mintzberg, 1973/1980; 1975/1989) which does not have contemporary relevance. More recently, it has been argued that Fayol's management functions 'still represent the most useful way of conceptualizing the manager's job' (Carroll and Gillen, 1987: 38). Nonetheless, Fayol's management functions continue be presented in the literature and in the classroom more as a matter of historical curiosity than for any insights it may offer.

This paper re-examines Fayol's (1949) five-fold delineation of managerial functions: planning, organising, commanding, co-ordinating and controlling; and finds that the central criticisms—inaccuracy and irrelevance—are unfounded. It is argued that these criticisms are based on a combination of misrepresentation and misunderstanding of the central ideas. It is concluded that Fayol's contribution remains relevant for management theory and practice.

Fayol on Management

Fayol (1949: 3) identified six groups of activities or essential functions to which all industrial undertakings give rise—technical, commercial, financial, security, accounting, and managerial activities. His primary concern is with the last of these, the managerial activities, which are 'concerned with drawing up the broad plan of operations of the business, with assembling personnel, co-ordinating and harmonizing effort and activity' (Fayol, 1949: 5). For Fayol (1949: 5-6)

> To manage is to forecast and plan, to organize, to command, to co-ordinate and to control. To foresee and provide means examining the future and drawing up the plan of action. To organize means building up the dual structure, material and human, of the undertaking. To command means maintaining activity among the personnel. To co-ordinate means binding together, unifying and harmonizing all activity and effort. To control means seeing that everything occurs in conformity with established rule and expressed command.

Fayol (1949: 19-20) identifies the 14 principles of management which he has most frequently applied, including the more commonly known division of work, authority, unity of command, centralisation, and scalar chain (line of authority); and then proceeds to elaborate them. They do not, he says, constitute an exhaustive list, since it has no precise limits, but they are a set of principles which 'aim at the success of associations of individuals and at the satisfying of economic interests' (Fayol, 1949: 41-42). The rest of Fayol's work (1949: 43-110) is taken up with detailing what he calls the elements of management—planning, organising, commanding, co-ordinating and controlling.

Planning

Planning is 'to assess the future and make provision for it' (Fayol, 1949:43). The plan of action—'the result envisaged, the line of action to be followed, the stages to go through, and the methods to use'—is at once the chief manifestation and most effective tool of planning (Fayol, 1949: 43). It is in taking the initiative for the plan of action that managers carry out the managerial function.

Fayol (1949: 45) recognises the benefits of what we would call today 'benchmarking', saying that 'it would be most useful for those whose concern is management to know how experienced managers go about drawing up their plans'. He also says that good specimen plans should be made generally available (Fayol, 1949: 51).

Fayol sees planning as more than 'the document' though. Planning is a process which requires important personal and interpersonal competencies, including those related to managing the organisation's internal stakeholders. In order to achieve a 'good' plan, Fayol (1949: 50-51) says the personnel in charge (managers) need

- the art of handling people (to gain active cooperation of all those involved in the planning process)
- considerable energy
- moral courage (to meet the obligation of making every preparation and seeking out optimum results rather than producing a plan aimed at minimum exposure to criticism)
- some continuity of tenure (so as to develop corporate knowledge and understanding)
- professional competence and general business knowledge

Organising

To organise is to provide the undertaking 'with everything useful to its functioning: raw materials, tools, capital, personnel' (Fayol, 1949: 53). Fayol (1949: 53-54) divides organisation into material and human organisation and focuses on the latter. He then lists the managerial duties associated with organising as

- Ensuring the plan is judiciously prepared and strictly carried out
- Matching the resources to the plan
- Leadership ('a single, competent energetic guiding authority', 'unity of command', control, supervision)
- Harmonising and co-ordinating activities
- Decision making
- Job analysis and design; staffing selection
- Empowerment (encouraging a 'liking for initiative and responsibility')
- Performance management—fair and appropriate remuneration; maintenance of discipline and sanctions against faults and errors; subordination of individual interests to the general interest
- Fighting against excess regulations, red tape and paper control.

Fayol devotes nearly 40 percent of his book to issues associated with organising. To the extent that he sees having the right people with the right skills in the right jobs, he spends much of the time here discussing the kinds of qualities managers and employees should possess and the kinds of education and training and development programs that will contribute to those qualities. In so far as Fayol saw the task of the book as presenting an argument for the importance of management as an organisational activity and making a contribution to the theory of management as it would be taught, this is not surprising.

Fayol (1949: 60-76) details his appreciation of the relationship between size, structure and processes in organisations as he discusses the different kinds of members of the 'body corporate'. It is worthy of note that his preference is for a 'flat' structure with, for example, only two layers of management between the lowest level of employees and the CEO (Fayol, 1949: 55). The general manager (or general manager group where an organisation is sufficiently large) is the executive authority drawing up the plan of action, selecting personnel, determining performance, ensuring and controlling the execution of all activities.

In his discussion of the search for improvements, Fayol (1949: 64-65) appears to foreshadow the total quality management (TQM) movement. Managers, he says, must have an active, unrelenting intention to effect improvements. The method of effecting these improvements includes 'observing, collecting and filing facts, interpreting them, trying out experiments if need be, and from the study as a whole, deducing rules which, under the manager's impetus, may be introduced into business practice.

Fayol (1949: 57) argues that beyond the size and shape of the organisation, what is more important is the substance:

> to create an organization it is not enough to group people and distribute duties; there must be knowledge of how to adapt the organic whole to requirements, how to find essential personnel and put each where he can be of most service; there are in sum numerous qualities needed.

Here, Fayol (1949: 78) points to the value of the organisation chart as a 'precious managerial instrument', not simply as a statement of what is, but because of its value when modifications to the organisation, as a result of changes in circumstances or people, become necessary. As Fayol (1949: 78) says, 'any modification in one part of the organization can have wide repercussions and influence the general running of the whole'. It should be noted that, in Fayol's (1949: 78) organisation chart and its accompanying documents, not only 'the whole of the personnel is shown, the constitution and demarcation of each department, who is in each position, the superiors from whom an employee takes orders, and the subordinates to whom he gives them …[but also] … the individual value of employees …their functions, … the physical limits of their responsibility, … [and] …who shall deputise for them.'

Command

The *mission* of command is to set the organisation going (Fayol, 1949: 97). The *object* of command is to get the optimum return from all employees, while the *art* of command rests on certain personal qualities and a knowledge of general principles of management (Fayol, 1949: 97). To the extent that managers aim at 'making unity, energy, initiative and loyalty prevail among the personnel' (Fayol 1949: 98) modern writers would more properly describe this managerial function as concerned with motivation, leadership and empowerment.

According to Fayol (1949: 98-103) one exercises command through a thorough knowledge of the personnel; by elimination of the incompetent; by balancing the interests of the organisation and its employees through a 'strong sense of duty and of equity' (Fayol, 1949: 100); through good example; through periodic audit of the organisation; through well developed organisational communication systems; through delegation of tasks; and through adopting the principles of a learning organisation (developing initiative among subordinates 'by allowing them the maximum share of activity consistent with their position and capability, *even at the cost of some mistakes'* (Fayol, 1949: 103, emphasis added).

Co-ordination

In co-ordination, we find Fayol's commitment to the principles of balance and contingent action. For Fayol (1949: 103), to co-ordinate is to 'harmonize all the activities of a concern so as to facilitate its working and its success …. to accord things and actions their rightful proportions, and to adapt means to ends'. Co-ordination is achieved, *inter alia,* by the 'precious instrument' of team meetings (weekly conferences of departmental heads). It is effected generally by 'combined action on the part of general management which supervises the whole, plus local managements whose efforts are directed towards the successful working of each particular part' (Fayol 1949:106).

Control

Control means 'verifying whether everything occurs in conformity with the plan adopted, the instructions issued and principles established' (Fayol, 1949:107). To the extent that the objective is to 'point out weaknesses and errors in order to rectify them and prevent recurrence … to contribute to the smooth working of each department in particular and of the concern in general' (Fayol, 1949: 107-108), there is a strong sense of total quality management and the learning organisation in Fayol's principles here. Control is a 'precious auxiliary' to management because it can provide necessary data that supervision may fail to furnish and because it provides against undesirable surprises (Fayol, 1949: 109).

This section has outlined Fayol's (1949) delineation of the managerial functions of planning, organising, command, co-ordination and control. The next section will examine the major criticisms of this approach and evaluate the veracity of their claims.

Commentary on Fayol

Hales (1993: 3) says that, if all philosophy is a set of footnotes to Plato, then management theory can be seen as a reply to Fayol's original memo. Part of the reply has been critical while another part has been reaffirming. Both parts of the reply are considered. The reader is then taken back to the original as the point of reference making a judgement as to reasonableness of the replies.

Fayol's Critics

Of Fayol's critics, Henry Mintzberg (1973/80; 1975/1989; 1979) is probably most well known. In *The Nature of Managerial Work,* Mintzberg (1973/1980) dismissed as 'folklore' Fayol's (1949) view of managerial work. This work, Mintzberg (1973/1980) said, is not about planning, organising, commanding, co-ordinating and controlling. Rather, it is what managers do. Other authors who share this criticism include Carlson (1951), Sayles (1964) and Stewart (1983).

Mintzberg (1973: 9) began his critique of Fayol by referring to the classical school of management as concerned with managerial work 'in terms of a set of composite functions' and characterised Fayol as the father of this school. Mintzberg (1973: 10) then claimed that the functional categories were not useful because they cannot be linked to specific activities:

> Which of these activities may be called planning, and which may be called organizing, coordinating or controlling? Indeed, what relationship exists between these four words and managers' activities? These four words do not, in fact, describe the actual work of managers at all. They describe certain vague objectives of managerial work.

Sayles (1964: ix) is also keen to distance himself from the classical school, whose concepts he describes as 'often abstruse with no obvious or definable referent in human behaviour'. Carlson (1951: 24), is similarly critical of the categories:

> If we ask a managing director when he is co-ordinating, or how much co-ordination he has been doing during a day he would not know, and even the most highly skilled observer would not know either. The same holds true for the concepts of planning, command, organization and control...

In a later book, Mintzberg (1979: 9) wrote that

> The 'principles of management' school of thought, fathered by Henri Fayol
> … was concerned primarily with formal authority, in effect with the role
> of direct supervision in the organization. These writers popularized such
> terms as *unity of command* (the notion that a 'subordinate' should have
> a single 'superior'), *scalar chain* (the direct line of this command from chief
> executive through successive superiors and subordinates to worker), and
> *span of control* (the number of subordinates reporting to a single superior.

Mintzberg (1979: 9, 319) also criticised Fayol's (1949: 34-36) concept of the
scalar chain because the idea of a direct line of command from superior to
subordinate and the transmission of communications up and down these lines
of command did not reflect the reality (indeed necessity) of cross
functional/divisional communication.

Thus the essence of the critique against Fayol (and others said to be of the
classical/principles of management school) is that he offers a set of prescriptions
about what managers ought to do, which bear no relationship to the reality
of what managers actually do.

Responding to the Critics

As well as his critics, Fayol also has his 'champions', such as Carroll and
Gillen (1987: 48), who conclude from their evaluation that Fayol's
characterisation of management still represents 'the most useful way of
conceptualizing the manager's job'. Defences of Fayol's taxonomy have been
of two kinds—one which says that the empirical evidence is there, if one
searches for it, and the other which says that the absence of the empirical
evidence does not really matter.

An example of the first defence is given by Mahoney, Jerdee, and Carroll
(1963/1987: 40) who reported a work study in which they were able to
relate specific manager behaviours to management functions by simply
asking the managers why they were carrying out specific activities. In an
example of the second, Hales (1993: 3) responded to the critics simply by
stating that they were wide of the mark—Fayol did not aim to list specific
managerial *behaviours* but to set out the requisite management *functions* of
an undertaking. In this regard, Tsoukas (1994) has argued that Mintzberg
and Fayol dealt with issues arising at a different ontological layer of
management such that their views are complementary rather than antithetical.

While these responses are reasonable of themselves, they still do not deal
effectively with the lingering idea that Fayol's (1949) work remains as some
kind of list of admonitions, as the product of an 'armchair theorist'. It is to
Fayol (1949) himself that the paper now turns for the strongest defence
against his critics.

The 'Original Memo'

Fayol (1949: 19-42) devoted considerable space to his 'principles of management', but if Fayol is the father of the 'principles of management' school, I imagine he would see it as a 'bastard child', since his own treatment of the functions of management went much beyond the several notions attributed to them. Indeed, I concur with Carroll and Gillen's (1987: 48) observation primarily because he was not just concerned with these matters and, in fact, anticipated many of the so-called 'modern' management ideas.

Unlike many of those who followed him, Fayol (1949: 6) recognised that

> Management … is neither an exclusive privilege nor a particular responsibility of the head or senior members of the business; it is an activity spread, like all other activities between head and members of the body corporate …. but it has such a large place in the part played by higher managers that sometimes this part seems exclusively managerial.

Fayol's (1949: 15-16) appreciation of his work was somewhat more circumspect than the claims of prescription levelled by others. Recognising the importance of an accepted theory ('a collection of principles, rules, methods, procedures, tried and checked by general experience') to the development of management teaching, he summarised his efforts in the following terms:

> It is a case of setting it going, starting general discussion—that is what I am trying to do by publishing this survey, and I hope that a theory will emanate from it.

Indeed, far from promoting a 'one best way' approach, Fayol (1949: 19) stated early in his work that he adopted the term 'principles' out of preference 'whilst dissociating it from any suggestion of rigidity, for there is nothing rigid or absolute in management affairs, it is all a question of proportion'.

It is also clear from Fayol's work that, to the extent that his is a metaphorical view of organisations (*cf.* e.g. Bolman and Deal, 1991; Morgan, 1986), he offered a systems based, organic model of organisations within which to frame his analysis. This is exemplified in a number of locations throughout the book. He noted early in his work that 'there is nothing rigid or absolute in management affairs (p 19) and discussed the importance of contingency planning. Fayol utilised the biological metaphor for the organisation, referring on several occasions specifically to the 'social organism' (p 24) and, in anticipation of Morgan's (1986) organism and brain metaphors, the centralisation of control in the 'organism' (pp 33, 69). Fayol (1949: 20) even used the term 'corps social' (translated as 'body corporate') to refer to all those engaged in a given corporate activity. It is therefore ironic that Morgan (1986: 25-29) equated Fayol's approach as more consistent with a bureaucratic machine metaphor. Indeed, Fayol (1949: 57-58) expressed concern at the use of the machine metaphor because it failed to acknowledge the importance of intermediates as generators of power and ideas.

Fayol considered 'intermediates' when he discussed the limitations of the chain of command. Rather than being blind to the concerns expressed by Mintzberg (1979: 9), Fayol (1949: 34) said that because there are many activities whose success turns on speedy execution, respect for the lines of authority must be reconciled with the need for swift action. Indeed, he stated that departing needlessly from the line of authority is an error, 'but it is an even greater one to keep to it when detriment to the business ensues' (Fayol, 1949: 36). In fact, he argued that the chief cause of the rigid adherence to the lines of authority had more to with 'insufficient executive capacity on the part of those in charge' than fear of responsibility on the part of the subordinates (Fayol 1949: 36).

His most obvious preference for the organism metaphor came when he discussed the managerial task of organising and said that 'to create a useful organization, it is not enough to group people and distribute duties; there must be knowledge of how to adapt the organic whole to requirements, how to find essential personnel and put each where he *(sic)* can be of most service' (p 57)

Further, while Fayol (1949: 66-70) declared his admiration for Taylor as a person, he expressed significant reservations regarding Taylor's 'scientific or functional management' and would hardly count himself as an adherent. This is significant for understanding Fayol's approach to the management processes embedded in the organisational framework. Instead of being wedded to an approach to management characterised by 'time and motion', Fayol (1949: 84*ff*) waxed eloquent on the 'misuse of mathematics', paraphrasing Comte's observation that 'mathematical facts are the simplest, least complex, and most 'crude' of phenomena, the most abstract, barren and remote from reality in contradistinction to social facts, which are the most complex and subtle'.

Clearly what Fayol displayed here is more than just a 'principles' approach to management. It is suffused with a sense of management as praxis, as a process embedded in its organisational and broader operating context and which is clearly a *human* endeavour rather than a dispassionate decision-making and order giving activity. Indeed, he introduces his general principles of management with the statement that the 'managerial function finds its only outlet through the members of the organization (body corporate)' (Fayol, 1949: 19). Planning, organising, commanding, co-ordinating and controlling are the ways in which ideas are developed and translated into reality via people. This philosophy was played out in his elaboration of his general principles.

Bases for Misinterpretation

If we see this kind of misinterpretation of Fayol as obvious, why is it apparently so widespread? There appear to be several possible reasons why this is so—

the timing of the translation of Fayol's book; the tendency for latter day scholars to use previous works as 'straw men' to knock down, rather than as foundations upon which to add to the edifice of knowledge; and the reliance on secondary rather than primary sources in the elaboration and appreciation of scholars' theoretical positions.

Fayol's work was published in the United States, largely through the efforts of Luther Urwick, an adherent of the classical school of management (*cf.* Gulick and Urwick, 1937). In the Foreword to *General and Industrial Management,* Urwick described Fayol as a man who, 'applied the scientific approach to problems in every direction' (Urwick, 1949: ix). This was at the time when German sociologist Max Weber's theory of bureaucracy was being translated and popularised by other members of the classical management school. Morgan (1986: 349) suggested that, as a result, Weber's theory of bureaucracy has been interpreted as belonging to the classical school and his theory thus (incorrectly) understood through the lens of classical management theory (see also Lamond, 1990). It would seem that Fayol has been similarly classified with an eye to the messenger rather than the message.

The second reason appears to be that, in their manic determination to make an original contribution to knowledge (a prerequisite to credentials and publication), commentators are inclined to represent earlier theories in a way which best suits commentator's 'new' approach rather than being faithful to the work being represented. It would appear that this is not uncommon in regard to European authors who have been set up as 'straw men' to be knocked down by others in the development of 'new' insights (see, for example, Lamond, 1990; Morgan, 1986: 350; Szasz, 1996: 106, 117-118). Mintzberg (1996/1997) suggested, in talking about the creation of knowledge, that 'that little boy did not have the courage to say that the king wore no clothes; he had the courage to see it. After that, saying it was easy.' One must also have the courage to accurately reflect what one sees.

The third reason appears to be because, on the basis of extensive anecdotal evidence, the majority of academics and students who discuss Fayol's contribution have never actually read *General and Industrial Management* (Fayol, 1949). Instead, these discussants rely on secondary sources, like Mintzberg (1973; 1975/1989), for their appreciation. In classes and discussions with academic colleagues around the world, the most common response to challenges about the contemporary value of Fayol is a sheepish admission that 'Well, no, I haven't actually *read* his book'. This omission enables commentators like Mintzberg to draw their conclusions with impunity.

Conclusion: Lessons for the New Era of Management

At a time when we are being encouraged to examine new approaches to management theory and practice, we should remain cognisant of the contribution that existing theory and practice can make to the so-called 'new era' of the next century. This paper has examined the work of Henri Fayol (1949) and concluded that, when the 'straw man' is swept away, his insights remain useful as a basis for understanding management and managerial behaviour. Indeed, given that the work was written in France nearer the beginning of this century (in 1916), it is a surprisingly 'current' text which deals in what writers would describe as an enlightened way with such recent 'discoveries' as employee participation, profit sharing, leadership and empowerment. We have reached a time when we are being encouraged, inappropriately, to throw off the shackles of old theories and embrace new paradigms (cf. Lamond, 1996). We would be better advised to re-read Fayol and others of our primary sources and so, to paraphrase Doris Lessing (1969), be led to an understanding of something that we have understood all our lives in a new way.

References

Bolman, L. and Deal, T. 1997. Reframing Organisations (2nd Ed) San Francisco: Jossey-Bass.

Carroll, S.J. & Gillen, D.J. 1987. Are the classical management functions useful in describing managerial work? Academy of Management Review, 12(1), 38-51.

Carlson, S. 1951. Executive Behaviour: A Study of the Workload and Working Methods of Managing Directors. Stockholm: Strombergs.

Fayol, H. 1949. General and Industrial Management. (trans. C Storrs). London: Pitman.

Gulick, L. and Urwick, L. (Eds.) 1937. Papers on the Science of Administration. New York: Columbia University Press.

Hales, C. 1993. Managing Through Organisation. London: Routledge.

Lamond, D.A. 1990. The irrational use of Weber's ideal types. Australian Journal of Public Administration, 49(4), 464-473.

Lamond, D.A. 1996. Karpin on management: Is that all managers should be doing? Journal of the Australian and New Zealand Academy of Management, 2(1), 21-35.

Mahoney, T.A., Jerdee, T.H. and Carroll, S.J. 1963. Development of managerial performance: A research approach. Cincinnati: South-Western; cited in Carroll, S.J. & Gillen, D.J. 1987. Are the classical management functions useful in describing managerial work? Academy of Management Review, 12(1), 38-51.

Mintzberg, H. 1973. The Nature of Managerial Work. New York: Harper & Row.

Mintzberg, H. 1975/1989. The manager's job: Folklore and fact. Harvard Business Review, 53(4), July-August, 49-61; reprinted in Mintzberg, H (1989) Mintzberg on Management: inside our strange world of organizations. New York: The Free Press, 9-24.

Mintzberg, H. 1979. The Structuring of Organizations. Englewood Cliffs, NJ: Prentice Hall

Mintzberg, H. 1980. The Nature of Managerial Work. Englewood Cliffs, NJ: Prentice Hall.

Mintzberg, H. 1996/1997. OMT Distinguished Scholar Address, Academy of Management Conference, Cincinnati, August; cited in Organisation and Management Theory Division Newsletter, Winter.

Morgan, G. 1986. Images of Organisation. Newbury Park, Ca.: Sage.

Sayles, L.R. 1964. Managerial Behaviour: Administration in Complex Organisations. New York: McGraw-Hill

Szasz, T. 1996. The Meaning of Mind: Language, Morality and Neuroscience. Westport, Conn.: Praeger.

Tsoukas, H. 1994. What is management? An outline of a metatheory. British Journal of Management, 5, 289-301.

Urwick, L. 1949. Foreword. In H. Fayol General and Industrial Management. (trans. C Storrs). London: Pitman, v-xvi

Economists' Evolving Conceptualisations of Management: Opening the 'Black Box'

Kyle Bruce

Abstract

This paper demonstrates that the recent mutual interest shown by evolutionary economists and strategic management scholars toward each other's work is not a novel development A panoramic journey through the history of economic thought reveals that economists across the spectrum of thought and ideology have considered the coordinating role of management as crucial to the processes of generating and sustaining competitive advantages and to the creation of wealth. The paper concludes by acknowledging that the recent contribution of evolutionary economists and their 'conversation' with strategic management scholars owe a great debt to earlier economic thinkers.

Introduction

Radner (1992) observed that 'quantitatively as well as functionally, 'managing' has become a significant activity in our economy'. Further, he asserted that:

> (t)his function has not escaped the attention of our colleagues in schools of business and management, where many courses are devoted to the subject. The pure science of economics, however, has been slower to focus on this phenomenon, and pure theory even slower (Radner, 1992: 1383).

The theoretical lag that Radner highlighted is reflected, to some extent, in the apparent exodus of both undergraduate and postgraduate students from economics to business and management departments, and in the concurrent expansion of economics curricula into business or management areas. As management economist John Kay (1991: 60) has observed, '(w)hile business education as a whole has been expanding, the role of formal economics within it has generally been contracting'. Kay added that in the arena of actual business or managerial practice the role of economic theory is limited, there being a widening gap between the study of economics and business practice that is indicative of a failure in communication and probably a failure of relevance by the economics profession. This is manifest, above all, in the fact that although '(e)conomics dominates public policy and every country's chief executive regards his (or her) macroeconomic adviser as a vital aide..., economics has almost no influence on business policy, and only in a small minority of companies does the chief executive have an economic adviser at all' (Kay, 1991: 57).

This may be the case in management practice, but is not quite so in the realm of management thought, particularly in research recently being conducted in the area of strategic management, notably the resource-based view of the firm. Scholars in this emergent field have been and continue to be profoundly influenced by certain strands of economic thought; in particular, the transactions costs and contractual approaches of 'new' institutionalists like Ronald Coase and Oliver Williamson, and the evolutionary approaches of the likes of Richard Nelson and Sidney Winter, William Lazonick, and David Teece (Mahoney & Pandian 1992; Foss, Knudsen & Montgomery 1995). Strategy scholar Nicolai Foss, echoing an earlier observation of Mahoney and Pandian (1992), recently asserted that 'economics is thought of as being able to further 'conversation' within the strategy discipline and management studies in general, rather than to block it' (Foss, 1996: 5). Even an 'icon' in the strategy field, Alfred Chandler, has emphasised the merits of evolutionary economics in understanding firms' organisational capabilities (1992; 1996). It is apparent then, that the interdisciplinary interest is not all unidirectional and that a competence or capabilities perspective on firms and firm strategies is a central feature of evolutionary economics.

This paper demonstrates that despite this apparently recent discovery by management and economics of each other's disciplines and also the general antipathy shown by mainstream economists to concerns of management scholars, not all economists necessarily share the view (inherited from John Stuart Mill) that economic growth emanates from an easily taught and modelled production-function or 'black box' approach (Winter, 1988; Knudsen, 1995). The paper explores the shortcomings of that approach from the viewpoint of strategy scholars and reveals that even within the ranks of the economics mainstream there have been economists interested in the coordinating role of management as they have attempted to paint a more realistic theory of firm behaviour than that which they have inherited from Mill. The paper demonstrates that the fundamental building blocks of evolutionary economics were laid over a half a century ago and that the 'conversation' between the disciplines owes a great debt to economists long since gone. But first, a quick word on the treatment of the firm and management by business schools.

The Business School Approach to the Firm and Management

Peter Drucker and Alfred Chandler have both asserted that any realistic theory of the firm must take into account the dynamics of entrepreneurship and innovation (Drucker, 1992: 9; Chandler, 1992; 1996). This is why Chandler has discounted the potential worth of the transaction costs economics of Ronald Coase and Oliver Williamson to a complete understanding of firm strategy. In this vein, one commentator has observed that while the 'desire of agents to minimize transactions costs through internal organization represents one way in which firms generate cost economies that enhance their profitability and competitive position', a more 'fully developed theory of the firm must, however, account for innovative behaviour, technological change, and, in general, the evolutionary character of the business environment' (Medema, 1994: 38). It will be argued that inroads in this direction were made by economists like Alfred Marshall and Joseph Schumpeter, and that their evolutionary approach developed as a result of placing the entrepreneur, management, and innovation at the forefront of analysis.

In *Scale and Scope*, Alfred Chandler (1990) criticised the economics profession for its lack of explanatory theory for the evolution and dominance of the industrial enterprise. He noted that in the industries at the core of the rapidly growing and industrialising American economy, the critical decisions concerning current operations and the allocation of resources were made by salaried managers of the modern industrial enterprise, not by markets:

The rise and continuing growth of this type of enterprise and its contribution to American economic expansion cannot be fully explained by orthodox economics. For economists of the conventional school a statement that economic growth was paced by a few hierarchical enterprises competing in an oligopolistic manner is a contradiction in terms. For them and for most scholars, bureaucracy means inefficiency and oligopoly means misallocation of resources. Market power did indeed bring oligopoly; yet such power rested far more on the development of organisational capabilities than on creating 'artificial' barriers to the allocative effectiveness of market mechanisms such as patents, advertising, and interfirm agreements (Chandler, 1990: 227).

The long term growth of these enterprises meant that major sectors of the US economy came to be administered through a system of managerial capitalism, where managers with little or no equity made operational and strategic decisions that determined each firm's competitiveness, the prosperity of the industry, and in part, the industrial performance of the national economy (Chandler, 1990: 232).

Chandler believes that the collective histories of these enterprises provide a story of economic growth and transformation. Economists, particularly those of the more traditional mainstream, have not developed a theory of the evolution of the firm as a dynamic organisation. Yet in the story conveyed by Chandler, the modern industrial enterprise played a central role in creating the most technically advanced and fastest growing industries of their day. These industries were in turn the pace-setters of the industrial sectors of their economies - the sector so critical to the growth and transformation of national economies into their modern, urban industrial form. They provided an underlying dynamic in the development of modern industrial capitalism (Chandler, 1990: 593). The core dynamic in this history, according to Chandler, was the organisational capabilities or competences of the enterprise as a unified whole — the collective physical facilities and human skills as they were organised in the enterprise. Only if these were carefully coordinated and integrated by management could the enterprise achieve the economies of scale and scope needed to compete in national and international markets and for continued growth. Such capabilities meant that the basic goal of the modern industrial enterprise became long-term profits based on long-term growth — growth that increased the productivity, and hence the competitive power, which drove the expansion of industrial capitalism (Chandler, 1990: 594).

For Chandler, the one branch of economics adequately dealing with these issues was the evolutionary theory of the firm. What sets these thinkers apart, he believes, is that they place the firm, and its specific and human assets, at the centrepiece of their analysis. The evolutionary approach provided a better understanding of why firms in the past emerged via the process of integrating production and distribution, and also why and how they grew by expansion into new markets. This approach was better equipped to achieve this goal, according to Chandler, because of its emphasis on continuous learning that makes a firm's assets dynamic. For members of the evolutionary approach, practised or learned routines are the essence of a firm's core capabilities or competences. They are crucially acquired in functional activities (production, distribution and marketing, improving existing products and processes, and developing new ones), they are even more importantly acquired in the coordination of these functional activities, and they are essential in the area of strategy: responding to moves by competitors, carrying out the long, costly, and risky process of moving into new markets, and in adjusting to the constantly changing economic, social and political environment (Chandler, 1992: 86; 1996).

Another Harvard Business School stalwart, William Lazonick, in his 1991 volume, *Business Organization and the Myth of the Market Economy*, picked up on Chandler's analysis by explaining the changes in industrial leadership from Britain to the US earlier in this century, and from the US to Japan more recently, in terms of the changing investment strategies and organisational structures of business enterprises in these nations. Like Chandler, he was critical of mainstream economists for their ignorance of, and inability to explain, these developments. Lazonick attacked the shibboleth of neoclassical economists which holds that the analysis of the optimal allocation of scarce resources commences by assuming a given endowment of productive resources and a given technology. Accordingly, these economists fail to inquire how society overcomes such scarcity by changing the quality/quantity of resources that it uses — that is, by developing and utilising its productive resources, questions that were once central to economic analysis. He continued:

> I would argue, moreover, that the propensity of mainstream economists to look first and foremost to market coordination to allocate resources serves as an intellectual barrier to perceiving the changing institutional reality of successful capitalist development; for as history shows, this changing institutional reality is characterized by the growing importance of planned coordination within the business organization and the growing dominance of business organization over the determination of economic outcomes. Through the process of innovation, particular business organizations gain competitive advantage, thus driving the development process. Mainstream economics offers no theory of innovation and no theory of competitive advantage. ...History shows that the driving force of successful capitalist development is not the perfection of the market mechanism but the building of organizational capabilities. ...(W)hat mainstream economists view as 'market failure' I view as 'organizational success' (Lazonick, 1991a: 7-8).

For Lazonick then, as for Chandler, traditional microeconomics, or what Sidney Winter calls 'textbook orthodoxy', has no theory of the innovative business organisation that generates higher quality products at lower unit costs — issues at the heart of the process of economic development (Lazonick, 1991a: 9, 16). As Winter (1988: 171) observed, textbook orthodoxy delivers a theory of the firm mainly for economists who are not really interested in the theory of the firm *per se*. That is, by assuming identical demand and cost conditions, it 'fails to provide a basis for understanding the incentives and processes in business firms that produce technological and organizational change'.

Also relevant for the focus of the present paper is Lazonick's assertion that the failure of mainstream economists to construct a relevant theory of capitalist development cannot be blamed on a lack of theory in the history of economic thought. As he noted; Marx, with his focus on the utilisation of resources; Schumpeter with his focus on the development of the same; and Marshall with his distinction between planned and market coordination in the generation of cost reductions, all provided relevant arguments that constitute a point of departure for a theory of capitalist development that is of use today (Lazonick, 1991a: 10). This history is brought out by Schumpeter.

Entrepreneurship in the History of Economic Thought

Exploring the treatment of entrepreneurship in the history of economic thought is assisted by a paper Joseph Schumpeter read before the Research Center in Entrepreneurial History at Harvard in 1949, entitled 'Economic Theory and Entrepreneurial History'. In the paper, Schumpeter undertook 'a brief survey of the history, within the economics literature, of the notions that economists have formed at various times on the subject of entrepreneurship and economic progress' (Schumpeter, 1949: 63). Tracing the term 'entrepreneur' to Cantillon, Schumpeter asserted that the former's recognition of business activity as a function *sui generis* was accepted by the Physiocrats and carried on by J. B. Say who, from his own business experience, 'had a lively vision of the phenomenon which most of the other classical economists lacked. With him, then, the entrepreneur is the agent that combines the others into a productive organism' (64). Schumpeter further noted that Say 'put the entrepreneur into the center stage of both the productive and the distributive theory which, though it disfigured many slips, first adumbrated the analytic structure that became fully articulate in the hands of Walras, Marshall, Wicksell, Clark, and the Austrians' (64).

Yet, in spite of the immense influence of the Physiocrats and of Cantillon on Adam Smith, Schumpeter argued further, English thought took quite a different approach towards the entrepreneur. Though Smith repeatedly discussed the employer (master, merchant, undertaker), 'the leading or directing activity as a distinctive function played a surprisingly small role in his analytic scheme of the economic process' (65). This was because Smith's natural law preconceptions led him 'to emphasize the role of labor to the exclusion of the productive function of designing the plan according to which this labor is being applied' (65). For Smith, the businessman provided capital and nothing else. This conception of the entrepreneur continued in the thought of Ricardo and Marx, Schumpeter surmised, where the 'designing, directing, leading, co-ordinating function has practically no place at all in their analytic schemata' (65). And also in John Stuart Mill, whose entrepreneur 'does a type of non-manual work that does not essentially differ from other types, and therefore reaps a return that is analogous to wages' (66). These are the views inherited by the mainstream as received wisdom. They are views that economic 'dissenters' had trouble believing and hence, what prompted them to question the status quo and develop different views and different schools of thought.

Alfred Marshall and Business Management

Alfred Marshall in his monumental *Principles of Economics* (first published in 1890), 'embedded his analysis of marginal adaptation in response to market forces within an evolutionary institutional setting in which business organization was central' (Lazonick, 1991b: 261). Or as Brian Loasby (1989: 48) observed, 'Marshall, like Smith, was primarily concerned with a topic alien to modern microeconomics, namely the nature and causes of the wealth of nations'. In *Industry and Trade* Marshall (1919) undertook, as the subtitle suggests, 'A study of industrial technique and business organisation; and of their influences on the conditions of the various classes and nations'. He also grappled with 'the issue of the relative importance for national economic performance of internal and external economies of scale' (Lazonick, 1991b: 261-262).

In the relatively neglected Book IV of his *Principles* , 'The Agents of Production. Land, Labour, Capital and Organization', there is no mistaking Marshall's recognition of the principle of organisation. Even his taxonomic choice of the term 'Agent' instead of 'Factor' lends credence to the fact that Marshall was well aware of the existence of a legitimate owner of a resource that somehow created value in the production process. In fact, one of the five chapters in Book IV is devoted entirely to 'Business Management'. In this chapter Marshall noted that 'the central problem of the modern organization of industry, (is) that which relates to the advantages and disadvantages of the subdivision of the work of business management' (Marshall, 1961: 283). Further, he observed that

> in the greater part of the business of the modern world the task of so directing production that a given effort be most effective in supplying human wants has to be broken up and given into the hands of a specialized body of employers, or to use a more general term, of business men. They 'adventure' or 'undertake' its risks; they bring together the capital and the labour required for the work; they arrange or 'engineer' its general plan, and superintend its minor details (Marshall, 1961: 293).

Marshall called this breed of economic animal 'Managers' and clearly perceived them as distinct from 'Owners' of businesses, as 'they are not required to bring any capital into it' but instead carry out 'a great part of the work of engineering the business, and the whole of the work of superintending it' (Marshall, 1961: 302). Management was perceived by Marshall as a specialised form of activity requiring specialists to undertake it (O'Brien, 1990: 74). He explicitly recognised the multi-faceted nature of the business management function: the risk element, the personnel element, the planning element, and the authority element. Furthermore, Marshall was clearly of the view that these 'managed' organisations were more efficient resource allocators than the market. This was because the functions of management were divided up, and carried out, by a specialised hierarchy.

Marshall also identified the economies associated with the increase in the scale of production and distinguished two classes of such economies: those emanating from internal organisation and those arising from external or regional conditions. He called the latter 'external economies' as they were 'dependent on the general development of the industry' which were 'often secured by the concentration of many small businesses of a similar character in particular localities: or, as is commonly said, by the localisation of industry' (Marshall, 1961: 266). The former he termed 'internal economies', as they were 'dependent on the resources of the individual houses of business engaged in (the industry), on their organization and the efficiency of their management' (Marshall, 1961: 266). As Lazonick has observed, Marshall recognised that internal economies 'result from organizational coordination of productive resources within a firm that spreads the fixed costs of that specific firm over more output, thus lowering unit costs' and that external economies 'result from market coordination within a specific region...that spreads the fixed costs of that specific region over more output, thus lowering costs'. Such that '(i)n the one case, organizational coordination fosters economic development; in the other case, it fosters market coordination' (Lazonick, 1991b: 261-262). In relation to scale economies, Marshall was of the opinion that the business enterprise was the fundamental organisational form for economic progress. As highlighted by O'Brien (1990: 74), Marshall perceived that the future of industry depended less on owner-manager entrepreneurs than on the large joint-stock companies, because of their superior technical and managerial abilities. Whilst his concept of 'external economies' has since formed the nucleus of research conducted in the related areas of 'industry capabilities', 'industrial districts', and Michael Porter's notion of 'clusters' (Foss & Eriksen, 1995; Best, 1990; Porter, 1990).

Joseph Schumpeter, Entrepreneurship, and Innovation

In a recent paper on evolutionary and neo-Schumpeterian economics, William Lazonick (1994) asserted that the study of innovation, and so economic development, demands a methodology that integrates theory and history. And further:

> Innovation must be studied as an evolutionary process in which strategic decision makers learn to manage the sources of uncertainty that they face in transforming innovative investments into higher quality/lower cost products than would otherwise exist...Innovation is a social process that requires the conscious involvement — or what I call the planned coordination — of many people with a variety of specialized skills and

functions. Innovation requires collective organization because it is complex, cumulative, and continuous (Lazonick, 1994: 246-247).

Lazonick claimed that throughout the work of Joseph Schumpeter, despite his initial focus on the centrality of the entrepreneur, there is an evolving realisation of the growing tendency of innovation to be a more collectivised process in the manner described above. And yet despite the legacy of Schumpeter — and Marx and Marshall for that matter — economists have ignored this evolving reality, being 'intellectual prisoners of the ideology of individualism'. Consequently, 'in pushing this research agenda forward, it has been the work of historians rather than economists that has led the way' (Lazonick, 1994: 259-260). Lazonick attributed this development to Schumpeter's legacy at the Research Center in Entrepreneurial History at Harvard Business School, which launched the careers of Alfred Chandler and the economic historian David Landes, both of whom have focused on structures of economic relationships other than market-mediated ones in their work.

In the second chapter of his *Theory of Economic Development* first published (in German) in 1911, Schumpeter laid the groundwork for his theory of entrepreneurial activity and innovation in positing that development (following Marx) results from 'changes in economic life...not forced upon it from without but (that which) arise by its own initiative, from within' (Schumpeter, 1961: 63; parentheses added). Furthermore, as Lazonick (1994: 249) has highlighted, the 'Fundamental Phenomenon of Economic Development' for Schumpeter, was entrepreneurial activity or enterprise that leads to innovation or the 'carrying out of new combinations' of the factors of production. This included the introduction of new products or methods of production; the opening of new markets; the conquest of new sources of factor inputs; and the creation of new organisations (Schumpeter, 1961: 66, 74). This notion of innovation was a clear improvement on the 'stationary state' view inherited from Mill which had nothing to say about the source of new businesss, new products, or new ways of doing things (Rumelt, 1987: 138).

The important point here is that Schumpeter explicitly recognised the existence of an economic agent, the entrepreneur, who coordinated the traditional factors of production, and innovated to create value and drive economic development. Entrepreneurship for Schumpeter 'constitutes a distinct economic function...primarily responsible for the recurrent 'prosperities' that revolutionize the economic organism' (Schumpeter, 1961: 132). Furthermore, for performing such a function, an entrepreneur received a return or profit, 'since the new combinations which are carried out if there is 'development' are more advantageous than the old, total receipts must in this case must be greater than total costs' (Schumpeter, 1961: 129). Yet this profit 'is certainly not a simple residuum; it is the expression of the value of what the entrepreneur contributes to production in exactly the same sense as that wages are the value expression of what the worker 'produces", it is a 'special and independent value phenomenon...fundamentally connected with the role of leadership in the economic system' (Schumpeter, 1961: 147, 153). This meant that Schumpeter believed that entrepreneurial profits were determined outside of the complex of market forces constituting his circular flow of income, because innovational activity is treated as an internal factor in economic change. It is also where he 'takes leave of the neoclassical theory of the market economy' (Lazonick, 1994: 250; Magnusson, 1994: 2).

Schumpeter further elucidated these concepts 28 years later in *Business Cycles* and included under the banner of innovation, 'Taylorization of work, improved handling of material, (and) the setting up of new business organizations' (Schumpeter, 1939: 84), demonstrating his recognition of changes in the industrial landscape. In Chapter Three of *Business Cycles*, Schumpeter defined innovation 'more rigorously', first, by justifying innovation as a 'distinct internal factor of change' and as 'the outstanding fact in the economic history of capitalist society', stating:

> It is an internal factor because the turning of existing factors of production
> to new uses is a purely economic process and, in capitalist society, purely
> a matter of business behaviour (Schumpeter, 1939: 86).

In tackling the neoclassical production function approach head-on, Schumpeter suggested that instead of varying quantities of factors to vary output, if 'we vary the form of the function', then 'we have an innovation'. In other words, innovation can be simply defined as 'the setting up of a new production function' (Schumpeter, 1939: 87). Furthermore, innovation for Schumpeter, 'dominates the picture of capitalistic life' by causing the 'intrusion into the system of new production functions which incessantly shift existing cost curves' (Schumpeter, 1939: 91), a point neglected by most economists, but less by the likes of Chandler and Lazonick.

Further to Lazonick's (1994) claim that Schumpeter's views on innovation evolved so as to necessitate a collective rather than an individual character, in *Business Cycles*, he introduced a new stage of capitalism, 'Trustified Capitalism' as opposed to 'Competitive Capitalism'. In fact, Schumpeter had recognised that such a transition had taken place earlier in 1928, in a paper published in the *Economic Journal* debating increasing and decreasing returns in the Marshallian firm. In that paper, he argued that in this new period of 'increasingly 'trustified', or otherwise 'organised', 'regulated', or 'managed' capitalism', '(i)nnovation is...not any more embodied typically in new firms, but goes on, within the big units now existing, largely independently of individual persons' (Schumpeter, 1928: 362, 384). Later, in *Capitalism, Socialism, and Democracy,* first published in 1942, he went even further by admitting that 'technological 'progress' tends, through systematization and rationalization of research and management, to become more effective and sure-footed' when it becomes 'the business of teams of trained specialists who turn out what is required and make it work in predictable ways' (Schumpeter, 1966: 118, 132). Schumpeter here explicitly recognised 'The Obsolescence of the Entrepreneurial Function' stating that the 'romance of earlier commercial adventure is rapidly wearing away, because so many more things can be strictly calculated that had of old to be visualized in a flash of genius' such that 'innovation itself is being reduced to routine' (Schumpeter, 1966: 132). The import of this recognition, especially for the evolutionary approach, has been highlighted above by Chandler (1992). Further, it is the opinion of Nathan Rosenberg (1994: 53-54), a leading contemporary theorist of innovation and technical change, that it was Schumpeter's view of innovation which made him very much an anti-neoclassicist:

> The nature of the innovation process, the drastic departure from existing routines, is inherently one that cannot be reduced to mere calculation, although subsequent imitation of the innovation, once accomplished, can be so reduced. Innovation is the creation of knowledge that cannot, and therefore should not, be 'anticipated' by the theorist in a purely formal manner, as is done in the theory of decision-making under uncertainty (Rosenberg, 1994: 53-54).

Therefore, as Lazonick (1994: 251) has highlighted, towards the last decade of his life 'Schumpeter had apparently abandoned his earlier ideology that attributed innovation to the entrepreneurial individual'. Again, according to Rosenberg (1994: 58), between the publication of *The Theory of Economic Development* (1911) and *Capitalism, Socialism and Democracy* (1942), 'the economic world, the object of Schumpeter's studies, had changed substantially during the period between the publication of the two books. Schumpeter's altered views were an acknowledgment of empirical changes that had occurred during his own professional lifetime'. This surfaced clearly in the 1949 paper mentioned in opening this section. Therein, Schumpeter explicitly recognised the evolution of entrepreneurial activity and innovation into a cooperative rather than individual activity:

> (A)s has often been pointed out, the entrepreneurial function need not be embodied in a physical person and in particular a single physical person. Every social environment has its own ways of filling the entrepreneurial function...The entrepreneurial function may be and often is filled co-operatively. With the development of the largest-scale corporations this has evidently become of major importance: aptitudes that no single individual combines can thus be built into a corporate personality... In many cases, therefore, it is difficult or even impossible to name an individual that acts as 'the entrepreneur' in a concern (Schumpeter, 1949: 71-72).

In the words of Lazonick (1994: 256), 'In an age of collective capitalism, as in an age of managerial capitalism, individual entrepreneurship still counts for something', yet 'for innovation to occur, the individual entrepreneur must build an organization that can develop and utilize productive resources in ways that have not been done before'. Schumpeter apparently was aware of this, however, unlike business historians and management scholars, not many other economists have caught the drift.

Ronald Coase and the Theory of the Firm

After doing extensive 'fieldwork' in American industry during the early 1930s, British economist Ronald Coase could not reconcile the mainstream idea of market coordination with the fact that all around him he saw a factor of production — management — whose function was also to organise or coordinate the factors of production (Coase, 1988a: 7; 1992: 716). He observed that 'this fact has not been ignored by economists' and cited Marshall, J. B. Clark, Frank Knight, and Dennis Robertson, as positing a fourth 'factor' of production in the guise of 'organisation' or 'coordination' as carried out by managers or entrepreneurs. This posed the question, Coase asked in his 1991 Nobel Lecture, 'why was it needed if the pricing system provided all the coordination necessary?' (Coase, 1992: 716). What he saw was that factors (or owners of such) did not always move between competing uses according to changes in relative prices but that they were sometimes directed to do so by an entrepreneur/coordinator. Coase later remarked that what he meant by 'entrepreneur' 'is the hierarchy in a business which directs resources and includes not only management but also foremen and many workmen' (Coase, 1988b: 29). It was evident to Coase then, that there were at least two mechanisms to coordinate resources: via markets wherein the price mechanism signalled resource allocation and opportunities; or via the firm which employed hierarchy (or management) as an organising principle — whereupon authority is used to effect the allocation of resources (Williamson, 1991: 3).

In the course of discovering why there were alternative modes of coordination and why in fact there are such things as firms, Coase unravelled the notion of marketing, or as they were later called, transactions costs. As he stated, '(t)he main reason why it is profitable to establish a firm would seem to be that there is a cost of using the price mechanism' (Coase, 1937: 389). And further, these costs could be lessened by the erection of a firm with a manager, rather than relative prices, directing resources between competing uses, for 'the operation of a market costs something and by forming an organization and allowing some authority (an 'entrepreneur') to direct resources, certain marketing costs are saved' (Coase: 1937, 400). He also asserted that such costs are not unique to the price mechanism but are associated with using internal organisation as well. Other manager-entrepreneurs may be able to organise a given transaction at a lower cost than the firm in question. In sum, '(w)hether a transaction would be organized within the firm...or whether it would be carried out on the market depended on a comparison of the costs of carrying out these transactions with costs of carrying out these transactions within an organization, the firm' (Coase, 1988a: 15-16). Such that '(t)his results in the institutional structure of production being that which minimizes total costs for the output produced' (Coase, 1988c: 38).

Yet although Coase recognised that erecting a firm would be profitable only when the costs avoided were greater than the costs that would be incurred by the firm in coordinating the activities of the factors of production, by his own admission, he 'did not attempt to uncover the factors that would determine when this would be so'. Nor did he 'investigate the factors that would make the costs of organizing lower for some firms than for others' (Coase, 1988c: 39, 45). 'This was quite satisfactory', Coase says, ' if the main purpose was, as mine was, to explain why there are firms. But if one is to explain the institutional structure of production in the system as a whole it is necessary to uncover the reasons why the cost of organizing particular activities differs among firms' (Coase, 1992: 45). This is precisely what Chandler and Lazonick have attempted to do in their work.

Coase was also critical of the approach taken by mainstream economists in their conception of management and business organisation. The firm-as-production function, which dominates orthodox thinking, with its emphasis on choice in factor substitution has reduced the firm to a series of exchange relationships (not unlike the market itself) such that the exact nature of the firm and the entrepreneur has been obscured. As Oliver Williamson has said, '(w)hat was an analytically convenient theory of the firm for purposes of studying markets and equilibrium came to be treated as an adequate theory of the firm for purposes of understanding economic organization' (Williamson, 1991: 10), which, as the analysis above has demonstrated, is simply not the case. For Coase, 'industrial organisation has become the study of the pricing and output policies of firms' and further, that 'it is clear that modern economists writing on industrial organization have taken a very narrow view of the scope of their subject' (Coase, 1972: 62). For Coase, economists have not concerned themselves with internal arrangements within organisations, but rather have limited their attention to market activity — the buying of inputs and the selling of outputs — totally neglecting what occurs in the interim. Such that they have ignored the very heart of industrial organisation: how and why industries are organised (Medema, 1994: 22). As Coase put it, 'what was lacking in the literature, or so I thought, was a theory which would enable us to analyze the determinants of the organization of industry' (Coase: 1972, 62).

Coase made his dissatisfaction with the mainstream treatment (or lack thereof) of industrial organisation very clear in his 1991 Nobel Lecture, asserting that economists have overlooked the institutional structure of production, which is crucial for its successful operation.

> What is studied is a system which lives in the minds of economists but not on earth. I have called the result 'blackboard economics'... . The firm in mainstream economic theory has often been described as a 'black box'. And so it is. This is very extraordinary given that most resources in a modern economic system are employed within firms, with how these resources are used dependent on administrative decisions and not directly on the market. Consequently, the efficiency of the economic system depends to a very considerable extent on how these large organizations conduct their affairs...Even more surprising, given their interest in the pricing system, is the neglect of the market or more specifically the institutional arrangements which govern the process of exchange. As these institutional arrangements determine to a large extent what is produced, what we have is a very incomplete theory (Coase, 1992: 715).

He asserted that '(i)t makes little sense for economists to discuss the process of exchange without specifying the institutional setting within which the trading takes place since this affects the incentives to produce and the costs of transacting' (Coase, 1992: 719). This has been the research focus of another Nobel prize winner in economics, Douglass North.

Evolutionary Economics and Strategic Management

Strategy scholars have made the case that the dynamic or evolutionary approach to economic routines, capabilities and competences represents a possible area for fruitful dialogue or 'conversation' between economics and strategic management. In an evolutionary approach the concept of strategy shares much common ground with scholars of management and has a great deal to offer to the emerging resource-based approach to the firm (Teece, 1984, 1990; Best, 1990; Chandler, 1992; Earl, 1995; Foss, Knudsen & Montgomery, 1995; Foss, 1996). In fact, both approaches have common intellectual antecedents. The evolutionary approach to economics can be traced back to Smith, Marshall and Schumpeter. Recent and present day analysts working in this tradition include G. B. Richardson, George Shackle, Edith Penrose, Richard Nelson and Sidney Winter, Brian Loasby, David Teece, Richard Langlois, and to some extent, Chandler and Lazonick. It is no surprise that the majority of economists working in this area do so from the vantage of business schools and management departments, rather than economics departments.

Broadly expressed, members of this research program share a concern with the patterns of organisation most conducive to innovation and economic growth and development. They suggest that a theory of the firm ought to be informed by the questions that entrepreneurs and managers ask: How is new value created? How do social institutions and forms of business organisation lead to growth and competitiveness? In turn, how are these institutions shaped by growth and competition? (Langlois and Robertson, 1995: 9). In other words, instead of assuming homogeniety amongst firms, they recognise differences and attempt to discover where the differences come from, placing organisational capabilties at the centrepiece of their understanding of firm behaviour (Foss, Knudsen & Motgomery, 1995: 3). In their summary essay of the program, Langlois and Everett (1994: 11) maintained that the essence of the evolutionary approach to economics 'lies in the variation exhibited by cultural artifacts'. That is, following Darwin, selective evolution is said to be impossible without variation, but variation alone is not sufficient in this process. Differences arising amongst individuals must be heritable such that there must be a mechanism to transmit variations to offspring. 'Institutions and routines — which we more broadly call rules, maintain Langlois and Everett (1994, 11), 'perform this function in economic evolution: Rules are 'reproduced' as actors imitate or borrow knowledge from others. Institutions are, after all, stored knowledge ready and waiting for individuals to adopt'. This is very much the central concern of Nelson and Winter's (1982) germinal *An Evolutionary Theory of Economic Change*. Focusing on the nature and meaning of economic capabilities and how innovations create new capabilities, Nelson and Winter reduced capabilities to path-dependent knowledge bases or learned routines (Foss, Knudsen & Montgomery, 1995: 4-6). Better routines, first introduced as innovations, are selected by the market environment and then propagated by replication in firms, and imitation between firms. This results in the differential survival of firms as reflected in their differing profitability. 'Through the process of competition, the better rules survive', such that routines 'function as the coordinative element in a firm, thus providing the continuity of the firm in a sea of change' (Langlois and Everett, 1994: 21-22). Knowledge or know-how then, is transformed into a key 'strategic asset' (Winter, 1987) and firms are 'repositories of productive knowledge' (Winter, 1988). Furthermore:

> The firm, then, is a special way to organize knowledge: It links together various kinds of intimate knowledge (capabilities) to coordinate productive activities. Much of the knowledge firms possess is tacit and empirically derived through trial-and-error learning processes. Since these capabilities often come in discrete, lumpy bundles, firms often find themselves with surplus capabilities for performing certain tasks. These firms may then expand their operations and take on additional similar activities (Langlois and Everett, 1994: 27-28).

Langlois and Robertson's (1995: 1) stated objective in *Firms, Markets and Economic Change* is to 'carry evolutionary economics more forcefully into the traditional bailiwicks of transaction-cost theory by presenting and applying an evolutionary theory of economic capabilities'. For them, the 'new' institutionalism has focused on organisational form, but largely through the eyes of the transactions-cost approach, such that the existence of business institutions, namely the firm, has been reduced to an optimal response to incentive problems. For these authors, this approach shrouds the question as to why coordination is necessary, and ignores the vital role of resource coordination for strategic uses that require new, and not always readily evident, combinations of resources. 'In a world of fundamental uncertainty', they continued, 'in which capabilities and knowledge differ among actors, this, rather than incentive questions, may be the central role of such institutions' (Langlois and Robertson, 1995: 3).

Langlois and Robertson (1995) further posited that the repertoire of routines used by organisations (or networks of such) represent their capabilities, or their 'core competences' to utilise Prahalad and Hamel's (1990) oft-cited phrase. And further, those business institutions that can create and utilise superior capabilities tend to perform better, and this is the essence of Schumpeterian 'destructive competition', or competitive advantage. As they stated:

> This picture of the rationale for the firm is what we might legitimately call a strategic, entrepreneurial, or Schumpeterian theory of vertical integration. The superiority of centralized control of capabilities lies in their ability to redeploy those capabilities in the service of an entrepreneurial opportunity when such redeployment would otherwise be costly. The firm overcomes the 'dynamic' transaction costs of economic change. It is in this sense that we may say that the firm solves a coordination problem: it enables complementary input-holders to agree on the basic nature of the system of production and distribution of the product. It provides the structure in a situation of structural uncertainty (Langlois and Robertson, 1995: 4).

In other words, unlike the 'new' institutional view in the Coase-Williamson tradition — where the firm is viewed as a 'second-best' solution to market failure and firm management is viewed as a functional equivalent to the 'invisible hand' for coordination — the evolutionary approach in contrast, sees the firm as a vital construct for the planning of competitive strategy and management as much more than hierarchical authority. As Michael Best (1990: 133) observed:

> For Schumpeter and Penrose, management shapes a company's vision, organization, and culture, anticipates change, designs competitive strategies, and searches for opportunities in a future for which no crystal ball or probability functions exist. With the inclusion of management as an explanatory variable the grip of static equilibrium theory gives way to that of dynamics of adjustment to environmental change, and the notion of profits as a return to capital is replaced by profit as, on the one hand, a

quasi-rent for superior organizational capability and, on the other, a financial resource for innovation, investment, and organizational development.

In *The New Competition* (1990), Michael Best stated that the term 'strategic' refers to market-shaping (ex-ante) activities in contrast with market-reacting (ex-post) responses, the latter being the typical approach to management by mainstream economics. Neil Chamberlain (1962: 10-11), in a largely overlooked microeconomics text, had a similar conception of strategic planning. '(M)anagement', he said, 'must adjust — ex post — to changes which had not been expected and must lay plans — ex ante — to deal with expected future events or to realize future aspirations'. He said that by and large economists have overlooked the planning characteristics of business enterprises because it has been 'slotted in' to the profit maximisation concept. He did not mention the socio-political implications of the word 'planning', but this aspect did not escape Phillips' (1985) analysis. Chamberlain observed that 'if one admits a larger area of managerial discretion, if (one) credits management with some capacity to make, build, affect, or control markets, then the institutional mechanisms for planning become of greater interest' (Chamberlain, 1962: 11).

The strategic approach to the firm adopted by those in the evolutionary program cuts straight across economics and strategic management, otherwise known as the capabilities, competence — or resource-based view of the firm. Like many other concepts in management theory, this approach has its roots in economic theory, namely that of Edith Penrose (1968) and G. B. Richardson (1972). Penrose suggested viewing the firm as a collection or 'pool of resources' and Richardson introduced the term 'capabilities' to encapsulate 'knowledge, experience and skills' accumulated by a firm. The firm then, for Langlois and Robertson (1995: 7), consists of an intrinsic core of capabilities that are 'idiosyncratically synergistic, inimitable, and noncontestable' — they cannot be duplicated or exchanged on the market, and they create more value when combined in a firm than when utilised separately; the remainder of the firm consists of ancillary capabilities that are contestable and may not be unique. For these analysts, idiosyncratic knowledge and ways of acting — a firm's routines and capabilities — are at the heart of the firm as an organisation (Langlois & Robertson, 1995: 13, 16).

Without getting caught in the mire of definitions and analyses of strategy, the crucial point posited by Langlois and Robertson is that corporate strategy is one of the most important variables affecting the boundaries between firm and market, or the 'make-or-buy' decision. For them, strategy formulation (and formation) and implementation involves finding a match between what a firm can do, or induce others to do on its behalf, and the technical requirements that such a strategy imposes. This in turn requires a command over, or privileged access to, resources. 'Since different firms have different bundles of capabilities', they argued, 'they vary in their ability to implement any given strategy' (18). And further:

> Questions of firm strategy and firm boundaries are thus closely related. Strategy implementation requires that firms compare their existing resources to their future needs and then determine how to make up any shortfall by either generating new resources internally or arranging to purchase them through the market (Langlois & Robertson, 1995: 18-19).

New resources are generated internally, following Penrose (1968), by 'transforming articulated and formalized knowledge about the best way to solve a certain problem into routines containing a strong element of tacit knowledge' such that they are hard to imitate (Knudsen, 1996: 19).

David Teece, a strategy scholar at Berkeley and an exponent of the evolutionary approach of economics, has a similar conception of strategy, and importantly for the present focus, links this formulation with economic theory. For Teece, the basic idea behind strategic management is 'that a firm needs to match its capabilities to its ever-changing environment' and that this involves 'the formulation and execution of plans relating to the establishment and deployment of a firm's assets' (Teece, 1984: 87). Implicit here is the notion that resource allocation is a function of strategic management, so that there should exist a set of economic principles to guide strategic decision makers. But as is well known by now, there is no such set of principles. As a consequence Teece sought to examine why this was the case. In a later conceptualisation, Teece (1990) defined strategy as managerial actions that enhance the value of a business enterprise, such that value creation is another function of strategic management. He identified several key issues of strategic management that directly coincide with the concerns of the evolutionary and neo-Schumpeterian economics programs: identifying the source of economic rents and differential performance of individual firms and protecting the source of these rents from rivals; identifying the differences between contracting arrangements and internal organisation, and assessing how the firm's boundaries affect performance; and assessing the importance of institutional context. Furthermore, the key issue of strategic management — positioning and managing the firm so as to generate, augment, and preserve economic rents — constitutes, for Teece, entrepreneurship (Teece, 1990: 46).

Conclusion

In the foregoing, it has been demonstrated that despite the apparent contemporaneity of economists' interest in management and more importantly, the reciprocal interest it has sparked amongst strategy scholars, an interest in the important resource-coordinating function of management has a long history. It was also established that among the most promising developments in economic thought towards a 'conversation' with strategic management, was the evolutionary approach which can be traced back to Marshall, Schumpeter, and Edith Penrose. This approach was seen to share much common ground with strategic management particularly the fact that both approaches conceive the firm as the basic unit of analysis and conceptualize the firm in terms of differentiated and inimitable stocks of knowledge capital — capabilities or competences — which are capable of generating competitive advantages, and so are central to a realistic theory of the firm.

Acknowledgments

The author has benefited greatly from conversations with Alfred D. Chandler and A. W. (Bob) Coats, and from comments on drafts of this paper from Peter Earl, Paul Robertson, Michael Browne, Rob Castle, and Chris Nyland.

References

Best, M. (1990), *The New Competition: Institutions of Industrial Restructuring*. Harvard University Press, Cambridge, Mass.

Caves, R. E. (1984), 'Economic Analysis and the Quest for Competitive Advantage', *American Economic Review*. Supplement, 74(2), pp 127-132.

Caves, R. E. (1984a), 'Industrial Organization, Corporate Strategy and Structure' in R. B. Lamb (ed) *Competitive Strategic Management*. Prentice Hall, Englewood Cliffs.

Chamberlain, N. (1962), *The Firm: Micro-Economic Planning and Action*. McGraw Hill, New York.

Chandler, A. D. (1977), *The Visible Hand: The Managerial Revolution in American Business*. Harvard University Press, Cambridge, Mass.

Chandler, A. D. (1990), *Scale and Scope: The Dynamics of Industrial Capitalism*. Harvard University Press, Cambridge, Mass.

Chandler, A. D. (1992), 'Organizational Capabilities and the Economic History of the Industrial Enterprise', *Journal of Economic Perspectives,* 6(3), pp 79-100.

Chandler, A. D. (1996), Interview with Author, May, Cambridge, Massachusetts.

Coase, R. (1937), 'The Nature of the Firm', *Economica,* v. 4, pp 386-405.

Coase, R. (1972), 'Industrial Organization: A Proposal for Research' in V. Fuchs (ed) *Policy Issues and Research Opportunities in Industrial Organization*. National Bureau of Economic Research, Cambridge, Mass.

Coase, R. (1988a), 'The Nature of the Firm: Origin', *Journal of Law, Economics and Organization,* v. 4, pp 3-17.

Coase, R. (1988b), 'The Nature of the Firm: Meaning', *Journal of Law, Economics and Organization,* v. 4, 19-32.

Coase, R. (1988c), 'The Nature of the Firm: Influence', *Journal of Law, Economics and Organization,* v. 4, pp 33-47.

Coase, R. (1992), 'The Institutional Structure of Production: Nobel Speech', *American Economic Review,* v. 82, 713-719.

Conner, K. R. (1991), 'A Historical Comparison of Resource-Based Theory and Five Schools of Thought Within Industrial Organization economics: Do We Have a New Theory of the Firm?', *Journal of Management,* 17(1), pp 121-154.

Drucker, P. (1955), *The Practice of Management.* Pan Paperback, London.

Drucker, P. (1981), 'Toward the Next Economics', in Bell, D. and I. Kristol (eds) *The Crisis in Economic Theory.* Basic Books, New York.

Drucker, P. (1992), *Managing For the Future.* Buterworth-Heinemann. London.

Earl, P. (1995), 'Shackle, Entrepreneurship, and the Theory of the Firm'. Paper presented to the 8th HETSA Conference, University of Queensland, 12-14 July.

Foss, N. J. & B. Eriksen (1995), 'Competitive Advantage and Industry Capabilities' in C. Montgomery (ed) *Resource-Based and Evolutionary Theories of the Firm: Toward a Synthesis.* Kluwer Academic Publishers, Boston.

Foss, N. J., C. Knudsen, & C. Montgomery (1995), 'An exploration of common ground: integrating evolutionary and strategic theories of the firm' in C. Montgomery (ed) *Resource-Based and Evolutionary Theories of the Firm: Toward a Synthesis.* Kluwer Academic Publishers, Boston.

Foss, N. J. (1996), 'The emerging competence perspective' in N. J. Foss & C. Knudsen (eds) *Towards a Competence Theory of the Firm.* Routledge, London.

Kay, J. (1991), 'Economics and Business', *Economic Journal,* 101(404), pp 57-64.

Knudsen, C. (1995), 'Theories of the Firm, Strategic Management, and Leadership' in C. Montgomery (ed) *Resource-Based and Evolutionary Theories of the Firm: Toward a Synthesis.* Kluwer Academic Publishers, Boston.

Knudsen, C. (1996), 'The Competence Perspective: A Historical View' in N. J. Foss & C. Knudsen (eds) *Towards a Competence Theory of the Firm.* Routledge, London

Langlois, R. N. and M. Everett (1994), 'What is Evolutionary Economics?' in L. Magnusson (ed) *Evolutionary and Neo-Schumpeterian Approaches to Economics.* Kluwer Academic Publishers, Dordrecht.

Langlois, R. N. and P. L. Robertson (1995), *Firms, Markets and Economic Change: A Dynamic Theory of Business Institutions.* Routledge, London.

Lazonick, W. (1991a), *Business Organization and the Myth of the Market Economy.* Cambridge University Press, New York.

Lazonick, W. (1991b), 'Organizations and Markets in Capitalist Development' in Bo Gustaffson (ed) *Power and Economic Institutions: Reinterpretations in Economic History.* Edward Elgar, Aldershot.

Lazonick, W. (1994), 'The Integration of Theory and History: Methodology and Ideology in Schumpeter's Economics' in L. Magnusson (ed) *Evolutionary and Neo-Schumpeterian Approaches to Economics.* Kluwer Academic Publishers, Dordrecht.

Loasby, B. (1989), *The Mind and Method of the Economist: A Critical Appraisal of Major Economists of the 20th Century.* Edward Elgar, Aldershot.

Mahoney, J. T. and J. R. Pandian (1992), 'The Resource-Based View Within the Conversation of Strategic Management', *Strategic Management Journal,* v.13, pp 363-380.

Marshall, A. (1919), *Industry and Trade.* Macmillan, London.

Marshall, A. (1961) [1890], *Principles of Economics.* 9th (variorum) edition. Macmillan, London.

Medema, S. (1994), *Ronald H. Coase.* Macmillan, London.

Nelson, R. (1991), 'Why do Firms Differ, and How Does it Matter?', *Strategic Management Journal,* v. 12, pp 61-74.

Nelson, R. and S. Winter (1982), *An Evolutionary Theory of Economic Change.* Harvard University Press, Cambridge, Mass.

O'Brien, D. P. (1990), 'Marshall's Industrial Analysis', *Scottish Journal of Political Economy,* 37(1), pp 61-84.

Porter, M. E. (1990), *The Competitive Advantage of Nations.* Free Press, New York.

Penrose, E. (1968), *The Theory of the Growth of the Firm.* Basic Blackwell, Oxford.

Peteraf, M. A. (1993), 'The Cornerstones of Competitive Advantage: A Resource-Based View', *Strategic Management Journal,* v. 14, pp 179-191.

Phillips, R. J. (1985), 'Marx, the classical firm, and economic planning', *Journal of Post-Keynesian Economics,* 8(2), pp 266- 276.

Prahalad, C. K. and G. Hamel (1990), 'The Core Competence of the Corporation', *Harvard Business Review,* May-June, 79-91.

Radner, R. (1992), 'Hierarchy: The Economics of Managing', *Journal of Economic Literature,* v.30, pp 1382-1415.

Richardson, G. B. (1972), 'The Organisation of Industry', *Economic Journal,* v. 82, pp 883-896.

Robinson, E. A. G. (1934), 'The Problem of Management and the Size of the Firm', *Economic Journal,* v. 44, pp 242-257.

Rosenberg, N. (1994), *Exploring the Black Box;* Technology, Economics, and History. Cambridge University Press, New York.

Rumelt, R. (1984), 'Towards a Strategic Theory of the Firm' in R. B. Lamb (ed) *Competitive Strategic Management.* Prentice Hall, Englewood Cliffs.

Rumelt, R. (1986), 'Theory, Strategy, and Entrepreneurship' in D. J. Teece (ed) *The Competitive Challenge*. Ballinger Publishing Co., Cambridge, Mass.

Schumpeter, J. A. (1939), *Business Cycles*. McGraw Hill, New York.

Schumpeter, J. A. (1949), 'Economic Theory and Entrepreneurial History'. Paper presented to Research Center in Entrepreneurial History, Harvard University in Change and the Entrepreneur. Harvard University Press, Cambridge, Mass.

Schumpeter, J. A. (1961), *The Theory of Economic Development*. Oxford University Press, New York.

Schumpeter, J. A. (1966), *Capitalism, Socialism and Democracy*. Unwin University Books, London.

Teece, D. (1984), 'Economic Analysis and Strategic Management', *California Management Review,* 26(3), pp 87-110.

Teece, D. (1986), 'Firm Boundaries, Technological Innovation, and Strategic Management' in L. G. Thomas (ed) *The Economics of Strategic Planning*. D.C. Heath and Co., Lexington.

Teece, D. (1990), 'Contributions and Impediments of Economic Analysis to the Study of Strategic Management' in J. W. Frederickson (ed) *Perspectives on Strategic Management*. Harper and Row, New York.

Teece, D. (1993), 'The Dynamics of Industrial Capitalism: Perspectives on Alfred Chandler's 'Scale and Scope', *Journal of Economic Literature,* v. 31, pp 199-225.

Teece, D. and S. Winter (1984), 'The Limits of Neoclassical Theory in Management Education', *American Economic Review: Supplement,* 74(2), pp 116-121.

Williamson, O. (1993), 'Introduction' in Williamson, O. and S. G. Winter (eds) The Nature of the Firm: Origins, *Evolution and Development*. Oxford University Press, New York.

Winter, S. G. (1987), 'Knowledge and Competence as Strategic Assets' in D. J. Teece (ed) *The Competitive Challenge*. Ballinger Publishing Co., Cambridge, Mass.

Winter, S. G. (1988), 'On Coase, Competence, and the Corporation', *Journal of Law, Economics, and Organization,* 4(1), pp 163-180.

Towards A More Integrative Cross-Functional Approach to Management Education

Rhett H. Walker, Lindsay Nelson, Dallas Hanson and Cathy Fisher

Abstract

Management education that develops a deep understanding of one or more discipline areas, but does not encourage students to see connections between the courses that they study, may not meet current organisational needs. The present organisational trend towards agility and flexibility, demands not only that employees be equipped with necessary technical knowledge, but that they must be able to integrate and use that knowledge in a creative manner. This is supported by findings of the recent Karpin Report. A possible solution lies in integrated assessment patterns, with an emphasis on attitude change and integrative ability rather than a revolutionary alteration of the knowledge base.

Introduction

Organisational knowledge presented in discreet packets appeals to teachers and students because it is self-contained and the boundaries are well-defined. Unfortunately, this process results in a narrow, partial view of the workings of an organisation. Prior to the mid-1980s this may not have caused a major problem. Within the last ten or fifteen years, however, the business environment has changed dramatically. Organisations are expected to be organic, responsive and flexible (Limerick, 1992; Bahrami, 1992; Stone and Smith, 1996). This means that those who work within those organisations need to be well-equipped to fit within this dynamic environment.

This paper posits that our management education system may not have kept sufficiently abreast of developments in the business environment. Students may be exposed to a range of discipline areas but the predominant model may inadvertently encourage the apprentice to treat each area as a single disconnected module. Students are provided with a rich knowledge base but they may not necessarily learn how to integrate and use that knowledge, to cross boundaries and be flexible. In this paper we offer a way by which these problems may be overcome. Our intent in writing this paper is to raise, for discussion, debate and possible research, a matter impinging directly on how we as educators fulfil the needs and requirements of prospective employees and employers alike.

The paper is divided into four sections. First, we examine the nature of management education currently presented in Australia and New Zealand. Second, we comment on what the present business environment demands of graduates. Third, we discuss what an education in management in the 1990s should offer. Finally, we present some thoughts for a possible degree course that addresses the key concerns raised.

Management Education in Australia and New Zealand

Generally speaking, management education in New Zealand and Australia channels learning into one or two major disciplinary areas. Institutions vary in exactly what is offered and how it is offered and assessed. They also vary in the mix of theory and practical experience included in units. The basic offerings, however, are similar. Typically students are required to undertake a number of units in a prescribed hierarchy which specifies 'pre-requisites' for later units, building disciplinary knowledge gradually in a sequence of units that otherwise stand alone. This approach to course structure and delivery inclines students to regard subject areas as mutually exclusive rather that seeing them as an inter-connected whole. They grow away from a multi-disciplinary orientation and into a limited single, or at best, dual-disciplinary way of thinking.

The development of this limited perspective has profound consequences for the way students define and approach problems and develop solutions. The process of education they experience in a three or four year undergraduate degree program provides them with, in Senge's (1990) term a 'mental model' that is used to interpret the world. This interpretation includes the language learnt, the perceptions they share, the meanings they give events, the skills and attitudes they possess. Churchman (1971), building on insights from German philosophy, referred to the similar concept of *Weltanschauung*, or world view, which describes the network of beliefs and assumptions that people use to organise their perception of events. Together these concepts describe a very narrow focus for learning and development.

The process of disciplinary education specifically builds such a mental model (the preferred term here), teaching a vocabulary that creates a view of the world, reinforcing disciplinary lessons about how the world works, gradually adding new knowledge and new opinions about the nature of problems and solutions. One outcome of channelling knowledge into disciplines is that there is shared vocabulary and understanding that enable us to see events through a particular 'lens'. A downturn in profit, for example, may be seen by a marketer as a problem stemming from sales performance, insufficient or inadequate promotional support; whereas an accountant or human resource manager may perceive the problem to be caused by excessive overheads or a lack of motivated staff. Thus, solutions will be visualised in terms of that manager's discipline based training.

The result of this educational process is therefore a mental model which provides powerful insights into how the world of organisations operates coupled with restrictive limitations. The power comes from the extent to which the accumulated knowledge and skill that is resident within single disciplines can be brought to bear on problems. The limitations are, unfortunately, just as obvious. Students may be inadequately prepared to deal with the typically complex nature of the problems and challenges that characterise day to day business decision making. They may be seduced by single discipline solutions, which are inadequate for the challenges of a complex post-industrial world.

These arguments are echoed in perspectives on business education framed elsewhere. For example, Wright, Bitner and Zeithaml (1994: 5-6) point out that:

> the American Assembly of Collegiate Schools of Business (AACSB) claims that business schools fail to provide the necessary tools (in problem-finding, problem-solving, communication, and people skills) and perspectives (viewing functional areas as part of a whole and applying a global outlook) that are essential for college graduates. This approach has created graduates who are better suited to traditional hierarchical corporations than the more fluid organisational forms emerging today…Employees must be able to communicate across functional boundaries to solve problems. The days of being rooted in a single discipline (such as marketing or operations), working with information only from that function to make a critical decision, then 'throwing it over the wall' into other functional areas are over. Effective employees are ones who can integrate information across the walls. As industry has urged business schools: 'It's not just the skills. It's the inter-relationship of skills'.

This is not to say that the content of courses or what is taught is necessarily inappropriate, indeed discipline-based teaching is required to provide individuals with entry-level skills and knowledge in recognised functional areas. Rather it is to suggest that the segregated nature of course structuring and subject unit delivery may be inadvertently inculcating a blinkered rather than holistic perspective to what is taught and how it may be applied in practical situations.

In the discussion that follows we use the term management education as a synonym for business education, and in a way that is meant to embrace a range of functional responsibilities including, for example, marketing, production, sales, human resource, accounting and financial management. In the next section we explain the challenges of the current business environment in more detail, expanding on the claim that it requires of individuals a multi-disciplinary approach.

What Is Expected of Managers In The Present Environment

Descriptions of changes to organisational structure and work patterns are becoming familiar themes in the management literature. Agility and flexibility have become paramount as firms move away from monolithic, rigid and mechanistic forms towards organic, responsive structures and processes (Boynton, 1991; Limerick, 1992; Bahrami, 1992; Tiernan, 1993; Martin, 1995; Stebbins and Shani, 1995; Stone and Smith, 1996). Coupled with this emphasis on flexibility is the belief that an organisation's ability to adapt and learn faster than its rivals provides a powerful competitive advantage (Boxall, 1994).

The workplace of the 1990s therefore carries with it an expectation that workers will be multi-skilled and capable of taking greater responsibility and initiative. Information has replaced equipment as the firm's most important asset. Increasingly the knowledge that employees hold is the key to organisational success (Brooks, 1994). These 'knowledge workers' are expected to be able to absorb more information and be responsible and creative in solving problems and making decisions. Burgoyne (1995) describes this transition as a move away from manufacture (creation using physical tools) to 'mentofacture' (creation using the mind). Indeed a knowledge-based economy is emerging to accommodate the fast pace of technological change and global competition (Bahrami, 1992).

Key areas within the organisation such as human resource management have similarly been encouraged to adopt a completely new role. Dowling and Schuler (1990) and Dunphy (1987) have explained that the HR function that has managed the deployment and development of human resources within the firm, has moved away from a micro administrative, 'housekeeping' role to a much broader focus that involves strategic planning and design of the organisation. Sisson (1995) has reported that many have welcomed the move away from what Tyson and Fell (1986) have called 'clerks of the works', to the role of 'architect' where the former was largely involved in routine administration and record keeping and the latter would be involved in policy formulation and management matters.

Correspondingly, much day-to-day business problem solving is characterised by its complex multi-disciplinary nature. Practising marketers know that solutions to what may be defined *prima facie* as marketing-specific problems not uncommonly lie in non-marketing specific areas such as accounting policies and procedures, production management, and an organisation's contracts with its suppliers. Arts administrators are required to be effective marketers and sound financial managers. Small business owner operators need to be proficient in all facets of management. Furthermore, the dramatic increase in the participation of professional engineers, accountants and other professionals in MBA courses in recent years, especially those offering a marketing major, bears clear testament to the recognition that expertise within a single disciplinary area is not necessarily sufficient for effective and successful business practice.

This dramatic change in responsibilities and in what is required of an individual to function effectively in business today necessitates a new set of competencies. Employees are encouraged to initiate change, make suggestions and be creative (Coopey, 1987). This is seen to have advantages for the employee and for the employer. Employees enjoy the responsibility and autonomy to contribute in a meaningful way to organisational processes. The organisation benefits because workers become more involved in the work process and identify more strongly with the outcomes.

Nevertheless the changes outlined above place high expectations on workers' abilities. Bahrami (1992: 40), for example, has stressed the need for employees to be able to read situations and apply different capabilities depending on what is required: 'Effective employees have the flexibility and the confidence to leverage their knowledge and capabilities across different areas as and when conditions change and new needs arise'.

Limerick (1992: 45), when discussing the emergence of network firms, has advocated that managers need to: 'take responsibility for linking together with others-they do not rely on hierarchy, or on corporate staff to take the initiative for them'. Collins (1987) also has identified that the re-focus necessitates a new mindset that, among other things, can allow the manager to see the whole rather than the parts and move freely between short and long-term time horizons.

What Management Education in the 1990s Should Offer

Watson (1993:18) invokes Cardinal Newman's notion of a broadly-based liberal education in discussing the nature of management and its implications for management education, suggesting that making lists of qualities required of a manager 'may mislead by suggesting that they can be separately developed and assessed'. And elsewhere in the same paper he argues for 'education which leads to a sound body of knowledge, but studied in a way which develops the intellectual skills of criticism, analysis and synthesis'(25). We concur with these views and submit that synthesis, in particular, may warrant closer attention in the structuring and delivery of business management courses, to the end of encouraging students to see the complex cross-disciplinary or cross-functional nature typical of much business decision-making and problem-solving. In this way, we believe, students will be better prepared to fulfil the requirements and expectations of business and industry, to function more in what has been described elsewhere as a 'generalist' capacity, and to draw upon what they have learned in a more synergistic way.

Discussion to this point has support in findings contained within *Enterprising Nation* (1995), the report of the industry task force on leadership and management skills in Australia, chaired by David Karpin. Consider, for example, the following key conclusions (Vol. 2: 1422-1424):

- Cross-functional integration skills and the ability to motivate others are...high priorities
- interpersonal skills and commercial relationship building skills should be widely distributed across the population [of managers and all employees within a given enterprise].

Criteria sought in graduating MBA students, contained in Chapter 21 of Volume 2 of the Karpin report, and reproduced below in Table 1, highlight the respective emphasis given to suggested characteristics of university graduates by business and university respondents. The differences in priorities defined by business and universities are significant. Furthermore, the importance given by business to cooperation and teamwork, the capacity to make decisions and solve problems, and the ability to apply knowledge to the workplace raises questions as to how well equipped graduates are to fulfil these expectations in a meaningful cross-functional way.

Table 1. Criteria sought in graduating MBA students—emphasis given to suggested characteristics of university graduates business and university respondents

	By Business	By University
Communication skills	1	7
Capacity to learn new skills & procedures	2	5
Capacity for cooperation & teamwork	3	8
Capacity to make decisions & solve problems	4	3
Ability to apply knowledge to workplace	5	4
Capacity to work with minimum supervision	6	6
Theoretical knowledge in professional field	7	1
Capacity to use computer technology	8	2
Understanding of business ethics	9	12
General business knowledge	10	11
Specific work skills	11	9
Broad background of general knowledge	12	10

1 = most emphasis; 12 = least emphasis
Note : the correlation between the two columns is not statistically significant.
(Source: Enterprising Nation (1995), p.931)

Characteristics of the 'ideal manager', summarised in Table 2 of Chapter 13 in Volume 1, also reproduced below, highlight again the importance placed by business leaders on people skills, strategic thinking, the capacity for visionary thinking, flexibility, and the ability to solve complex problems, all of which require a synergistic cross-functional orientation.

Later in this same chapter of the Karpin report the authors make the key point that 'Current programs offered should take a broader, more generalist approach, to avoid creating technical specialists...' (Enterprising Nation, Vol. 1, p. 564), a recommendation echoed by Midgley in the report's conclusions, 'Cross-functional integration skills...are...high priorities' (Vol. 2, p. 1422).

Table 2. Characteristics of the 'Ideal Manager'

Characteristics	% of participants
1. 'People skills'	75%
2. Strategic thinker	58%
3. Visionary	52%
4. Flexible and adaptable to change	50%
5. Self management	33%
6. Team player	32%
7. Ability to solve complex problems and make decisions	25%
8. Ethical/high personal standards	23%

(Source: Enterprising Nation (1995:.535)

Similar conclusions are reached by Barry (1996), who has also found problems with the standard of management and has emphasised the need to improve its quality. Both Karpin and Barry (1996) call for higher levels of management education as the remedy, observing that in any event the educational level of managers in Australia is not as high as in some other countries such as Germany, Japan and the USA.

These calls for higher levels of education in Australian and New Zealand management find a willing audience in our culture. Government and industry provide broad support, students continue to be keen to enrol in Commerce and Business degrees and management academia prospers. However, the very success of this response creates a difficulty.

This education produces more and more knowledge about specific topic areas, but not necessarily always with the integration needed to produce flexibility. In other words, in the face of growing evidence that managers require generic, integrated knowledge and skills, education has responded by becoming more specialised. The demand for specialisation is being driven, at least in part, by the professions such as accounting, human resource management and marketing which pressure institutions of higher education to include topics they feel are relevant. In a sense, the professions are their own worst enemy because on the one hand they desire flexible managers with integrated skills but on the other hand demand higher levels of specific knowledge which precludes the integration they so highly value.

Overwhelmingly, it is held, management courses have concentrated on knowledge-based study. This is both convenient and easy for staff. It is convenient because it suits academics who teach discipline-based topics such as law, economics, accounting and psychology. It is easy due to the fact that each topic can be treated as a separate unit for purposes of setting assignments and examinations. Moreover, as professional bodies exert pressure for new topics within, say, marketing, financial or human resource management, university departments find it relatively simple to accommodate them.

The mental models provided by much conventional education actually inhibit real world problem-solving because, whilst powerful, they tend to limit the view of graduates. More than this, within the relatively limited scope of the world view educationally provided, the orientation is disproportionately biased towards knowledge content, rather than skill development and the inculcation of attitudes called for in the new world economy.

The shape of this problem becomes clear if the various requirements of the good management education, outlined in earlier discussion of Barry and Karpin, are summarised in Table 3, using the distinction between knowledge, skills and attitudes:

Table 3. Knowledge, Skills and Attitudes Required for a Business Education

Knowledge	• of specific discipline areas (for example human resources, marketing) • of multi discipline oriented approaches to problems (for example via use of simulation software)
Skills	• logical thought • analysis • in obtaining information (research skills) • in disseminating information (in writing, verbally, and in variety of styles and with the aid of a variety of information technology applications) • independent thought • problem • negotiation • team building • leadership (or potential for leadership in entry level staff)
Attitudes	• curiosity • global orientation • problem (rather than knowledge) focus • entrepreneurial approach • that learning is life-long • confidence

Our current education system aims to deliver knowledge and skills, and to inculcate something of what we as educators believe to be worthy attitudes in students. The process of doing so, however, tends to be rooted in individual and individually taught subject units. What is required, however, is a pattern of education that meets the complete set of challenges in a manner that engenders multi-disciplinary, integrative knowledge. This, we suggest, will better equip students for dealing with issues which require problem solving skills, will facilitate the development of a global focus, and will engender a more widely-scoped approach to later (life long) learning.

A Way Forward

To this point we have suggested that:

- managers must be flexible, adaptive, life long learners with strategic skills and a problem solving orientation;
- they must also have higher levels of education with a sound knowledge of at least one of the discipline areas centred on functional areas of management;
- this may create an education problem, because the tiers of study to gain disciplinary expertise tend to narrow vision, constrain flexibility and adaptability.

What are the possible solutions that we offer? A return to Newman's liberal education is both unlikely and unwarranted. Unlikely because it runs counter to the interests of professional bodies, counter to the demands of firms seeking technically skilled entry-level staff, and counter to the interests and expertise of academics. It is unwarranted because the current system can be changed to resolve the problem, so that we produce highly skilled, flexible, adaptable discipline expert graduates. This does not mean that the spirit of enquiry and mental thinking that Newman advocated should be ignored; indeed the system we outline seeks to build such activities.

This is a challenging task especially given that the established knowledge based teaching takes up almost all (conventionally) available teaching time. One possible solution that we advance here, whilst retaining the core of current disciplinary study, is to add just a little to the knowledge content but to make more substantial alterations to the way units are taught and assessed. We also acknowledge that the calls for flexibility/adaptability involve higher order skills that need to be developed sequentially from year to year.

The focus of assessment patterns as a tool for change is fundamental to the process we propose in what follows. Currently, students often know more about the matter chosen as central to essays and projects than about almost any other area of their units. Assignments that are part of ongoing assessment provide deep and concentrated learning and, therefore, provide powerful levers to use in developing a multi-disciplinary mindset without directly challenging the need for ongoing development of specialist skills. Consequently, specifically multi-disciplinary subjects and forms of assessment play a vital part of the suggested system summarised below, but are not intended to dissipate the time that might otherwise need to be devoted to more concentrated subject units. In the second year of the proposed program there is a one semester multi-disciplinary unit that extends students beyond the boundary of a conventional Commerce course; and in the third year we have made provision for conventional 'capstone units' that could easily adopt multi-disciplinary approaches, as well as a research unit.

In the suggested three year course structure summarised below then, it can be seen that standard discipline based teaching is retained, but that this is augmented in such a way as to provide for the multi-disciplinary integration for which we have argued above.

In Year 1, conventional courses, but including:

- A research assignment (aimed at developing electronic database skills, referencing skills, reporting skills).
- A requirement that at least two assessment requirements be verbal (dissemination and discursive skills).
- One case analysis of a global problem, involving numerical analysis (requiring a global orientation and multi-disciplinary approach in answering)
- At least two assessment requirements in the form of short essays each of around 1000-1500 words (analytical, dissemination and argumentive skills)
- One team based assessment exercise (team skills)
- Introduction to computer simulations, for example a two hour program within one subject.

This year is intended to provide a foundation for building both discipline-based knowledge and communication skills, team skills, global orientation, research skills and multi-disciplinary thinking. It is not considered necessary to provide any multi- disciplinary subjects in this first year because students will tend to study a wide range of foundation units. The multi-disciplinary element is provided by the suggested changes to the assessment patterns.

In Year 2, conventional courses, but including:

- Two research assignments, at least one group based (developing team skills, research and analytical skills)
- Longer essays (2000-2500 words)
- At least three cross-disciplinary case studies, one focused on an aspect of the Asia-Pacific region.
- A compulsory, multi-disciplinary, integrating unit. This should be an accredited one semester unit focussing on skill development. Content would include: public speaking, abstract logical thinking and brief coverage

of either ecology or aesthetics. The intention would be to 'stretch' developing disciplinary thinking and develop two skills areas that may not be adequately covered by conventional courses.

This year includes five assignments that involve multi-disciplinary thinking, and a short course aimed at 'stretching' students by augmenting the more conventional single disciplinary model.

In Year 3, conventional courses, but including:

- Two research based assignments that are issue-centred.
- At least two 'capstone' units that are multi-disciplinary.
- Computer simulation as a significant assessment component in two units, in both cases with a multi-disciplinary requirement for problem solving.
- An emphasis on problem related analysis in all assignments.
- Provision of a 'special topic' unit that allows for individual curiosity driven research.
- Facilitation of entrepreneurial activity by students with appropriate unit accreditation

We believe that this proposed course structure adequately addresses the needs for disciplinary knowledge and skill development, but also provides one answer to the call for targeted attitude development, including global orientation and the fostering of curiosity. The mental model that results is powerful because it facilitates both single and multi-disciplinary thought.

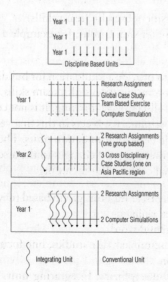

Figure 1
Contrast between existing and proposed courses

Figure 1 illustrates conceptual differences between the two types of degree courses. It has been argued that one effect of channelled, discipline-based learning is that it may produce graduates unable to cross those boundaries when faced with managing in the world of business. In the model put forward here, they would gain the skills and attitudes which permit an integrative, multi-disciplinary view of problems and issues, and would benefit from a global approach in which knowledge and skills could be drawn from a number of appropriate disciplines. Students would learn to apply a macro as well as a micro view to problems with which they are faced. The outcome is one of synergy; by learning to apply and integrate information from a number of areas, students would draw from a much richer base and develop more appropriate solutions in a shorter amount of time. The global focus encourages a *gestalt* effect where the whole becomes greater than the sum of the individual parts. Students would more likely enter organisations as valuable, flexible productive employees rather than carriers of specialised packets of knowledge.

Conclusion

Business management and marketing students may be inadvertently and unintentionally encouraged to segment their learning into discrete subject areas that are considered to be largely independent of each other. This mindset is inappropriate in a business environment that is characterised by flexibility and innovation. A short analogy may assist in making the point clearer. A motor mechanic receives training on a range of specific knowledge and skills: the cooling system, electrical circuits, fuel system, operation of the pistons, valves and so on. As cars become more complex, additional knowledge is needed such as for fuel injection, disc brakes, power-assisted steering and air-conditioning. As useful and necessary as specific knowledge for each area might be, we still expect our mechanic to have the integrated, overall knowledge to be able to diagnose problems and understand how the car works. This is knowledge on a global, holistic level that will enable the mechanic to visualise the car as a complete unit rather than a number of disjointed parts. Of course, (s)he will need to analyse sub systems and components from time to time in order to isolate problems, but (s)he will still need to understand a motor car as a complete, functioning unit.

In the study of management it is argued that there is a tendency to take an atomistic approach to arranging curricula, to the point where students may be unable to see management as an integrated whole. Instead, management problems are seen as fragmented, disconnected items and thus flexibility is displaced by rigidity in thinking and problem solving when faced with management issues in organisations. This may help to explain why students see little if any connection between university studies and the 'real world'.

The course structure that has been tentatively put forward in this paper is aimed at redressing what are perceived as limitations of the current focus of management and marketing education. The use of integrative assessment attempts to develop an attitude within students that discipline areas are interlinked. The course does not detract from the current commitment to specialised knowledge but, rather, challenges the notion that this knowledge is neatly segmented.

References

Bahrami, H. (1992), 'The Emerging Flexible Organisation: Perspectives from Silicon Valley', *California Management Review* Vol 34 No 4 pp 33-52.

Barry, B. (1996), 'The Development of Management Education in Australia', *Asia Pacific Journal of Human Resources* Vol 34 No 2 pp 44-56.

Boxall, P. (1994), 'Placing HR Strategy at the Heart of Business Success', *Personnel Management* Vol 26 No 7 pp 32-35.

Boynton, A. (1991), 'Beyond Flexibility: Building and Managing the Dynamically Stable Organisation', *California Management Review* Vol 34 No 1 pp 53-66.

Brooks, D. (1994), 'HR in the 90s: From Tacticians to Strategists', *HR Focus* Vol 71 No 9 pp 12-13.

Burgoyne, J. (1995), 'Feeding Minds to Grow the Business', *Personnel Management* Vol 1 No 19 pp 22-25.

Churchman, C. (1971), *The Design of Enquiring Systems*, New York: Basic Books.

Collins, R. R. (1987), 'The Strategic Contributions of the Human Resource Function', *Human Resource Management Australia* November pp 5-20.

Commonwealth of Australia (1995), *Enterprising Nation: Renewing Australia's Managers to Meet the Challenges of the Asia-Pacific Century*. Report of the Industry Task Force on Leadership and Management Skills (Chair: David Karpin), April.

Coopey, J. (1987), 'The Case for Creativity in Complex Organisations', *Personnel Management* Vol 19 No 3 pp 30-33.

Dowling, P. J. and R. Schuler (1990), 'Human Resource Management'. In Blancpain, R. (ed.) *Comparative Labour Law and Industrial Relations in Industrialised Market Economies* (4th ed.) Volume 2, pp. 125-149, Boston: Kluwer Law and Taxation Publishers.

Dunphy, D. (1987), 'The Historical Development of Human Resource Management in Australia', *Human Resource Management Australia* Vol 25 No 2 pp 40-47.

Limerick, D. (1992), 'The Shape of the New Organisation: Implications for Human Resource Management', *Asia Pacific Journal of Human Resources* Vol 30 No 1 pp 38-52.

Livingston, J. S. (1971), 'The Myth of the Well-educated Manager'. *Harvard Business Review* Vol 49 No 1 pp 79-89.

Martin, F. (1995), 'Leading the Knowledge of Workers of the 1990s', *Journal of Services Marketing* Vol 9 No 3 pp 5-6.

Mintzberg, H. (1973), *The Nature of Managerial Work*, New York: Harper & Row.

Power, P. and P. Kennet (1996), 'Top CEOs Develop Two Special Dimensions of Leadership', *HR Monthly* October, pp 22-24.

Purcell, J. (1995), 'Corporate Strategy and its Link with Human Resource Management Strategy', in J. Storey (ed.) *Human Resource Management: A Critical Text*, pp. 63-86, London: Routledge.

Senge, P. (1990), *The Fifth Discipline: The Art and Practice of The Learning Organisation*, New York: Doubleday.

Sisson, K. (1995). 'Human Resource Management and the Personnel Function', in J. Storey (ed.) *Human Resource Management: A Critical Text*, pp. 87-109, London: Routledge.

Stebbins, M. and A.B. Shani. (1995), 'Organisational Design and the Knowledge Worker', *Leadership and Organisation Development Journal* Vol 16 No 1 pp 23-30.

Stone, T. and L. Smith (1996), 'A Contingency Theory of Human Resource Management Devolution', *Canadian Journal of Administrative Sciences* Vol 13 No 1 pp 1-12.

Storey, J. (1995), 'Human Resource Management: Still Marching On, or Marching Out?', in J. Storey (ed.) *Human Resource Management: A Critical Text*,. London: Routledge.

Tiernan, S, (1993), 'Innovations in Organisational Structure', *Ibar* Vol 14 No 2 pp 57-68.

Tyson, S. and A. Fell (1986), *Evaluating the Personnel Function.*, London: Hutchinson.

Watson, S.R. (1993), 'The Place for Universities in Management Education', *Journal of General Management* Vol 19 No 2 (Winter) pp 14-42.

Wright, L.K., Bitner, M.J. and V.A. Zeithaml (1994), 'Paradigm Shifts in Business Education: Using Active Learning to Deliver Services Marketing Content', *Journal of Marketing Education* Fall pp 5-19.

Section B
Leadership and teams

4

Examining a Full Range Leadership Development System

Bruce J Avolio

Introduction

During the 1990s, there are fundamental changes occurring in many organisations, which have significantly redefined the relationship between leaders and followers in those organisations. This transformation has involved a move away from authoritarian, command and control systems, towards more collaborative and inclusive network-based systems.

What we are witnessing today in many organisations, is the advent of more *dispersed leadership*, rather than less leadership, although it's not always in the most organised form. Leadership has been migrating to levels of organisations where it had been previously blocked, stifled and/or vigorously challenged in the past. Yet, in many organisations, the migration of leadership 'south', is still not evident at senior to middle levels of management.

The ongoing migration of leadership is fuelled, in part, by the advanced information technology revolution, in which leadership itself has become embedded in the new systems available within many organisations (Sosik, Avolio & Kahai, 1997). Today, groups and larger collectivities have near instant access to a tremendous range of information that has made it possible for people at the lowest levels of organisations to influence key decisions traditionally reserved for senior management. More people can now lead intelligently, and have the information and knowledge to support their leadership potential.

Taking an optimistic view of the future, we may be witnessing the full development of an 'empowered workforce', 'empowered electorate' and 'empowered citizenry', who are each more likely to question, challenge and offer their own unique solutions to problems. Furthermore, the follower as leader has become a reality in many institutions. Yet, there are some 'leaders' that still treat followers as 'subordinates', offering them little opportunity to provide input and to participate in critical decisions. Part of the foot dragging can be attributed to some people not yet realising they do have more discretion to lead, which is a 'habit' still reinforced and embedded in their past styles of interaction.

Organisational and Leadership Transformations

One of the greatest difficulties in changing and advancing human versus technical systems, is that human systems are embedded in old ways of behaving, long after the 'technical' change has 'supposedly' taken place. Stated another way, the transformation of leadership processes and systems has to overcome its own 'installed base', which currently resides in the minds and hearts of people who are still leading *and* following. There appears to be a 'residual software' in many organisations, that represents a major obstacle to any successful transformation in thinking and behaving.

We fully expect that the transformations in organisations today will be associated with a significant amount of friction regarding questions such as 'who is in charge, who is responsible, and who is best able to move us forward?' Yet, these questions are quite reasonable, if one simply considers we are making fundamental changes in the leadership practices and philosophy that have dominated institutions and organisations throughout this century.

Looking back over the last decade, we have seen a surge of interest around the world in exploring the components of leadership that appear to have the greatest impact on human motivation and performance. Some authors have labelled these components charismatic or inspirational leadership, others have called them the "neo-charismatic" models of leadership, while in our work we have referred to them as transformational leadership.

My purpose in this paper is to review where we stand with our conceptualisation and measurement of a 'full range' of leadership styles, by including transformational at the highest end of the full range of leadership. Let me begin by explaining why we chose the term 'Full Range', and then move on to describing its components.

We chose the term 'Full Range' to challenge ourselves and colleagues to continue to expand the range of inquiry into examining what constitutes the highest levels of leadership potential, perspective, and capacity. We've attempted to broaden the scope of inquiry, by examining multiple dimensions or components comprising a full range of leadership at three distinct levels of analysis. These levels include: the *individual, group* and *organisational culture*.

One unique aspect to our approach is that we have taken the same leadership components developed at an individual level of analysis, and have applied those components to exploring leadership processes observed at the group, organisational and/or cultural level. This strategy was not used as a matter of convenience, rather, we escalated the full range model because we felt that it provided the best overall framework for explaining the range of leadership styles that could be potentially observed in individuals, groups and across organisational cultures. In sum, we will begin where most others have started their inquiries into leadership, viewing the individual leader. We then take the same leadership model and examine shared leadership in teams and use it to discuss differences in organisational culture.

Focusing on the 'Individual' as Leader

In 1991, we put forth a leadership model later published in Bass & Avolio (1994), which identified 9 theoretical components or styles of leadership. These components fell into three general categories: transformational, transactional, and non-transactional/laissez-faire leadership. These 9 components became the basic framework for revising the Multifactor Leadership Questionnaire to its current version (Form 5X). The MLQ survey has now been used extensively throughout the world in order to measure the components contained in the full range leadership model (Avolio, Bass & Jung, 1996).

Based on results using different versions of the MLQ, transformational leadership on average, has a more positive relationship than transactional and nontransactional/laissez-faire leadership with individual, group, and organisational measure of performance. We have referred to this pattern of relationships, as a hierarchical ordering of relationships. Bass (1997) recently extended the discussion of the hierarchical ordering of leadership styles by arguing that the model is robust and universal in its relevance across all cultures.

Three recent meta-analyses of the military and broader organisational psychology literature reported that correlations between transformational leadership and rated performance, as well as objectively-measured performance at both individual and group levels, were consistently stronger and more positive than with transactional leadership (Gaspar, 1992; Patterson, Fuller, Kester & Stringer, 1996; Lowe, Kroeck & Sivasubramaniam 1996). Passive and more avoidant styles of leadership were generally negatively correlated at both levels of performance. This hierarchical pattern of relationships has been found in a broad range of cultures, including those that are highly individualistic through to highly collectivistic (Bass, 1997). A summary of the meta-analysis results are presented in figure 1 below.

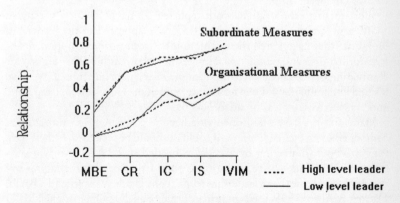

Figure 1 The moderating effect of types of performance measures (subordinate perceptions/ratings vs. organisational measures) on the relationship between MLQ scales and high and low level leader effectiveness.

MLQ Factor Structure

Since the very first results were published using the MLQ (Bass, 1985), there have been differences in opinion about the underlying factor structure of the instrument. Generally, most authors accept the distinction that we've made between transformational, transactional and laissez-faire leadership styles, causing some to argue for a three-factor model of leadership. However, our position on this issue has been consistent, that even though we can always fall back to a more general model of leadership, we've argued for retaining components that are conceptually more highly differentiated. For assessment and development purposes, we believe the more highly differentiated the components contained in the leadership model, the more likely future research and its application in organisations will be advanced. The debate concerning what are the distinct construct valid components contained in the full range model is far from settled at the present time.

The Multi-factor Model.

The original multi-factor model proposed by Bass (1985) was based on a qualitative analysis of Burns' (1978) distinctions between transactional and transformational leaders, as well as results obtained by surveying 198 U. S. Army field grade officers using the MLQ Form 1 to describe their immediate supervisors. The MLQ Form 1 was an outgrowth of the components that had been discussed by Burns as well as by House (1977), in his theory of charismatic leadership. Five leadership components and a non-transactional or laissez-faire component were extracted from a preliminary factor analysis. The six factors described in more detail by Bass (1985) were Charisma/Inspirational, Intellectual Stimulation, Individualised Consideration, Contingent Reward, Active Management-by-Exception and Avoidant or Laissez-faire leadership.

Subsequent to the original work reported by Bass (1985), a variety of analyses of various versions of the MLQ have appeared in the leadership literature, that have tested the distinction between various components of transformational and transactional leadership. Many authors have argued for eliminating laissez-faire leadership from the instrument and model. We have resisted its elimination for one reason: we wanted the range of leadership styles and perspectives to be as broad as possible.

Many authors have questioned whether the correlated transformational components and contingent reward could or should be separated. Others have suggested that managing-by-exception needed to be split into two sub-factors: *active* and *passive*. Still others found that passive managing-by-exception and laissez-faire leadership formed one factor. Most recently, Bycio, Hackett & Allen (1995) used confirmatory factor analysis of the original MLQ Form 1, producing a factor structure comprised of three transformational and two transactional leadership factors, similar to the original structure presented by Bass (1985). However, Bycio et al. (1995) followed the pattern described above, and did not include in their analysis the original laissez-faire scale. We believe its elimination could potentially alter the resulting factor structure of the model.

Conceptual and Empirical Sources of the Competing Factor Model Solutions

Following the strategy we articulated in 1993 (see Bass & Avolio, 1993), regarding alternative conceptualisations of a full range model and valid criticisms of the MLQ survey, I will present a brief summary of different competing models of leadership, ending up with the most highly differentiated 9-factor model that has been discussed in detail by Bass and Avolio (1994).

Basis for a 9 Factor Solution.

Based on results reported by Hater and Bass (1988), the original 6-factor model was expanded when management-by-exception was split into active and passive dimensions (MBEA, MBEP). We also chose to evaluate charisma (CH) and inspirational motivation (IM) as two separate, but correlated, factors because we observed that leaders who were inspirational were not always seen as charismatic. The charisma scale was further divided into attributed charisma (AC) and charismatic behaviour (CB) based on recommendations by House, Spangler and Woyke (1991) to differentiate attributed from behavioural charismatic leadership.

Basis for a 7 Factor Solution.

A seven factor solution has emerged when we combined attributed charisma (AC), charismatic behaviour (CB) and inspirational motivation (IM) into a single higher order factor. Repeatedly, despite the proposition that measure of attributed charisma, charismatic behaviour and inspirational leadership are conceptually distinct, correlations of 0.80-0.90 are found when differential measure of each have been attempted.

Basis for a 5 Factor Solution.

As noted above, Bycio et al. (1995) produced a five-factor solution using confirmatory factor analysis of the MLQ Form 1. Form 1 did not contain independent scale scores for active and passive management-by-exception, but rather a single score for both combined. Bycio et al. (1995) provided support for Bass's (1985) original model containing three independent transformational factors and two independent transactional factors without including items tapping laissez-faire leadership. The authors qualified their conclusions indicating that a simple factor structure may also be appropriate given the high correlation between transformational and contingent reward leadership. An alternate five factor solution also emerged out of the work of Howell and Avolio (1993), which comprised a single higher order transformation factor, three transactional factors, and a laissez-faire factor.

Basis for a 3 Factor Solution.

Prior to any factor analytic results, conceptually, the range of leadership factors discussed by Bass (1985), included transformational, transactional, and non-transactional or laissez-faire leadership. This 3-factor solution has often been discussed in the literature as representing transformational and transactional leadership factors, as the two main higher-order constructs of leadership, with some brief mention of laissez-faire leadership.

Basis for a 2 Factor Solution.

The research and models presented by House (1977), and Conger and Kanungo (1987), exemplify two factor solutions of charismatic and non-charismatic leadership, although, as noted by House (1995), Conger and Kanungo have frequently included the components of transformational leadership in their descriptions of charismatic leadership.

Rationale for a 1 Factor Solution.

A single general factor would be confirmed if all of the leadership factors were seen as a single bundle of behaviours and attributes. In other words, it's either leadership, or it's not leadership in the eyes of the raters.

A recent study was undertaken, analysing data collected using the MLQ Form 5X in fourteen independent samples (Avolio, Bass, & Jung, 1996). The purpose of this study was to examine the factor structure of this newly revised instrument to determine how many components were empirically distinguishable from each other within the 9-factor model. Exploratory and confirmatory factor analysis were used here to test the factors contained in the MLQ Form 5X.

The factor analysis included 14 samples with a total of 3,786 respondents. All 14 samples contained MLQ rater evaluations of a target leader. The first 9 samples were used as our derivation sample. This was the first set of samples received from researchers using the MLQ Form 5X in their own research programs. The remaining five samples were obtained following the collection of the first set of samples, and were used for replicating the factor structure in the first set. Results of our analyses for both the initial and replication sets, including four items per scale were taken from the original pool of items contained in the MLQ Form 5X survey.

The final set of 36 items came from the larger pool of items contained in the MLQ, after trimming items based on results from the first factor analysis.

These 36 items were retained from the analyses in the initial set of samples in order to replicate the results using the same items in the second set of samples. Intercorrelations among the transformational scales were generally high and positive, similar to the intercorrelations reported for the MLQ 5R survey (see Bass & Avolio, 1990). There were also positive and significant correlations between the transactional contingent reward (CR) scale, and each of the scales comprising transformational leadership in both the initial and replication set of samples.

The positive and significant correlations between the transformational and transactional contingent reward leadership scales were expected for several reasons. First, *both* transactional and transformational leadership represent active, and constructive forms of leadership. Second, as noted numerous times, effective leaders display varying amounts of both transactional and transformational leadership (Bass & Avolio, 1993, 1994). Third, a consistent honouring of exchanges and transactional agreements builds trust, dependability, and perceptions of consistency among associates of their leaders, which can form the basis for the higher levels of trust and respect associated with transformational leadership (Shamir, 1995). Therefore, although conceptually unique, one could expect to obtain a positive correlation among these factors.

Based on prior research with earlier versions of the MLQ, we expected active *corrective* transactional leadership, or active management-by-exception, to exhibit either low positive or negative correlations with the transformational and the more *constructive* form of transactional leadership (CR). Active management-by-exception also was excepted to correlate with the more passive form and avoidant laissez-faire leadership (LF). Consistent with many previous studies of earlier forms of the MLQ (See Bass & Avolio, 1990, 1993), the passive and avoidant leadership factor was expected to correlate negatively with the transformational and transactional contingent reward leadership scales.

Summary of MLQ Results

We used structural equations modelling to examine whether the data from the initial and replication sample sets best confirmed either five or six factor models of leadership. The six factor model did not produce an adequate fit due to high intercorrelations among the transformational leadership factors, and positive correlations with contingent reward leadership when the total item set was examined. To improve the psychometric properties of the instrument, without altering the six factor model, we utilised the Modification Indices (MI) provided by LISREL to trim individual items contained in each scale. Refinements to survey instruments using 'item trimming' without altering the underlying model, can help further research on survey measures

Table 1 Mean, Standard Deviations, and Intercorrelations of MLQ 5X scores Among the Initial Set of Samples and Replication Set of MLQ 5X Scores

Variable	M	SD	1	2	3	4	5	6
1. Charisma	2.58,2.69	.87,.91	**.92,.92**					
2. Intellectual Stimulation	2.51,2.54	.95,.93	.82,.81	**.83,.78**				
3. Individualised Consideration	2.66,2.64	.99,.99	.81,.82	.74,.77	**.79,.78**			
4. Contingent Reward	2.51,2.40	.98,.99	.77,.71	.73,.67	.75,.68	**.80,.74**		
5. Management-By-Exception- Active	1.69,1.60	.85,.90	-.17,-.16	-.09,-.08	-.23,-.21	-.11,.02	**.63,.64**	
6. Passive/Avoidant	1.02,1.09	.79,.89	-.51,-.54	-.46,-.44	-.45,-.52	-.38,-.28	.24,.45	**84,,86**

Note: Each item was rated on the 5-point scale from 0 (not at all) to 4 (frequently, if not always). Coefficient alphas are reported values in boldface along the diagonal. First values in each column show correlations from the original set of samples (N=1,394 after listwise deletion) and the second value in each column show correlations from the replication set of samples (N=1,706 after listwise deletion.).

such as the MLQ (Podsakoff & Organ, 1986), without modifying the conceptual model it was designed to assess.

Using an 'item-trimming' strategy was consistent with our goal of developing a reliable and valid multi-factor instrument with a minimum number of items per scale. We used the parameters on the MI to increase the measurement's overall fit to the original six factor model, by selectively eliminating items from each scale that had high cross-loadings with other factors, and/or did not load on the factor it was intended to measure. After we finalised the item selection process, we reran LISREL with the original sample set, to determine if the model fit had improved with a reduced set of items. We present in Table 1, a summary of descriptive statistics for the 6-factor model.

The 6-factor model produced fit indices exceeding the minimum cut-offs recommended in the literature (Anderson & Gerbing, 1998; Bentler, 1990; Bollen 1989; James, Mulaik, & Brett, 1982). However, for comparison purposes, we examined two alternative 5-factor models proposed by Bycio et al (1995) and Howell and Avolio (1993), in order to determine if they provided a better or more parsimonious fit for the data collected using the revised MLQ. Results reported in Table 1 indicated the best model fit was for six factors. Generally, the two alternative models did not meet the minimum cut-offs for adequate fit. This pattern was also true for models containing more than 6 factors.

Table 2 Summary of confirmatory factor analysis results for three alternative models

	Bycio et al. Model	Five Factor Alternative Model	SixFactor Model
Chi-Square	2854/454 (3122)	279/584 (3179)	2509/579 (2788)
GFI	87 (86)	89 (88)	91 (91)
AGFI	85 (84)	87 (86)	90 (89)
RMSR	05 (06)	04 (06)	04 (05)
NFI	90 (89)	90 (88)	91 (90)
TLI	85 (83)	88 (87)	89 (88)

Using these preliminary results as a basis, we attempted to replicate the revised MLQ survey in a second and independent set of samples.

Replication Sample Tests of Fit.

We retested the six factor model solution using the 36 item shortened version of the MLQ (Form 5X) with the second set of samples. As noted earlier, the second set of samples was comprised of 1706 cases.

Tests from the initial set of nine samples, produced a similar pattern of results with respect to model fit in the replication set of samples. Although there was some minor shrinkage in the level of fit for the six-factor model on several indices, the six factor solution appeared to produce the best absolute fit, over the two alternative five-factor models. For each of the 5-factor models, none of the indices reached adequate levels of fit.

Based on results from the initial set and the replication samples, evidence was found that the best model fit was associated with a six-factor model. However, although a better absolute fit, the six factor model was not dramatically different in fit than the more parsimonious alternative five-factor model. For the most part, the five and six-factor models held up with relatively little shrinkage when tested in the replication sample.

Taken together, these results provided a broader base of evidence for the original factor structure underlying the MLQ survey, while also expanding the range of leadership styles that have been examined in prior research based on earlier models of leadership (Bass, 1990). Yet, differentiating each of these factors from one another still poses a difficult challenge given the typical problems associated with any survey measure, for example general impression and halo errors. In our opinion, the full range 9 factor model still remains an ideal to strive for in future research using the MLQ.

We now recommend enlarging the range of samples to replicate the present results testing the construct validity of a six-factor model. By broadening the sample base, we can provide a better test of the underlying theoretical model, while also enhancing the generalisability of the findings reported above by Avolio et al (1996). Eventually, extensions to the data base should include leaders from different cultures, using translations of the MLQ Form 5X survey. Along these lines, preliminary analyses of ratings of platoon commanders in the Israel Defence Forces, with a Hebrew translation version of the MLQ, provided support for a 6-factor model of leadership. It is our contention that, as we approximate the population of raters evaluating all respective leaders, we will be better able to uncover finer distinctions between the factors comprising what has been labelled here as a 'Full Range' model of leadership.

We must reiterate that although the transformational leadership components are generally highly correlated for assessment, counselling and training purposes, it is definitely more useful to assess each of these components as separate factors. For example, using an earlier MLQ (Form 8Y), Den Hartog, Van Mujen & Koopman (1997) came to a similar conclusion after reporting evidence for a Dutch sample of managers, for a 3-factor (transformational, transactional and passive leadership) and a 4-factor model of leadership (transformational, contingent reward, active management-by-exception and passive leadership). Den Hartog et al. (1997) stated, 'although the three factor solution provides a useful research solution, distinguishing between different components of transformational leadership may remain useful, particularly for training purposes.' (p.32).

Instead of limiting future leadership research and practice to a global charismatic and/or transformational leadership factor, researchers and practitioners ought to continue to examine separately, each of the components that others describe as a 'global' factor. Our reasoning for this argument is that it is easier to describe to people how to be more *intellectually stimulating,* or how to be more *individually considerate,* than how to be more inspirational or *charismatic.* In the same way, how a trainee has used different forms of transactional leadership such as *contingent reinforcement,* is quite important feedback, if the trainee underutilises contingent reinforcement or over utilises *active-managing-by-exception.*

Implications for Individual Level Leadership Development

There are several implications from these preliminary results for assessing and developing individual-level leadership. First, by measuring a wider and more detailed range of leadership factors, we increase our chances of tapping into the actual range of leadership styles that are exhibited across different cultures and organisational settings. Second, to the extent this range of leadership styles holds up in future research, we have moved closer to developing a basis for a more effective and comprehensive means for leadership assessment, training and development. Third, while the transactional leadership factors included here have been discussed in the leadership literature for at least fifty years (Bass, 1990), little attention in the aggregate had been paid to measuring and understanding the transformational components until the last ten to fifteen years.

The Migration of Leadership to Group Systems and Teams.

As some leading organisations have transformed into intelligent network systems, the positive influence of leadership has come to reside more in their networks than in any one single individual. Call it alliances, ensembles, teams, or cells, what is happening today is a fundamental change in the way leadership is exercised in organisations and institutions. It is far more shared within and between levels, and may have far greater potential and substantially less risk, as a consequence of it being embedded in networks versus any one person (Avolio, Jung, Murry and Sivasubramaniam, 1996). Today, we have flatter hierarchies, virtual information retrieval and dissemination, enhanced autonomy, a more rapid pace of change and much greater need for interdependencies in organisations throughout the global marketplace. The question we address next, is whether the 'shared' leadership systems in organisations has changed to accommodate these dramatic transformations?

A secondary question is whether we can measure such collective or *shared leadership,* and in more practical terms describe it to others using a full range model of leadership.

Although technical and social trends are rapidly transforming organisations today, placing greater importance on understanding the 'collective forces' of leadership, we can't neglect the individual, who remains a potent and fundamental force in an expanded leadership system and/or framework. With this orientation in mind, a whole new frontier for dialogue on leadership systems and practices has emerged - one that is now *both* multi-dimensional along the full-range model, and multi-level with respect to individuals and groups.

Although there has been a surge of interest around building and rebuilding organisations utilising teams (Amason, Thompson, Hochwater & Harrison, 1995; Hackman, 1990), relatively little attention has been given to understanding what constitutes 'shared leadership' in teams. Ilgen, Major, Hollenbeck & Sego (1993) indicated there was relatively little research that had examined shared leadership processes in teams, as compared with the majority of research on 'team leadership', such as project leaders.

It is somewhat surprising that more attention has not been paid to leadership in teams, since several authors have concluded that one of the major contributing factors to the failure of teams is its ineffective leadership (Cummings, 1978; Klein, 1984; Sinclair, 1992; Steward & Manz, 1994). Sinclair (1992) was specific on this point, suggesting the most critical ingredient in team success is its leadership, both within the group and through its supervision.

For our purposes, shared leadership has been defined as a group-level leadership behaviour exhibited in a collective sense by all members of a team. We represent such leadership here as the average of all member's evaluations of the team's leadership style. This operational definition was used as a crude initial measure of what will eventually emerge as a measure of shared leadership within teams.

Groups, Teams and Shared Leadership

We begin with a rather basic notion, that 'while all teams are groups, not all groups are teams' (Tannenbaum, Beard, & Salas, 1992, p.118). A collective goal, alignment of interests, an adequate level of cohesion, and shared leadership are each necessary, but not sufficient conditions for team effectiveness. Moreover, high performing teams continuously develop over time, while working towards sharing in responsibilities, building a sense of collective meaning and purpose, and identifying with the teams' common goals and central purpose (Shamir, House & Arthur, 1993). Interestingly enough, all of these characteristics are also associated with effective individual leadership and the quality of the relationship built with each follower (Avolio et al., 1996). For example, Kozlowski, Gully, Salas & Cannon-Bowers (1996a; 1996b), have discussed each of these characteristics with respect to an effective team leader or supervisor, versus leadership within a team exhibited collectively by all team members.

In line with current African humanistic theories of group behaviour, we believe the 'vital force' in teams comes from optimising the relationships among individuals in the team, and in developing its collective efforts and abilities (see Christie, Lessem, & Mbigi, 1993). This philosophy parallels discussions of 'group potency' (see Guzzo, Yost, Campbell & Shea, 1993), as well as Bandura's (1986) concept of 'collective efficacy.' By developing relationships among members of the group to work more effectively towards a common goal, we can begin to describe how shared leadership processes play a central role in the development of a high performing team.

A Preliminary Examination of A full Range of Leadership in Teams.

When operationalising transforming leadership, Burns (1978) discussed how such leaders are able to get members of their group to willingly sacrifice personal gain for the gain of others. This level of sacrifice was expected to occur when members identified with what the leader was striving to accomplish.

We now extend Burns' argument suggesting that high performing teams collectively display transformational leadership, as well as transactional and laissez-faire leadership. Many examples of transformational leadership and its effects on individual willingness to sacrifice are depicted in the team literature, including references to 'high performing' teams (such as Katzenbach & Smith, 1993).

It is interesting to note that shared leadership has been discussed many times in terms of shared responsibility for transactional agreements or contracts in groups (Bass & Avolio, 1994), with respect to the development of a vision (Nanus, 1992), in terms of developing creative and innovative solutions (McGrath, 1984), and in terms of addressing conflicts and disputes in groups (Amason et al., 1995). Here we intend to examine how transformational, transactional and nontransactional (laissez-faire) leadership as operationalised by Bass and Avolio (1994) can be applied to measuring the collective leadership observed in high performing teams. We briefly discuss below a newly designed team leadership survey that attempts to assess the main components comprising Bass and Avolio's (1994) 'full-range' leadership model.

Parallels Between Individual and Team Leadership

At a very basic level, most authors would agree that it is essential for groups or teams to establish a means for clarifying their expectations of each other, and to design ways to regulate interactions within the group or team, and within the context of a larger organisation. According to socio-technical systems theory, effective group performance minimally requires that groups regulate themselves (Trist, 1977), which typically occurs by setting norms and expectations that group members must understand and uphold (Manz & Sims, 1987). One can view this process as an early transactional phase in the emergence of becoming a transformational team. Establishing a base of expectations for appropriate internal or external transactions begins to establish some sense of coherence regarding how groups should function within themselves, and in transactions with other groups (Avolio et al., 1996; Kozlowski et al., 1996a, 1996b). To the extent that transactions and agreements are honoured over time by group members, a basis for trust and commitment to the group can be established (Shamir et al., 1993). Where transactions are missing, groups are likely to spin out of control, failing to accomplish even rather simple objectives.

Like effective leaders, effective teams also develop and enforce norms that clearly identify what is expected of members, and what members can expect to receive for satisfying expectations. Effective teams establish goals, provide timely feedback, set up contingencies to address changes in their context, punish members or take corrective action for members who violate rules, and reward those who meet objectives, if not exceed them. Guidelines are created to differentiate 'good' versus 'bad' behaviour. Such rules and/or guidelines are not so different than what one would expect to observe with more traditional transactional styles of leadership (Bass & Avolio, 1994), however, here transactions are among team members oftentimes of equal or similar status, as opposed to being between a leader and follower.

Moving up the continuum of leadership, highly effective teams have been characterised as having a clear central focus or vision, and comprised of members who identify with the team's vision (Katzenbach & Smith, 1993); members actively build each other's potential; they are cohesive, and over time build a framework of coherent values and beliefs (Cohen, Ledford, & Spreitzer, 1996; Kozlowski et al. 1996b). One can easily say that all of these characteristics are also important and frequently discussed in the context of more traditional models of individual inspirational and transformational leadership (Avolio et al., 1996; Bass & Avolio, 1994; Hogan, Curphy & Hogan, 1994; Yukl, 1994). Exemplary and/or transformational leaders develop in their followers a shared sense of purpose and/or vision, they work towards developing followers to their full potential, they are the 'keeper', if not champion, of their group's values, and often it is because of the leader's efforts or sacrifices that followers come to identify with the vision or goals being pursued.

The first study to use the TMLQ, which was conducted by Jung, Avolio, Murry and Sivasubramaniam (1997), included 186 business-major undergraduate students enrolled at a large public university in the Northeastern United States. Participants were registered in two introductory organisational behaviour courses, in which they were involved in semester-long groups working on class projects. Four of five students were randomly assigned to 37 groups of mixed gender at the beginning of semester. The mean age of the participants was 20, and 54% were females.

In study 2, conducted by the same authors, students came from two introductory organisational behaviour classes at a large public university in the Northeast of the United States. The total number of students participating in study 2 was 169 of which 52% were males. The mean age was 21. All participants were randomly assigned to 42 groups of mixed gender at the beginning of the semester to complete group projects.

For study 1, group-level leadership data using the TMLQ were collected from subjects after all group projects were completed. Items were rated on five-point response scales: (1) not at all, (2) once in a while, (3) sometimes, (4) fairly often, and (5) frequently, if not always. All participants were asked to evaluate each statement in terms of the team's collective leadership behaviour.

The same procedures used in study 1 were also used in study 2, except that the group potency scale was added as an outcome measure. Guzzo and his colleagues have argued that transformational leadership can enhance group potency and effectiveness through the use of intellectual stimulation, by promoting a consideration of different member's viewpoints and by inspiring collective action for higher levels of group motivation (Guzzo et al., 1993; Shea & Guzzo, 1987).

A third study involved U.S. Army enlisted men, who each rated the collective leadership of their platoons using a military version of the TMLQ. There were several hundred soldiers from 18 platoons, involved in the third study conducted by Bass, Avolio, Jung and Berson (1997).

The items in the TMLQ were written based on four sources. The first source was from the definitions of the constructs comprising Bass and Avolio's full range leadership model. The second source was the MLQ Form 5X survey. Items were reviewed by the first author for their suitability for inclusion in the TMLQ. The third source was from individuals who had worked in teams for at least one year. These teams came from four different organizations including: a large financial services firm; two global manufacturing operations, one high technology-based and the other, a low technology assembly plant; and the fourth was a theatre group. Each team (total = 20) was interviewed for approximately two hours on videotape, describing stages of team development, how to effectively lead teams, how to reinforce high potential, etc. The first author reviewed each videotape for leadership content and developed sample items for inclusion in the preliminary version of the TMLQ. The last source for developing team leadership items was the team literature. This literature was reviewed focussing on discussions of leadership indicators in teams.

Measuring Team Leadership.

A factor analysis was conducted for the first sample of students, including all 40 leadership items included in the TMLQ. With the entire set of 40 items, the model failed to converge after 10 iterations, due to high intercorrelations among the transformational and transactional leadership factors. We selected three items to represent each leadership construct, based on the Modification Indices (MI) produced by LISREL VII, active management-by-exception, was represented by two items.

After finalising the selection of items, we then retested the original and several competing models to determine the best model fit. Similar to our results with the MLQ, all of the fit indices, as well as chi-square tests improved, going from a one-factor to a six-factor model. The team leadership scales produced adequate levels of internal consistency, except for the MBEA and MBEP/LF scales, which were below 0.7.

As noted earlier, the main purpose of study 2 was two-fold: (1) to replicate the results reported from study 1; and (2) to further assess the psychometric properties of the revised TMLQ survey, adding in a team-oriented outcome measure of group potency as the criterion measure (Guzzo et al, 1993).

Again, most team leadership subscales indicated adequate levels of reliability except active management-by-exception (=.52). Similar to research conducted at an 'individual level' of analysis, most transformational leadership scales were highly correlated with ratings of effectiveness and group potency.

Based on results reported in study 1, we retested the same models with the revised TMLQ survey. Results of the analysis in study 2 again supported the six-factor model. None of the fit indices improved beyond the six factor model. Reliabilities produced were nearly identical to those reported for Study 1.

In a separate study conducted with soldiers rating their platoons using the TMLQ, additional support was found for the six factor model. These results are still preliminary in that they are based on a relatively small sample of US Army personnel. However, unlike studies 1 and 2, this sample represents organisational units which contained members who had a history of interactions with each other. On average, 15 members of each platoon evaluated the 'platoon's leadership' using a slightly modified version of the TMLQ for military contexts. Thus in three separate instances the 'shortened' full range model held up for group-level measure of transformational, transactional and non-transactional/laissez-faire leadership.

Overall, a primary assumption that we had in developing the TMLQ was that leadership constructs operationalised at an individual level could be employed at a group level (Avolio & Bass, 1995). With respect to the 'full range' leadership model discussed by Bass and Avolio (1994), constructs such as 'individualised consideration' can be examined in terms of a dyadic relationship between a leader and his or her follower, or in terms of how each team member on average, treats others in terms of recognising the needs, ability and motivation of each other.

Preliminary evidence has now been provided here supporting a six-factor model of group/team leadership styles. The six factors included three transformational leadership styles, one transactional or contingent reward/exchange style, a corrective or active management-by-exception style and a combination of the passive corrective/laissez-faire style. Perhaps most important, the factors comprising the range of leadership styles included in this study were very similar to results reported earlier for the MLQ completed by individual followers rating their respective focal leaders.

Applying Team Leadership to the Prediction of Potency and Performance

Current research on teams indicates that exemplary leadership can have a positive impact on group motivation, efficacy and performance (Kumpfer, Turner, Hopkins, & Librett, 1993). A substantial amount of literature that has qualitatively examined high performing teams has come to the same conclusion (Hackman, 1990; Katzenbach & Smith, 1993; Manz & Sims, 1993). It seems reasonable to conclude that effective if not exemplary leadership in teams, is required for achieving the highest levels of performance. Based on the current team literature, the type of leadership that we predict makes a difference between a collection of individuals being a group versus a highly effective team, is leadership which is more transformational (Avolio et al, 1996).

Several components of Klimoski and Mohammed's (1994) model of team performance were tested in the next study to be reviewed. (The full description of this study can be obtained in Sivasubramaniam, Jung, Avolio & Murry, 1997). In their model, they begin with each individual's potential to contribute, team composition, size and resources available. Each of these factors contribute to a 'team's capacity'. In the study conducted by Sivasubramaniam et al. (1997), these variables were controlled by randomly assigning members to their respective groups, and limiting group size to four or five members. Next in their model they specify team leadership. For the purposes of preliminary research with the TMLQ, team leadership was operationalised here as transformational versus avoidant/laissez-faire leadership. This was done to address the typical high correlation between transactional and transformational leadership. While Klimoski and Mohammed (1994) identified several process variables, including level of collective effort and quality of interpersonal relations, the 'collective effort' variable was operationalised as potency, while the measure of performance represented each group's overall performance over a four month period.

Shamir et al (1993) argue that transformational leadership can enhance the potency of group or teams by making participation in a group's efforts more meaningful and tied to the collective identity of the group. Leadership in groups can highlight the importance of the task and how the group has greater capability to take on difficult challenges. Going back to Burns (1978), by collectively building faith in a better future, transformational leadership among team members is expected to enhance the overall feelings of potency within a team. To the degree that transformational leadership builds personal identification within a group (Shamir, et al., 1993), and a sense of confidence, a group's level of potency and performance is expected to be higher (Guzzo et al., 1993).

Laissez-faire leadership represents a passive and/or avoidant style of leadership in groups where it is likely that no one will take responsibility for structuring the group's agenda, agreements or expectations. In such situations, the group becomes over time more passive, less potent and generally ineffective (Hackman, 1990; Silver & Bufanio, 1996). At the individual level, avoidant leadership has been consistently shown to lead to lower follower satisfaction and effectiveness, as well as lower organisational performance (see Lowe et al., 1996).

Guzzo, et al., (1993) identified group efficacy and potency as an important cognitive influence on team performance, reporting a positive relationship between group potency and team performance (Guzzo et al., 1993; Shea & Guzzo, 1987). Several others have also reported support for the potency/efficacy - performance relationship (Arad & Drasgow, 1994; Cohen & Denison, 1990; Spink, 1990). Silver and Bufanio (1996) examined the relationships among group potency, group goals and task performance among 25 student groups. Their results showed that group potency was significantly and positively related to subsequent task performance.

Direct and Indirect Effects of Team Leadership on Group Performance

Since the development of teams represents a time-based process, one should examine how the group's leadership and level of potency were manifested over time. Specifically, Sivasubramaniam et al. (1997) predicted that groups that were initially more transformational, would also exhibit higher initial levels of potency. These initial levels of potency would then positively predict the group's continued use of transformational leadership behaviours, potency, and beliefs as well as overall performance (Guzzo et al., 1993). Alternatively, groups that were characterised by laissez-faire leadership would fail to establish clear expectations, and the basis for determining each other's contributions to the group. Such groups would flounder and not exhibit high levels of potency either initially or over time. These groups would be expected to exhibit more laissez-faire leadership over time and less effective levels of performance.

Summary of Results

A total of 182 undergraduate students majoring in business management enrolled at a large public university in the Northeastern United States participated in phase 1 of data collection. Of the total number of students, there were 155 who completed both phases of the study. Participants completed all survey measures individually during class time roughly three weeks into the semester (time 1), and ten weeks after the initial assessment (time 2). The groups interacted on a weekly basis to complete case assignments and experiential exercises during the first three weeks of the semester. They were also required to turn in the first of several assignments before the first phase of the survey assessment (time 1) was completed. None of the groups received any feedback on their first assignment before completing the survey instruments. The second phase of data collection was completed two weeks before the end of the semester (time 2), and a week before the groups' final project was due. Students were not given grades for group projects until the last day of classes. While not monitored systematically, all of the groups met regularly outside class hours to discuss and complete the assigned projects.

In all, there were 12 items included from the TMLQ that measured transformational leadership. The transformational scale reliability was 0.90 for time 1, and 0.90 for time 2. Laissez-faire/avoidant leadership was assessed by three items. The mean score on these three items was used as the indicator of team laissez-faire leadership. The scale reliability was 0.69 for time 1 and 0.70 for time 2. Group Potency was assessed by using the measure developed by Guzzo and his colleagues (Guzzo et al., 1993). The scale reliability was 0.91 for time 1, and 0.92 for time 2. To minimise any confounding effects due to practice or order, item-order was scrambled for the two administrations of the survey at times 1 and 2. The time between the two survey administrations was approximately ten weeks.

For measuring team performance, each group's grade assigned by the respective instructors in the two classes, was used as a measure of performance. The final group grades were determined at the end of semester well after the second phase of data collection was completed. Grades were standardised within each section. The subsequent Z-scores were then used as the standardised measure of performance for all subsequent analyses.

Team leadership significantly predicted group potency beliefs. Team transformational leadership positively predicted potency in both time periods, as well as across the three month interval of this study. Potency beliefs in time 1 did not predict team transformational leadership in time 2, but was significantly and negatively related to team laissez-faire leadership in time 2. Group potency positively predicted group performance. The relationship between leadership and performance was mediated by group members' perception of their level of potency beliefs. Direct effects of team leadership style on performance were not significant, when taking into consideration the indirect effects.

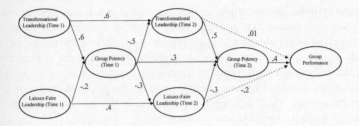

Figure 2 Results of the longitudinal LISREL Model of effects of Leadership

Note: Indicators and other model parameters not shown to improve clarity

These preliminary findings indicated that transformational leadership can occur early on in teams, and it can impact group potency and performance in ways that parallel individual leader and follower interactions. Indeed, it appears, as has been suggested by Kozlowski et al. (1996b), Manz and Sims (1987), and Shamir et al. (1993), that team or collective leadership is at least one factor in predicting the subsequent effectiveness of teams.

Preliminary results using the TMLQ survey with the platoon sample described earlier parallel the results reported by Sivasubramaniam et al. (1997). Platoon members rated their collective leadership three months prior to going through what is called Joint Readiness Training. The intensive training involves two weeks of simulated missions in the field that is used to test the overall performance of platoons. When we examined the top and bottom three performing platoons out of 18 who had gone through JRTC, we found that the top platoons were significantly more transformational than the bottom, confirming the patterns noted above. Individual leadership as displayed by the platoon's lieutenant and sergeant also differentiated between high versus low platoon performance.

Next Steps in Research on Team/Collective/Shared Leadership

There are a number of interesting avenues that can be pursued in future research on team leadership. First, the current results need to be replicated on other samples who have a more diverse membership with respect to age, ethnicity and work experience. Second, measures of team leadership should be further refined, with specific emphasis on measuring the more transactional components of team leadership. Measures of transactional leadership, as noted above, were not included in the study by Sivasubramaniam et al. (1997), since items representing contingent reward leadership were too highly correlated with the transformational scale.

Another area for potential future research is to tease out the actual patterns of behaviour that result in groups becoming teams, and teams becoming more transformational. For example, to build trust, the group may first establish expectations via contracts and agreements with its members over time. As members fulfil their obligations to agreements, they may begin to exhibit higher levels of trust in each other. This may partially explain the typical high correlation between team transformational and transactional leadership. The speed at which this occurs will likely depend on the nature of the group and its membership. More heterogeneous groups, with little history of being together, may take longer to work through agreements and to build trust with each other. These groups may also require more external leadership initially to launch the group, but, over time, may establish enough trust to be self-sufficient with the leadership within the group.

At present, we do not know whether the members of the groups or platoons that were more transformational had higher levels of identification and commitment to their work, as Shamir et al., (1993) would predict. Future research needs to examine how groups that described themselves as more transformational built trust, identification and commitment to their tasks. For instance, did one member make a difference in getting the group to identify with its work? How did the formal leadership of the platoon influence the development of collective leadership? Was it a collection of members that each made the difference in terms of identification? Or, in different groups, did both occur and have a similar impact on the group's level of development with respect to transformational leadership, identification and high levels of performance? It seems safe to say that, at the present time, we know very little about these dynamics in terms of team formation processes, which also has implications for viewing leadership at the next level of analysis, which includes organisational systems/culture.

Some Practical Implications for Teams

The current work on team leadership has reaffirmed the importance of examining the effects of collective leadership on subsequent levels of group potency and performance. Moreover, these findings indicated that if some groups were simply left alone, they might become increasingly less effective over time, and that 'good' leadership does not necessarily 'spontaneously' emerge in all groups. Based on these results, there is some reason to believe that appropriate and early leadership interventions could have a significant and positive impact on subsequent group/team performance. What appears to be clear from the work on team leadership is that the characteristics which authors such as Katzenbach and Smith (1993) discussed with respect to high performing teams are very similar to those characteristics that have often been attributed to exemplary leaders in organisations. It is these transformational characteristics that Burns (1978) first identified for individual leaders, that appear to now apply equally well to describing high performing teams.

The Next Level: Organisational Culture

Paralleling our efforts at the individual and team level, we have also attempted to examine the full range leadership model at the organisational or culture level. We have produced a 28 item survey called the Organisational Description Questionnaire (ODQ), which assesses transactional versus transformational leadership cultures.

A preliminary and exploratory factor analysis of this instrument based on data collected from a sample of 500 community leaders (see Avolio & Bass, 1991; 1995), resulted in two distinguishable factors: a global transformational versus transactional factor. In this sample, we found positive relationships between ratings of transformational leadership on the MLQ, and ratings of transformational cultures, from a separate group of raters completing the ODQ survey. A similar pattern emerged for ratings of individual level transactional leadership and the cultures observed in a broad range of community organisations.

These initial results indicated that it may be feasible to differentiate transactional versus transformational cultures in the same way that we have differentiated transactional versus transformational teams and leaders. Extending the leadership model to the organisational cultural level, provides us with a parsimonious framework to examine leadership at three distinct levels of analysis. This multi-level/muiltidimensional framework also can facilitate an examination of how different leadership styles at individual and group levels have an impact on motivation and performance when the cultural context is either aligned with or in conflict with the respective leadership styles. Also, one can track the emergence of styles of leadership as organisations grow from enterprise startups to larger complex systems.

Obviously, the area in which we have done the least work, is that of organisational culture. This in no way indicates that measuring cultural-level leadership is any less important than team or individual level leadership. In fact, just the opposite may be true; as organisations transform their structures into more boundary-less and networked enterprises, cultured leadership is bound to become even more relevant to organisational effectiveness (Shamir, 1997). Moreover, as the rate of forming strategic alliances grows around the world, studying culture-level leadership becomes extremely timely. Specifically, one could ask how difficult it will be to merge a highly transactional with a high transformational culture? What are the strategies organisations should pursue to optimise the merger of such dissimilar cultures? How can individual and group-level leadership in those organisations contribute to the eventual convergence of those disparate cultures? These and many other questions remain unanswered, because there has been relatively little emphasis on directly examining the leadership culture of organisations.

With the rapid transformations going on in organisations today, the time seems propitious to explore this next level of leadership in organisational systems. In doing so, we must realise, as we have done for teams, that the emergence of different types of cultural leadership will, no doubt, take time. Perhaps the time it takes for such cultures to emerge and differentiate themselves may be an important indicator in the future of an organisation's capability to handle rapid transformations in the markets.

Conclusions and Implications

Our intent was to present a broad overview of the work being currently undertaken to examine the full range leadership model at three over lapping levels of analysis. As can be surmised, additional work is needed to fully validate the model at each of these three respective levels. However, it seems fair to say, that there are many more consistencies as opposed to discrepancies across these respective levels with regards to the results reported in this paper. Most importantly, once we are able to assess the full range of leadership factors at each level, we will have created a more dynamic framework for examining the complete leadership system within any organisation. From a practical perspective, having developed a total leadership framework based on the composition of these three levels, it should be easier to develop individuals and groups to higher levels of leadership potential. Indeed, if being an effective individual leader is the basis for effective team leadership and cultures, starting at the individual level is a great place to begin developing the full potential of organisations.

References

Amason, A.C., Thompson, K.R., Hockwarter, W.A., & Harrison, A.W. (1995). Conflict: An important dimension in successful management teams. *Organizational Dynamics,* 24, 20-35.

Anderson, J., & Gerbing, D.W. (1988). Structural equations modeling in practice: A review and recommended two-step approach. *Psychological Bulletin,* 103, 411-423.

Arad, S., & Drasgow, F. 1994. *Empowered work groups: Conceptual framework and empirical assessment of empowerment processes and outcomes in organizations.* Paper presented at the Annual Conference of the Society for Industrial and Organizational Psychologists, Nashville, TN.

Avolio, B.J. & Bass, B.M. (1995). Individualized consideration is more than consideration when viewed at multiple levels of analysis. *Leadership Quarterly,* 6, 199-218.

Avolio, B.J. & Bass, B.M. (1991). *The full-range of leadership development,* Center for Leadership Studies, Binghamton, NY.

Avolio, B.J., Bass, B.M. & Jung, D. (1996). Confirmatory factor analysis of MLQ5X for measurement requirement. *Paper, Society for Organizational and Industrial Psychology Conference,* San Diego, CA.

Avolio, B.J., Jung, D.I., Murry, W.D. & Sivasubramaniam, N. (1996). Building highly developed teams: Focusing on shared leadership processes, efficacy, trust, and performance. In M.M. Beyerlein, D.A. Johnson, & S.T. Beyerlein (Eds.), *Advances in Interdisciplinary Studies of Work Teams* (pp.173-209), Greenwich, CT: JAI Press.

Bandura, A. (1986). *Social foundations of thought and action: A Social cognitive theory.* Englewood Cliffs, MJ: Prentice Hall.

Bass, B.M. (1985). *Leadership and performance beyond expectations.* New York, NY: Free Press.

Bass, B.M. (1990). *Bass and Stogdill's handbook of leadership.* NY Free Press.

Bass, B.M. (1997). Does the transactional-transformational leadership paradigm transcend organizational and national boundaries? *American Psychologist,* 52, 130-139.

Bass, B.M., & Avolio, B.J. (1994). *Improving organizational effectiveness through transformational leadership.* Thousand Oaks, CA: Sage.

Bass, B.M., & Avolio, B.J. (1993), Transformational leadership: A response to critiques. In M.M. Chemmers & R. Ayman (Eds.), *Leadership theory and research: Perspective and directions* (pp. 49-88). San Diego, CA: Academic Press.

Bass, B.M. & Avolio, B.J. (1990). *Transformational leadership development: Manual for the Multifactor Leadership Questionnaire.* Palo Alto, CA: Consulting Psychologist Press.

Bass, B.M., Avolio, B.J., Jung, D.I. & Berson, Y. (1997) *A research report on platoon leadership.* Unpublished paper.

Bentler, P.M. (1990). Comparative fit indices in structural models. *Psychological Bulletin, 107,* 238-246.

Bollen, K.A. (1989). *Structural equations with latent variables.* New York, NY: Wiley.

Burns, J.M. (1978). *Leadership.* New York, NY: Harper & Row.

Bycio, P., Hackett, R.D., & Allen, J.S. (1995). Further assessments of Bass' conceptualization of transactional and transformational leadership. *Journal of Applied Psychology,* 80, 468-478.

Christie, P., Lessem, R. & Mbigi, L. (1993). *African management: Philosophies, concepts and applications.* Randsburg, South Africa: Knowledge Resources.

Cohen, S.G. & Denison, D.R. 1990. Flight attendant teams. In J. R. Hackman (Ed). *Groups that work (and those that don't): Creating conditions for effective teamwork.* (pp. 382-397). San Francisco, CA: Jossey-Bass.

Cohen, S.G., Ledford, G.E. Jr., & Spreitzer, G.M. 1996. A predictive model of self-managing work team effectiveness. *Human Relations,* 49, 643-676.

Conger, J.A. & Kanungo, R.A. (1987). Towards a behavioral theory of charismatic leadership in organizational settings. *Academy of Management Review.* 12, 637-647.

Cummings, T.G. (1978). Self-regulating work groups: A sociotechnical synthesis. *Academy of Management Review,* 3, 625-634.

Den Hartog, D.N., Van Muijen, J.J., & Koopman, P.L. (1997). Transactional versus transformational leadership: An analysis of the MLQ. *Journal of Occupational and Organizational Psychology,* 70, 19-34.

Gaspar, S. (1992). *Transformational leadership: An integrative review of the literature.* Doctoral dissertation. Western Michigan University, Kalamazoo, MI.

Guzzo, R.A., Yost, P.R., Campbell, R.J., & Shea, G.P. (1993). Potency in groups: Articulating a construct. *British Journal of Social Psychology,* 32, 87-106.

Hackman, J.R. 1990. *Groups that work (and those that don't): Creating conditions for effective teamwork.* San Francisco, CA: Jossey-Bass.

Hater, J.J., Bass, B.M. (1988). Superiors' evaluations and subordinates perceptions of transformational and transactional leadership. *Journal of Applied Psychology,* 73, 695-702.

Hogan, R., Curphy, G., & Hogan, J. 1994. What we know about leadership effectiveness and personality. *American Psychologist,* 49, 493-504.

House, R.J. (1977). A 1976 theory of charismatic leadership. In J. G. Hunt & L. L. Larson (Eds.), *Leadership: The cutting edge.* Carbondale: Southern Illinois University Press.

House, R. J. Spangler, W. D. & Woycke, J. (1991). Personality and charisma in the U.S. presidency: A psychological theory of leadership effectiveness. *Administrative Science Quarterly,* 36, 364-396.

Howell, J.M., & Avolio, B. J. (1993). Transformational leadership, transactional leadership, locus of control and support for innovation: Key predictors of consolidated-business unit performance. *Journal of Applied Psychology,* 78, 891-902.

Ilgen, D., Major, D., Hollenbeck, J., & Sego, D. (1993). Team research in the 1990s. In M. Chemers, & R. Ayman (Eds.), *Leadership theory and research: Perspectives and directions,* (pp.245-270). New York, NY: Academic Press.

James, L.R., Mulaik, S.A., & Brett, J.M. (1982). *Causal analysis: Assumptions, models, and data.* Beverly Hills, CA: Sage.

Jung, D., Avolio, B., Murry, W., Sivasubramaniam, N., & Sosik, J. 1996. Leadership in work groups: *An empirical investigation of leadership style, collective efficacy, collective identity, and group performance.* Paper, Annual meeting of the Academy of Management, Cincinnati, OH.

Katzenbach, J.R. & Smith, D.K. (1993). *The wisdom of teams.* Boston, MA: Harvard Business School Press.

Klein, J.A. (1984). Why supervisors resist employee involvement. *Harvard Business Review,* 62, 87-95.

Klimoski, R., Mohammed, S. 1994. Team mental model: Construct or metaphor? *Journal of Management,* 20, 403-437.

Kozlowski, S.W.J., Gully, S.M., Salas, E., & Cannon-Bowers, J.A. 1996a. Team leadership and development: Theories, principles, and guidelines for training leaders and team. In M.M. Beyerlein, D.A. Johnson, & S.T. Beyerlein (Eds.), *Advances in interdisciplinary studies of work teams.* (pp.253-291). Greenwich, CT: JAI Press.

Kozlowski, S.W.J., Gully, S.M., McHugh, P.P., Salas, E., & Cannon-Bowers, J.A. 1996b. A dynamic theory of leadership and team effectiveness: Developmental and task contingent leader roles. In G.R. Ferris (Ed.), *Research in personnel and human resource management,* 14, 253-305. Greenwich, CT: JAI Press.

Kumpfer, K. L., Turner, C., Hopkins, R., & Librett, J. 1993. Leadership and team effectiveness in community coalitions for the prevention of alcohol and other drug abuse. *Health Education Research,* 8, 359-374.

Lowe, K. B., Kroeck, K.G., & Sivasubramaniam, N. 1996. Effectiveness correlates of transformational and transactional leadership: A meta-analytic review of MLQ literature. *Leadership Quarterly,* 7, 385-425.

Manz, C. C., & Sims, H.P. Jr. 1993. *Business without bosses: How self-managing teams are building high performance companies.* New York: Wiley.

Manz, C.C., & Sims, H. P. Jr. 1987. Leading workers to lead themselves: The external leadership of self-managing work teams. *Administrative Science Quarterly,* 32, 106-128.

McGrath, J.E., (1984). *Groups: Interaction and performance,* Englewood Cliffs, NJ: Prentice Hall.

Nanus, B. (1992). *Visionary leadership: Creating a compelling sense of direction for your organization.* San Francisco: Jossey-Bass.

Patterson, C., Fuller, J.B., Kester, K., & Stringer, D.Y. (1995). *A meta-analytic examination of leadership style and selected follower compliance outcomes.* Paper, Society for Industrial and Organizational Psychology, Orlando, FL.

Podsakoff, P.M. & Organ, D.W. (1986). Self-reports in organizational research: Problems and prospects. *Journal of Management,* 12, 531-544.

Shamir, B. (1997). *Leadership in the boundaryless organization. Disposable or indispensable.* Unpublished paper.

Shamir, B. (1995). Social distance and charisma: Theoretical notes and an exploratory study. *Leadership Quarterly,* 6, 19-47.

Shamir, B., House, R.J. & Arthur, M.B. (1993). The motivational effects of charismatic leadership: A self-concept based theory. *Organizational Science,* 4, 577-594.

Shea, G.P., & Guzzo, R.A. 1987. Group effectiveness: What really matters? *Sloan Management Review,* 28, 25-31.

Silver, W.S. & Bufanio, K.M. 1996. The impact of group efficacy and group goals on group task performance. *Small Group Research,* 27, 347-359.

Sinclair, A. (1992). The tyranny of team ideology. *Organization Studies,* 13, 611-626.

Sivasubramaniam, N., Jung, D.I., Avolio, B.J. & Murry, W.D. (1997). *A longitudinal model of the effects of team leadership and group potency on group performance.* Unpublished paper.

Sosik, J.J., Avolio, B.J., & Kahai, S.S. (1997). The impact of leadership style and anonymity on group potency and effectiveness in a GDSS environment. *Journal of Applied Psychology,* 82, 89-103.

Spink, K.S. 1990. Group cohesion and collective efficacy of volleyball teams. *Journal of Sport and Exercise Psychology,* 12, 301-311.

Stewart, G., & Manz, C. (1994). Leadership for self-managing work teams: A theoretical integration. Paper, Annual Conference of the Society for Industrial and Organizational Psychologists, Nashville, TN.

Tannenbaum, S., Beard, R., & Salas, E. (1992). Team building and its influence on team effectiveness: An examination of conceptual and empirical developments. In K. Kelley (Ed.), Issues, theory and research in industrial/organizational psychology (pp. 117-153). Amsterdam: Elsevier.

Trist, E. 1997. Collaboration in work settings: A personal perspective. *Journal of Applied Behavioral Science,* 13, 268-278.

Yukl, G. 1994. *Leadership in organizations.* Englewood Cliff, NJ: Prentice Hall.

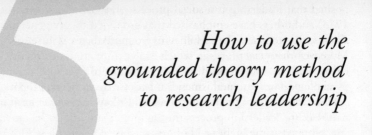

How to use the grounded theory method to research leadership

Ken W. Parry

Abstract

The use of the grounded theory method has not characterised the study of leadership to date. However, there is a strong argument that because leadership can be viewed as a process of social influence, the grounded theory method is suitable. The literature on this topic is not strong on detailing how the grounded theory method may be used to research the social influence processes of leadership. This article goes some way toward redressing that shortfall by proposing some procedures and considerations by which the grounded theory analysis of leadership can be undertaken validly and reliably.

Introduction

A strong case has been put forward to justify the use of the grounded theory method as both valid and reliable for the study of leadership (Parry, 1997a). Parry proposed that because leadership can be viewed as a process of social influence, and because grounded theory identifies social processes as research outputs, grounded theory is a useful method with which to advance our understanding of leadership. Although the practical application of grounded theory has already been written up (e.g. Pidgeon and Henwood, 1996), this article deals specifically with the application of grounded theory to the study of leadership. Parry (1997a) generated a number of conclusions about the use of grounded theory for the study of leadership, and these conclusions will elaborated in this article into a clearer framework and procedure with which to apply the grounded theory method.

The suggested context of the proposed research is one of change. Grounded theory is a method used in some qualitative research. Although the use of grounded theory has not characterised leadership research to date, it has been argued there is a clear justification for its use. Scholars as eminent as Bass

(1990), Hunt (1991), Rost (1993), Yukl (1994) and Alvesson (1996) have posited that leadership is a social process, and Glaser and Strauss (1967, 1978) and others have emphasised that grounded theory generates theory about social processes. The usefulness of grounded theory is therefore manifest. Moreover, the social processes which evolve from grounded theory analysis help with our understanding of leadership not because they exclude psychological or structural issues, but because they integrate them.

However, much of the use of grounded theory has not yet examined the nature of the leadership process throughout organisations. Its use has been concentrated at the higher end of organisational hierarchies. Such research has examined leaders or senior managers, and has neglected the process of leadership throughout the organisational hierarchy. It is assumed that leadership can be exhibited at all levels of an organisation. Other published 'grounded theory' research has not utilised the full method proposed by Glaser and Strauss, or has not progressed past the descriptive stage of analysis. Still other grounded theory leadership research has concentrated on specific elements of the leadership paradigm, thereby excluding other essential elements from consideration. Finally, some grounded theory research has studied structural elements of leadership while neglecting essential consideration of the social and psychological elements. This article will attempt to identify some methodological considerations which will redress these shortfalls.

Parry (1997a) proposed a number of research objectives to drive future leadership research and to build upon the large volume of quality leadership research which has been generated to date. By suggesting strategies and tactics with which to operationalise these research objectives, this article will attempt to show how the above shortfalls in the grounded theory research of leadership as a social process can be overcome. The following research objectives relate to the research problems associated with theorising adequately about the nature of leadership as a social influence process.

1. Investigate change incidents in organisations. The social influence and leadership processes at work during those change incidents will be the focus of investigations. Resultant changes in the perceptions, attributions, beliefs and motivations of followers will be investigated. Semi-structured and unstructured in-depth interviewing should be the predominant source of data, supplemented with observation and document analysis. People and incidents from all levels of the organisation should be the subject of investigation. Inquiry should be about who did what, when and where. Importantly, it also should be about why, and more importantly how outcomes were achieved.

2. Use an analytical method which is appropriate to the study of social processes in organisations. Grounded theory is the suggested sociological research method, and will involve the qualitative analysis of qualitative

data. The full, iterative Glaser and Strauss (1967) methodology must be utilised to build rigour into the research. Computer software such as NUD*IST or Ethnograph can be used to assist with the recording and analysis of data, and to enhance the rigour of the analysis.

3. Generate an integrative theory of the social influence processes at work in the substantive organisational setting under investigation. Grounded theory analysis of qualitative data will help to ensure that the theory considers all the relevant variables which impact on leadership within that substantive setting. The purpose of the research will be to generate theory, not to test theory. The resultant theory should then be compared with the extant leadership literature. Replication of the research should be attempted in a range of substantive settings with the aim of moving toward a more formal theory of leadership.

By using these conclusions as a start point, this article will attempt to elaborate upon ways in which such a research method can be operationalised effectively.

Leadership as Social Process

Parry (1997a) concluded that there is a case for considering leadership as a process of social influence. Support has come from Hunt (1991) and Locke, *et al.* (1991). Yukl (1994: 3) suggested that there is a strong view among leadership theorists that leadership is a social influence process that occurs naturally within a social system, and is shared among various members of that social system. This implies that leadership needs to be researched as a process, rather than through the study of leaders alone (Yukl, 1994).

Although the literature mentions social process frequently, there is no clear definition of the term. This is a problem for leadership scholars to resolve because a number of authors have used psychological and other quantitative methods to research leadership and claim to have investigated social influence processes (Conger, 1989; House and Mitchell, 1977; Meindl, Ehrlich and Dukerich, 1985). However, it can be concluded that because leadership can be viewed as a social influence process, grounded theory is a particularly useful method of data analysis and theory generation.

Relevance of the Grounded Theory Method

Because leadership is a social process, and because grounded theory has as an outcome the emergence of a social process (Fagerhaugh, 1986; Glaser, 1992; Glaser and Strauss, 1967), grounded theory is a relevant method.

Moreover, Glaser (1992: 13) has observed that grounded theory, in particular, is useful to 'researchers and practitioners in fields that concern themselves with issues relating to human behaviour in organisations, groups, and other social configurations'. Because leadership can be viewed as a process of social influence, this implies clearly that grounded theory can play a significant role in the study of leadership.

Further, Hunt and Ropo (1995) posited that there is and should be an increasing emphasis on processual analysis in organisational research, including leadership research. Also, Glaser (1992) noted that the contribution of grounded theory to well-worked areas of research is not the generation of a new concept or pattern, since these are usually saturated, but a better conceptual grasp of the basic social processes which might be missing. Leadership is a well-worked area of research, and grounded theory may give a better conceptual grasp of the basic social influence processes associated with leadership.

One of the originators of grounded theory insisted that 'grounded theory research is the study of abstract problems and their *processes,* not units' (Glaser, 1992: 24). 'Units' would include people, or leaders, or managers, or CEOs. Because research needs to investigate the *process* of leadership (Parry, 1997a), the relevance of grounded theory is manifest.

Strauss and Corbin (1990: 7) have asserted that if carried out correctly, and by using the full grounded theory method as detailed by Glaser and Strauss (1967, 1978), as opposed to the 'partial' grounded theory method which has been identified by Parry (1997a: 8), the findings will possess the characteristics of 'good' scientific research. Those criteria are significance, theory-observation compatibility, generalisability, reproducibility, precision, rigour, and verification.

Sources and form of Data

It is contended that change incidents can be the basis for data gathering for researching leadership as a social influence process via the grounded theory method. Change is an enduring and integrative theme in the leadership literature (Bass, 1990; Parry, 1997a). Change incidents are inherently longitudinal, and an appropriate methodology is needed to reflect this. The methodology used traditionally to investigate longitudinal phenomena is the longitudinal case study, utilising predominantly positivist data and analysis. However, non-positivist methods (including grounded theory) are equally relevant for longitudinal work.

Also, the major dimension of organisational change relevant to leadership is the use of influence to change the activities and relationships of people organisations. Because leadership involves a transformation in the views, beliefs, attitudes and motivations of followers (Bass, 1990; Rost, 1993; Yukl, 1994), it is about change. Leadership induces others to take action (Locke, et al., 1991), it involves a restructuring of a situation (Bass, 1990), and it is differentiated from management by its capacity to produce change (Kotter, 1990). Therefore, it is axiomatic that change is an essential aspect of the process of leadership. Hence, as Parry (1997a) concluded, change incidents can be the basis of investigation of the leadership process.

It is proposed that unstructured and semi-structured interviews be the main source of data, supported by observation and participant observation as subsidiary sources of data. A preference for interviewing over participant observation helps to overcome the potential validity problem of researcher reactivity, or the impact that the researcher's presence has on the phenomenon under investigation. Reactivity can be seen as interference, or it can be seen as data (Chenitz and Swanson, 1986). However, by utilising in-depth interviewing over participant observation as the predominant source of data, the direct involvement of the researcher in the phenomenon under investigation is reduced.

Furthermore, participant observation is of a particular observable setting or of a physical process. This especially is so in the nursing industry, a particularly fertile area for grounded theory research (Boyd, 1993; Chenitz and Swanson, 1986; Irurita, 1990; Lundrigan, 1992; Munhall, 1994), and the education industry (Conrad, 1978; Eichelberger, 1989; Guba, 1978; Millett, 1994). In both nursing and education, social processes are at least as important as technical processes. Hence, grounded theory has correctly been found to be beneficial there.

The use of participant observation to gather data for grounded theory analysis is also prevalent in cultural anthropology (eg Henrickson, 1989; Lantis, 1987; Stewart, 1990), where the situations and processes are easily observable. Indeed, Strong (1984) recommended the use of observation to gather data for the study of leadership, but explicit within this recommendation is that the researcher observes managers. The point has been well made that managers can be observed but a process such as leadership cannot be observed easily (Parry, 1997a). Therefore, the social processes of leadership are not easily observable. A social process is being researched, not a physical setting. Therefore, unstructured and semi-structured interviewing is suggested as the predominant form of data gathering, with observation as the secondary or supplementary form of data gathering.

Sampling Strategy

The proposed method will use a combination of statistical and theoretical sampling to select interviewees (Glaser and Strauss, 1967). The initial interview subjects should be statistically random in that they came from a range of levels in the hierarchy; from a range of functional areas; and from different stages of the change process. The use of this stratified random sampling strategy is supported by Law (1994). Bryman (1993) suggested that subjects for the present research should be 'everyday people in everyday situations'. By randomly selecting people from all levels of the organisational hierarchy in the initial stages of data gathering, this can be achieved. More importantly, this strategy will ensure the integration of the entire range of leadership variables that impact on the organisation.

As the data analysis progresses and conceptual categories emerge, the sampling strategy will mature. The initial stratified random strategy will give way to a theoretical sampling strategy. Strauss and Corbin (1990: 176) defined theoretical sampling as 'sampling on the basis of concepts that have proven theoretical relevance to the evolving theory.' Concepts have proven theoretical relevance when they are consistently present or consistently absent during the process of constant comparison. When these concepts are found to be of sufficient importance, they are given the status of 'categories'. Hence when interviewing, the researcher will seek out subjects who will help to provide information about theoretically relevant concepts such that these concepts can ultimately be given the status of 'saturated categories'. Also, the researcher will vary the questions asked of these subjects such that the true nature of concepts and categories can be ascertained.

One way in which theoretical sampling can be achieved is to interview people who were mentioned in prior interviews as having contributed to the leadership process. By doing this, comparison groups (Glaser and Strauss, 1967: 49) can be identified and data gathered from them. These comparison groups are not known in advance, but will emerge as respondents talk about particular people and particular incidents through which they see a leadership process in action.

In this way, the meanings attributed to an event by both potential leader and potential follower can be understood. This approach will help to identify aspects of leadership that are not directly observable by followers. It also helps to identify aspects of following that are not immediately observable by leaders. This approach is also an example of 360 degree data gathering, which has been identified as an important contribution to leadership research (Avolio, 1993). The issue of 360 degree data gathering is especially important in view of the established capacity of leadership influence to be exerted upwards and horizontally as well as downwards through organisations (Yammarino, 1994).

Interview Strategy

Parry (1997a) has identified the problems associated with questioning respondents about leadership per se. The main problem is that respondents' implicit theories of leadership will subvert the objectivity of their responses.

Some ways in which this interviewing strategy can be enacted are now discussed. One suggested way to circumvent this potential problem is to interview people in depth about concepts which are subordinate to the overarching concept of leadership, but which have been confirmed in the extant literature as being closely associated with it (Parry, 1997a). For example, rather than asking interviewees about 'leaders' or 'leadership', they can be asked about people who are going to get them through a particular change process, who they look to for a lead, who have the most impact on their attitudes and motivation at work, or who they see as being exceptional or influential. Further in-depth interviewing about the processes by which these outcomes are achieved can shed light on the social influence processes at work in organisational settings.

Second, it is well established in the leadership literature that leadership involves the use of influence to effect real change (Yukl, 1994). Therefore, an initial question of respondents could be 'Who has had most effect in creating, driving or stifling these changes?', followed by 'How have they had that effect?'. Similarly, it is well established that leadership can be interpreted as an attribution of exceptionality by followers (eg. Conger and Kanungo, 1987; Conger, 1989). Therefore, an initial question might be 'Do exceptional people stand out as affecting your application, motivation, or your ability to get things done?', followed by 'How have they had that effect?'.

Fourth, it is well established that the leadership process results in extra effort from followers (Bass, 1985). Therefore, an initial question might be 'Are there people you would do that bit extra for?', followed by 'How do they get that bit extra from you?'. Fifth, an *a priori* aspect of leadership is that other people follow. Therefore, an initial question might be 'Who do you look up to and who do you follow?', followed by 'How do they get you to do that?'. For all four examples, intervening and supplementary questions might relate to expanding and giving detail on incidents, processes, and the impact of particular people, as well as specifying the role of people at senior and junior levels in the organisation. The supplementary and elaborative questioning is quite unstructured. The interviewee drives the content, but the researcher keeps the content within general guidelines.

However, it may quickly become apparent to the researcher that there are no people who stand out as being 'exceptional' to the interviewees. Also, it may quickly become apparent to the researcher that no-one generates extra effort from potential followers and there is no-one that interviewees can look up to for a lead. In these instances, subsequent interviews must concentrate on asking interviewees how and why they perceive that the required leadership outcomes have not been achieved.

Therefore, Glaser (1978) has acknowledged that some *pre-emergent analytic thinking* is necessary for the *'emergent fit'* model of grounded theory. A researcher cannot come into a topic like this completely cold. The researcher must have some predetermined idea of the things about which the subjects will be questioned, without asking explicitly about esoteric topics from the existing leadership literature. Thus, questioning of subjects should revolve around a range of leadership-related topics including those indicated above. A range of suggested questions is included in Appendix A. Having said this, existing leadership theories must not be considered until after the grounded theory has been generated. Obviously, the emergent theory must be compared with the extant leadership literature. This delay will avoid the possibility of existing theories or biases being 'forced' into the data being gathered.

Conversely, the benefits to grounded theory research of investigating the implicit theories of participants were identified by Bresnen (1995) and Bryman, Stephens and à Campo (1996). The methodological implication of recognising these contrasting viewpoints about esoteric terminology is that generic terminology should be relied upon as the basis of the interview questions, but that in addition, esoteric terminology should be used as a supplement in order to gauge the impact of the implicit theories of participants upon their interpretation of reality.

The implicit leadership theories of interviewees help to give an indication of the values that they hold dear (Millett, 1994). Hence, there is merit in asking supplementary questions of interviewees about their implicit definitions of leadership, and asking for elaboration on the manifestation of such leadership in the organisational setting under investigation. Also, subjects could be asked about people who they believe are obvious leaders and people who are not obvious leaders.

Subsequent theoretical sampling would ensure that other perspectives are gained on the identified people and also that the identified people are interviewed about their own leadership styles and behaviours. This type of sampling helps to achieve the 360 degree research which is so essential to the understanding of social processes. Dawson (1994) has emphasised the importance of this contextualist issue in a processual approach to organisational change research. It is also necessary to ensure that such questioning relates to all levels of the organisational hierarchy to avoid the previously acknowledged problem of concentrating on senior management positions.

Coding for Concepts

Coding is the process of analysing data, and open coding is the initial process of breaking down, examining, conceptualising, and categorising data (Strauss and Corbin, 1990). Glaser (1978) and Turner (1981) recommended that incidents be coded into more than one category, if appropriate, during the early stages of concept, or category generation. A category is a classification of concepts. Such classification is discovered when concepts are compared against one another and appear to pertain to similar phenomena. In this way, 'concepts are grouped together under a higher order, more abstract concept called a category' (Strauss and Corbin, 1990: 61).

The researcher must be wary also of creating too many categories or too few categories in the initial coding. The former will clog the system and stifle the emergence of higher level categories (Millett, 1994). The latter will pre-empt or force the emergence of higher level categories, which is a major methodological mistake (Glaser and Strauss, 1967).

The problem of creating too many or too few conceptual categories can be overcome by two procedures. The first is to create properties for each category (Strauss and Corbin, 1990). In this way, categories could become progressively more abstract by incorporating new properties rather than by creating new categories of equally low levels of abstraction. For example, in the work of Parry (1997b), the category of *change* had the following properties associated with it: *uncertainty, scope, variety/complexity, cultural variation, and avoidability.* These properties were progressively added as theoretical sampling added more data to the category over time. Through the identification of these properties, the category became more abstract as the analysis progressed over time.

The second procedure is to compare the categories generated by open coding from the very first interview transcript. Each subsequent datum should be coded openly, and that coding compared to categories generated previously. If the same, the item can be classified as part of the existing category. If found to be a property of a previously generated category, the item can be allocated to the category, and a new property recorded in the memo for that category. If the newly coded item is conceptually different from the categories generated previously, a new category can be created and recorded within the computer software file. In this way, the process of comparative coding is begun with the initial data collection, and carried out for the duration of the analysis process. Initially, it is likely to be found that categories and their properties are created frequently. Gradually, the categories and their properties became saturated, and over time the rate of creation of new conceptual categories slows. This level of rigour and detail is necessary to identify and incorporate the full range of variables which impact on the leadership process.

There are differing arguments as to whether or not individual categories should be defined. Glaser (1978) has played down the importance of category definitions because the concepts remain in a state of flux until theory is generated; certainly until the categories are saturated. On the other hand, Martin and Turner (1986) favoured defining categories because the process of definition forces the theorist to express explicitly and at length the relationships between themes which are grouped together into categories.

It is this author's belief that attempting to define concepts has a beneficial effect on clarifying the nature of categories. Definition should be done mainly within the context of theoretical coding and the comparison, reduction, and linking of categories. However, it must also be recognised that the definitions of categories can vary as their character changes over time during the process of theoretical coding.

The Use of Software

The use of appropriate software will help to achieve the precision and rigour which is required of good-quality scientific research. There has been considerable anecdotal debate about the extent to which computer software will help with the generation of theory. However, it can be stated with some confidence that programs such as NUD*IST and Ethnograph will ensure that all recorded data will be retained and accessed effectively. On the other hand, it can also be stated with confidence that the primary responsibility for theory generation lies with the researcher, and not with the computer software.

The Use Of Diagrams

Diagrams are visual representations of one's analytical scheme. They are also visual representations of the categories and how they link together (Corbin, 1986a). During the process of theoretical coding, diagrams are very helpful by enabling the researcher to illustrate the relationships between categories. As the researcher asks questions about the nature of categories, and the relationships between them, diagrams help to clarify thoughts on these matters.

When researching the social influence processes of leadership with the grounded theory method, it will be beneficial to diagrammatically represent the concepts apparent in each interview transcript. From the analysis of the very first document, a diagram can be drawn representing the ideas present. With each succeeding transcript, the new diagram can be compared with all previous diagrams as part of the process of constant comparison. This procedure enables the researcher to build up a progressively more detailed and accurate diagram of categories and the relationships between them.

The Use Of Memos

Memos form the basis of the emergent theory, and should be written during the process of data gathering and analysis. Memos should be detailed descriptions of the phenomenon under investigation (Martin and Turner, 1986). Spradley (1979) suggested that researchers keep four separate sets of memos.

1. Short memos made at the time of observation or interviewing.
2. Expanded memos made as soon as possible after the field session.
3. A fieldwork journal that records problems and ideas that arise.
4. A provisional running record of analysis and interpretation.

The use of a word processor and the relevant software enables the researcher to incorporate all four sets of notes/memos into concurrent documents. All four types of memos can be recorded and integrated continuously in word processing format.

When investigating leadership processes, memos can be recorded via two formats. The first format involves memos being spoken into the tape recorder at the completion of interviews. In this way, these memos are transcribed at the same time as the interviews are transcribed. This process is beneficial because it allows the researcher to recite freely and in detail the nature of the theme as it occurred to her or him. The importance of this detailed, immediate, and *in situ* memoing has been stressed by Glaser (1978). Fieldnotes in memo form are published rarely. This is because they are temporary and usually unintelligible to anyone but the researcher (Kirk and Miller, 1986). However, it is the testing of the field notes, and their elaboration during theoretical coding and category comparison that needs to be recorded and detailed.

The second format involves memos being written up under the heading of each category, as each category emerges during analysis. Therefore, memos are created in accordance with the coding of data, and with the creation of categories. These memos are indexed within the data files of the computer software for easy access and elaboration during theoretical coding. During theoretical coding and the comparison, reduction and linking of categories, memos can be readily altered, added to, elaborated upon, split, and merged as the theory emerges from the analysis.

The above prescriptions for the use of memos would hold whether the researcher is investigating leadership or some other sociological phenomenon.

Theoretical Coding and Generation of Basic Social Process

Selective sampling is akin to theoretical sampling. This involves the sampling of respondents according to the evolving theory. The questions asked of respondents also depend upon the evolving theory. This procedure helps to clarify the nature of categories, and the relationships between and among categories, until such time as the categories are saturated. Hence, the data set is progressively selected according to the need to clarify and tighten theory. Selective sampling ceases when no new data are found to generate new categories or properties of categories. This situation represents saturation of the categories.

Saturation of categories

Sampling, data gathering and coding will continue iteratively until all categories are saturated. Saturation means that all levels and properties of categories seem complete, and that new data add no new insights to the categories or the relationships between them (Glaser and Strauss, 1967; Strauss and Corbin, 1990). Saturation represents a sense of closure, by which all data fit into existing categories and behaviour within the context of a category could be predicted (Hutchinson, 1986). In other words, the category is closed.

Theoretical coding

As categories become saturated, the researcher needs to determine the relationships among those categories, and the characteristics of categories which allow them to relate to other categories in some way. The investigation of the relationships among categories is known as theoretical coding because discussion of the relationships between categories forms the basis of theory (Glaser and Strauss, 1967). Strauss and Corbin (1990) distinguished further between axial coding and selective coding and component parts of theoretical coding. Axial coding elaborates upon the nature of categories, and selective coding elaborates on the relationships between categories with the aim of determining core or near-core categories. As Swanson observed (1986:125):

> Theoretical codes allow the researchers to organise the categories, to clarify what each category is in relation to other categories, and thus, to develop theoretical links between the categories. These links will lead to the development of a process or processes and the generation of theory.

Glaser (1978) nominated a family of theoretical codes to assist the researcher to undertake theoretical coding. He referred to this family of theoretical codes as the '6 C's' (Glaser, 1978:74) and they help the researcher to conceptualise how categories relate to each other and are integrated into theory (Swanson, 1986). This family of theoretical codes is represented in Table 1.

Table 1 A Family of Theoretical Codes: The Six C's

1. Causes	4. Consequences
2. Contexts	5. Covariances
3. Contingencies	6. Conditions

Source: Glaser, 1978:74

Theoretical coding using the six C's allows the researcher to ask a number of questions of the data and categories to help clarify their relationship with one another. Those questions are:

- Is it a *cause* or a *consequence* of some other category?
- What are the intervening *conditions* between the causes and consequences?
- Within what *context* does this category emerge? Context refers to the location of events or incidents pertaining to a phenomenon (Strauss and Corbin, 1990).

- Is this category a *contingency* (having a bearing on another category)? In other words, what is change in this category dependent upon? This refers usually to unplanned change (Strauss and Corbin, 1990; Swanson, 1986).
- Is there *covariance* between this category and other categories? Covariance occurs when one category changes with the changes in another category (Strauss and Corbin, 1990).

The 6 C's have been found to be particularly productive for social research into leadership processes (Parry, 1997b). In particular, such interrogation of the data enables determination of dependent, independent, intervening and moderating variables. It also identifies conceptual categories which might explain the nature of the links between leadership categories and followership categories.

For example, in the work of Parry (1997b) a range of categories were found to represent the independent variables associated with leadership. Another range of categories were found to represent the consequences of leadership, and represented dependent variables associated with followership. A third range of categories were found to represent the change context within which leadership processes operated. Effectively, these were moderating variables.

Also, the leader-follower relationship was found to be contingent upon a fourth group of categories which reflected the extent to which leaders and followers were adaptable to the change environment with which they were faced. These categories represented intervening variables. Fifth, a group of categories were found which had covariance between the leadership and the followership categories. These covariant categories represented a reciprocal relationship between leadership and followership.

By asking the above questions of the data, and seeking answers, the level of abstraction of the categories increases progressively. During open coding, the conceptual labels attached to each category must reflect an appropriate level of abstraction (Martin and Turner, 1986). Too low a level of abstraction, and one would have a separate label for each datum. Too high a level of abstraction, and all data would fit within it, thereby creating the methodological problem of forcing the creation of a core category. However, during theoretical coding, the level of abstraction of conceptual labels must increase progressively (Martin and Turner, 1986).

These questions must be asked from an early stage in the data gathering process. By doing so, the researcher can maintain a balance between the number of emerging categories and the complexity of properties attributed to each category.

As a consequence of answering these questions, category memos can be added progressively on the computer, and diagrams drawn and redrawn to reflect the emerging relationships between categories. The asking of these questions directs the researcher to undertake further selective sampling to gather data which will provide more accurate answers.

The result of this theoretical coding is the comparison, linking and reduction of categories such that a core category and basic social process will be uncovered. This technique reflects the emergence of theory to explain the leadership phenomenon under investigation.

Comparison, linking and reduction of categories

Part of the theoretical coding process results in the comparison of categories to look for similarities and differences. If categories are similar according to a number of properties they can be merged or linked to form a new category. In this way the number of categories can be reduced. Corbin (1986b) warned against linking categories too early in the analysis process because it might inhibit the emergence of other categories.

If similarities or differences between categories can be explained by another conceptual code, this new conceptual code becomes a category at a higher level of abstraction. By this means the number of categories is reduced progressively, but their explanatory power is increased.

Use is made of memos and diagrams when comparing, linking and reducing categories. Also, new data are obtained through selective sampling and data are reinterrogated in accordance with the process of theoretical coding. This progressive movement to a higher level of abstraction will result in the emergence of a core category, which is the central phenomenon around which all the other categories are integrated (Strauss and Corbin, 1990). It also will result in the emergence of a basic social process, which also can be a core category.

Core categories

The core category integrates all other categories at the highest level of abstraction. Corbin (1986b:99) suggested a number of questions, the answers to which would indicate the identity of the core category. Those questions are:

- In all of these interviews or observations, what seems to be the main story line, the main pattern or theme that I see happening over and over again?
- What category do all other categories seem to be pointing to or leading up to?
- Which category seems to be of a higher level of abstraction than the others?
- Which category could the others be subsumed under?

The researcher needs to reinterrogate the data to gain answers to these questions. Reinterrogation of the data involves reading memos, reading transcripts, continued theoretical coding, posing and testing operational hypotheses about the phenomenon under investigation. Core categories can emerge at higher and higher levels of abstraction. Consequently, researchers may be able to identify near-core categories as well as core categories.

Most of the grounded theory procedures outlined in this paper are valid whether leadership or some other social process is being researched. However, apart from identifying relevant change incidents and a sampling and interviewing strategy to investigate leadership, the full rigorous grounded theory method of analysis must be followed, as detailed in this paper.

Basic social process

The aim of grounded theory is to derive a core category which explains the phenomenon under investigation (Glaser, 1992; Glaser and Strauss, 1967). Fagerhaugh (1986: 135) emphasised that most, but not all core categories will be social processes. Core categories will be social processes if they account for process, that is change which occurs over time. Most grounded theory does investigate social processes. Because the research outlined in this paper will investigate social influence processes, the emergent core category must be a basic social process.

Process involves change which occurs over time (Fagerhaugh, 1986: 135) and the linking of action/interactional sequences (Strauss and Corbin, 1990: 143). Therefore a social process is a process which is concerned with human beings in their relations to each other. Fagerhaugh (1986:135) has noted that basic social processes should be expressed as gerunds, which means that they should end in 'ing'. She provided examples such as 'becoming', 'limiting' and 'routing'. Irurita (1990:248) theorised around a basic social process called 'optimising'. Parry (1997b) theorised around a basic social process called *enhancing adaptability*. A gerund suggests movement and change, or process, over time. As explained earlier, the emergent social process is entirely representative of the phenomenon of leadership. Within the emergent social process will be incorporated a range of psychological, structural and other impacting variables.

Conclusion

The theme of this conference is 'Management Theory and Practice: Moving to a New Era'. It is my conclusion that by using the method detailed in this paper, the study of leadership as a crucial component of effective management will be enhanced substantially for progress into the new era of management research.

References

Alvesson, M. (1996) Leadership studies: from procedure and abstraction to reflexivity and situation. *Leadership Quarterly,* 7 (4), 455-485.

Avolio, B. J. (1993). Personal correspondence. State University of New York at Binghamton, NY, September 30.

Bass, B. M. (1990). *Bass and Stogdill's handbook of leadership: Theory, research and managerial applications.* New York: Free Press.

Bresnen, M. J. (1995). All things to all people? Perceptions, attributions and constructions of leadership. *Leadership Quarterly,* 6 (4), 495-513.

Bryman, A. (1993). Personal correspondence. Loughborough University, Loughborough, Leicester, UK, September 23.

Bryman, A. E. and Burgess, R. G. (Eds.) (1994). *Analysing Qualitative Data.* London: Routledge.

Bryman, A., Stephens, M. and à Campo, C. (1996). The importance of context: Qualitative research and the study of leadership. *Leadership Quarterly,* 7 (3), 353-370.

Chenitz, W. C. and Swanson, J. M. (1986). *From practice to grounded theory: Qualitative research in nursing.* Menlo Park, California: Addison-Wesley.

Conger, J. A. (1989). *The Charismatic Leader: Behind the Mystique of Exceptional Leadership.* San Francisco: Jossey Bass.

Conger, J. A. and Kanungo, R. N. (1987). Toward a Behavioral Theory of Charismatic Leadership in Organizational Settings. *Academy of Management Review,* 12 (4), 637-647.

Conrad, C. F. (1978). A Grounded Theory of Academic Change. *Sociology of Education,* 51 (2), 101-112.

Corbin, J. (1986a). Coding, writing memos, and diagramming. In W. C. Chenitz and J. M. Swanson (Eds). *From Practice to Grounded Theory: Qualitative Research in Nursing.* Menlo Park, CA: Addison-Wesley.

Corbin, J. (1986b). Qualitative data analysis for grounded theory. In W. C. Chenitz and J. M. Swanson (Eds). *From Practice to Grounded Theory: Qualitative Research in Nursing.* Menlo Park, CA: Addison-Wesley.

Dawson, P. (1994). *Organisational Change: A Processual Approach.* London: Paul Chapman Publishing.

Eichelberger, R. T. (1989). *Disciplined Inquiry: Understanding and doing Educational Research.* White Plains, NY: Longman.

Fagerhaugh, S. Y. (1986). Analysing data for basic social processes. In W. C. Chenitz and J. M. Swanson. *From Practice to Grounded Theory: Qualitative Research in Nursing.* Menlo Park, CA: Addison-Wesley.

Glaser, B. (1978). *Theoretical Sensitivity.* Mill Valley, CA: Sociology Press.

Glaser, B. G. (1992). *Emergence vs forcing: Basics of grounded theory analysis.* Mill Valley, CA: Sociology Press.

Glaser, B. and Strauss, A. (1967). *The Discovery of Grounded Theory.* Chicago: Aldine Press.

Glaser, B. G. and Strauss, A. L. (1978). Grounded theory. In N. K. Denzin (Ed.), *Sociological Methods.* New York: McGraw Hill.

Guba, E. G. (1978). *Toward a Methodology of Naturalistic Inquiry in Educational Evaluation.* CSE Monograph Series in Evaluation, No. 8. Los Angeles: UCLA Graduate School of Education.

Henrickson, R. L. (1989). *Leadership and Culture.* Doctoral dissertation. San Diego: University of San Diego.

House, R. J. and Mitchell, T. R. (1977). Path-Goal Theory of Leadership. *Journal of Contemporary Business,* 3, Autumn, 81-97.

Hunt, J. G. (1991). *Leadership: A New Synthesis.* Newbury Park, CA: Sage.

Hunt, J. G. and Ropo, A. (1995). Multi-level Leadership: Grounded Theory and Mainstream Theory Applied to the case of General Motors. *Leadership Quarterly,* 6 (3): 379-412.

Irurita, V. F. (1990). *Optimizing as a Leadership Process: A Grounded Theory study of Nurse Leaders in Western Australia.* PhD Thesis, Perth: The University of Western Australia.

Kirk, J. and Miller, M. (1986). *Reliability, validity and qualitative research.* Beverly Hills, CA: Sage.

Kotter, J. P. (1990). *A Force for Change: How Leadership Differs from Management.* New York: Free Press.

Lantis, M. (1987). Two important roles in organizations and communities. *Human Organization,* 46 (3), 189-199.

Law, J. (1994). Organisation, narrative, and strategy. In J. Hassard and M. Parker (Eds.). *Towards a New Theory of Organisation.* London: Routledge.

Locke, E. A., Kirkpatrick, S., Wheeler, J. K., Schneider, J., Niles, K., Goldstein, H., Welsh, K. and Chah, D. O., (1991). *The essence of leadership: The four keys to leading successfully.* New York: Lexington Books.

Lundrigan, C. B. (1992). *Chief nurse executive leadership in small rural hospitals.* Doctoral dissertation, University of Colorado.

Martin, P. Y. and Turner, B. A. (1986). Grounded Theory and Organisational Research, *Journal of Applied Behavioural Science,* 22 (2), 141-157.

Meindl, J. R., Ehrlich, S. B. and Dukerich, J. M. (1985). The romance of leadership. *Administrative Science Quarterly,* 30 (1), March, 78-102.

Millett, B. (1994). *Identifying a Model of Institutional Change: The Transition from College of Advanced Education to University.* PhD Thesis, Brisbane: Griffith University.

Munhall, P. L. (1994). *Revisioning Phenomenology: Nursing and Health Science Research.* New York: National League for Nursing.

Parry, K. W. (1997a), Grounded theory and social process: A new direction for leadership research, *Leadership Quarterly* (accepted for publication).

Parry, K. W. (1997b). Enhancing adaptability: Leadership strategies to accommodate change in local government settings. *Journal of Organizational Change Management* (submitted for publication).

Rost, J. C. (1993). *Leadership for the Twenty-First Century*. Westport, Connecticut: Praeger.

Spradley, J. P. (1979). *The Ethnographic Interview*. New York: Holt, Rinehart and Winston.

Stewart, A. (1990). The bigman metaphor for entrepreneurship: A 'library Tale' with morals on alternatives for further research. *Organization Science*, 1 (2), May, 143-159.

Strauss, A. and Corbin, J. (1990). *Basics of Qualitative Research: Grounded Theory Procedures and Techniques*. Newbury Park, CA: Sage Publications.

Strong, P. M. (1984). On qualitative methods and leadership research. In J. G. Hunt, D. M. Hosking, C. A. Schriesheim, and R. Stewart (eds), *Leaders and managers: An international perspective on managerial behavior and leadership*. New York: Pergamon Press, 204-208.

Swanson, J. M. (1986). Analysing data for categories and description. In W. C. Chenitz and J. M. Swanson (1986). *From Practice to Grounded Theory: Qualitative Research in Nursing*. Menlo Park, CA: Addison-Wesley.

Tesch, R. (1991). Software for qualitative researchers: Analysis needs and program capabilities. In N. G. Fielding and R. M. Lee (Eds.), *Using computers in qualitative research*. London: Sage.

Turner, B. A. (1981). Some practical aspects of qualitative data analysis: One way of organising the cognitive processes associated with the generation of grounded theory. *Quality and Quantity*, 15, 225-247.

Yammarino, F. J. (1994). Indirect Leadership: Transformational Leadership at a Distance. In Bass, B. M. and Avolio, B. J., *Improving Organisational Effectiveness Through Transformational Leadership*. Thousand Oaks, California: Sage Publications.

Yukl, G. (1994). *Leadership in Organizations* (3rd edn). New Jersey: Prentice Hall.

Appendix A
Introductory questions asked in unstructured interviews

These are indicative questions only. The exact wording, and the wording of intervening and supplementary questions, is determined by the direction of the interview and the responses of interviewees.

Questions relating to leadership processes occurring in critical incidents

- What are the major changes that are affecting you at the moment?
- How do these changes affect your motivation, attitude to work, performance?
- Who has had most effect in creating, driving or stifling these changes?
- How have they had that effect?
- What effect have you had on these changes?
- How have you had that effect?
- Do exceptional people stand out as affecting your application, motivation, or your ability to get things done?
- How have they had that effect?
- How have you had that impact on others?
- Who has had most influence on you in this organisation?
- How have they had that effect?
- Who do you look up to and who do you follow?
- How do they get you to do that?
- How do you get people to look up to you and follow your lead?
- Who do you look to to get you through the change process?
- How are they going to get you through the change process?
- Are there people you would do that bit extra for?
- How do they get that bit extra from you?
- Intervening and supplementary questions relate to
- expanding and giving detail on incidents, processes, and the impact of particular people.
- specifying the role of people at senior and junior levels in the organisation.

Questions relating to implicit theories and their effect on values

- What does leadership mean to you? What is your philosophy of leadership?
- Have you seen evidence of such leadership in this organisation recently?
- How has this leadership been evidenced?
- Compare and contrast two obvious leaders in the organisation.
- Can you think of examples where leadership is obviously lacking?
- How and why is it lacking?
- If you were running a leadership course in this organisation, what content would you include?

Theoretical sampling dictates that subsequent and ongoing questions be directed at particular people, and about particular incidents; with the aim of clarifying and saturating the nature of concepts, and the theoretical relationship between concepts.

Key incidents should be identified early in the interviews. Key people should also be identified. These people need not be referred to by name, in an attempt to maintain confidence in the confidentiality of the interview, and to enhance the richness of the responses. Once key incidents and key people are identified, the detail of leadership processes is examined. This is reflected in the abundance of 'how?' and 'why?' questions. The importance of these questions for understanding and theorising about process has been emphasised by Tesch (1991) and Bryman and Burgess (1994).

The relevance of the Team Management Index® for recruitment and teams in an R&D environment

John Chapman and Bruce Acutt

Abstract

The need for better practices in recruitment and team formation is evident in both the private and public sector, as both sectors become more competitive. To maximise employee productivity, the selection of individuals for specific job types and the placement of them with other employees, demands careful consideration. This paper examines the use of a behaviour based personality test, the Team Management Index (TMI) which identifies preferred work styles in individuals. The Index was applied to three generic positions in a public research and development organisation. They were Research Scientist, Extension Officer and Technician/ Experimentalist. Preferred workstyles of the most outstanding operatives in each of these three job types showed that a clear model exists for Technician/Experimentalist which might be used in recruitment. No single clear model was found to exist for Research Scientists or Extension Officers. An analysis of psychological subscales showed that Scientists were more often introverted rather than extroverted and analytical rather than belief orientated. Technicans were more often introverted than extroverted, practical rather than creative, analytical rather than belief orientated and structured rather than flexible in their approach to work. Extension Officers showed no significant preferences on the psychological subscales. The less complex a job's requirements the more effective the TMI appears to be for recruitment. If used correctly the TMI can be a useful tool for team building.

Introduction

For an industry or company to compete successfully, research and development is often a critical success factor. The primary production sector is no different. Historically, the bulk of research and development in primary production in Queensland has been provided by the Department of Primary Industries (DPI). Increasing competition from other providers such as universities and the Commonwealth Scientific and Industrial Research Organisation (CSIRO) and greater expectations from industry clients, have contributed to the need for more effective outcomes. It is therefore vital that every effort be made to select the applicant most likely to prove most suitable for the job, when hiring.

Research and development work is, in most cases, conducted in teams, sometimes known as organisational task groups, because the range of skills and effort required to complete complicated projects is normally beyond one individual. During the selection process, consideration should be given to the ability of the individual to function effectively in teams during their employment with the organisation. If the selection process is poor, then teams can become dysfunctional, even when filled with talented people. As Margerison and McCann (1993: 29) noted, "Some teams fit together well by chance, while others learn to work together. Too many however, are totally misfits, never learn to work together and are ineffective".

Three generic positions conduct research and development work within the Department of Primary Industries. The Research Scientist gathers the ideas for projects, seeks approval and funding, gathers resources required to do the job, provides the scientific expertise and manages the project through to completion. This position usually requires a minimum of a Masters degree and, increasingly, a Doctorate. The position of Technician/Experimentalist requires a lesser qualification such as an Associate Diploma or a base degree and carries out the functions of assisting the Scientist in experiment establishment, data collection, data measurement and data processing. Extension Officers in agriculture usually have a degree or a Masters and are key purveyors of attitude change in clients. They are the specialists in technology transfer and need effective skills in interpersonal relations.

In reality few officers hold all the skills that are described for a position and consequently need the abilities of others to provide the missing links. The base model for the Department suggests that a project team needs at least one of each of the three generic positions to function properly. However, it is common for teams larger than three to be put together because of the geographic location and the technical and personality skills requirements.

The selection of personnel for the Department of Primary Industries involves standard techniques (Department of Primary Industries, 1994). These are formation of an interview panel, shortlisting from written applications, interviewing, verifying information via referees reports and background information and final selection based on a rating system. The use of other selection methods is often approved but seldom used. Any form of testing in the employment of research and development staff has been rarely been used.

This study was aimed at enhancing the process of staff selection for Research and Development teams by using a personality based instrument, to assist in the assessment of how people prefer to work. While the use of personality tests is not well regarded by some (Blinkhorn and Johnson, 1990; Stone, 1991) they are strongly supported by others (Guion, 1965; Gulliford, 1992; Ffrench, 1988). Robertson (1994) also supported personality testing in personnel selection, but believed that insufficient research evidence was available. Research has uncovered linear relationships between various, specific personality constructs and either overall work performance or specific work-related competencies. However, this is not sufficient to solve the problems of selection and team building.

The study investigated the use of one test with three job types. The test selected, the Team Management Index, has been the subject of considerable research and widespread use in the public and private sector (Margerison and Davies, 1987; Davies, Margerison and McCann, 1987; Davies, Margerison and McCann, 1988; Ffrench, 1988). The Team Management Index provides information about an individual's preferred workstyles.

Traditional Staff Selection

Stone (1991) suggested that Australian organisations had not significantly changed their selection methodology in the previous thirty years. The written application, personal interview and reference check constitute an almost universal selection process in the majority of firms (Patrickson and Hayden, 1988). Survey evidence produced by Wright and Thong (1989) for the Victorian private sector showed that for the selection of professional/administrative staff, the most commonly used technique was a simple person-to-person interview (45% of sample) or a series of person-to-person interviews (46% of sample).

Vaughan and McLean (1991) summarised a survey of Australian firms and their selection practices. They found that practices were technically and scientifically unsophisticated and highly susceptible to error. They suggested that firms preferred to use ad hoc and relatively unstructured interviews and reference checks, reserving more sophisticated techniques such as psychological testing and assessment centres to senior executive selection. They found that even at the senior executive level, sophisticated testing was not common.

Personality Testing Theory

Early testing for recruitment tended to focus on cognitive tests (Guion, 1987) largely because they revealed high validity coefficients in research. Personality measurements had been little used during the 1970s and 1980s. An attempt to review test validation for selection, since the mid 1960s, was abandoned because of the low number of tests reported used. It was the late 1980s and the early 1990s which saw a surge in the use of personality tests, at least in the Western World (Dakin, Nilakant and Jensen, 1994).

According to Gulliford (1992) the conceptualisation of personality and how personality testing might be used in selection, has been approached in two different ways. One is the trait approach and the other is the behavioural approach. The trait approach emphasised the identification of candidates with an appropriate profile of personal characteristics. The behavioural approach emphasised the identification of observable behaviours appropriate to the job.

Many trait based personality tests exist and two of the most popular are the Minnesota Multiphasic Personality Inventory (MMPI), (Miller, 1977) and the Meyers-Briggs Type Indicator (MBTI) (Briggs Meyers, 1977).

Tests which take the behavioural approach are designed with more specific intent. For example, a range of instruments exist which assess how people perform and consequently fit in teams. Since work teams are an integral part of a Research and Development environment, instruments of this type were considered more likely to be relevant to the proposed research. Three instruments of this type which are used by the Department of Primary Industries include the Group Styles Inventory (Lafferty and Cooke, 1991), the Team Management Index (Margerison and McCann, 1993) and the Belbin Analysis (Belbin, 1981).

The Team Management Index

The Margerison-McCann Team Management Index was selected for this study because it is a behavioural test designed to indicate individual workstyle preferences. It is widely used in Australia (Margerison and Davies, 1987) and in Great Britain (Rushmer, 1994).

Margerison and McCann (1993) suggested that the Team Management Index is a useful recruitment and selection tool for teams. They summarised the use of the Index by applying what they call the law of the "Three P's". People have work preferences. They like to practice these on a regular basis. Where the job facilitates this, they perform well.

The Team Management Index is a sixty-item, self-report questionnaire based on Jung's theory of psychological types, adapted for a managerial work situation, (Margerison and Davies, 1987). The index uses eight types of work, which team members, from varied work backgrounds recognised as contributing in some form or other to effective teamwork. The eight types are:

- Advising – gathering and reporting information
- Innovating – creating and experimenting with ideas
- Promoting – exploring and presenting opportunities
- Developing – assessing and testing the applicability of new approaches
- Organising – establishing and implementing ways of making things work
- Producing – concluding and delivering outputs
- Inspecting – controlling and auditing the working of systems
- Maintaining – upholding and safeguarding standards and processes

After establishing the importance of work type as the foundation of teamwork, the developers of the Team Management Index (Margerison, McCann and Davies, 1995) used as a theoretical framework, Jung's key concepts:

- Extroversion and Introversion – describing how people prefer to relate with one another
- Sensing and Intuition – explaining how people prefer to relate to their world
- Thinking and Feeling – defining how people prefer to interpret their world

They were supported in this approach by Mitroff and Kilmann (1978) who believed that Jung's personality types provided an appropriate framework for typing; the two most important Jungian dimensions being informational and decision-making. The informational dimension reflects the individual's preference for seeking data, either from the individual's inner world or from the external environment. The decision-making dimension reflects the individual's choice of decision-making process which they brought to bear upon the preferred kind of data input. To Jung's concepts Margerison, McCann and Davies (1995) added extensions which included the Judging and Perceiving dimension on how people responded to their world.

With these concepts as a theoretical base, Margerison, McCann and Davies (1995) suggested there are four major work preferences that determine an individual's role preference. They are likely to go about establishing relationships in an introverted or an extroverted way. Secondly, they collect information in either a creative or a practical way. Thirdly, they make decisions by either utilising their beliefs or critically analysing the issues. Finally, they organise their work in either a structured or flexible manner. These four major preferences became the four psychological subscales of the TMI.

As Rushmer (1994) explained, effective teamwork is achieved by filling all the necessary work functions, indicated by the wheel (Figure 1) with people whose work preferences lie in those areas. Finally, the team is held together by a person who practices linking skills. A set of different individuals with preferences for working in a variety of ways are thus brought together as a team.

Figure 1 The Team Management Wheel

Method

Participants

The group selected for this study was a cluster sample (Emory and Cooper, 1991). It comprised staff in the South and South East Regions of the Queensland Department of Primary Industries. This was done for ease of access by the researcher and because a high percentage of the Department's technical staff were located in the two regions (>75%). Each officer (Scientist, Technician/ Experimentalist and Extension Officer) was employed by one of five sub-programs which were Sheep, Beef, Intensive Livestock, Field Crops and Horticulture. They were line managed by Industry Managers who were asked to review their staff lists to ensure that staff included in the study, performed roles which were typical of one of the generic positions of Scientist, Technician/ Experimentalist and Extension Officer.

The review of staff positions revealed a total of 128 Scientists, 112 Technicians/ Experimentalists, and 78 Extension Officers who could be included in the study. It was considered that a minimum working group of 25 from each generic position would be adequate for analysis. This group of 25 was to comprise the people considered by raters as the best performing individuals for the generic position.

Staffing Rating

In order to rate staff, a Likert Scale (Neuman, 1994) for each generic position was developed. The method used to develop the Likert Scales was a nominal group technique (Carmen and Keith, 1994) and involved the cooperation of a middle management group.

The group was asked to focus on one of the generic positions and to write characteristics associated with the proper functioning of that position until they had completed as many as they believed were relevant. The characterics were then collected and grouped for similarities and made into a list. Each of the group participants was then asked to vote for the characteristics they believed were most important. They were allocated one-third of the number of characteristics developed as votes.

To complete the staff ratings for the positions of Research Scientist and Extension Officer two senior staff were used. One was the Industry Manager who directly line-managed the officer and the other was an experienced officer in policy development who was employed in the same sub program as the staff member and who knew the performance of staff of the sub-program in both regions. Care was taken that the raters made overlapping assessments of staff so that a standardisation process could be used to correct for rater variation within each sub-program.

After the scoring of all 318 staff was completed the scores allocated to each officer were converted to ratings (score/maximum score) so that they were comparable. The rates in each sub program were analysed by fitting generalised linear models, assuming a normal distribution using the following model:

$$Y_{ijk} = U + R_i + C_j + O_{kj} + E_{ijk}$$

Where	Y_{ijk} =	rating
	U =	population mean
	R_i =	effect of rater
	C_j =	effect of category (j = Scientist, Extension, Technician)
	O_{kj} =	effect of officer nested within category$_j$
	E_{ijk} =	random errors which are assumed to be independent.

The mean for officer k in category j gives a standardised rating for that officer. Thus, although the officer may be rated by three, two or one raters, his/her standardised rating was estimated as though he or she was rated by all raters.

Through this process, a standardised rate, with a maximum of one was determined for all staff in each sub-program. They were then ranked from lowest to highest within their sub-program and the highest scorers selected for the next phase of the study.

Work Preference

The highest scoring 30 from each of the three generic positions were selected for the analysis of work preferences. This figure was based on an assumption that not all officers would agree to participate and this would help to ensure that at least 25 would be involved.

The Team Management Index questionnaire was then mailed to the 90 officers selected, along with an explanatory letter. At the end of the ten day turn around period, 24 Scientists, 19 Technicians and 17 Extension Officers had returned the index. All others were then followed up by a telephone call. The final returns numbered 27 Scientists, 26 Technicians and 26 Extension Officers which were then submitted to the Team Management Institute for analysis and determination of individual workstyles.

Each officer in the study was therefore allocated attributes, according to the four psychological subscales and the data for each of the three job types were analysed for differences. The counts of officers having the various combinations of these attributes were assumed to have a Poisson distribution and log-linear models were fitted for Scientists, Extension Officers and Technicians. The resulting analyses of deviance are analogous to analyses of variance of quantitative data. The deviance statistic is approximated and distributed as chi-squared statistics, with the approximation improving with increasing number of observations. The difference in deviance from models with and without a term also has an approximate chi-squared distribution and can be used to test the contribution of that term (Payne et al., 1994).

The Team Management Institute allocated work preference roles as denoted in Figure 1. Three roles were allocated to each individual. Of these three roles, one was the major role in which the individual was most comfortable working. Two related roles were also allocated indicating the next most comfortable roles the individual enjoyed working in. Chi-square tests were used to determine whether the patterns of occurrence of major roles for each job type were different from those expected from a no preference model or models developed from generic job types by Team Management Systems (Margerison and McCann, 1995). Chi-square analyses were also used to test whether the occurrence of related roles on either side of the major role was different from what would be expected if the relationship between major and related was random.

Results

Analysis of Psychological Subscales

The analyses of deviance of the counts of officers having the sixteen combinations of the four psychological subscales being introverted vs extroverted (I vs E); creative vs practical (C vs P); beliefs vs analytical (B vs A); structured vs flexible (S vs F) is shown in Table 1.

Table 1 Analyses of deviance of psychological subscales

	Scientists		Technicians		Extension Officers	
	DG^2	Significance	DG^2	Significance	DG^2	Significance
I vs E	4.62	*	3.95	*	1.40	ns
C vs P	.04	ns	17.45	***	.00	ns
B vs A	18.59	***	17.45	***	.62	ns
S vs F	.33	ns	7.95	**	.50	ns
I vs E - C vs P	6.36	*	.01	ns	.65	ns
I vs E - B vs A	.22	ns	.01	ns	.39	ns
I vs E - S vs F	.22	ns	1.29	ns	3.80	†
C vs P - B vs A	.30	ns	1.19	ns	.16	ns
C vs P - S vs F	3.02	ns	3.02	ns	2.52	ns
B vs A - S vs F	.17	ns	.19	ns	.54	ns
I vs E - C vs P - B vs A	.15	ns	5.35	*	3.71	†
I vs E - C vs p - B vs A	.86	ns	.47	ns	.98	ns
C vs P - B vs A - S vs F	2.44	ns	1.85	ns	.44	ns

Note: DG^2 change of deviance (df = 1)   ns effect not significant
   * significant effect (P<0.05)   ** significant effect (P<0.01)
  *** significant effect (P<0.001)   † approaching significance

Table 2 Analyses of deviance (final models)

| | Scientists | | Technicians | | Extension Officers | |
	DF	Deviance	DF	Deviance	DF	Deviance
I vs E	1	4.62	1	3.95		
C vs P			1	17.45		
B vs A	1	18.59	1	17.45		
S vs F			1	7.95		
Residual	13	13.86	11	12.01		
Total	15	37.07	15	58.80	15	17.76

As the models, including only the significant main order effects, provided adequate fits for these data, (Table 2) and given the small number of observations, higher order interactions have not been further considered.

For Scientists the decision making (change of deviance 18.59, df = 1, prob of c^2 <0.001) and relationship forming (change of deviance 4.62, df = 1, prob of c^2 = 0.03) sub scales were highly significant as shown by the analysis of deviance with Scientists being very analytical rather than belief oriented. They were also introverted rather than extroverted. The model with the decision making and relationship forming subscales fits the data adequately (residual deviance 13.86, df = 13, prob of c^2 = 0.38).

For Technicians, all attributes were significant as shown by the analysis of deviance. Technicians in the study were introverted (change of deviance 3.95, df = 1, prob of c^2 = .05), practical (change of deviance 17.45, df = 1, prob of c^2 < 0.001), analytical (change of deviance 17.45, df = 1, prob of c^2 < 0.001) and structured (change of deviance 795, df = 1, prob of c^2 = 0.005) in the way they approached their work, rather than being extroverted, creative, belief oriented and flexible. The model with these main effects adequately fitted the data (residual deviance 12.01, df = 11, prob of c^2 < 0.001).

Extension officers showed relatively evenly spread preferences, (residual deviance 17.76, df = 15 prob of c^2 0.28) with no significant differences.

A summary of the work preferences of the 27 Scientists, 26 Technicians and 26 Extension Officers in their psychological subscales is given in Table 3.

Major Work Preferences

In Table 4, the major work preferences for Technicians/Experimentalists in this study is compared with models developed by Team Management Systems in their research from all indexes (Margerison and McCann, 1995) and with no preference models.

The work preferences for Technicians were significantly different to those of the no preference model and also many of Team Management models.

Table 3 Psychological Subscale Preferences

		Scientist	Technician	Extension
Forming	Extroverted	8	8	10
Relationships	Introverted	19	18	16
		27	26	26
Gathering	Practical	13	23	13
Information	Creative	14	3	13
		27	26	26
Making	Analytical	24	23	15
Decisions	Beliefs	3	3	11
		27	26	26
Work	Structured	12	20	11
Organisation	Flexible	15	6	15
		27	26	26

However, the Technicians profile is not significantly different from that of the Team Management models of all people who have completed the Team Management Index, and positions in Administration, Finance/Accounting and Production/Construction. The Technicians bore the closest resemblance to the Production/Construction managers. Concluder-Producer was the preferred major role of Technician/ Experimentalists. The next most preferred roles were Thruster-Organiser and Controller-Inspector which are contiguous roles to Concluder-Producers on the Team Management Wheel (Figure 1).

The number of Scientists who preferred each major role was not significantly different to the numbers expected from the no preference model and the general population model. Differences did occur between the Team

Table 4 Significance of Various Models for Technicians Preferred Major Role

Major Role	Observed	Expected					
		No Preferred Role	Team Management Models				
			General	R&D	Production and Constr	Finance and Acct	Admin
Explorer-Promoter	0	3.25	1.98	4.38	0.76	1.33	1.56
Assessor-Developer	2	3.25	4.73	3.86	2.80	3.45	3.64
Thruster-Organiser	6	3.25	6.37	5.66	7.90	6.90	6.76
Concluder-Producer	12	3.25	6.84	5.41	10.45	8.76	8.84
Controller-Inspector	4	3.25	2.37	1.54	2.29	2.65	2.08
Upholder-Maintainer	0	3.25	0.47	0.26	0.25	0.53	1.30
Reporter-Adviser	0	3.25	0.55	0.51	0.25	0.27	0.52
Creator-Innovator	2	3.25	2.65	4.38	1.27	2.12	1.30
c^2 (df=7)		36.77	9.77	19.30	3.87	4.74	7.48
Significance		<0.001	0.202	<0.007	0.794	0.691	0.380

Management job type categories. A range of major workstyles were evident for Scientists and only Upholder-Maintainer was not preferred at all.

The number of Extension Officers preferring each major role was not significantly different to the numbers expected from the no preference model but was different to those expected from the Team Management model. Work preferences were well dispersed and none of the eight were significantly less common.

Discussion

Technicians

Of the three generic positions investigated, Technician/Experimentalist showed the clearest model of preferred workstyles. Concluder-Producer was the preferred major role for 12 of the 26 high performers while six preferred the Thruster-Organiser role and four the Controller-Inspector role. In all, 22 of the Technicians preferred either Concluder-Producer, Thruster-Organiser or Controller-Inspector. These roles are contiguous and became a model for the ideal Technician with Concluder-Producer the major role and Thruster-Organiser and Controller-Inspector the related roles. Analysis of the psychological basis for allocating work preferences revealed that the Technicians in the study were predominantly introverted in the way they formed relationships, highly practical in the way they gathered information, very analytical in decision making and structured in the way they organised their work.

Scientists

The absence of common, clearly preferred workstyles prevented any clear model of the ideal Research Scientist being developed. The most highly preferred major workstyles for the 27 Scientists were Concluder-Producer, Controller-Inspector and Creator-Innovator. Of the 27 individuals sampled, eight preferred major workstyles of either Concluder-Producer or Controller-Inspector. These individuals were similar to the Technician model of preferences.

Fifteen of the 27 Scientists in the study showed a preference for Creator-Innovator either as a major or a related role. Often Creator-Innovator would be a related role on the opposite side of the Team Management Wheel to the major role and the other related role. These results indicated that many Scientists have learnt to be creative in the way they gather information, to maximise their effectiveness and respond to the demands of the job.

Analysis of the four psychological subscales highlighted the differences and similarities between Technicians and Scientists in this study by revealing that, like Technicians, Scientists are often introverted in the way they form relationships at work and are usually analytical in their decision making.

The study population of Scientists was evenly split between taking either a practical or a creative approach to gathering information and was also evenly split between being structured and flexible in the way they organised their work. This highlighted a key difference between Scientists and Technicians. Ideas are a critical difference between the two job types, a Scientist must learn to gather and utilise ideas and information either from themselves or from others.

Extension Officers

Work preferences for Extension Officers were scattered through the eight workstyles with a trend towards the two organising styles of Concluder-Producer and Controller-Inspector. This trend is similar to the dominant preferences in the other two job types studied and reinforces the importance of these workstyles and their effectiveness across a wide range of job types.

This variation in workstyles preferences and lack of differences in the psychological subscales reflected the great range of skills and abilities that are expected of Extension Officers and indicated considerable variation in the way successful Extension Officers go about their work. For example they are expected to have skills in the social sciences as well as technical skills. This is reflected in a comparison of the psychological subscale for making decisions. The more technically orientated job types of Scientist and Technician are strongly analytical in their approach to decision making while Extension Officers are often more belief orientated than analytical.

Conclusion

Results of this study suggest that the work preference model for the job type of Technician/Experimentalist developed from using the Team Management Index, can be used as a recruitment and selection tool. The model shows that Technicians prefer Concluder-Producer as their major role with Thruster-Organiser and Controller-Inspector as the related roles. It is concluded that one of these workstyles preferences should be the major role and at least one other be a related role for acceptance into this job type.

No similarly clear model was found for Research Scientist and Extension Officer. The Index has potential use in project team formation for Research and Development. Results from this study have revealed how important the Technician model is for teams involved in Research and Development. It is suggested therefore that a person with these workstyle preferences should be among the first identified for a project team. Once this person is installed the search can begin to round out the team's performance capabilities by attempting to fill critical characteristics in the Team Management Wheel (Figure 1).

Often an individual has two workstyles which fit the Technician model but they have learnt the value of being creative in the way they seek information. This is also a highly acceptable model for Research Scientists and Extension Officers. Margerison and McCann (1995) called this the Research and Development Manager's split. They described people with this profile as having a preference for generating ideas but they have learnt that they must thrust, organise and finish the tasks and projects they generate. However, it appears from this study that the ability to develop a Creative-Innovative approach is not essential for Scientists and Extension Officers, since a considerable number of those in this elite study group have all their preferences in the Controlling-Organising sector of the Team Management Wheel and none in the Advising-Exploring sector.

The more complex the requirements of the job the more difficult it is to develop a straight-forward model of what an individual's behaviour should be. Therefore, it is likely that, the greater the complexity of the job, the less useful a behaviour based personality test such as the Team Management Index would be in selection and placement.

Potential exists for further research into the usefulness of the Team Management Index in a wide range of less complex job types.

References

Belbin, R.M. 1981. *Management Teams: Why they succeed or fail.* London: Heinemann

Blinkhorn, S. and Johnson, C. 1990. The insignificance of personality testing. *Nature,* 348:671-672

Briggs Meyers, I. 1977. *Meyers-Briggs Type Indicator.* North Carlton, Victoria: Australian Psychologists Press

Carman, K. and Keith, K. 1994. *Community consultation techniques: purposes, processes and pitfalls.* Information Series (QI 94030), Department of Primary Industries, Queensland

Dakin, S., Nilakant, V. and Jensen, R. 1994. The role of personality testing in managerial selection. *Journal of Management Psychology,* 9(5):3-11

Davies, R., Margerison, C., and McCann, D. 1987. *Validity and application of the Margerison-McCann Team Management Index.* Paper presented to the 22nd Annual Conference of the Australian Psychological Society, Australian National University, Canberra

Davies, R., Margerison, C., and McCann, D. 1988. *The development of psychological tests for applied organisational settings: The case of the Margerison McCann Team Management Index.* Paper presented to the XXIV International Congress of Psychology, Sydney, Australia

Department of Primary Industries 1994. *Recruitment and selection standard.* Brisbane, Australia: Queensland Government

Emory, W.C., and Cooper, D.R. 1991. *Business research methods.* Boston: Irwin

Ffrench, B.1988. The team management index in the recruitment process. *Management Decision,* 26(51):48-52

Guion, R.M. 1965. *Personnel Testing.* New York: McGraw-Hill

Guion, R.M. 1987. Changing views for personnel selection research. *Personnel Psychology,* 40:199-213

Gulliford, R.A. 1992. The role of personality in assessing management potential. *Management Decision,* 30(6):69-75

Lafferty, J.C., and Cooke, R.A. 1991. *Group styles inventory.* Plymouth, Michigan: Human Synergistics

Margerison, C., and Davies, R. 1987. *Team Mapping.* Paper presented to the Australian and New Zealand Association of Management Educators Conference and Exhibition, University of Sydney

Margerison, C., and McCann, D. 1993. How to map team effectiveness. *Executive Development,* 6(5):29-32

Margerison, C., and McCann, D. 1995. *Team management systems: A handbook for members of the TMS network.* Milton, Brisbane: Team Management Systems

Margerison, C., McCann, D., and Davies, R. 1995. *How the Team Management Index compares with the Meyers Briggs Type Indicator.* Brisbane, Australia: Institute of Team Management Studies

Miller, D.C. 1977. *Handbook of research design and social measurement.* New York: Longman

Mitroff, I.I. and Kilmann, R.H. 1978. *Methodological approaches to social sciences.* San Francisco: Jossey-Bass

Neuman, W.L. 1994. *Social research methods.* Massachusetts: Allyn and Bacon

Patrickson, M. and Hayden, D. 1988. Management Selection Practices in South Australia. *Human Resource Management Australia,* 26(4):96

Payne, R.W., Lane, P.W., Digby, P.G.N., Harding, S.A., Leech, P.K., Morgan, G.W., Todd, A.D., Thompson, R., Tunnicliffe Wilson, G., Welham, S.J., and White, R.P. 1994. *Genstat 5 Release 3 Reference Manual.* Oxford: Oxford University Press

Robertson, I.T. 1994. Personality and personnel selection. *Journal of Organisational Behaviour* No 1 (Supplement) :75-89

Rushmer, R.K. 1994. *Comparing and contrasting Belbin with TMS.* Paper presented to the British Academy of Management Conference, Lancaster University, Lancaster

Stone, R.J. 1991. *Human Resource Management.* Brisbane: John Wiley and Sons

Vaughan, E., and McLean, J. 1991. A survey and critique of management selection practices in Australian business firms In R.J. Stone (Ed.). *Readings in Human Resource Management:* 29-42. Brisbane: John Wiley and Sons

Wright, K., and Thong, M. 1989. *Recruitment channels and selection methods of Victorian private sector organisations.* (Occasional Paper No 6) Victoria: Phillip Institute of Technology

The management of teams and technology in small organisations: Moving to a new era

Stephanie Miller

Abstract

This study reports on the extent of the use of communication and information technologies to support teamwork within small to medium sized organisations in the western metropolitan region of Melbourne, Australia. The results of a survey of 156 organisations are presented. Computer-based technologies are regarded as essential contributors to efficiency but the benefits of collaborative work offered by these technologies are not being extensively exploited within the population. Responses to attitudinal statements indicate that teamworking is associated with improved organisational performance. Organisations using electronic mail report greater satisfaction with their teams than those which do not use electronic mail.

Introduction

This paper explores the behaviours and attitudes of small business managers to the role of information and communication technologies and teamwork as strategies to improve organisational capability. The literature suggests that team work improves employee motivation and makes better use of resources with resulting improvements in productivity (Galbraith, 1977; Senge, 1991; Morgan, 1988; Bolman & Deal, 1991; Hames, 1994; Limerick & Cunnington, 1993, Belbin, 1996). Information technologies which facilitate improved communication, coordination and collaboration enable teams to function more effectively (Sproull & Kiesler, 1991; Johansen, 1992; Orlikowski, 1993; Currie, 1995). The population selected for study is small to medium sized business within the western region of Melbourne. Teamwork, in some form, has been implemented in almost half of the research population and around one-third of the companies in the population have the network capability to enable computer supported collaborative work (CSCW).

However, only one-fifth of the research population are combining the two strategies of technology and teamwork.

Teamwork

> A team is a small number of people with complementary skills who are committed to a common purpose, performance goals and approach for which they hold themselves mutually accountable. (Katzenbach & Smith, 1993: 45).

Many organisations have implemented teamwork in some form in Australia. Those which have been written about include CSR, ICI, Arnott's Biscuits, Qantas, National Rail, the Department of Justice (Tasmania), the Department of Families, Youth and Community Care (Queensland), Central Highlands Water (Queensland) and Newcastle City Council (Self Managed Work Teams Conference, 1996). These organisations are all large but Katzenbach and Smith (1993: 15) argue that 'real teams should be the basic unit of performance for most organisations, regardless of size'.

Teamwork may be implemented at any level in an organisation. Self-managing teams are usually to be found at the operational level of an organisation, high-performance teams may be cross-functional teams operating projects or they may be executive-level teams. Much of the work discussed in the literature is based on teams at the operating level of the organisation, although there is a great deal of interest in senior management teams. Organisations have had greater difficulty in implementing the team concept at higher levels.

Teams also differ according to the degree of autonomy given to them. Teams may be limited to having the power to make suggestions, they may have the authority to schedule work and vacation times, they may have discretion over budget items, or they may have responsibility for complete self-management. Self-managing teams tend to improve the fit between the needs of individuals and the needs of their organisations (Bolman & Deal, 1991). When the fit is good both benefit: the individual finds satisfaction and meaning in work, while the organisation is able to optimise the creative talent of its managers and workers.

Many organisations continue to report failure after attempting to develop a team-based structure. Some writers believe that organisations ask too much too quickly of their employees. Lipnack and Stamps (1994) argue that team implementations will continue to fail at alarming rates unless organisations remove the impediments to corporate trust—outmoded reward systems, obsolete status symbols and outdated management practices. Their belief is that people are being asked to reach higher levels of performance and creativity when the framework for this is often not provided. Belbin (1996) believes that many organisations adopt teamworking without altering traditional hierarchical decision making processes. This can result in a lot of wasted energy. Teams find they are not empowered to act when they are frequently overruled by a member of the hierarchy. Most of the leaders of small business in Australia have no management training, but even if they did they would probably not learn enough about devolving decision-making power to employees. An examination of most undergraduate programs in Australia today will reveal that leadership, social and communication skills are still neglected. The Karpin report recommended that communication and leadership skills be incorporated into management training as one way of addressing the poor performance of Australian managers (Karpin, 1995). When power is appropriately devolved the pressure on leaders is relieved. Belbin (1996) and Jenkins (1996) agree that an organisation which empowers its teams no longer requires the services of superhuman managers.

> If you have a really effective team, the apparent weaknesses of any individual are made good by his or her colleagues, so they really do not matter. The search for the perfect manager—the motor which drives much management training—is a wild goose chase. Empowerment makes this evident for all to see. (Jenkins, 1996: 107)

Changing expectations from employees may also have an impact on the role of leaders and the degree of empowerment available to workers. Hames (1994) believes that the demand from all workers for greater levels of involvement in decisions relating to the fundamental purpose and direction of their organisations will continue to rise dramatically with a consequent need for more effective learning and improved life-style and support mechanisms within the organisation. In this type of organisation groupware, information technology to facilitate seamless communication, should fit naturally. The search for 'open, improved and more effective ways of working can only be achieved through co-operative processes in which all stakeholders are invited to contribute' (Hames, 1994).

In contrast with Hames' optimistic view of organisations, writers such as Clegg (1995), and Boje and Winsor (1995) argue that the experience of the vast majority of workers shows that the bureaucratic, hierarchical nature of modern organisations has not changed. Top down hierarchies have been a part of the culture of the western world for so long that it is difficult to change direction. Harrison (1992) observes that 'bureaucratic hierarchy currently forms the structural context for most of our conceptions of communication in organisations' (14). These contrasting views illustrate the continuing debate between theorists with an optimistic view of the transformation of work, usually referred to as 'post-Fordist' and those, such as Clegg (1995) who see an inevitable antagonism between the interests of workers and the interests of management. This latter approach, which conceptualises new workplace organisation as 'Neo-Fordism', informed by

Marxist theory, suggests that in practice flexibility and autonomy of employees will be associated with a strengthening of management control over the labour process (Harley, 1994). In a study of indicators of flexibility and autonomy drawn from the Australian Workplace Industrial Relations Survey, Harley (1994) found that while functional and procedural flexibility were associated positively with autonomy for workers this was only to the extent that management felt that autonomy contributed to better economic performance.

When implemented with appropriate changes to leadership and empowerment, teams can provide a more rewarding working environment for employees, along with a range of organisational benefits. Teams bring together a complementary mix of skills and experiences which are likely to exceed those of any individual in the group. This combination is likely to lead to improvements in work methods and processes, service and product quality, and productivity (Katzenbach and Smith, 1993; Shonk, 1992). Teams enable greater flexibility in staffing and employees are more likely to be attracted and retained in a company which supports a participative structure (Shonk, 1992). Teams provide a unique social dimension in the workplace which leads to a greater appreciation of the meaning of work and the effort brought to bear upon it until team performance becomes its own reward (Katzenbach and Smith, 1993). Teams also provide an environment which allows workers to have fun and to celebrate their achievements (Katzenbach and Smith, 1993).

Information Systems in Smaller Organisations

Studies in the United States, Canada and the United Kingdom indicate that the implementation of computer systems by small business has been extensive (Ray, 1994). Furthermore, it has been predicted that small companies will be well-placed to take advantage of information technologies to improve team effectiveness:

> In the future, small and midsize companies will be extremely active groupware users, as they discover that effective use of technology enables them to extend their resources to compete with larger organisations. Smaller size may even be an advantage because these companies can make quicker, clearer decisions on both infrastructure and groupware systems. (Opper & Fersko-Weiss, 1992: 35)

Information systems in small firms are becoming more sophisticated (Cragg & Zinnatelli, 1995). Research by Ray et al. (1994), conducted in Indiana with a survey of 231 smaller organisations, found that both small business owners and employees held a positive view of the value of office automation as a method of improving efficiency and therefore making the business more profitable and/or more efficient. Both owners and users also held some negative views of computers, often viewing computers as a source of stress.

Interestingly, both the owners and the employees agreed very strongly that computers improved communication (Ray et al., 1994).

Workers in small firms tend to use menu-based application packages and to rely on external sources for their application software. Training is typically limited to hands-on supervision when new applications are introduced (Cragg & Zinnatelli, 1995). In most firms computer expertise is limited to a very few personnel. As the software packages are easy to use and time is always a limited resource, training is often viewed as unnecessary (Cragg & Zinnatelli, 1995).

Small firms display a casual attitude to the management of information systems. Since top management support is a key factor contributing to the success of information systems the lack of effective planning and the lack of exposure to computers at senior levels in small firms is a problem (Cragg & Zinnatelli, 1995).

Small firms faced with national or international competition are tending to turn increasingly to new technologies (Julien, 1995). Smaller firms tend to modernise in a more incremental and less planned way than large firms. They may use networks of suppliers, research centres or public or private agencies transferring information, industry associations and contractors to assist with the acquisition of knowledge about new technologies (Julien, 1995). The cost of new equipment relative to the profitability of the business, the management profile or the owner-manager's personal characteristics, organisational complexity, the nature of the firm's strategy and the quality of technological information obtained, together with the capacity to process it, are all factors underlying the penetration of information technologies (Julien & Raymond, 1994).

Lefebvre (1995), in a Canadian study, found small manufacturing firms did best where the level of technological penetration was high and the computer-based applications were present across both administrative and production environments. The processes of organisational learning stimulated by information technology permeated all activities and the cycles of experimentation and action which arose from such environment were synergistic:

> In that respect, knowledge is tacit and part of an organisation's invisible assets embodied in the collective knowledge of the workers. There is no doubt that effective organisational learning is an essential ingredient to reap fully the benefits of innovative efforts (Lefebvre, 1995: 521).

In this way pervasive information technology can help to develop team capability.

A recent Committee for Economic Development of Australia (CEDA) Information Paper (1996) describes 'workgroup computing as underpinning the second wave of connectivity in the enterprises of the late 20th century'. Over 70 per cent of respondents (of which 13 per cent had between 1 and 50 staff) to the CEDA (1996) survey reported that 'all or most' of their

Australian sites were equipped with workgroup computing facilities. Electronic mail was the most widely accepted application, being available to 80 per cent of staff in professional and service organisations. However, penetration of other workgroup computing technologies was still relatively low. The most popular applications being used—electronic mail, telephone conferencing, electronic diaries and shared information databases—were not dependent on organisation-wide acceptance and did not necessarily require investment in new equipment or infrastructure (CEDA, 1996: 12) The CEDA report was optimistic about the future growth of groupware but the survey also showed only moderate acceptance of the newer technologies.

Workgroup technologies face far more obstacles to acceptance than individual applications. Grudin (1994) identifies a disparity in the additional work required from individuals using groupware and the benefits they may derive. Groupware may violate socially accepted behaviours through insensitivity. Moreover, groupware may not be capable of dealing with exceptions and improvisation that is common to group activity (Grudin, 1994). The result of such frustrations is that users will revert to single-user applications. To succeed groupware will have to be used by most or all group members. The application will have to appeal to people with different roles, backgrounds and preferences. For this reason a user centred approach to design is important (Grudin, 1994).

Chaudry and others (1996) observed that small businesses find the processes involved in designing, developing and implementing decision support systems problematic. In small business, where there is no specialist information technology department it is important to identify an individual in the organisation who will champion change and work with potential users in the development and implementation stages. This means allocating resources and time to develop internal information technology skills. It is hard for business managers to evaluate individual groupware products in a market place which is very confusing (CEDA, 1996).

Before team working technologies can be accepted a form of collaborative working must be established in the firm. Orlikowski (1993) observed two organisational elements which seem especially relevant in influencing the effective utilisation of groupware: people's cognitions, or mental models about technology and their work; and the structural properties of the organisation, such as policies, norms, and reward systems. She wrote:

> The findings suggest that where people's mental models do not understand or appreciate the collaborative nature of groupware, such technologies will be interpreted and used as if they were more familiar technologies, such as personal, stand-alone software (e.g. a spreadsheet or a word processing program). Also, where the premises underlying the groupware technology (shared effort, cooperation, collaboration) are countercultural to an organization's structural properties (competitive and individualistic culture, rigid hierarchy, etc.), the technology will be unlikely to facilitate collective use and value. (Orlikowski, 1993: 238)

Not only is there a need for education, training and support of organisation members to awaken notions of collaborative work, to develop new mental models, there is also a need for managers to critically assess their organisation's structure, the vision of the company and the ways in which their workers can participate in reshaping the workplace for cooperative effort and shared rewards.

The Research

Very little research into the use of technology to support teamwork in small business is available for Australia.

The area covered by this study has a population which continues to grow, while the rate of unemployment remains unacceptably high. The rate of unemployment in parts of the region is fifty percent higher than for the whole of Melbourne (Grant, 1995). Within the study environment there exists remnants of a working-class culture derived from the history of the western regions of Melbourne as the home of blue-collar workers. In more recent times, business people have found the region to be cost effective through being close to transport, having cheaper land than other urban areas of Melbourne and a ready supply of both skilled and unskilled labour.

This survey of small to medium organisations in the west of Melbourne was completed by 156 organisations across five industry sectors (Figure 1).

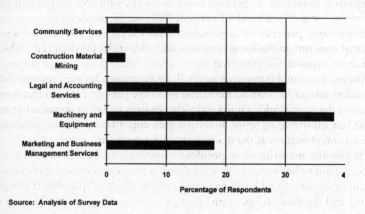

Source: Analysis of Survey Data

Figure 1 Profile of respondents by industry, n = 156
Source: Analysis of survey data

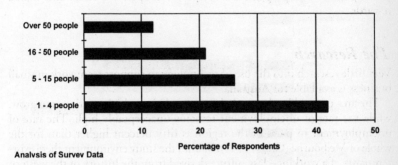

Analysis of Survey Data

Figure 2 Profile of respondents by number of staff, n = 156
Source: Analysis of survey data

Respondent organisations had staff numbers ranging from 1 to over 50 employees (Figure 2), 41 per cent had 4 or fewer employees, 47 per cent had between 5 and 50 staff and 12 per cent had over 50 employees.

Eighty-one per cent of respondents reported having a formal or semi-formal structure in their organisations with clear roles for their staff, which tends to support the view that bureaucratic hierarchies remain the most common structural framework in small organisations. Six per cent said their structure was *ad hoc,* with no formalised roles, five per cent reported that teams formed the main working units and eight per cent said their organisation was based on self-managing teams. In other words, only 13 per cent of organisations have team structures as the main form of organisation.

While the majority of respondent organisations have some forms of information technology, usually it is limited to the most common applications: word processing (used by 87 per cent of organisations), spreadsheet (68 per cent) and database (63 per cent) packages (Figure 3). This would seem to indicate that 13 per cent of respondent organisations have no computing resources. It is interesting to note that the fourth most popular technology is electronic mail (34 per cent). The Internet is also reported to be used by 23 per cent of respondents. Other applications, such as project management software, electronic scheduling and groupware are not well represented in smaller organisations.

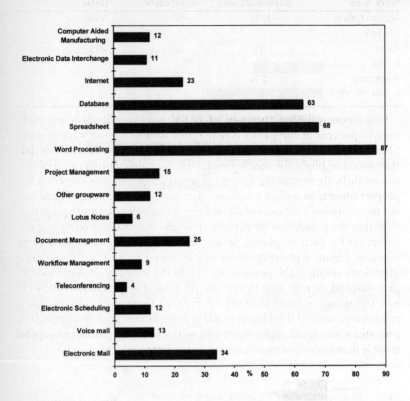

Figure 3 Profile of respondents by information technologies
Source: Analysis of Survey Data

These results tend to support the view expressed by Julien (1995), that small businesses work on very specific market niches, where competition is less strong and where new technologies are not as essential. Respondents indicated that new technology was very costly, that it took up a great deal of time, and that it required expertise which was not readily available within the firm.

The belief that expertise is not readily available is born out by the results shown in Table 1. Table 1 provides details of the business managers' perceptions of the competence of their staff's use of information technology. Details from three work areas, administration, sales and production are provided.

Table 1 Competence of technology use of respondents

Work Area	Sophisticated	Competent	Basic
Administration n = 145	17%	58%	19%
Sales n = 98	5%	31%	29%
Production n = 94	12%	25%	24%

Even amongst the most pervasive of the technologies, administrative tools, only 17 per cent of companies believed their technology use was proficient (Table 1). If these perceptions were shown to be based on measurable data they would highlight the need for more effective training programs. Training can be difficult to manage in a small organisation because there are few people available to replace a staff member involved in training. While cost is a factor, having staff unavailable is a greater barrier to training programs.

Within the population 40 per cent of organisations reported having one computer for each employee. Investment in technologies appears to be ongoing. Figure 4 presents details of past spending and future spending intentions amongst the population. While the majority of organisations plan to spend over the next three years, the total of intended investments in new technology is lower than for the previous three years. This may be a reflection of wishful thinking as much as firm planning commitments. The only area where small organisation managers say they are planning to spend more is in network communications, up by 3 per cent.

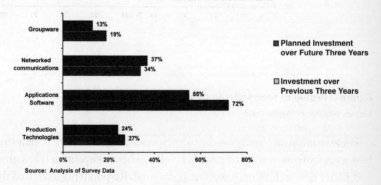

Source: Analysis of Survey Data

Figure 4 Past and intended technology expenditure
Source: Analysis of Survey Data

With 72 per cent of respondents indicating that they have invested in applications over the past three years and 34 per cent having invested in networked communications it would appear that the basic infrastructure required for computer supported team work is in place in over one-third of the population.

Statements relating to the use of technology to support teamwork were put to business managers in the final section of the survey. Only those respondents who believed that they used teamwork in their organisations were asked to respond. Seventy-four responses were received. In other words 48 per cent (74 of 156) of the sample considered that they used teamwork. A seven point Likert scale (Strongly Disagree (1) to Strongly Agree (7)) was used for each of 19 statements.

To identify the main factors emerging from the attitudinal survey, the data was examined using principal components analysis as the extraction technique and varimax as the method of rotation. Five factors, accounting for 51.3 per cent of the variance, were extracted. Three factors emerged with eigenvalues greater than 1 and accounted for 43 per cent of the variance. Factors 4 and 5 yielded eigenvalues of .93 and .65 respectively. Table 2 presents data from the factor analysis showing the five factors and their eigenvalues, the individual instrument items associated with each factor and the factor loadings for each item. The five factors are presented in decreasing order of importance.

Table 2 Principal components analysis of survey data

Factor/Survey Item	Loading	Eigenvalue
Factor 1: Technology has a positive impact on teamwork		4.58772
1 Technology helps us to work in teams.	.78387	
5 Teams rely on technology to communicate.	.76383	
19 Technology has enabled more effective teams.	.74142	
13 Technology is used to disseminate information quickly.	.70015	
4 Communications technology makes its easier to work in teams.	.61431	
18 We regularly communicate electronically with outside organisations.	.60181	
10 Network communications have improved our performance.	.54946	
Factor 2: Culture		2.47864
15 Teams are rewarded.	.69808	
9 Organisation culture enables good teamwork.	.51887	
17 Team manages flexible work times.	.51201	
Factor 3: Structure		1.09573
16 Teams have improved organisation's performance.	.66457	
2 Teams have clearly defined roles and responsibilities.	.58261	
7 Structure enables teamwork.	.50162	
12 Work better since teams were implemented.	.32825	
Factor 4: Management Support for Teams		.93089
8 Teams are used at management level.	.78353	
Factor 5: Training Supports Teamwork		.65373
6 Organisation invests in training.	.69206	
3 Employees like working in teams.	.55493	

The first factor relates to the pervasiveness, accessibility and consistency of information and communications technology to support teamwork. There is strong commonality amongst the responses relating to the effectiveness of teamwork and reliance on technology to achieve the work. Sixty per cent of respondents believed that *technology helps us to work in teams* and 60 per cent said *network communications have improved our performance.*

The second factor relates to organisation culture. Around 70 per cent of respondents believed that their *organisation culture enables good team work,* that the *teams are rewarded* and that the *teams have control over their work schedules.*

The third factor centres around structural issues. Eighty per cent of respondents agreed that their *structure suits teamwork,* that their *teams have clear roles and responsibilities* and that *the use of teams has improved their organisation's performance.*

The fourth factor, management teams, showed that 44 per cent of respondents believed that they *have teams at management level.* This reflects the difficulty indicated in the literature of developing teams at top management level. This may be compounded in smaller organisations where the manager is also the owner of the firm.

Factor five reveals a strong relationship between training and employees liking teamwork. Eighty per cent of respondents reported that they *invest in training* and over 70 per cent said that their *employees like working in teams.*

Overall the respondents endorsed teamwork as a means of enhancing performance. Statement 16, *I am confident that the use of teams has improved our organisation's performance,* received agreement from 83 per cent of respondents.

A large number of organisations were not using technology to support teamwork, even where teams were present. Statement 5, *Our teams rely heavily on information technology to communicate* was agreed to by only 38 per cent of respondents.

Within the group of respondents using teams 33 had access to email and 42 did not. For each of these subgroups, responses on two items relating to effectiveness and performance were compared. In response to Statement 19, *Information technology has enabled our teams to be more effective,* 80 per cent of email users agreed with the statement whereas only 52 per cent of non-users agreed (Figure 5).

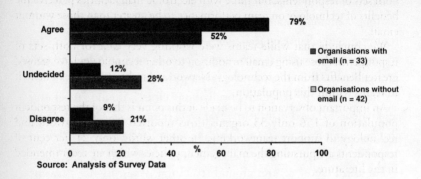

Figure 5 Information technology has enabled our teams to be more effective

Source: Analysis of Survey Data

Statement 16, I am confident that the use of teams has improved our organisation's performance resulted in almost identical, and very positive, means for both groups. The result is slightly more positive for the organisations using email (Figure 6).

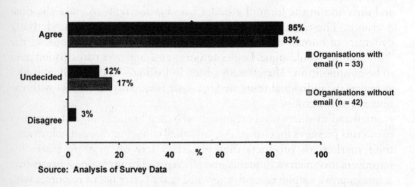

Figure 6 The use of teams has improved our organisation's performance

Source: Analysis of Survey Data

The two sets of results combined indicate that teams are working well for both sets of respondents, but those with electronic mail facilities perceive the benefits of technology on team performance to be greater than those without email.

We conclude that while teams were working very well for both sets of respondents, those using email in addition to other technologies have realised greater benefits from the technology. Networking technologies are of benefit to teams within this population.

An important observation to be made at this point is that of the respondent population of 156 only 33 organisations reported using teamwork and technology to support teamworking. In other words, only 21 per cent of respondents are pursuing the management policies which are recommended in the literature.

Conclusions

The results indicate the existence of an underlying conflict between team structures and traditional power relationships in the organisations sampled. The majority of organisations in this sample continued to operate within hierarchical structures. Eighty-one per cent of respondents have a formal, or semi-formal structure with clear roles for their staff. This is despite the fact that teamwork is reported to improve organisational capability amongst the majority of the firms which have tried it. Leadership is crucial in any team or group or 'family'. There can be no final resolution to the antagonism between the power held by an owner/manager and the need to devolve authority to team members. The literature reveals a moral dilemma for both management thinkers and business owners between the desire to give workers fair participation through team structures and the need to establish authority and direction in the form of a leader who has the right to make the final decisions. The team represents a microcosm containing the underlying dynamics of human culture and which may reflect class relations, as the 'Neo-Fordists' would argue. Leader authority and employee participation tend to be in opposition. The interests of the individual—the individual leader as well as the individual team member—are frequently in conflict with the interests of the group.

Small and medium sized organisations have a limited range of responses to external pressures for change. As most small companies are not able to alter their markets or products they generally rely on new processes for improvements in service, quality and efficiency. The literature suggests that teams improve employee motivation and make better use of resources with resulting improvements in productivity and organisational capability. It is also suggested that information technologies which facilitate collaboration, communications and coordination enable teams to function more effectively. Within this framework there are many variables which either hinder or promote teamwork. Effective leadership is required to provide a vision for teamwork. Training and team development is important for employees to understand how and why teams are used in the organisation. Reward systems should reflect the effort of teams as well as individuals. Rewards may include celebrations of the teams and more light-hearted social events. The research shows that teamwork is enjoyed in 80 per cent of organisations which have implemented teams. Perhaps the organisation of work into empowered teams is intrinsically rewarding.

Communication between and within teams supported by effective systems enables improved sharing of information. The results show that information and communications technology enables teams to be more effective. Communication from senior management needs to inform and involve employees. This is part of organisational learning, developing better processes to absorb experiences and knowledge from the workplace and through learning transfer from industry groups and parent companies which is indicated in the literature as a fundamental element of successful team development.

Amongst this sample there is an awareness of the need for technology to improve efficiency but the benefits to be derived from combining management techniques (such as team structures, collaboration and empowerment) with information technologies are yet to be realised. Only 21 per cent of respondent organisations are using information technologies to support teamwork.

Almost 40 per cent of respondent firms intend spending on networking technologies over the next three years but only 13 per cent plan to invest in groupware. The literature indicates that groupware is suited to the small to medium sized organisation and yet it has not been adopted in the past and it will be adopted by only a small percentage of organisations in the near future. Small businesses owners continue to demonstrate an incremental approach to technology implementation.

This study shows that the applications and the technical infrastructure required for collaborative computing is present in around 35 per cent of small to medium sized organisations. Team development processes appear to be reasonably mature in around half of the population. This study highlights the need to further develop our understanding of the decision making processes of small business managers. Clearly the decision to implement teamworking and to invest in teamworking technologies rests with the entrepreneur and a few key individuals. Just what catalysts are present for such decisions to be taken are unknown. Further research would clarify what motivated the one-fifth of small businesses who have adopted these strategies to develop the new 'mental models' required for the effective use of information and communications technology to support teamworking.

References:

Belbin, R. Meredith, 1996, *The Coming Shape of Organization,* Butterworth Heinemann, Oxford.

Boje, David M and Winsor, Robert D, 1995, `The Resurrection of Taylorism: Total Quality Management's Hidden Agenda', *Journal of Organizational Change Management,* Vol 6, No 4, pp 57-70.

Bolman, Lee and Deal, Terrence E, 1991, *Reframing Organisations, Artistry, Choice and Leadership,* Jossey Bass, San Francisco.

CEDA Information Paper No 48, 1996, *Exploiting the Benefits of Workgroup Computing, Survey of CEDA Members 1996,* Committee for Economic Development of Australia, Melbourne.

Chaudhry, S, Salchenberger, L and Beheshtian, 1996, 'A Small Business Inventory DSS: Design, Development, and Implementation Issues, *Computer Operations and Research,* Vol 23, Iss 1, pp 63-72.

Clegg, Stuart, 1995, `Postmodern Management?', *Journal of Organizational Change Management,* Vol 5, No 2, pp 31 - 49.

Cragg, Paul B, and Zinatelli, Nancy, 1995, 'The evolution of information systems in small firms', *Information & Management,* Vol 29, pp 1-8.

Currie, Wendy, 1995, Management Strategy for I.T., *An International Perspective,* Pitman, London.

Finholt, Tom and Sproull, Lee, (1990), 'Electronic Groups at Work', Organization Science, Vol 1 No l, in Halasz, F (Ed), CSCW 90: *Proceedings of the Conference on Computer Supported Cooperative Work,* Los Angeles, Oct 7 - 10, pp 431-442.

Galbraith, J, 1977, *Designing Complex Organisations,* Addison Wesley, Reading, Mass.

Grant, J, Watson, D and Sandy, G, 1995, *Economic Overview of the West and Northwest Region of Melbourne,* VUT, DEET.

Grudin, Jonathan, 1994, 'Groupware and Social Dynamics: Eight Challenges for Developers', *Communications of the ACM,* January, Vol 37, No 1, pp 92-105.

Hames, Richard, David, 1994, *The Management Myth,* Business and Professional Publishing, Sydney.

Harley, Bill, 1994, 'Post-Fordist Theory, Labour Process and Flexibility and autonomy in Australian Workplaces', *Labour and Industry,* Vol 6, No 1, October, pp 107-129.

Harrison, Teresa, M, 1992, 'Designing the post-bureaucratic organisation: Toward egalitarian organisation structure', *Australian Journal of Communication,* Vol 19 (2), pp 14-29.

Jenkins, David, 1996, *Managing Empowerment,* Century Business, London.

Johansen, Robert, 1988, *Groupware: Computer Support for Business Teams,* The Free Press, London.

Julien, Pierre-Andre and Raymond, Louis, 1994, 'Factors of New Technology Adoption in the Retail Sector', *Entrepreneurship: Theory and Practice,* Vol 18, Iss 4, pp 79-90.

Julien, Pierre-Andre, 1995, 'New Technologies and Technological Information in Small Businesses', *Journal of Business Venturing,* 10, pp 459-475.

Karpin, D, 1995, *Enterprising Nation: Renewing Australia's Managers to Meet the Challenges of the Asia Pacific Century,* Report of the Industry Task Force on Leadership and Management Skills, 3 vols, Canberra, AGPS.

Katzenbach, Jon R and Smith, Douglas K, 1993, *The Wisdom of Teams,* Harvard Business School, Boston, Mass.

Lefebvre, Elisabeth, Lefebvre, Louis and Roy, Marie-Josee, 1995, 'Technological Penetration and Organizational Learning in SMEs: the cumulative effect', *Technovation,* Vol 15, No 8, pp 511-522.

Limerick D and Cunnington, 1993, *Managing the New Organisation, A Blueprint for Networks and Strategic Alliances,* Business and Professional Publishing, Chatswood.

Lipnack, Jessica and Stamps, Jeffrey, 1994, *The Age of the Network,* Wiley, New York.

Morgan, Gareth, 1988, *Riding the Waves of Change,* Jossey Bass, Calif.

Orlikowski, Wanda J, 1993, 'Learning from Notes: Organizational Issues in Groupware Implementation', Vol 9, No 3, pp 237-250.

Ray, Charles, Harris, Thomas, and Dye, J Lee, 1994, 'Small Business Attitudes Towards Computers', *Journal of End User Computing,* Vol 6 No 1, pp 16-25.

4th Annual Australian Self Managed Work Teams Conference, 1996, Workplace Global Network, Melbourne, June.

Senge, Peter, 1992, *The Fifth Discipline: The Art and Practice of the Learning Organization,* Random House, Sydney.

Shonk, James, H, 1992, *Team Based Organizations,* Business One Irwin, Illinois.

Sproull, Lee and Kiesler, Sara, 1991, *Connections, New Ways of Working in the Networked Organisation,* MIT Press, Massachusetts.

Section C
Work forms and practices

Outsourcing: 'Functional', 'fashionable' or 'foolish'?

James D. Hunter and
G. Richard Gates

Abstract

The growth in popularity of the outsourcing phenomenon is obvious, yet questions remain as to the rationale for its adoption. Is it a 'blinkered' decision made by managers looking for a 'quick fix' solution in order to meet performance objectives set by their masters; or a decision reached through critical analysis of all the dimensions encompassed by the outsourcing process? An examination of current management practice and research suggests that managers are ill prepared to undertake the critical assessment required to fully comprehend the dimensions of outsourcing. This paper discusses these issues and their implications, urging caution in the unquestioning adoption of management fads that are short on critical thought and long on ideological rhetoric.

Introduction

The outsourcing phenomenon, also referred to as contracting out, is occurring almost everywhere. In recent years, there has been a dramatic increase in the use of third parties to provide a variety of products and services in the public, private and 'not-for-profit' sectors. As Domberger and Hall (1995: 1) note, it is happening 'in the private and public sectors, in Europe, America, Asia and Australia. It is becoming a widely used management tool'.

In Australia, a weak economic environment is unlikely to provide the necessary spark to result in dramatic recoveries in either private or public sector revenues. Such a lacklustre environment will inevitably lead to management becoming increasingly focused on reducing costs in order to meet performance objectives imposed by the relevant stakeholders. In these circumstances it is likely that outsourcing will become increasingly popular due to its apparent (and highly questionable) assumption that promises automatic cost reductions to management. Nowhere is this more evident than in the public sector.

All levels of government have embarked upon an aggressive outsourcing program under the rubric of 'competition policy' (see Hilmer, 1993) whereby services previously provided by the public sector and its agencies have been, or are being, transferred to the private sector. This change to the way in which governments manage and deliver their business has not gone unnoticed, with a growing chorus of voices raising concerns about the use of this management tool and its consequences.

A clear example of this concern is found in matters considered within the Commonwealth Ombudsman's *Annual Report* (1995-96). In this report, it was observed that complaints had increased 28 per cent over the previous year, a result largely attributed to quality issues and the lawfulness of agencies' actions. The Ombudsman recognised this to be of particular concern when it was realised that issues raised as a result of 'contracted out' services fell outside the Ombudsman's jurisdiction, leaving consumers with no avenue to public sector accountability mechanisms.

The Ombudsman questioned which functions and agencies 'should be subjected to the accountability and scrutiny of Parliament' and queried the public purpose and the ability of the marketplace to guarantee accountability in managing public assets. The culmination of such concerns has resulted in the Ombudsman recommending that its jurisdiction be extended to include contracting out.

The Ombudsman's voice is but one of many parties expressing concern about the outsourcing process yet there seems to be little evidence that the tide of outsourcing activity is about to turn. This criticism of outsourcing is embedded in a wider critique of current economic policy (labelled economic rationalism by many) of which outsourcing is but one dimension (see Rees and Rodley, 1995; Saul, 1997).

As mentioned above, outsourcing is not unique to the public sector but is also affecting the private sector. Many private companies are putting out a variety of services to tender. For example, the AMP Society is outsourcing most of its legal services and the banks have been outsourcing a range of management services such as payroll, security and cleaning. What is interesting is that an organisational tool long utilised by certain industries (such as the construction industry) is being applied in a range of circumstances. Two questions that immediately come to mind are (i) why is this occurring; and (ii) are these changes permanent?

The concept that organisations will often seek to utilise external parties in the process of providing goods and services has been around for a long time. Over two hundred years ago Adam Smith wrote that it is 'the maxim of every prudent master is never to attempt to make at home what it will cost him more to make than to buy' (quoted in Reilly & Tamkin, 1996: 1).

The growing popularity of outsourcing as a management tool is obvious. One has only to turn to the popular press to observe this. However, there seems to be little understanding of what outsourcing really is. Rothery and Roberts

(1995: 4) highlighted the results of a survey of fifty top executives and reported 'extensive ignorance' about outsourcing despite the fact that more than 20 per cent of the executives questioned were actively considering its adoption.

One of the interesting questions that arise from the outsourcing debate is whether managers have considered and fully understood the dimensions of outsourcing as a management tool? It might be suggested that they are caught up in a 'popular' tide of pluralistic ignorance stemming from, amongst other things, an adherence to 'popular' research methodologies overly-simplifying an inherently complex issue. As Henry Fielding observed, some two hundred and fifty years ago:

> Fashion is the great governor of this world: it presides not only in matters of dress and amusement, but in law, physics, politics, religion and all other things of the gravest kind. (quoted in Shiller, 1984: 457)

When assessing the background and implications of a particular management decision, such as the decision to outsource, the researcher cannot divorce the effects of outsourcing from the context within which the decision for it was made. To focus on outsourcing alone would suggest the role of management is insignificant.

Aulich and Reynolds (1993) support this view when they identify management as the real issue underlying the outsourcing decision:

> The debate on contracting out has too often focused on economic and financial issues rather than on management. Neo-classical economists make the assumption that the quality of management is homogeneous in the long run and that the inexpert are eliminated by market forces unless they learn to match the performance of those who excel. Howard (1989, 87-8) suggests that this is not a realistic assumption given that management as a variable is probably the most critical to the performance of business and industries.

Cooksey and Gates (1995), in proffering explanations for the apparent shortcomings of MBA programs in preparing individuals for the rigours of management, highlight the deleterious impacts of the unquestioning nature of management education. They argue (quoting from Richardson, 1993) that 'management education's priorities had become 'abstracted and irrelevant, reflecting and mirroring the interests of academics rather than world they try to describe".

This comment would suggest that the research relating to management decision making must embrace a more holistic stance. Such an approach would engender in management an appreciation for the consequences of relationships, the patterns arising from relationships and the importance of chaos and complexity (see Richardson, 1993). Adopting this view creates a compelling reason to view traditional management research that relies on a narrow discipline base, in the context of methodologies that more closely reflect the world in which managers operate.

The above discussion prompts a number of questions. Has the 'conformity' or 'fashion' that Fielding focused on and the 'research gap' that Cooksey & Gates (1995) talk about, manifested itself in 'the rise and rise' of outsourcing? Is outsourcing a truly functional management tool, a passing management fad or simply a foolish reaction by management (perhaps abrogating their responsibilities) attempting to come to terms with the chaos and complexities inherent in, and around, organisations today?

This paper seeks to shed some light on these questions by examining the management function and its relationship with the outsourcing decision. The first section seeks to develop a management theory appropriate for today's complexity, effectively establishing the context within which the issue of outsourcing will be considered. Section two examines the current research relating to outsourcing and explores how it relates to the management function. Finally, section three considers whether the relevant research adequately reflects the real world and explores the proposition that the outsourcing debate is symptomatic of a deeper malaise afflicting today's society: namely, a society driven by ideology rather than critical thought.

A Management Theory for Our Time

Outsourcing cannot be considered by itself. Building on the line of argument developed above, it is clear that there is benefit in contemplating the nature and impact of the management function in order to assess the merits, or otherwise, of outsourcing. Furthermore, it is necessary for the management function to be viewed in the wider context of a developing society responding to radical change. Indeed, the most important change to management in the twentieth century has not been in the management discipline per se but in the tools utilised by managers to achieve outcomes. Technology has been a driving force in this domain.

The impact of new technology is reshaping the world in which we live, revolutionising business processes, products, markets and even certain industries. Jones (1995: 5-6) noted the role of technology in economic history, when he identified its pivotal role in bringing about two significant 'cross-overs' and a likely third:

> Just as agriculture declined as a major employer in the nineteenth century to enable expansion in manufacturing to occur, and as manufacturing declined as a major employer in the twentieth century to enable expansion in services to occur, it now seems inevitable that market-based service employment will decline even more rapidly—in exactly the same way, and

for exactly the same reasons—due to the introduction of miniaturised, sophisticated, low-cost technology.

Freedman (1992) expanded this theme of a world dominated by technology when he observed that the more technology looms as a factor of competition, the more management education and training moves towards the 'soft sciences' such as leadership, change management and employee motivation.

This movement is a reflection of the fact that management does not always have the control it desires over a variety of matters it believes should be in control and therefore seeks other mechanisms, often blindly, to solve these problems. The utopia that is promised by embracing the 'soft sciences' is never realised; another case of looking good on paper but failing in application and outcome when the rough edges of the real world prevail.

Of course, care must be taken not to 'throw the baby out with the bath water', as some linear models provide the only explanation we have. However, it would appear that current management thinking is unable to separate itself easily from the comfort of an outdated and unrealistic management view in spite of abundant evidence to the contrary (see Saul, 1997). The smoothing of curves and the dropping of outlier observations are but two examples that all is not well. Average effects are rarely, if ever, found and there are many cases of outliers which are treated as anomalies rather than as the normal effects of non-linearity and complexity.

This raises the question as to the appropriateness of conventional management techniques which still rely on traditional 'scientific' approaches to management developed in the late nineteenth century (for example, the work of Frederick Taylor). Such approaches posit a neat correspondence between cause and effect, reducing even the most complex systems to the interaction of a few simple factors.

Is an unpredictable business world, characterised by dynamism and volatility, adequately accounted for by principles that promise managers the capacity to analyse, predict and control the organisation? At face value, the traditional forms of scientific management would seem extremely unhelpful.

Freedman (1992) suggested that perhaps management theory has not kept pace with scientific development, believing:

> the problem may lie less in the shortcomings of a scientific approach to management than in managers' understanding of science. What most managers think of as scientific management is based on a conception of science that few current scientists would defend.

Cooksey and Gates (1995) also highlight the inadequacies of the traditional scientific approach to management when discussing human resource management theory. They point out that human behaviour is complex and cannot be adequately modelled on linear relationships between cause and effect. They illustrate this by using the analogy of releasing a marble from the edge of a bowl; successive releases of the marble will never yield the same trajectories due to, amongst other things, small imperfections on the surfaces of the bowl and marble. Each release, even from what might appears to be the same point, may not be exactly the same point and the small surface imperfections of the bowl and marble can become exaggerated as the length of the trajectory increases. They conclude that it is impossible to predict exactly what will happen each time some program or option is put in place and believe that many managers do not appear to understand that this is the kind of operating environment in which they exist.

The above description is the hallmark of a chaotic, dynamic system whose behaviour is both sensitive to initial conditions and responsive to subsequent system changes.

It is clear that while the world of management has continued to apply concepts that do not accurately reflect the real world, scientific disciplines are developing theories that seek to explain the complexities of the real world and describe how these systems cope with uncertainty and change. These theories would appear to be appropriate in describing the complexities of organisations and their behaviour. It may also have ramifications for the linear thinking that attends outsourcing decisions and its projected outcomes. One might anticipate that outsourcing will not always 'work out' as it was intended and may, on occasions, yield precisely the opposite effects to that desired.

Rather than regarding these 'abnormal' outcomes as rare events, the newer management thinking would encourage us to expect that, on occasions, things will not turn out as expected. This is not because there is some deliberate attempt by an 'invisible hand' to thwart the outsourcing process but rather because it is simply a natural (or expected) outcome given the complex and non-linear character of the operating environment in which outsourcing operates.

So What is the Take-home Message from this Discussion on Management?

The suggestion is that management's outsourcing decisions are based on linear management thinking. This reliance on cause and effect is clearly not an accurate reflection of the real world. Such thinking which currently attends most management decision-making fails to look at the complex environment in which the outsourcing process sits and makes assumptions about outcomes which may not be valid. In other words, management often believes that it knows exactly what will happen when in fact nothing is further from the truth. Managers must take account of the complex environment in which outsourcing operates; to be prepared for outcomes which are not expected; and to be continually monitoring outcome so that adjustment may be made to process to accommodate the unexpected.

The above discussion is not merely academic speculation but grounded in practicality. It is all about attempting to match the non-linear environment with a management theory that will cope with it.

'Research' on Outsourcing

The view expressed earlier in this paper that contemporary management practice is founded upon a narrow discipline base is confirmed when one examines the research literature relating to outsourcing.

Debate has been largely limited to the disciplines of economics and finance with arguments from both sides apparently sustained by subjective research, analysis and interpretation. Ascher (1987: 2) states that 'both sides have supported their claims by documenting the experiences of organisations that have [outsourced] but the data employed in these exercises is uniformly partisan and highly suspect.'

Aulich and Reynolds (1993) sustain this view, observing that the debate appears more concerned about the 'thrust and parry' of ideological rhetoric than serious contemplation of outsourcing issues. This lack of adequate critical consideration creates a situation that has 'encouraged extrapolations and generalisations from often limited and regionally specific data.'

It seems incongruent that the experiences of organisations that have sought to contract out such activities as garbage collection, cleaning and catering services are deemed a worthy and reliable basis to assess other outsourcing decisions of an unrelated nature.

Borland (1994) would seem to support the criticism of over-generalisation, observing that the nature of human capital input is critical in determining the effects on costs and quality of output. In other words, activities such as cleaning and garbage collection are characterised by essentially non-specific human capital requirements (i.e. unskilled labour) and involve markets that possess an abundance of potential suppliers. In this instance, such conditions are likely to result in a reduction in the price of providing the service, but this effect is clearly not representative of all markets, particularly those where the human capital requirements are highly specific.

Furthermore, Paddon and Thanki (1995) argue that the relevance of international research to the Australian situation is diminished because of a divergence in economic, technological and institutional factors faced by other countries around the world but not necessarily seen in Australia. As mentioned previously contextual factors can make a significant difference to outcomes. In this case the contextual factor is not only the way in which management operates but, amongst other things, the manner in which a society or nation functions in terms of concepts of democracy, organisation of the public sector and related government, legal constructs and assumptions.

Overall, research seems to have been limited to the effects of outsourcing with little or no regard given to the array of factors underlying the decision to outsource. Domberger and Hensher (1993) present a view that encapsulates the general mood of research into outsourcing, reducing the decision to a simple two step process comprising:

- a 'make or buy' decision (costs); and
- the contract's structure, aiming to ensure satisfactory performance (quality?)

Some might wish to question the adequacy of such a simplistic process and might wish to broaden the debate about the adequacy of the measures being employed to ascertain whether outsourcing is worth doing or not from a systemic perspective (Cooksey and Gates, 1995). In looking at the available research, one wonders whether implicit in the great bulk of its limited commentary, is a belief that the issue is adequately addressed by focusing upon the mere comparison of costs (time series and cross sectional analysis) and consideration of its impact on 'quality'.

Furthermore, the inherent difficulties in defining and measuring changes in 'quality' has resulted in an additional research bias. This is to be seen in an abundance of studies focusing on the determination and subsequent justification of the potential savings accruing from a decision to outsource while quality measures suffer or are ignored.

The collective wisdom derived from 'outsourcing' research suggests that cost improvements generally flow from such decisions but the size of ongoing cost savings is highly variable. The Industry Commission (1996) concludes that there is no automatic level of savings to be derived from contracting-out. In other words, the mere act of contracting out does not guarantee that there will be a cost saving of a particular size, or indeed any cost saving at all.

Some critics have argued that the purported gains derived from contracting out are illusory. For instance, Quiggin (1996) believes that the debate has been driven by the desire to reduce service costs, frequently without regard for its impact on employees. He argues that the measured gains from contracting out arise from reductions in wages and increases in work intensity, with the 'net social gain' attributable to such a decision being significantly less.

Chalos (1995) adopting a slightly different perspective, believes outsourcing decisions are generally based on short term cost and cashflow considerations rather than long term strategic planning. He argues that as a consequence of this myopia, organisations underestimate transaction and co-ordination costs and distort the true marginal costs of production by including non-value-adding activities and applying arbitrary cost allocations. As a result, cost justifications of outsourcing decisions are frequently inaccurate and may underestimate true costs and exaggerate benefits.

On the issue of quality, there appears to be only preliminary and inconclusive research. The Industry Commission Report (1996: 546) stated that 'The available evidence on the effect of contracting on the quality of service provision is varied, ranging from quite significant deterioration to substantial improvement in quality.'

Despite the heterogeneity of the research findings with regard to both savings and quality, the general movement towards embracing outsourcing by both private and public sectors would suggest that either:

• management possesses some other source of information which promotes the unquestioning adoption of outsourcing; or
• management is proceeding to adopt outsourcing in the hope that it will provide the panacea to their problems.

In other words they are working off an ideological rather than empirical base. 'It seemed like a good idea at the time' is the prevailing motivational force for implementation of the strategy (see Gates and Cooksey, 1996).

What Does It All Mean?

This paper has sought to develop a line of thought which hopefully prompts the 'critical thinkers' amongst us to look beyond the boundaries imposed by the current outsourcing research and debate. It encourages managers to embrace a systemic approach to considering the merits, or otherwise, of management decisions in general and outsourcing in particular.

We have identified the existence of three 'research gaps', or apparent failings of the research effort to adequately reflect the real world situation. It is here contended that such anomalies could significantly alter the basis upon which managers have traditionally handled the outsourcing decision.

The first 'gap' identified relates to the glaring disparity between the traditional 'scientific' approaches to management, embedded in assumed linear relationships, and a management theory that will cope with all the complexity and chaos that is characterised by the world in which management decisions are made.

The second 'gap' springs from the adoption of the proposed approach to management in this paper. The 'richness' of the management theory proposed, reflecting a non-linear and chaotic operating environment, highlights a discrepancy between it and the narrow contemplation attending to outsourcing as a research issue.

The final 'gap' arises from the narrow discipline base upon which current outsourcing research is based and the inherent complexity of the outsourcing process itself. The ramifications of any outsourcing decision are far more than simply economic or financial in nature with consequences for the culture of the organisation, the individuals who make up that organisation and ultimately the society within which they exist.

Decisions made on such a questionable base are further magnified by the human condition. When faced by uncertainty and chaos there is a natural tendency to cling to the comfort of ideological frameworks that can be used to justify decisions outside the knowledge, scope and experience of decision-makers. Interestingly, such a process can never prove a decision's efficacy, merely promote its unquestioning adoption. This, in turn, promotes the conformity that Fielding alluded to, an innate desire to be part of the group and the fear of potential rejection by that group.

Costa (1996, p. 372) reflected:

> for a moment about how information appears to be replacing thought, and how ideology appears to be replacing scientific inquiry and responded that perhaps the age of reason has.....become passé. Let us dedicate ourselves to assuring that neither of these predictions turns out to be true.

It is also our heart-felt hope that this is not, and will not, be the case.

In a sense we are urging substantial caution in the 'blind' adoption of any popular management fads (including outsourcing). The worry is that eventually someone gets to pay the piper and the piper in this case may be the very organisations which has embraced their new-found partner with such uncritical abandon. We wish to encourage managers to not only question the efficacy of the mechanisms, which are often foist upon them by unknowing politicians, boardrooms or senior management, but also to learn the necessary critical tactics for questioning and assessing these experiments. In doing so managers need to move from being trained technicians to critical thinkers.

Whether or not business schools are doing this is moot. It would appear that our MBA and commerce programs are failing badly in this regard as there is little evidence suggesting that the current pandemic of outsourcing activity is about to cease or come under critical scrutiny.

We would suggest that such scrutiny would only begin to occur when organisational injury has occurred and then it may be too late. Samuel Johnson's notion that 'when a man knows he's about to be hanged in a fortnight, it concentrates his mind wonderfully', comes to mind here. In fact it may be the case that the reason that outsourcing is so readily embraced without a 'credit check' is that managers are 'about to be hanged' because of pressure from the ultimate decision-makers (politicians or shareholders) to produce beneficial short term outcomes. In that case, one can quite understand the adoption of simplistic, short term solutions, such as outsourcing, as such solutions are just what the doctor ordered.

It is a pity that neither the patient nor the doctor seems to have adequately researched the effect of the drug before administration. The market place solution does not seem to mind that a number of patients (organisations that experiment with the outsourcing medicine) will die along the way.

It is only a matter of time before issues raised here become clearer. In the meantime, we must continue to ask the hard questions so that in the event that outsourcing does not deliver all that it promised, we could minimise the damage and save the organisational patient (and its relatives) from a premature and painful death.

Finally, to the title of our paper. On the critical management scorecard, outsourcing is functionally questionable; certainly fashionable and the existence of considerable evidence to suggest that its current, unquestioning application is foolish.

References

Ascher, K. 1987. *The Politics of Privatisation*. London: Macmillan Education.

Aulich, C. & Reynolds, M. 1993. Competitive tendering and contracting out. *Australian Journal of Public Administration,* 52: 396-400.

Borland, J. 1994. On contracting out: Some labour market considerations. *Australian Economic Review,* 3rd Qtr: 86-90.

Chalos, P. 1995. Costing, control, and strategic analysis in outsourcing decisions. *Journal of Cost Management,* 8: 31-37.

Commonwealth of Australia. 1996. *Commonwealth Ombudsman Annual Report 1995-96*. Canberra: Australian Government Publishing Service.

Cooksey, R.W. & Gates, G.R. 1995. HRM: A management science in need of discipline. *Asia Pacific Journal of Human Resources,* 33:15-38.

Costa, L. 1996. Lifespan neuropsychology. *The Clinical Neuropsychologist,* 10:365-374.

Domberger, S. & Hensher, D. 1993. Private and public sector regulation of competitive tendered contracts. *Empirica,* 20: 221-240.

Domberger, S. & Hall, C. 1995. *The Contracting Casebook*. Canberra: Australian Government Publishing Service.

Freedman, D. 1992. Is management still a science? *Harvard Business Review,* 70:26-39.

Gates, G.R. & Cooksey, R.W. 1996. Karpin and Hilmer: Classic cases of 'it seemed like a good idea at the time'. *The Journal of SEAANZ,* 4:7-16.

Hilmer, F. 1993. *The National Competition Policy. Canberra:* Australian Government Printing Service.

Industry Commission 1996. *Competitive Tendering and Contracting by Public Sector Agencies*. Melbourne: Australian Government Publishing Service.

Jones, B. 1995. *Sleepers, Wake! Technology & the Future of the World* (4th ed.). Melbourne: Oxford University Press.

Quiggin, J. 1996. *Great Expectations: Microeconomic Reform and Australia*. Sydney: Allen and Unwin.

Rees, S. & Rodley, G. 1995. *The Human Cost of Management*. Sydney: Pluto Press Australia Ltd.

Reilly, P. & Tamkin, P. 1996. *Outsourcing: A Flexible Option for the Future*. Brighton: The Institute for Employment Studies.

Richardson, H. 1993. Weak outdo the strong. *Times Higher Education Supplement,* 28 May: 4.

Rothery, B. & Robertson, T. (1995). *The Truth About Outsourcing.* London: Gower Publishing.

Saul, J.R. 1997. *The Unconscious Civilization.* Melbourne: Penguin Books Australia Ltd.

Shiller, R.J. 1984. Stock prices and social dynamics. *Brookings Papers on Economic Activity,* 2:457-510.

Taylor, F. 1911. *The Principles of Scientific Management.* New York: Harper.

Contexts, cultures and forms of teleworking

David Lamond, Peter Standen and Kevin Daniels

Abstract

The fusion of information and communication technologies (ICTs) is creating a radical change in the ways we do business, and even in the way we understand the concept of work. Teleworking is one of a suite of so-called flexible work practices now gaining widespread acceptance, but it appears to be favoured more as an idea rather than as a practice. This paper proposes a conceptual model for understanding the differential incidence of teleworking between companies and between countries and for understanding the various forms that telework can take.

Introduction

Initial interest in telework and teleworking was kindled in the 1970s, when the term 'telecommuting' was used to denote working away from the office, primarily by way of telephone communication, as a substitute for physical travelling (Nilles, Carlson, Gray & Hanneman, 1976). By the 1980s, teleworking was being described as the 'next workplace revolution' (Kelly, 1985), and interest in teleworking continued to grow among workers, employers, transportation planners, communities, the telecommunications industry, and others (Handy & Mokhtarian, 1996). More recently, we have begun referring to the 'virtual organisation', where information and telecommunications technology (ICT) is allowing work to be widely dispersed over space and time (Handy, 1995; Van der Weilen, Taillieu, Poolman, & Van Zuilichem, 1993).

If, as Jackson (1997: 355) suggests, teleworking has 'the potential to transform the very experience and meaning of work', there is an urgent need to gain an understanding of this phenomenon. However, most writing on telework has involved prescriptions based heavily on the experience of individuals and does not use existing theory or recent research. This paper examines the available research and finds a differential incidence of telework, between countries and companies; mixed claims about advantages and disadvantages; and differences in the forms of telework that are employed. A conceptual framework, which considers the cultural and organisational contexts within which teleworking takes place, is proposed as basis for explaining and predicting the differential incidence and forms of telework.

Teleworking: Incidence, Benefits and Costs

It is estimated that in 1993 there were up to 1.27 million teleworkers in the UK and up to 5.89 million teleworkers in the USA (Gray, Hodson & Gordon, 1993). More recent figures suggest that there are now between 8 and 9 million US teleworkers (Glosserman, 1996; Rourke, 1996). Other studies indicate that teleworking is also likely to increase in the future. For example, Huws' (1994a,b) survey of 1000 employers in the UK indicated that, while 6 per cent already employed staff who used information technology to work remotely from the work place, a further 8 per cent expected to introduce teleworking. In a survey of 305 senior US executives, 70 per cent predicted that teleworking would increase in their companies throughout 1996 (Frazee, 1996)

There are many reasons to expect organisations and their employees to experiment with this type of work organisation, particularly given the rapid growth of affordable telecommunications technology. These reasons include improved flexibility for organisations and employees, as well as more general social benefits (Andriessen, 1991; Anon, 1994a; IRS, 1996d; Blodgett, 1996; Gillespie, Richardson and Cornford, 1995; Glosserman, 1996; Grant, 1985; Gray et al., 1993; Gurstein, 1991, Hamblin, 1995; Kelly, 1985).

For organisations, the benefits are seen in terms of the positive impact on what are often their two largest overheads—their work force and accommodation costs—improved productivity, improved employee retention, greater staffing flexibility and cost control, and office space control (Blodgett, 1996; Kelly, 1985; Grant 1985). In an IRS (1996c) survey on teleworking in the UK, these were among the main reasons cited by companies for initiating teleworking.

The feminisation of the work force, and changing social attitudes towards work and family, has been matched by shifting expectations of the work/non-work balance. Teleworking is attractive as a way to balance work and non-work/family goals. One case study of a teleworking venture found that the majority of the teleworkers were married women with childcare responsibilities (Crossan & Burton, 1993).

Another group of European teleworking employees cited the main advantages of teleworking as flexibility, especially in the context of juggling family commitments; and avoiding commuting or minimising work-related travel (IRS, 1996d). Specific individual benefits are thought to include more flexible working hours; more time for home and family; reduced commuting; greater job autonomy; less disturbance whilst working; and the chance to remain in work despite moving home, becoming ill or taking on family care roles. Many of these direct benefits would have indirect consequences for job and life satisfaction and possibly physical health.

At a social level, forces acting to promote telework include concern with pollution and urban congestion (Glosserman, 1996) and a need to provide employment opportunities for rural areas. For example, the introduction of 'telecottages' (centres offering communications and general workplace facilities to remote workers), is seen as a vehicle for bringing employment to remote and economically deprived areas with high unemployment (IRS, 1996a). The list of perceived societal benefits includes increased community stability; increased entrepreneurial activity; less pollution; and more efficient use of energy resources.

Whilst the list of perceived benefits is impressive, the potential negative consequences of teleworking have also been acknowledged. For the individual, these consequences can include: fewer chances for development or promotion; increased conflict between work and home (and, indeed, potential for conflict with other household members in the home); limited face-to-face contact with colleagues, and questions of employment status; lower job security; social isolation; more time spent working; routinisation of tasks; and a perception that teleworkers are not valued by their managers (Andriessen, 1991; IRS, 1996d; Crossan and Burton, 1993; Grant 1985; Gurstein, 1991; Gillespie *et al.*, 1995; Hamblin, 1995).

Then there is the organisational challenge of transferring all or part of the work involved in business transactions, which may involve many people, to the home (Grant, 1985). Negative organisational consequences may include increased selection, training and support costs; difficulty supervising and motivating; difficulty socialising new employees to the organisation; health and safety consequences; security issues; the costs of additional equipment and office space; and the costs involved from the requirement to improve planning and performance measures (*cf.* Huws, 1994a; Littlefield, 1995; McClelland, 1995). Indeed, research suggests that the advantages of telework may not outweigh the social and organisational problems linked with this 'radical relocation of office space' (Van der Weilen, Taillieu, Poolman and Van Zuilichem, 1993: 146). These may well be some of the reasons why, although there appears to be significant support for the idea of teleworking, actual levels of teleworking appear to be increasing only slowly.

For example, while 62 per cent of US executives reported that their companies were encouraging telecommuting arrangements for their employees, only 42 per cent of their companies had teleworking programs in place. Further, only 7 per cent of workers were taking advantage of the available programs (Frazee, 1996). In Western Europe, Brewster, Mayne and Hegewisch (1994) estimate that less than 1 per cent of organisations use teleworking practices. Similarly, Korte, Kordery and Robinson (1994) estimate that teleworkers comprise less than 1 per cent of the work forces in European Community member states, and only up to 7 per cent in the most industrialised states. Meanwhile, Australian research estimates around that about 1 per cent of the work force is engaged in non-trivial telework (McLennan, 1996). Smith (1995) observes that, in New Zealand, while many companies pay lip service to teleworking, few seem willing to implement the practice as a central business strategy.

It should be said that precise estimates of current teleworker numbers are difficult to find, due to the limitations of survey methodologies and use of non-comparable definitions. For example, surveys frequently cover only large organisations and often have limited sampling frames, while definitions frequently do not specify whether telework requires a minimum number of hours spent off-site, whether teleworkers are permanent employees, and whether a computer linked to the office is a prerequisite. (*cf.* Standen, 1997). For the same reasons, it is not possible to directly compare published estimates of telework uptake in Europe, the US, Canada, Australia, Japan and other relevant countries

Whilst exact figures are not available, it has been suggested that the most prevalent forms of telework are home based and mobile telework (Gray *et al.,* 1993), with only a small fraction of all teleworkers in North America, Europe and Australia using remote offices (Gillespie *et al.,* 1995; IRS, 1996d). It has also been argued that it is reasonable to assume the majority of teleworkers do not spend all of their working time engaged solely in one form of telework (Gray *et al.,* 1993).

On the basis of these findings, it is clear that the phenomenon of telework is not a straightforward one. The extent and forms of teleworking vary between different contexts, and telework itself has received mixed endorsement. Indeed, a significant gap between support for telework as an idea and the utilisation of telework as a practice is discerned. There is a need for a framework to delineate and link these variables.

In the following sections, theoretical and empirical considerations from the literature are used to develop predictions about the relationships between the sets of contextual factors and the various forms of telework. These predictions set an agenda for future research and build on recent attempts to develop a framework for integrating current knowledge and guiding future teleworking research and practice (Lamond, Daniels & Standen, 1997; Standen, Daniels & Lamond, 1997).

Teleworking: What Exactly is It?

For all the attention that has been paid to it, there is still no 'official' definition (IRS, 1996a; Moon and Stanworth, 1997). Until recently, attempts at defining telework have focussed on location (remote from the office) and/or

ICT usage. In a recent review and synthesis of the literature, Lamond *et al.* (1997) argued that, to adequately address the organisational behaviour issues raised by telework, it is necessary to develop a more fine grained typology involving several additional dimensions. They suggest that teleworking needs to be understood, not just in terms of where work is done or what equipment is used, but as a process that involves a series of dimensions:

- *ICT usage*—extent of use of telecommunications/IT links—home/mobile computer, fax, modem, phone, mobile phone, use of WWW sites
- *Knowledge intensity*—extent of knowledge required, ease of output measures and autonomy of work
- *Intra-organisational contact*—extent (range and intensity) of intra-organisational contact
- *Extra-organisational contact*—extent (range and intensity) of extra-organisational contact
- *Location*—the amount of time spent in the different locations: traditional office, home, remote office/telecottage, nomadic.

These dimensions have been used to develop a typology of telework, together with exemplar jobs, as shown in Table 1. Further differentiation could be developed by noting that these jobs can be permanent, temporary or *ad hoc;* that they can involve the use of ICT to a greater or lesser extent; and that the remote offices can be further divided, for example, into satellites, telecentres, telecottages, and so on.

Table 1 Types of teleworking and sample jobs

High Knowledge Intensity (Type A)

	Intra-Organisational Contact			
	High		Low	
	External Contact		Internal Contact	
	High	Low	High	Low
Home-based	Sales Managers	Accountant/Programmer	Lawyer	IS Developer/Architect
Remote office	Sales Managers	Programmer	Lawyer	IS Developer
Nomadic	Sales Managers	Internal consultants	Community nurse	IS Developer

Low Knowledge Intensity (Type B)

	Intra-Organisational Contact			
	Low		High	
	External Contact		Internal Contact	
	High	Low	High	Low
Home-based	Customer Enquiries	Secretarial/Clerical	Phone Sales	Clerical/Data Entry
Remote office	Customer Enquiries	Secretarial/Clerical	Phone Sales	Clerical/Data Entry
Nomadic	Service Persons	Secretarial/Clerical	Sales Representative	Clerical/Data Entry

Source: Lamond et al., 1997.

Using this typology allows us to say that

- teleworking is a process which involves a bundle of practices;
- there is no *one* form of teleworking and, as a corollary, there is no one best way of teleworking;
- teleworking is best thought of as a multidimensional phenomenon, its character varying along five dimensions—ICT usage, knowledge intensity, intra-organisational contact, extra-organisational contact, and location.

The five dimensions also allow us to describe and make predictions about teleworking in different national and organisational contexts. It is to these descriptions and predictions that we turn in the next section.

Teleworking in Context

Teleworking is a set of work practices that exists at the juncture of a wide variety of organisational, social, individual and historical forces. Figure 1 presents our initial attempt to capture in a schematic diagram what we consider to be the major contexts within which teleworking is embedded—the national and organisational contexts. This schema has been developed by way of close analysis and synthesis of the currently available empirical data. The macro level context is set by national variations in legislation, geography, culture and industrial relations, while the organisational level comprises both structure and culture. Looking within organisations, there are also social (group) factors, such as socialisation and communication; and individual factors such as personality, job characteristics, the home/work interface and the psychological character of work (including job satisfaction, motivation, and the nature of the psychological contract). Our focus in this paper though, is on the contextual factors that impact on teleworking.

It was noted earlier that, while there has been a lot of interest expressed in the literature about teleworking, most of this has been descriptive or in the form of exhortation, and there has been little research. As such, the following discussion is exploratory, aiming to contribute to theory development by identifying variables likely to impact on the form of teleworking. The factors identified below are not an exhaustive list, and we do not attempt a full treatment of their complex interactions. Rather, we present an initial set of predictions based on existing evidence or theories from related domains.

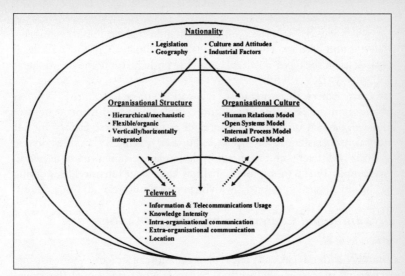

Figure 1 A conceptual overview of the contexts and forms of teleworking

Note: Bold lines reflect expected strong relationships; dotted lines reflect expected weak relationships.

National Context

A fundamental implication of the contributions by Hofstede (1980; 1983; 1991), and Hampden-Turner and Trompenaars (1994) to the developing body of knowledge about international culture and management is that cultural interpretation and adaptation are a prerequisite to the comparative understanding of national and international management practices—what works well in one country may be entirely inappropriate in another (Morden, 1995). The empirical evidence suggests that this is true of teleworking.

It is clear that some countries are making more use of telework than others, and differential growth rates exist (DiMartino and Wirth 1990; Brewster, Hegewisch and Mayne, 1994; IRS 1996a-d). For example, in Europe the Scandinavian countries and the UK appear to have greater uptake than the central and southern countries (Brewster *et al.,* 1994; IRS, 1996a-d).

These differences are partly due to national culture (e.g. Scandinavian organisations are more egalitarian and hence more trusting of teleworkers; *cf.* Hofstede, 1983; 1991); industrial profiles (eg. northern Europe has more 'knowledge workers'); geographical issues (e.g. the existence of sparsely populated areas in Scandinavia); governmental pressure to bring marginal groups into the workforce (*cf.* DTI, 1986; Gillespie *et al.,* 1995); changes in societal attitudes (e.g. in the UK knowledge workers are moving from cities to rural areas for quality of life reasons; *cf.* Gillespie *et al.,* 1995); changing labour force characteristics (e.g. greater participation of women in the workforce in northern Europe, including those with child care roles; *cf.* Hegewisch and Mayne, 1994); differences in industrial relations (*cf.* Gunnigle, Brewster and Morley, 1994) and legislative climates (eg. there are legal restrictions on the types of work that can be conducted at home are prevalent in Germany (IRS, 1996d)).

We may expect, therefore, to see teleworking more in countries with less urbanisation, more egalitarian cultures, proactive governments, extensive knowledge based industries, and greater affluence. These factors are not necessarily coexistent in any instance. Further, it is likely that these diverse factors may differentially encourage or discourage certain forms of telework. For example, Type B (non-professional/low knowledge intensity) teleworking may be discouraged in countries with hierarchical cultures and strong unions.

Organisational Context—Structure and Culture

Structure

A number of trends currently affecting organisational structure—downsizing, delayering, process re-engineering, replacement of traditional functional departments with team-based or project-based structures, the shift to a core/periphery model with a greater role for contingent workers, and growth in inter-organisational networks (Dess, Rasheed, McLaughlin, and Priem, 1995)—point to a rise in teleworking. The reasons here appear to be twofold.

On the one hand, the rise in knowledge work and the increased sophistication of information technology make it easier for organisations to develop virtual structures that transcend traditional space and time limits (Reich, 1992; Handy, 1995). These structures can often be characterised as loose federations of groups and individuals. Building on the contingency approach to organisational structure (Dess, *et al.,* 1995), it could be expected that such flexible, 'organic' organisations are more likely to move towards teleworking and are more likely to have effective teleworkers. The reciprocal relationship is likely to exist here too, as growth in teleworking encourages wider experimentation with flexible structures.

On the other hand, teleworking might be introduced by organisations where the primary attraction is the promised cost reductions referred to earlier. Here there may be a distinct lack of interest in flexibility issues and notions of 're-engineering' may be code for cost-cutting. The impact on teleworking is likely to be quite different to that of the organic orientation and so the reasons for introducing teleworking need to be carefully explored.

Again, the consequences of these factors are different for the types of telework identified above. For example, the growth of virtual teams may shift teleworking more towards a full time option for Type A (high knowledge) workers, while the greater use of the contingent workforce is likely to see a rise in Type B (low knowledge) teleworkers. We might also expect a rise in both home and nomadic working (as opposed to telecottage and remote office working) in virtual organisations as workers are tied less to one organisation or location of the main office.

Culture

A number of predictions follow from the view that teleworking forms are related to organisational cultures. We have utilised Quinn's (1988) Competing Values framework as a basis for classifying cultures. Based on empirical studies in American firms, Quinn's (1988) framework identifies organisations on two dimensions—flexibility vs. control and internal vs. external focus—creating four potential organisational archetypes. An adapted version of Quinn's (1988) framework is presented in Table 2, which also includes some of the predicted impacts on forms of teleworking.

HRM authorities emphasise the importance of supportive organisational cultures for flexible working practices (e.g. Guest, 1990). Accordingly, organisations whose internal processes are characterised by flexibility, trust and openness (see the Human Relations model in Table 2) would be expected to move towards home based or remote office teleworking practices for all types of workers (Standen, 1997). Organisations whose cultures have an external focus (Open Systems) are similarly more likely to support telework when the cultures are also more flexible. These organisations are focused on expansion and adaptation, and may see telework as a competitive business tool to increase flexibility and communication.

Conversely, cultures focused on flexible external goals but which have a bureaucratic control-based internal focus (Rational Goal), are likely to support only Type A teleworkers. Clerical and other non-professionals may not be considered to be trustworthy off-site, thus reducing possibilities for teleworking. Finally, organisations lacking flexibility in both internal and external perspectives (Internal Process) are focussed on stability and would be considered least likely to experiment with radical practices like telework. With both types of control-oriented cultures, Type B teleworkers may be very rare. Where Type B teleworkers are employed, it is likely to be only in home based or remote office contexts, where outputs from workers can be easily measured. For both Type A and Type B workers, control-oriented organisations may only employ teleworkers where other factors (such as structure) support such practices.

As in the case of organisational structure, there are reciprocal relationships between teleworking and culture—introducing teleworking practices necessitates changes in people's attitudes, and affects on culture. It is likely however, that most telework programs are currently small scale and that 'feedback' effects will be found more in the future. There will be limits to culture effects—eg, nomadic workers (sales staff and consultants) get to work off-site more from practical necessity which may override cultural factors. Indeed, these groups were allowed to roam off-site long before telework was considered as an organising strategy.

Table 2 Predicting telework from Quinn's (1988) Competing Values framework

	Internal Focus	External Focus
Flexibility	**Human Relations Model** Goal: human commitment Values: human resources, training, cohesion, morale	**Open Systems Model** Goal: expansion & adaptation Values: adaptability, readiness, growth, resource acquisition, external support
	Telework: Types A and B; all types of intra- and extra-organisational contact; all locations	Telework: Type A; all types of intra- and extra-organisational contact; bias towards nomadic
Control	**Internal Process Model** Goal: consolidation & continuity Values: information management, communication, stability, control	**Rational Goal Model** Goal: maximisation of output Values: productivity, efficiency, planning, goal setting
	Telework: Limited Type B; home, remote office, telecottage	Telework: Limited Type A; extra-organisational contact; mainly nomadic

Conclusion

Telework is one of the most radical departures from standard working conditions in the suite of flexible work practices now gaining widespread acceptance, and presents unique challenges to both managers and employees. This paper has examined the incidence and forms of teleworking and presented a framework for understanding the impact of national and organisational contexts.

It has also proffered directions for research by making a series of predictions about the relationship between context and form. Armed with these new insights, researchers should be looking to move beyond initial qualitative exploratory work, through larger scale quantitative survey work toward quasi-experimental evaluation of intelligently designed telework interventions. Given the rapid change in technology and the expected changes in work practices, new research approaches will be required and these will need to be sensitive to the multiple realities (of Type A and B workers, of males and females, of nomadic and home based teleworkers and so on) that telework encompasses.

As we noted in our introduction, the future of teleworking depends on whether employers provide the opportunity to telework and whether workers take advantage of this opportunity. To realise the full benefits of telework there must be a dialogue between teleworkers, those that manage teleworkers, and researchers. The new communications media that support telework also allow researchers to interact with management and teleworker communities in new ways, bringing exciting possibilities for the research community to assist in the evolution of this new work practice.

References

Andriessen, J.H.E. 1991. Mediated communication and new organizational forms. In C.L. Cooper and I.T. Robertson (Eds.), *International Review of Industrial and Organizational Psychology.* Chichester: Wiley.

Anonymous 1994. Homeworking agreement. *European Industrial Relations Review,* 249, 12-13.

Blodgett, M. 1996. Lower costs spur move to more telecommuting. *Computerworld,* 30(45), 8.

Brewster, C. Hegewisch, A. and Mayne, L. 1994. Flexible working practices: the controversy and the evidence. In C. Brewster and A. Hegewisch (Eds) *Policy and Practice in European Human Resource Management:* 168-193. London: Routledge.

Crossan, G. and Burton, P.F. 1993. Teleworking stereotypes: A case study. *Journal of Information Science Principles & Practice,* 19(5), 349-362.

Department of Trade and Industry (DTI), Information Technology Division (1986.—*Remote Work Units Project for Disabled People: Evaluation Study.* London: DTI.

Dess, G.G., Rasheed, A.M.A., McLaughlin, K.J. and Priem, R.L. 1995. The new corporate architecture. *Academy of Management Executive,* 9(3), 7-20.

Di Martino, V. and Wirth L. 1990. *Telework: Conditions of Work Digest* 9(1). Geneva: International Labor Office.

Elling, M. 1985. Remote work/Telecommuting—A means of enhancing the quality of life, or just another method of making business more brisk? *Economic and Industrial Democracy,* 6(2), 239-249.

Frazee, V. 1996. Support for telecommuting is on the rise. *Personnel Journal,* 75(10), 22.

Gillespie, A.E., Richardson, R. and Cornford, J. 1995. *Review of Teleworking in Britain: Implications for Public Policy.* Report to the Parliamentary Office of Science and Technology.

Glosserman, B. 1996. How green is my cyberspace? *Japan Times Weekly International Edition,* 36(44), 15.

Grant, K.A. 1985. How Practical Is Teleworking? *Canadian Datasystems,* 17(8), 25.

Gray, M., Hodson, N. and Gordon, G. 1993. *Teleworking Explained.* Chichester: Wiley.

Guest, D. 1990. Human resource management and the American dream. *Journal of Management Studies,* 27(4), 377-397

Gunnigle, P Brewster, C and Morley, M (1994) European industrial relations: change and continuity. In C. Brewster and A. Hegewisch (Eds.) *Policy and Practice in European Human Resource Management:* 139-153. London: Routledge,

Gurstein, P. 1991. Working at home and living at home: emerging scenarios. *Journal of Architectural and Planning Research*, 8, 164-180.

Hamblin, H. 1995. Employees' perspectives on one dimension of labour flexibility: working at a distance. *Work, Employment and Society,* 9, 473-498.

Hampden-Turner, C. and Trompenaars, F. 1994. *The Seven Cultures of Capitalism* London: Piatkus.

Handy, C. 1995. Trust and the virtual organization. *Harvard Business Review,* 73(3), 40-50.

Handy, S.L. and Mokhtarian, P.L. 1996. The future of telecommuting. *Futures,* 28(3), 227-240.

Hiemstra, G. 1982. Teleconferencing, concern for face, and organizational culture. In M.Burggon (Ed.) *Communication Yearbook 6,* Beverly Hills, CA: Sage, 874-904.

Hofstede, G. 1980. *Cultures Consequences: International Differences in Work-related Values* London: Sage.

Hofstede, G. 1983. The cultural relativity of organisational practices and theories. *Journal of International Business Studies,* 13(3), 75-90.

Hofstede, G. 1991. *Cultures and Organisations* London: McGraw-Hill.

Huws, U. 1994a. Teleworking: Facing up to the future. *Industrial Relations Review & Report,* 563, 9-11.

Huws, U. 1994b. *Teleworking.* Brussels: European Commission's Employment Task Force (Directorate General).

Huws, U., Korte, W.B. & Robinson, S. 1990. *Telework: Towards the elusive office.* John Wiley & Sons.

IRS 1996a. Teleworking in Europe: part one. *European Industrial Relations Review,* 268, 17-20.

IRS 1996b. Turn on, tune in, churn out--a survey of teleworking. *IRS Employment Review,* 609, 6-15.

IRS 1996c. IRS survey on teleworking in the UK. *European Industrial Relations Review,* 271, 22.

IRS 1996d. Teleworking in Europe: Part three. *European Industrial Relations Review,* (271), 18-23.

Jackson, P.J. 1997. Changes in work and organisations: new faces and new phenomena? In F. Avallone, J. Arnold and K. De Witte, (Eds.) *Quaderni di Psicologia del Lavoro* (Volume 5: Feelings Work in Europe), 351-356.

Kelly, M.M. 1985. The Next Workplace Revolution: Telecommuting. *Supervisory Management,* 30(10), 2-7.

Korte, W. B., Kordey, N. & Robinson, S. 1994. *Telework penetration, potential and practice in Europe.* TELDET Report No. 11. Bonn: Empirica.

Lamond, D.A., Daniels, K. and Standen, P. 1997. *Virtual working or working virtually?: An Overview of Contextual and Behavioural Issues in Teleworking.*

Presented at the Fourth International Meeting of the Decision Sciences Institute, Sydney, Australia, 20-23 July.

Littlefield, D. 1996. Council asks workers to log into PC centre. *Personnel Management,* 2(17), 9

McClennan, W. 1996. *Persons employed at home, Australia.* Australian Bureau of Statistics Catalogue No. 6275.0. Canberra: AGPS.

Moon, C. and Stanworth, S. 1997. Flexible working in Europe. The case of teleworking in the UK. In F. Avallone, J. Arnold and K. De Witte, (Eds.) *Quaderni di Psicologia del Lavoro* (Volume 5: Feelings Work in Europe), 337-344.

Morden, T. 1995. International culture and management. *Management Decision,* 33(2), 16-21.

Nilles, J.M., Carlson, F.R., Gray, P. and Hanneman, G.J. 1976. The *Telecommunications-Transportation Trade-Off.* Chichester: John Wiley and Sons

Quinn, R. 1988. *Beyond rational management: Mastering the paradoxes and competing demands of high performance.* San Francisco: Jossey-Bass.

Reich, R. 1992. The *work of nations.* NY: Vintage.

Smith, A. 1995. Is teleworking really taking off? *Management-Auckland,* 42(9), 118.

Standen, P. 1997. Home, work and management in the information age. *Journal of the Australian and New Zealand Academy of Management,* 3(1), 1-14.

Standen, P., Daniels, K. and Lamond, D.A. 1997. *A Conceptual Framework and Research Agenda for Organisational Behaviour Issues in Teleworking.* Presented at the Second Australian Industrial and Organisational Psychology Conference, Melbourne, 27-29 June.

Van der Weilen, J.M.M., Taillieu, T.C.B., Poolman, J.A. and Van Zuilichem, J. 1993. Telework: Dispersed organizational activity and new forms of spatial temporal co-ordination and control. *European Work and Organizational Psychologist,* 3(2), 145-162.

Individual–organisational value congruence in human resource practitioners

Ann Lawrence

Abstract

Using a survey questionnaire developed from the McDonald & Gandz list of values and the 'Competing Values Framework' of Quinn & McGrath, this study examines the extent to which the individual values of Australian human resource practitioners are perceived to be congruent with those of their employing organisations. Findings indicate that this occupational group place high importance on the individual Clan and Adhocracy values ('developmental humanism') and Market values and low importance on Hierarchy values ('utilitarian instrumentalism'). By contrast, human resource practitioners in Australia perceive organisational values in practice to be more consistent with Hierarchy and Market values than Clan and Adhocracy values. Consequently human resource practitioners experienced low levels of individual - organisational value congruence. The implications of these findings for organisational strategy and the roles of human resource practitioners are briefly discussed.

Introduction

Over the past two decades changing market conditions have precipitated large scale organisational culture changes which require organisations to take a strategic, proactive, and systematic approach to human resource management and place a greater emphasis on the integration of human resource activities with corporate strategy. Many organisations have embraced new approaches to managing human resources which recognise the contribution of people and their values and attitudes as well as their skills, knowledge and abilities in achieving a competitive advantage (Tyson & Fell, 1986; Becker & Gerhart, 1996). As prior research has indicated (Feather, 1992, 1994; Rokeach, 1973, 1979; Schein, 1992; Schwartz, 1992), values are important influences on a person's beliefs, attitudes, perceptions, actions and decisions. They operate as criteria for decision making processes, judgement, preference and choice, are intimately connected with moral and ethical codes, and can be used to predict behaviour in specific situations. In addition to developing or remoulding the organisation's core cultural values in an attempt to fit with the corporate strategy (Stace & Dunphy, 1994), emphasis has been placed upon the importance of achieving congruence between the core values[1] of the individual and those of the organisation (Adkins, Russell & Werbel, 1994; Chatman, 1991; Entrekin & Pearson, 1995; Kabanoff, Waldersee & Cohen, 1995; McDonald & Gandz, 1992; Posner & Schmidt, 1993; Schein, 1992; Whitely, 1995).

Some of the core values now cited as important for organisational success include humanistic and developmental values such as organisational learning, development, innovation, creativity, increased participation and equity, teamwork, high trust between employer and employee, respect, openness, honesty, commitment, cooperation, flexibility, diversity, and a recognition of equal opportunity (Field & Ford, 1995; Enterprising Nation: Report of The Industry Task Force on Leadership and Management Skills (1995); McDonald & Gandz, 1992; Senge, 1990; Storey, 1992). These values are consistent with the organisational culture perspective of 'developmental humanism' and 'soft' human resource management (Hendry & Pettigrew, 1990; Legge, 1989; Storey, 1987) where the emphasis is placed on the term 'human resource management' (Legge, 1995a, p. 35).

Proponents of management by shared values argue that there are benefits that can accrue to both the individual and the organisation when there is congruence between their core values (Chatman, 1991; McDonald & Gandz, 1992). This has been supported by empirical evidence that indicates that individual - organisational value congruence has a positive impact on work adjustment, levels of job satisfaction and career success (Bretz & Judge, 1994; Meglino, Ravlin & Adkins, 1989). Value congruence can also result in higher levels of organisational performance, employee commitment, loyalty, employee involvement in decision making, and influence intention to remain with the organisation and actual turnover (Chatman, 1991; Deal & Kennedy 1982; Karathanos, Pettypool & Troutt, 1994; Peters & Waterman, 1982; Posner, Kouzes & Schmidt, 1985). It has also been suggested that individual–organisational value congruence may represent a means whereby the integration of business strategy and *human resource management* can be articulated (McDonald & Gandz, 1992).

However, the values and philosophy espoused as important by an organisation may not always be consistent with, nor support, the organisational behaviour and practices that actually develop (Argyris & Schön, 1978; Kabanoff, 1993). In examining this difference between the organisational rhetoric and reality, Legge (1995a, 1995b) and Storey (1987; 1995) have argued that the values of 'utilitarian instrumentalism' rather than 'developmental humanism' may more often than not be seen to be reflected in organisational practice. 'Utilitarian instrumentalism' focuses upon competitiveness and accountability, as does 'developmental humanism', however, values such as cautiousness, economy, formality, obedience, and order are seen as more important (McDonald & Gandz, 1992; Quinn & McGrath, 1985). This perspective of human resource management and organisational culture 'places emphasis on the idea of resource - that is, something to be used dispassionately and in a calculative, formally rational manner' (Sisson & Storey, 1993, p. 17) and the human resource is often seen as an 'expense of doing business'. Any policy or practice which fits the business strategy is therefore admitted (Sisson, 1994) and its focus is ultimately 'human *resource management*' (Legge, 1995a, p. 35).

These two theoretical perspectives of organisational values, 'developmental humanism' and 'utilitarian instrumentalism', share many similarities with the view of individual and organisational values proposed by McDonald and Gandz (1991; 1992) for Quinn and McGrath's (1985) 'Competing Values Framework' of organisational culture forms. The forms are described as: 'The Clan', 'The Adhocracy', 'The Hierarchy' and 'The Market'. Many of the values and practices of Clan cultures, which focus on relationships, morale, and the group, and Adhocracy cultures, which emphasise the values of change, transformation and growth, are consistent with the perspectives of 'developmental humanism'. Many of the practices and values of Hierarchy cultures, which value order, stability and the execution of regulations, are consistent with the perspective of 'utilitarian instrumentalism' (see Figure 1). However, it could be argued that the practices and values of Market cultures are not unique to either 'developmental humanism' or 'utilitarian instrumentalism' and may be shared to varying degrees by either perspective.

RELATIONSHIPS	CHANGE
THE CLAN The Consensual Culture Purpose: Group Cohesion Salient Values: Broadmindedness, Consideration, Cooperation, Courtesy, Fairness, Forgiveness, Humour, Moral integrity, Openness, Social equality (Developmental Humanism)	**THE ADHOCRACY** The Developmental Culture Purpose: Broad Purposes Salient Values: Adaptability, Autonomy, Creativity, Development, Experimentation (Developmental Humanism)
THE HIERARCHY The Hierarchical Culture Purpose: Execution of Regulations Salient Values: Cautiousness, Economy, Formality, Logic, Obedience, Orderliness **(Utilitarian Instrumentalism)**	**THE MARKET** The Rational Culture Purpose: Pursuit of Objectives Salient Values: Aggressiveness (Ambition), Diligence, Initiative **(Shared with Utilitarian Instrumentalism and Developmental Humanism)**
STATUS QUO	TASK

Figure 1 Overlap between value concepts embedded in 'The Competing Values Framework' and the perspectives of 'Development Humanism' and 'Utilitarian Instrumentalisation'

Source: Adapted from Quinn, R.E., & McGrath, M.R. (1985) and McDonald, P., & Gandz, J. (1992). p. 69.

Virtually every occupational group is involved in and affected by these widespread organisational culture and value changes. However, it could be argued that human resource practitioners[2] are central to many of these changes. The human resource function and profession has undergone massive change over the past decade (Smart & Pontifex, 1994; Dowling & Fisher, 1997; Ulrich, Brockbank & Yeung, 1995). There is evidence of a growing strategic involvement in organisational planning and organisational change and development by employees in this function (Conner & Ulrich, 1996; Dowling & Fisher, 1997; Ulrich et al. 1995). To promote people as a source of competitive advantage, Ogbonna (1992) has argued that the human resource function is required to develop programs which integrate the interests of the goals of management, employees and other key constituents, as well as promote a committed, flexible and adaptable workforce with a concern for quality and excellence (Ogbonna, 1992). To do this human resource practitioners must have a solid understanding of the organisation's culture and values they are presenting to employees and organisational stakeholders and how to influence greater congruence between the desired and actual organisational culture. They must also understand how to add value in the organisation by helping line management align HR strategies, processes, and practices with business needs.

It is possible, however, that a tension or a paradox exists between these roles of human resource practitioners and the values underpinning them and the values of the organisation (Conner & Ulrich, 1996; Ulrich, 1997). The tensions between these values have serious implications for the design, implementation and ultimate success of corporate strategy.

It is generally assumed that, based on the roles played by Australian human resource practitioners and the focus of their professional educational and training up to the present time (Smart & Pontifex, 1994; Dowling & Fisher, 1997), this occupational group will place more importance on humanistic and developmental focussed Clan and Adhocracy values and on Market values than on Hierarchy values (Guest, 1987; Hendry & Pettigrew, 1990; Legge, 1995a & 1995b). In addition, accepting that the argument regarding organisational rhetoric versus reality put forward by Legge and Storey is applicable to Australian organisations, it could be assumed that Hierarchy values will be perceived to be more important to organisations than Clan and Adhocracy values. It follows therefore that the levels of individual - organisational value congruence for Clan and Adhocracy values will be lower than the levels for Hierarchy values. However, there is little Australian research to support these assumptions and they remain to be tested empirically. Therefore the current study explores these predictions and the following hypotheses have been formulated:

Hypothesis 1: Human resource practitioners will rate Clan and Adhocracy values ('developmental humanism') and Market values as personally more important than Hierarchy values ('utilitarian instrumentalism').

Hypothesis 2: Human resource practitioners will perceive Hierarchy ('utilitarian instrumentalism') and Market values as more important to their employing organisations than Clan and Adhocracy values ('developmental humanism').

Hypothesis 3: The levels of individual - organisational value congruence in human resource practitioners for Clan and Adhocracy ('developmental humanism') values will be lower than Hierarchy values ('utilitarian instrumentalism').

Research Method

This research was part of a wider study exploring individual - organisational value congruence among occupational groups. The total sampling frame included employees in the accountancy profession, managers and human resource practitioners, and was recruited in two ways. The first group was recruited from students undertaking the Graduate Diploma of Business at Deakin University, Burwood Campus, Melbourne, during 1995 and 1996. These students were chosen as participants because they were predominantly part-time students who were in full time employment in a wide variety of organisations, in occupations related to their course of study (Accounting, Management or Human Resources). The second group of respondents was recruited directly from organisations listed as Victorian members of the Institute of Chartered Accountants in Australia (ICAA, 1994) and from those firms listed as employers of Victorian members of the Australian Human Resources Institute (AHRI, 1995). Agreement to circulate the survey questionnaires was obtained from 10 organisations, representing the banking, finance, insurance, retail and services industries, and the public sector. The questionnaires were mailed out to the nominated contact person within the organisation with instructions to distribute to all personnel within the accountancy, human resource and management functions. These two groups of respondents, Graduate Diploma students employed in the professions, and employees in the professions within organisations, were considered as part of one sample. Participation in the study was voluntary. Neither individual respondents nor their organisations could be identified, and return of the completed questionnaire was taken as consent to be included in the study.

The Questionnaire

The questionnaire, based on the McDonald and Gandz (1991) list of values, was developed using a focus group consisting of accounting, human resource and general management academic staff, accounting and human resource and management professionals, and post graduate business students. Minor changes were made to the original McDonald and Gandz list of values. In the final version the value of 'aggressiveness' was changed to 'ambition', and the value 'development' was changed to 'development of skills'. However, the original explanatory phrases used by McDonald and Gandz were retained for each of these values (see Appendix 1). A four point Likert scale with the categories: 'not at all important' (1), 'slightly important' (2), 'fairly important' (3), and 'extremely important' (4), was used to measure the intensity levels of each of the values.

All respondents were asked to spend approximately 15 minutes responding to the self administered questionnaire to indicate the importance to themselves of each of the 24 values by choosing from four categories using the scale described above. Respondents were subsequently asked to rate the importance of the same 24 values to their employing organisations. The respondents were also asked to respond to a range of demographic questions.

Response Details

In total, 900 questionnaires were distributed and 456 useable responses were received, a response rate of 50.6 per cent. Of these 456 responses, 87 were from human resources practitioners and the data from this group form the basis of this study. A summary of the demographic characteristics of the 21 male and 66 female respondents is presented in Table 1.

Table 1 Demographic characteristics of Human Resource Practitioners

Demographic Characteristics of Human Resource Practitioners		N	%
Sample size		87	100
Age	18-29 years	40	46.0
	30-39 years	31	35.6
	40 years or more	16	18.4
Gender	Male	21	24.1
	Female	66	75.9
Highest level of education attained	High School/TAFE	26	29.9
	Bachelor's degree	38	43.7
	Post graduate	23	26.4
Number of years in organisation	< 1 year	18	20.7
	1 to < 4 years	29	33.3
	4 years or more	40	46.0
Number of years in profession	< 1 year	10	11.5
	1 to < 4 years	29	33.3
	4 years or more	48	55.2
Employment status	Full time	83	95.4
	Part-time	4	4.6
Organisation size (number of employees)	1-499	23	26.4
	500-999	16	18.4
	1000 or more	48	55.2

Data Analysis Procedures

In testing the hypotheses Confirmatory Factor Analyses (CFA) using maximum likelihood estimates through LISREL were performed separately on the 24 individual and organisational value items to confirm the individual and organisational factor structures (Joreskog & Sorbom, 1988). Scores were computed for each of the four individual value factors and the four organisational value factors ('Clan', 'Adhocracy', 'Hierarchy', and 'Market' values) by taking the arithmetic mean of the items contained in the factor. Paired sample *t*-tests were used to determine withingroup differences between the particular value factors. Levels of congruence were measured by calculating the difference between the mean scores for the individual value factor and the mean scores for the organisational value factor, with a mean score of zero indicating no difference (Weiss, 1978; Meglino et al., 1992). A positive score indicated that the individual rated the value factor higher than the organisation, while a negative score indicated that the organisation rated the value factor higher than the individual. As this was an exploratory study and a large number of comparisons were made, levels of significance of p £ .01 were considered to be highly significant; however, levels of $p < .05$ have also been reported to illustrate differences.

Results

A summary of the means and standard deviations for each of the individual and organisational value factors and levels of individual–organisational value congruence is presented in Table 2.

Value Factors	Individual Value Factors		Organisational Value Factors		Individual-Organisational Value Congruence	
	M	SD	M	SD	M	SD
CLAN: (Broadmindedness, Consideration, Cooperation, Courtesy, Fairness, Forgiveness, Humour, Moral integrity, Openness, Social equality)	3.41	.39	2.58	.62	.83	.66
HIERARCHY: (Cautiousness, Economy, Formality, Logic, Obedience, Orderliness)	2.65	.46	3.04	.51	-.41	.60
ADHOCRACY: (Adaptability, Autonomy, Creativity, Development, Experimentation)	3.31	.38	2.72	.67	.59	.74
MARKET: (Ambition, Diligence, Initiative)	3.33	.47	3.08	.63	.25	.70

Table 2 Means and standard deviations for individual values, organisational values and individual–organisational value congruence

The hierarchy of individual values for human resource practitioners reveals strong preferences and confirms the view that human resource practitioners self report Individual Clan and Adhocracy ('developmental humanism') values and Market values as more important than Individual Hierarchy ('utilitarian instrumentalism') values. These findings support many of the assumptions and the findings from the literature suggesting this occupational group places high importance on personal values which are human and development centred (McDonald & Gandz, 1991; 1992; Mill, 1994). Both Individual Adhocracy values and Clan values were rated as more important than Individual Hierarchy values. The results indicate strong support for hypothesis one as statistically significant differences were found between Individual Clan and Adhocracy values and Hierarchy values ($p <. 001$) for the human resource practitioners. Significant differences were also found to exist between Individual Market Values and Hierarchy Values ($p <.001$). Clan values were rated as more important than Adhocracy values although at the more conservative level ($p <. 05$). There were no statistically significant differences between Individual Adhocracy values and Market values, or between Clan values and Market values (see Table 3).

In addition, the values of human resource practitioners appear to be congruent with the requirements of their role of 'employee champions', and 'change agents' (Conner & Ulrich, 1996; Dowling and Fisher, 1997; Smart & Pontifex, 1994; Ulrich, 1997). However, the scores for Individual Hierarchy values, which are rated between 'slightly important' and 'fairly important', are much lower in importance than the other three values. These results suggest that human resource practitioners do place some importance on what could be perceived as traditional business oriented values but not as much as other values. However, the lower scores may be considered as internally consistent with the higher importance placed on Clan and Adhocracy values, as these are argued to be competing rather than complementary to Hierarchy values (McDonald & Gandz, 1992; Quinn & McGrath, 1985). Ulrich (1997) adds support for this view as he cites these apparent contradictions or competing roles as a paradox in the role of the human resource practitioner. Significant differences were also found between Individual Market values and Hierarchy values. This may relate to the small number and type of items (ambition, diligence, and initiative) in the Market values factor, and the argument made earlier that some of these items may be perceived to constitute part of the other value factors and fit with either or both 'developmental humanism' or with 'utilitarian instrumentalism'. In particular, the value of initiative could be seen as a competing value to some of the Hierarchy values.

Organisational Values

The results also offer support for hypothesis 2 (see Table 2). Overall the perception of the importance of organisational Hierarchy values by human resource professionals indicates that the values of Australian organisations are perceived to be more consistent with the perspective of 'utilitarian instrumentalism' than that of 'developmental humanism', supporting the views of Legge (1995a) and Storey (1987, 1995). Both Organisational Hierarchy values and Market values are rated higher than Organisational Clan values and Adhocracy values. A comparison between each of the value factors indicate statistically significant differences between five of the six pairs of values (see Table 3). Organisational Hierarchy values were rated as more important than both Adhocracy values ($p <. 01$) and Clan values ($p <. 001$). Organisational Market values were rated as more important than both Adhocracy values ($p <. 001$) and Clan values ($p <. 001$). Organisational Adhocracy values were rated slightly more important than Clan values, but at the less conservative level of significance ($p <. 05$). There was no statistically significant difference between Organisational Hierarchy values and Market values.

Individual–Organisational Value Congruence in Human Resource Practitioners

As a result of the differences between individual and organisational values human resource practitioners appear to experience low levels of individual-organisational value congruence for all the values. The direction of these results offer support for hypothesis 3 (see Table 2). The lowest to highest congruence was experienced for Clan values, followed by Adhocracy values, Hierarchy values and Market values in that order (see Table 3). In addition there are significant differences between the measures of individual-organisational value congruence for the six measures. The levels of congruence for Clan values were lower than Adhocracy values ($p < .01$); Adhocracy values were lower than Hierarchy values ($p < .001$) and Clan values were lower than Hierarchy values ($p < .001$). However, it is noteworthy that the levels of congruence for Adhocracy, Clan and Hierarchy values were all lower than Market values (all $p < .001$).

Discussion

This study raises a number of issues in relation to the widely espoused organisational culture changes which recognise the contribution of people in achieving a competitive advantage and the benefits of individual–organisational value congruence. The implications of these findings need to be taken into consideration, as both strengths and weaknesses, first by those responsible for the development and implementation of corporate strategy and, second, by those responsible for the education, training and development of human resource practitioners.

Value pair	Individual Values			Organisational Values			Individual - Organisational Value Congruence		
Value pair	M	SD	t-test (2 tailed)	M	SD	t-test (2 tailed)	M	SD	t-test (2 tailed)
Adhocracy	3.31	.38	$t\,(df\,1,82)=-2.20$, p < .05	2.73	.67	$t\,(df\,1,84)=2.07$, p <.05	.58	.75	$t\,(df\,1,80)=-3.57$, p <.01
Clan	3.41	.39		2.58	.62		.85	.66	
Adhocracy	3.32	.38	$t\,(df\,1,84)=12.88$, p <.001	2.74	.65	$t\,(df\,1,84)=-3.24$, p <.01	.58	.72	$t\,(df\,1,82)=8.32$, p <.001
Hierarchy	2.65	.46		3.05	.51		-.41	.60	
Adhocracy	3.31	.38	$t\,(df\,1,85)=-.37$, p >.05	2.72	.67	$t\,(df\,1,85)=-5.86$, p <.001	.60	.74	$t\,(df\,1,84)=4.56$, p <.001
Market	3.33	.47		3.08	.63		.25	.70	
Clan	3.41	.39	$t\,(df\,1,84)=13.74$, p <.001	2.60	.61	$t\,(df\,1,83)=-5.49$, p <.001	.84	.65	$t\,(df\,1,79)=11.43$, p <.001
Hierarchy	2.65	.46		3.05	.51		-.39	.60	
Clan	3.41	.39	$t\,(df\,1,83)=1.37$, p >.05	2.58	.62	$t\,(df\,1,84)=-7.14$, p <.001	.84	.66	$t\,(df\,1,81)=6.53$, p <.001
Market	3.33	.47		3.08	.64		.25	.70	
Hierarchy	2.65	.47	$t\,(df\,1,85)=-15.73$, p <.001	3.05	.51	$t\,(df\,1,84)=.70$, p >.05	-.41	.60	$t\,(df\,1,83)=-6.77$, p <.001
Market	3.34	.47		3.10	.61		.22	.66	

Table 3 Comparison of means, standard deviations and *t*-values for individual, organisation, values and individual–organisational value congruence for pairs of values

These findings suggest organisational cultures which emphasises the core values of Clan and Adhocracy values, and 'developmental humanism' (Hendrey & Pettigrew, 1990; Quinn & McGrath, 1985; McDonald & Gandz, 1991,1992), do not yet appear, at least to the Australian human resource practitioners surveyed, to underpin the dominant organisational practice. This group perceives that low importance is placed on many of the values which are argued to be crucial to gaining a competitive advantage such as the Organisational Clan values of Broadmindedness, Consideration, Cooperation, Courtesy, Fairness, Forgiveness, Moral integrity, Openness, Social equality (Tyson & Fell, 1986). This group also perceives that organisations place low importance on those values that are crucial to organisational learning such as the Organisational Adhocracy values of Adaptability, Autonomy, Creativity, Development, and Experimentation (Senge, 1990; Field & Ford, 1995) and which demonstrate the ability of organisations and their leaders to be proactive, flexible and responsive to the turbulent environments predicted for the future (Enterprising Nation, 1995). These findings would indicate therefore that, to date, there has been a failure by these organisations to either wholly adopt, implement or to integrate the values that underpin such culture change strategies.

By contrast, with high importance on Individual Clan, Adhocracy human resource practitioners' values are self reported as consistent with a humanistic and developmental approach to human resources management and with their emerging role in a climate of organisational change and organisational learning. The value hierarchies of this occupational group will influence organisational change and development decisions, organisation structures, and the type of reward, recruitment, selection, evaluation and control systems being designed and implemented in organisations. However, this occupational group may find it more difficult to carry out their roles effectively, particularly that of 'change agent' and 'employee champion', without experiencing conflict in organisational cultures that are strongly underpinned by a philosophy and values of 'utilitarian instrumentalism', or where the espoused organisational values conflict with the values in action, and where these values are highly inconsistent with their own. The cognitive dissonance that emerges as a result of value incongruence may cause a strain on employees and create unnecessary conflict and stress, and ultimately have a negative impact upon organisational effectiveness (Chatman, 1991; McDonald & Gandz, 1992).

In addition it appears that the benefits of shared values for both the individual and the organisation argued earlier, such as high levels of job satisfaction (Meglino, Ravlin & Adkins, 1989), higher levels of organisational performance, employee commitment, loyalty, employee involvement in decision making, intention to remain with the organisation (Chatman, 1991; Deal & Kennedy 1982; Karathanos, *et al.,* 1994; Peters & Waterman, 1982; Posner, Kouzes & Schmidt, 1985) that are critical for organisational success in such cultures will be at risk. It also appears that these organisations are failing to tap into the potential strengths inherent in their employees' Adhocracy values such as creativity, development and experimentation, as well as humanistic values which underpin team processes such as consideration, cooperation, openness, and moral integrity. These lost opportunity costs have serious implications for maintaining organisational effectiveness.

The high levels of incongruence of individual-organisational values, especially for Clan, Adhocracy and Hierarchy values, also suggest that these organisations may not have adequately developed a consistency between many of their human resource policies and practices or integrated their strategic human resource planning. For example, these findings suggest that they may not be using the notion of core values 'fit' as part of their recruitment policy or among their specific selection criteria, at least in relation to their human resource practitioners (Chatman, 1991).

The implications of these findings need to be taken into consideration, as both strengths and weaknesses, by educators and the designers and facilitators of human resource development interventions in both the public and private sectors so as to meet the new demands being made of this occupational group. The broad range of key competencies and skills required for the changing roles of human resource professionals must be addressed (Ulrich et al, 1995; Ulrich, 1997). In particular, educators need to address the paradox in the competing HR roles of the necessity to be a 'strategic partner' on one hand and 'employee champion' on the other; and also the need to act as a 'change agent' and role of 'administrative expert' which requires a need for 'continuity, discipline and stability'. Appropriate human resource development strategies are necessary to balance these conflicting demands (Ulrich, 1997, p. 46). More seriously, the findings underline the strategic importance of management development which recognises the need for management education as a process of continuous improvement, particularly in the 'soft' skills and an understanding of the linkages between strategic choices, organisational culture, values and HRM practices (Barry, 1996; Enterprising Nation, 1995).

This exploratory research is subject to some limitations. Although the McDonald and Gandz items were based on in-depth interviews, and these have some overlap with other value taxonomies in the literature, the number and type of items on the draft scales cannot be considered exhaustive. While the work of Hofstede (1980) and Hampden-Turner (1994) have suggested that there are different value characteristics for national cultures, there are many similarities between Australia, Canada, the United States of America and the United Kingdom. The items for this scale were developed on one population, namely managers and human resource practitioners from organisations in Canada and the United States of America, and the instrument scale was developed on a small Australian sample of management, accounting professionals and human resource practitioners. However, there may be other individual, occupational organisational and national cultural differences which need to be taken into consideration.

As with any study where respondents are asked to rate themselves, there is the possibility of social desirability bias, where respondents may have presented a favourable impression of their individual values. The findings in relation to the self report of individual value hierarchies of human resource practitioners in this study should not be generalised without validation on a much larger and more broadly based sample of organisational constituents, from wider occupational representation and levels within the organisation.

Organisational culture and value change often takes many years and a great deal of time, effort and resources to achieve. Cross-sectional study does not reveal information about whether organisations are generally evolving towards placing importance on a particular set of values. An organisation's values may be in a transitional state and therefore may lag behind the changes in the individual, personal values of the occupational groups that make up the organisation and society in general. Therefore the findings in this study should not be generalised without validation on a much larger and more broadly based sample of organisational constituents, from wider occupational representation and levels within the organisation.

Finally, while human and development centred organisational cultures may exist, given the complexity of factors that impinge on organisations, this may not be an appropriate human resource strategy for more than a few organisations, or subcultures within organisations, even if it is an 'ideal' to be espoused. A more pluralist perspective may be necessary in the study of individual and organisational values to reflect the true diversity of the organisation.

Notes:
1. The definition of values used in this perspective are consistent with Rokeach (1973; 1979) and pertain to desirable end states or behaviours, transcend specific situations, guide selection or evaluation of behaviour and events, and are ordered by relative importance. They also involve a clear preference between specific mode of behaviour and its opposite or between a general goal and its opposite (Feather, 1994).
2. The term 'practitioner' is used as there are many specialist and generalist areas of practice within the human resource management profession.

References

Adkins, C.L. Russell, C.J. & Werbel, J.D. (1994). Judgements of fit in the selection process: The role of work value congruence. *Personnel Psychology,* Autumn, 47, 605-623.

Argyris, C. & Schön, D. (1978). *Organizational Learning.* Reading, Mass.: Addison -Wesley.

Australian Human Resources Institute (1995). *Australia's who's who in HR: The 1995 Networking Directory.* Neutral Bay, NSW: AHRI.

Barry, B. (1996).Management Education in Australia. *Asia Pacific Journal of Human Resources,* 34, 44 -56.

Becker, B., Gerhart, B. (1996). The impact of human resource management on organisational performance: Progress and Prospects. *The Academy of Management Journal,* 39, 4, 779-801.

Burns, T. & Stalker, G.M. (1961). *The Management Of Innovation.* London: Tavistock.

Cascio, W.F. (1989). *Managing Human Resources: Productivity, Quality Of Work Life, Profits* (2nd edn.). New York: McGraw-Hill.

Chatman, J. A. (1991). Matching people and organisations: Selection and socialising in public accounting firms. *Administrative Science Quarterly,* 36, 459-484.

Child, J. (1988). *Organization: A Guide to Problems and Practice* (2nd edn.). London: Paul Chapman Press.

Conner J. & Ulrich, D. (1996) Human Resource Roles: creating value not rhetoric. *Human Resource Planning* 19, 3, pp. 38-49.

Dowling, P. J., & Fisher, C. (1997). The Australian HR Professional: a 1995 profile. *Asia Pacific Journal of Human Resources,* 35, 1-20.

Dunphy, D. & Stace, D. (1992). *Under New Management: Australian Organizations in Transition.* Sydney: McGraw Hill.

Enterprising Nation: Report of The Industry Task Force on Leadership and Management Skills. (1995). (Karpin Committee). Canberra: AGPS.

Entrekin, L.V., & Pearson, C.A. (1995). Comparison of values espoused by quality and other managers. *Asia Pacific Journal Of Human Resources,* 33, 130-139.

Feather, N.T. (1992). Values, valences, expectations and actions. *Journal Of Social Issues,* 48, 109-124.

Feather, N.T. (1994). Values and Culture. In W.J. Lonner & R.S. Malpass (Eds.), *Psychology and Culture* (183-189). Needham Heights, MA.: Allyn and Bacon.

Field, L. & Ford, B. (1995). *Managing Organisational Learning: From rhetoric to reality.* Melbourne: Longman Australia.

Guest, D.E. (1987). Human resource management and industrial relations *Journal Of Management Studies,* 24, 503-521.

Hendry, C., & Pettigrew, A. (1990). Human resource management: An agenda for the 1990's. *International Journal Of Human Resource Management,* 1, 17-44.

Hampden-Turner, C. (1994) *Corporate Culture: From Vicious to Virtuous Circles* London: Hutchinson Books Ltd.

Hofstede, G. (1980). *Culture's Consequences, International Differences In Work Related Values.* London: Sage Publications.

Howes, P. & Folley, P. (1993). Strategic Human Resource Management: An Australian case study., *Human Resource Planning,* 16, 3, 53-64.

Institute Of Chartered Accountants In Australia Members Handbook (1994). Sydney: ICAA.

Joreskog, K.J. & Sorbom, D. (1988). LISREL 7: *A Guide to the Program and Applications* (2nd edn.). Chicago, Ill: SPSS.

Kabanoff, B. (1993). An exploration of espoused culture in Australian organisations (with a closer look at the banking sector). *Asia Pacific Journal of Human Resources,* 31, 1-29.

Kabanoff, B., Waldersee, R., & Cohen, M. (1995). Espoused values and organizational change themes. *Academy of Management Journal,* 38, 1075-1104.

Karathanos, P., Pettypool, D.M., Troutt, M.D. (1994). Sudden lost meaning: A catastrophe? *Management Decision,* 32, 15-19.

Legge, K. (1989). Human Resource Management - a critical analysis. In J. Storey (Ed.), *New Perspectives on Human Resource Management* (19-40). London: Routledge.

Legge, K. (1995a). HRM: rhetoric, reality and hidden agendas. In J. Storey (Ed.), *Human Resource Management: A critical text* (33-59). London: Routledge.

Legge, K. (1995b). *Human Resource Management: Rhetorics and Realities.* Houndmills, London: Macmillan Press Ltd.

McDonald, P., & Gandz, J. (1991). Identification of values relevant to business research. *Human Resource Management,* Summer, 217-236.

McDonald, P., & Gandz, J. (1992). Getting value from shared values. *Organizational Dynamics,* 20, Winter, 64-77.

Meglino, B., Ravlin, E.C., & Adkins, C.L. (1989). A work values approach to corporate culture: A field test of the value congruence process and its relationship to individual outcomes. *Journal of Applied Psychology,* 74, 424-432.

Mill, C. (1994). Using principles to win respect. *Personnel Management,* April, 19.

Ogbonna, E. (1992). Organization culture and human resource management: Dilemmas and contradictions. In P. Blyton & P. Turnbull (Eds.), *Reassessing Human Resource Management* (74-96). London: Sage Publications.

Peters, T.J. & Waterman, R.H. Jr. (1982). *In Search Of Excellence.* New York: Harper Row.

Posner, B.Z., Kouzes, J.M., & Schmidt, W.H. (1985). Values make a difference: An empirical test of corporate culture. *Human Resource Management,* 24, 293-310.

Posner, B.Z., & Schmidt, W.H. (1993). Values congruence and difference between the interplay of personal and organizational values. *Journal of Business Ethics,* 12, 341-347.

Quinn, R.E., & McGrath, M.R. (1985). The transformation of organizational cultures: A competing values perspective. In P.J. Frost, L.F. Moore, M. R.

Louis, C.C. Lundberg, & J. Martin (Eds.), *Organizational Culture* (315-334). Beverley Hills, Calif.: Sage Publications.

Rokeach, M. (1973). *The Nature of Human Values.* New York: Free Press.

Rokeach, M. (1979). *Understanding Human Values.* New York: The Free Press.

Schein, E. (1992). *Organisational Culture and Leadership* (2nd edn.). Jossey-Bass: San Francisco.

Schwartz, S.H. (1992). Universals in the content and structure of values: Theoretical advances and empirical tests in 20 countries. In M. P. Zanna (Ed.), *Advances In Experimental Social Psychology* (1-65). Orlando FL.: Academic Press.

Senge, P. M. (1990). *The Fifth Discipline: The Art and Practice of the Learning Organisation.* New York: Doubleday.

Sisson, K. (Ed.), (1994) *Personnel management: A comprehensive guide to theory and practice in Britain.* Oxford: Blackwell.

Smart, J., & Pontifex, M. (1994). Human resource management and the Australian Human Resources Institute: The profession and its professional body. In A.R. Nankervis & R.L. Compton (Eds.), *Readings in Strategic Human Resource Management* (185-205). Melbourne: Thomas Nelson.

Stace, D. & Dunphy, D. (1994). *Beyond The Boundaries: Leading And Re-Creating The Successful Enterprise.* Australia: McGraw-Hill Book Company.

Storey, J. (1987). Developments in the management of human resources: An interim report. *Warwick Papers in Industrial Relations.* 17, IRRU, School of Industrial and Business Studies, University of Warwick, November.

Storey, J. (1992). *Developments in the Management of Human Resources.* Oxford: Blackwell.

Storey, J., & Sisson, K. (1993). *Managing Human Resources and Industrial Relations.* Buckingham: Open University Press.

Tyson, S. & Fell, A. (1986) *Evaluating The Personnel Function.* London: Hutchinson.

Ulrich, D. (1997). *Human Resource Champions: the next agenda for adding value and delivering results.* Boston, Mass: Harvard Business School Press.

Ulrich, D., Brockbank, W., Yeung, A.K., & Lake, D.G. (1995). Human resource competencies: an empirical assessment. *Human Resource Management,* Winter, 34, 473-495.

Weiss, N.M. (1978). Social learning of work values in organisations. *Journal of Applied Psychology,* 63, 711-718.

Whiteley, A. (1995) *Managing Change: A Core Values Approach.* South Melbourne: Macmillan Educational Australia Pty Ltd.

Appendix One

Table 4 McDonald & Gandz (1991, 1992) shared individual and organisational value concepts

Shared value concept: Defined as an enduring mode of behaviour which emphasises:*

Adaptability	being flexible and changing in response to new circumstances
Ambition	being aggressive and pursuing goals vigorously
Autonomy	being independent and free to act
Broadmindedness	accepting different viewpoints and opinions
Cautiousness	being cautious and minimising exposure to risk
Consideration	being caring, kind and considerate
Cooperation	being cooperative and working well with others
Courtesy	being polite and having respect for individual dignity
Creativity	developing new ideas and applying innovative approaches
Development	achieving personal growth, learning and development
Diligence	working long and hard to achieve results
Economy	being thrifty and careful in spending
Experimentation	taking a trial and error approach to problem solving
Fairness	being fair and providing just recognition based on merit
Forgiveness	being forgiving and understanding when errors occur
Formality	upholding proper ceremony and maintaining tradition
Humour	creating fun and being lighthearted
Initiative	seizing opportunity and taking responsibility without hesitation
Logic	being rational and thinking in terms of facts and principles
Moral Integrity	being honourable and following ethical principles
Obedience	complying with directions and conforming to rules
Openness	being straightforward, sincere and candid in discussions
Orderliness	being neat, tidy and well organised
Social Equality	being equal to others and avoiding status differences

Note: *These definitions are consistent with behavioural descriptions mentioned by respondents during the interviews.
Source: McDonald, P., and Gandz, J. (1992). Getting Value from Shared Values. Organizational Dynamics. 20, 3, Winter, p. 67

Business process reengineering: Application and success in Australia

Peter O'Neill and Amrik S. Sohal

Abstract

This paper presents the results of a study undertaken in Australia which investigated the extent of Australian thinking and experience with Business Process Reengineering (BPR). The data for the study was gathered through a postal questionnaire survey which was mailed to 535 of Australia's top businesses. The findings of the survey are compared with earlier studies on BPR conducted in the United States and the United Kingdom/Europe. The hypothesis that 'expectant business process change is not significantly related to business improvements along dimensions of benefits and corporate impact' is tested. Finally the paper provides recommendations for mangers which are seen as important for successfully implementation of BPR projects.

Introduction

Since the late 1980s businesses have been making radical operational changes, referred to as Business process Reengineering (BPR). BPR is the fundamental rethinking and radical redesign of business processes to achieve dramatic improvements in critical, contemporary measures of performance, such as cost, quality, service and speed (Hammer and Champy, 1993). There have been only a limited number of empirical studies investigating the application of BPR amongst businesses.

Commentary on the subject commenced in Australia around 1990 mostly in the professional journals and magazines and had almost ceased by the end of 1994. This could lead one to believe that BPR in Australia no longer has any business performance relevance, or alternatively that it has become so entrenched in business practice that it is second nature. Except for a study of BPR in the Australian banking industry conducted by KPMG (1996), to date no other empirical study has been conducted in Australia which has investigated the extent of Australian thinking and experience with BPR. To fill this gap a questionnaire survey was conducted in late 1996 and the results of this survey are presented below. The aim of the survey was not only to quantify the use and success of business process reengineering within Australian organisations, but also to establish if there are lessons to be learned from the experiences. In presenting the results of the Australian survey, the paper also compares the findings with earlier studies on BPR conducted in the USA and the UK. These includes:

- the Guimaraes and Bond (1996) survey conducted in 1996 in which they surveyed 586 randomly selected manufacturing organisations in the USA, obtaining a response rate of 22 per cent (135 questionnaires). For their survey BPR was defined as dramatic changes (paradigm shifts) to business processes, in contrast with incremental improvements.
- the Carr and Johansson (1995) study of 47 American and European firms conducted in 1995. Their 90 minute telephone survey consisted of 81 questions grouped into broad sections covering; consultants, teams, roles, change readiness, IT, implementation, education, benefits, and success factors.
- the Zairi and Sinclair (1995) survey of 500 managers in manufacturing, services, public sector organisations (including local and national governmental bodies), and National Health Service Trusts (hospitals) which resulted in 65 responses, giving an overall response rate of 13 per cent. The aim of this survey was to identify the use of business process reengineering within different industries in the UK, and to attempt to ascertain the level of integration between business process reengineering and total quality management.
- The KPMG (1996) study of Australia's 28 major banks and finance houses. Following screening interviews to ensure a common understanding among all survey participants, ten institutions were deemed not to be undertaking BPR. Surveys were then mailed to 18 institutions, with 17 responding.

Further this paper also tests the hypotheses that *expectant business process change* is *not* significantly related to *business improvement* along the dimensions of benefits and corporate impact. Lastly the paper aims to provide recommendations for managers. These cover those factors seen as important for successfully implementing BPR projects. With this information managers should be able to minimise risk, and thus focus attention and resources on those factors important to success.

Research methodology and survey respondents

The questionnaire used for this study was developed from the literature and particularly based on the work of Carr and Johansson (1995) and Guimaraes and Bond (1996). The questionnaire together with an introductory letter and a pre-paid reply envelope was mailed out to Australia's top 500 companies, as reported by Dunn and Bradstreet (1996). An extra 35 surveys were sent out to companies that are wholly owned subsidiaries, or divisions of the top 500 companies. A follow-up letter was sent out three weeks after the mail out of the questionnaire.

The entry point into each company was through their strategic planning manager, as experience with most of Australia's leading companies tells us they have a dedicated position for planning, other than with the Managing Director or CEO. Nineteen questionnaires were returned undelivered and a total of 100 responses were received (one questionnaire was received too late to be included in the analysis), giving an overall response rate of 19 per cent, which is considered satisfactory for an exploratory study, and is comparable to other studies of this nature conducted overseas.

Respondents represented a broad range of functions, however senior managers including managing directors, chief executives, and general managers, made up the majority. The remaining respondents were from functional areas such as finance, operations management, quality, human resources management , and information systems. This skew towards top management is a partial explanation for the slightly lower response rate, but also exemplifies the responsibility necessary at the highest levels to under such project activity.

Figure 1 shows the survey respondents classified by industry sector and Figure 2 shows the respondents classified by company size measured by the number of employees.

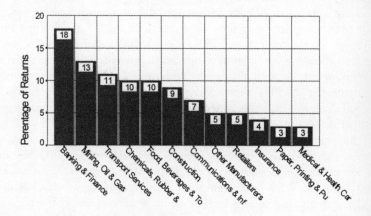

Figure 1
Respondents by primary business

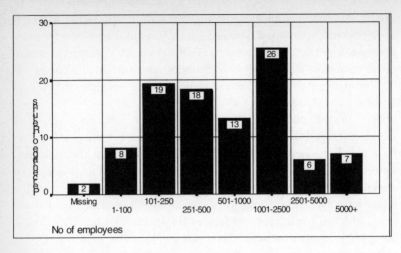

Figure 2
Respondents grouped by number of employees

Survey Results
Extent of BPR Activity

The first question in the questionnaire asked whether or not the company had undertaken BPR. Nearly sixty per cent (58%) of the sample have undertaken BPR, which if applied across the population of companies represents a significant amount of BPR activity. Only 9 per cent of respondents indicated that they would be undertaking a project in the near future. The data confirms anecdotal evidence that Australian companies have been much slower to reengineer than their counterparts in the US and Europe with BPR take up rates of 69% and 75%, respectively. What this result indicates is that although 67 per cent of companies in Australia will have experience with reengineering within the next 12 months, 33 per cent see no reason to reengineer at all. This implies a cautious Australian business attitude to radical change—despite the potential benefits—and may simply be a case of the benefits do not yet out-weigh the pain and disruption.

The results show that the Banking, Insurance, Chemicals, Food, Mining, Paper, and Medical were more likely to have undertaken BPR, than the sectors of Retailing, Communications, Other Manufacturers, Construction, and Transport. What seems significant in this information is that Retailers and Communications companies in Australia see less competitive pressure for radical change than other sectors. This may indeed be due to the oligopolies present in these sectors and their isolation from direct international competition. Furthermore, the Food, Beverage and Tobacco companies intend to move toward BPR with the next 12 months, and the Communications and Transport sectors would seem intransigent to change, compared to other sectors.

The results presented below are based on the 58% of the sample which had BPR experience. Note that in Figures where Means and Standard Deviations are presented the responses were given on a five-point Likert scale ranging from 1 for 'Not at All' to 5 for 'Great Extent'.

Two questions asked were when the organisation started their change project and whether this was their first BPR effort. Figure 3 shows that BPR activity in Australia peaked at the end of 1995. Fifty-seven per cent of the respondents had been involved in more than one BPR projects. Analysis of previous BPR experience by industrial sector reveals that the new adherents to BPR are Other Manufacturers, Retailers, Medical and Health Care, and Insurance, while Communications, Banking, Mining, and Construction have had previous BPR exposure compared to other sectors. Two points of note; firstly that the insurance sector would seem to be behind banks in BPR experience, but may be gaining in anticipation of deregulation within the banking sector.

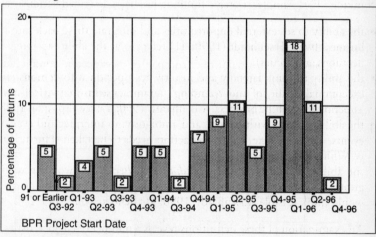

Figure 3
BPR project start date

Company's BPR Project Stage

As shown in Figure 4 approximately half (47%) of respondents have indicated that they are in the implementation phase of their projects, while almost a third were already into the improvement phase. The improvement phase is somewhat swelled by companies who believe that the project will never really be over (see Figure 5), instead believing that their initiative will be absorbed into a Continuous Improvement program. Significantly only one company or 2 per cent of the sample indicated that they had abandoned their project during the planning phase because top management (one must assume stakeholders), could not accept the significant amount of internal pain it would cause.

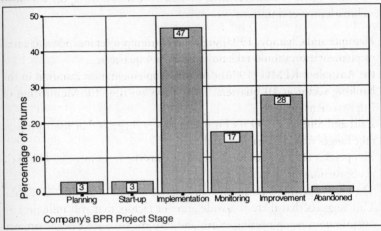

Figure 4
Company's BPR project stage

Figure 5 shows that the majority of companies are expecting completion of their BPR projects in 1997. However more significantly is that 17 per cent of companies responded that their BPR efforts would never end, instead believing that it will be improved on through Continuous Improvement efforts.

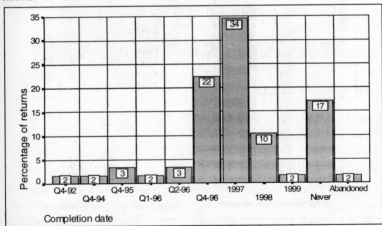

Figure 5
Company's expected or actual completion date

The actual time scale of reengineering projects always exceeded the expected time-scale.

Figure 6 shows that in 91 per cent of cases an Australian BPR project is expected to be in the Monitoring or Improvement phases after 16 quarters or 4 years. There is however little consistent data available on which to benchmark project duration;

- Hammer and Champy (1993) suggest that from project inception to a trial implementation should take no more than 4 quarters,
- the Australian KPMG (1996) data puts implementation duration in the banking sector at 10 quarters, (but allows no time for Monitoring or Improvement phases)
- Zairi and Sinclair's (1995)'s European survey suggests that most projects take longer than 12 quarters, and
- Zampetakis (1994) anecdotal summary puts the reengineering like cycle at approximately 20 quarters.

  The present result of 16 quarters thus agrees broadly with the above data. This suggests that there is a wide array of factors that will influence an organisations reengineering effort, and thus the time-scale of the project. Such factors as the following are typical are
- magnitude and extent of the business process changes,
- inexperience in BPR implementation, or
- unexpected problems faced during the BPR project.

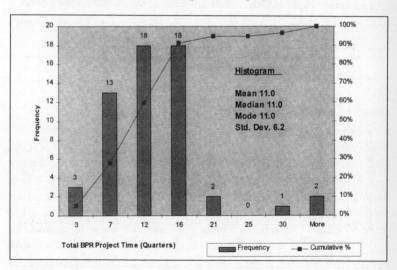

Figure 6
Histogram of company's actual BPR project duration

Events as Triggers to BPR

Figure 7 shows the mean and standard deviations of event triggers which lead to business process reengineering being used within the respondent company. The two most significant triggers in Australian companies are *competitive pressures* and an *intense need to cut costs*. This result agrees with the Carr and Johansson (1995) response for competitive pressures but there is a marked dissimilarity for cost cutting. Confirmation of the result does occur in the KPMG study, and suggests that Australian process costs are well behind those of World Best Practice, relegating proactive approaches such as Benchmarking to a secondary status. The reason for this can again be attributed to the isolation of Australian businesses from global competition.

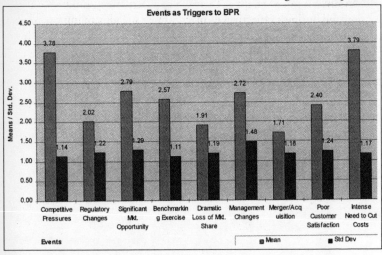

Figure 7 Statistics of event triggers

Focus of Corporate Strategy

Most authors agree that if BPR is to be successful in terms of goal attainment, it must be driven by strategy (Gadd and Oakland, 1996; Zairi and Sinclair, 1995). Respondents were thus asked to identify which of the four strategic possibilities were the focus for their organisation (multiple responses were allowed). Customer service was indicated by 81.0% of the respondents as their main strategic focus, whilst cost reduction was also indicated by 58.6% of the respondents. Quality achievement and time reduction were identified by 37.0% and 17.2% of the respondents, respectively. This implies that Australian organisations place cost above quality and cycle time reduction as competitive strategies, a result that is at odds numerically and in a ranked sense with the Carr and Johansson (1995)study.

Expectant Change in Business Processes

Respondents were asked to identify the degree of *Expected Change to Business Processes,* as such they were asked to rate a subset of the business processes listed by Guimaraes and Bond (1996). As can be seen from Figure 8, most change was expected in Business Planning, Inventory Management, and Production Scheduling. This is distinct from Guimaraes and Bond study which found sales and order entry, production scheduling, and product design and development were the business processes with the greatest expected change. The difference and the larger standard deviation can be attributed to the homogeneity of the Guimaraes and Bond population. However, the difference in Business Planning is significant and suggests that in general Australian organisations are not as adept as their US counterparts in linking strategic direction and business objectives to business plans. This finding would also help explain why the cost structures in Australian organisations have been allowed to fall behind that of International Best Practice.

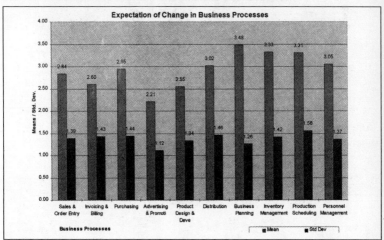

Figure 8
Statistics of expectant change in business processes

Extent Goals and Objectives Included in BPR

Respondents were asked to rate the *Extent to which 14 Goals and Objectives* were included by their organisation in the BPR Plan. The results are shown in Figure 9a and Figure 9b. The primary uses of goals and objectives were found to be focusing on end results, reducing costs and production times, improving competitiveness via cost reduction, and redesigning end-to-end processes improvement for success. The only commonality with Guimaraes and Bond (1996) is that of focusing on end results and objectives, though more emphasis is placed on time as a competitive weapon. Significantly the means for each goal and objective (except product development) was well above the moderate extent level (3.0), whereas in the Guimaraes and Bond sample each was below 3.0, suggesting that Australian organisations are expecting much more from their BPR effort than US companies. Given that costs feature in goals ranked two and three, it is plausible to suggest that the response overall is a catch-up plan, rather than a proactive plan for innovation.

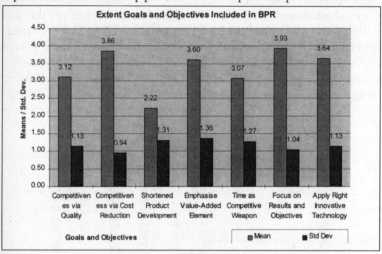

Figure 9a
Statistics of goals and objectives included in BPR

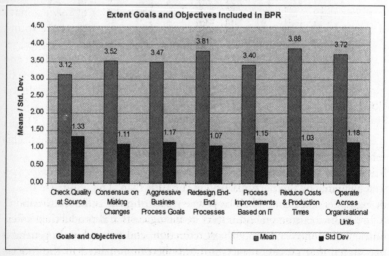

Figure 9b
Statistics of goals and objectives included in BPR (cont.)

View of Information Technology within BPR

Respondents were asked to list their view of Information Technology from within the BPR program. Almost three quarters of respondents listed IT as an Enabler of BPR, 17.2 per cent a driver, and almost 9 per cent saw it as irrelevant. This confirms the view of most authors, that IT should be positioned as an enabler, even if the extent of the IT change necessary is great (Carr and Johansson, 1995). That is IT should be used to enhance the value of BPR, and should never drive the changes without a clear business strategy for change. Even if the IT potential drives the initial thinking about change, it is necessary to step back from the technology, understand the current process, and reengineer before automating, or before adding or enhancing present information systems (Devonport, 1993). In this light it is alarming that almost a fifth of Australian respondents see IT as a driver in their strategy of customer service and cost reduction, but in doing so may be automating processes without the true benefit of reengineering.

A significant point is that almost a tenth of respondents believe IT is irrelevant to their program. This is a very sound and mature view of BPR, and correctly implies that major process improvements can be achieved within existing IT structures.

Effectiveness of Consultants

Respondents were asked to quantify the effectiveness of consultants in their BPR programs along six role dimensions. As can be seen from Figure 10, consultants had moderate impact on project and change management, IT implementation and to a lesser extent the formulation of management strategy. It would thus seem that Australian organisations have found consultants less effective in the formulation of management strategy, and yet more effective in the management of change, than companies in the Carr and Johansson (1995) study. Consultants could thus add more value (hence be more effective) to Australian BPR programs by improving the clients conceptual linkage between change management and strategic direction— including IT strategy. Of particular concern is that consultants have had a minor to moderate impact on the provision of training in both studies. This may imply that:

1. internal resources and expertise are available,
2. consultants do not have the expertise, or
3. the trainer's expertise and process ownership are linked (positive correlation).

In the latter case, several comments were received that indicated clients were particularly concerned about the perceived process ownership. In general it was stated that process ownership must be clearly linked to the process stakeholder, with the converse—*consultant ownership*—*implying project failure.*

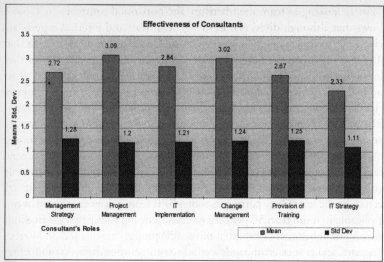

Figure 10
Statistics for effectiveness of consultant's roles

Selection Of BPR Team Members

Respondents were next asked to indicate which people were selected on their BPR teams, and to qualify the selection in terms of seven qualities. The results presented in Table 1 show the number of internal staff, consultants and external stakeholders who initiate, lead and participate in BPR programs. It should be noted that the figures are not mutually exclusive (multiple selections were possible), and the size of teams was not specified. The aim was to gain an insight into the roles of different individuals in BPR project teams, rather than to uniquely define team membership and roles.

Table 1 Selection of BPR team members

Number Selected viz Team Members	Expert	Thinker	Proj. Mgmt	Stake Holder	Authority	Team Player	Not Applic.	Percent Selected Selected	Percent of Responses
Division Heads	8	10	3	24	35	7	6	20.2%	89.7%
Staffers General	11	16	13	11	1	24	6	17.6%	89.7%
Experts Internal	29	26	16	5	2	8	7	20.0%	87.9%
Consultant External	28	14	23		1	1	9	15.5%	84.5%
IT Staff	20	12	10	11	1	5	10	13.7%	82.8%
Customers	3	3	0	22	1	2	31	7.2%	46.6%
Suppliers	3	2	0	16	1	3	35	5.8%	39.7%
TOTALS	102	83	65	89	42	50	104	431	58
Per cent	19.1%	15.5%	12.1%	16.6%	7.9%	9.3%	19.4%	100%	

Firstly looking at team membership, the horizontal summary in Table 1 shows that although divisional heads, general staff and internal experts are selected at an equal rate, it is clearly divisional heads and internal experts that offer BPR teams the greatest number of qualities. The table shows that divisional heads are valued for their authority and as stakeholders, while internal experts are valued for their creative expertise and as project thinkers. The data tends to agree with that of Zairi and Sinclair (1995) in the case of divisional heads but disagrees in that here internal consultants or experts are seen as more 'valuable' than general staff. The difference appears to be rooted in ownership of the process, which in the UK study would seem to be general staff, whereas in Australia it is primarily with divisional heads and secondarily with customers. Despite this fact Australian customers and suppliers are seen to be the least likely participants of a BPR team, on average listed as not applicable in more than 50 per cent of cases. The data confirms the findings of Carr and Johansson (1995) that most BPR projects are focused on internal processes, and as such erroneously exclude customers or suppliers, and further entrench Australian top management's centralised process ownership

Secondly, looking at the mix of qualities which are considered valuable to BPR teams. From the vertical summary shown in Table 1, the most valued qualities are those of business process expertise, process ownership, overall creativity and to a lesser extent project management skills. The data confirms the finding of Carr and Johansson, (1995) and the assertion of Talwar (1993), that expert knowledge of the business system is an essential ingredient to the successful reengineering of business processes. However, there is no such agreement on other qualities. Noteworthy are those of project management and team skills, which although identified as valuable qualities, are not rated highly, further indicating that the emphasis is on selecting and redesigning the right processes, rather than on implementation skills.

Time Devoted to BPR by Team Members

Figure 11 shows that in 57 per cent of cases, team members have committed up to 60 per cent of their time on BPR assignments, with the remaining 40 per cent on their existing workloads. The data compares favourably to that of Carr and Johansson's (1995) study where 58 per cent cases committed up to 75 per cent of their time, and emphasises the finding that in the majority of cases BPR projects are very much a part-time activity. It also implies that Australian organisations are less inclined to allow for total staff commitment than their US and European counterparts, and would explain why in Australia, consultants are selected almost twice as often (84.5 per cent versus 47 per cent). It is thus quite possible that internal team demands from 'real jobs', do not represent the major project constraints, but perhaps project duration, financial resources and cultural backlash do.

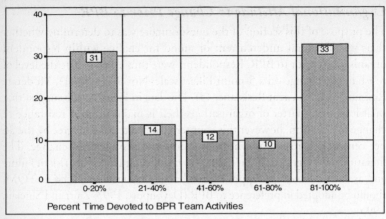

Figure 11
Time devoted to BPR by team members

Organisational Position as Primary Sponsor of BPR

Figure 12 shows that divisional general managers and directors are the primary initiators of BPR projects in Australia. The data are at odds with the study of Carr and Johansson (1995) which suggests that the CEO plays the sponsorship role, while Zairi and Sinclair's (1995) data indicates that it is directors in the UK who play the lead role. In all cases top management is seen as playing the lead role and suggests at the outset that management commitment at the highest levels is required for successful BPR. The distinctive managerial levels within the three data sets maybe linked to a difference in project scope, necessitating a broader managerial scope in projects that encompass the whole organisation.

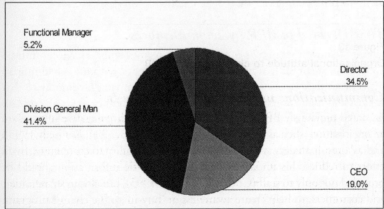

Figure 12
Organisational position as primary sponsor of BPR

Organisational Attitude to Change Prior to BPR

The purpose of this section of the questionnaire was to determine whether their was a natural undercurrent or mood for change within respondent organisations prior to BPR. Respondents were thus asked to rate the level of resistance to change on a 5-point Likert scale: Not Resistant (1), Moderate Resistance (3), to Great Resistance (5). The data in Figure 13 do suggest that in at least one quarter of organisations their is major or great resistance to change of any form, however this counterbalanced to some degree by the 36 per cent of organisations who show very little resistance to change. The literature has suggested that resistance to change implies higher risk of failure and as such a lower risk approach to change management, such as TQM, should be adopted in preference to BPR (Devonport, 1993; Zairi and Sinclair, 1995).

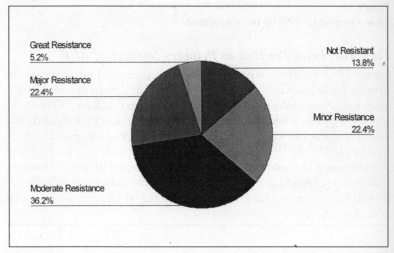

Figure 13
Organisational attitude to change prior to BPR

Communications used to Create BPR Buy-In

As stated previously BPR programmes frequently have negative impacts on an organisation, such as fewer staff (Coulson-Thomas, 1994; Kennedy, 1993), and as a result anxiety which may suspend their ability to co-operate. In an effort to reduce this impact regular and authentic information should be provided not only to staff (Coulson-Thomas, 1993), but also to shareholders and customers, to help create awareness or 'buy-in' to the change program. As one respondent commented *'communication at such times is not an overhead, it is as fundamental as the chief executive's personal involvement.'* While another commented that the 'media had a great impact on creating the burning platform necessary for employee, shareholder and customer buy-in.'

Figure 14 shows that the three communications methods which had the greatest impact were kick-off meetings, workshops and Q&A sessions. When compared with the Carr and Johansson (1995) study it can be seen that company newsletters are used to a great extent in US and UK organisations to create buy-in, and yet less so in Australia. Despite the fact that newsletters can be a cheap and convenient method of communication, it would seem that in Australia, if the communication is negative it is best done on a face to face basis. Perhaps what is missing from the Australian ethos is that newsletters are an effective mode to establish a bulk head or burning platform picture of the company's situation—good or bad.

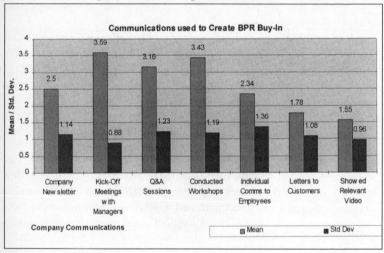

Figure 14
Statistics of organisational attitude to change prior to BPR

Process Redesign Method Adopted

Carr and Johansson (1995) summarise the literature on BPR methodology as one that attempts to start with a clean slate, or at best as an understanding of current processes. The reasoning for this is to enable original design as opposed to conventional design, and in so doing optimise the usage of technology leverage and organisational restructuring.

Sixty per cent of Australian respondents believe BPR starts with a complete knowledge of existing processes, instead of the prevailing best practice which calls for an overview. One respondent put the Australian view very succinctly as a *clean slate redesign also comes with expert knowledge of existing processes*. This view however does agree with the high value placed on experts on the

BPR team, and further confirms the authors view that BPR in Australia is very much a conservative, best practice catch up, rather than radical redesign.

Implementation Problems Experienced within BPR

The data in Figure 15a, and Figure 15b shows the ratings of BPR problems classified broadly into the groupings of; *planning, operational, up-front costs, side effects, organisation environment, and problems due to lack of results* from BPR projects. It shows that the most severe problems in Australian BPR implementations were in the minor to moderate levels, and are summarised below:

1. In general the *BPR project was larger than originally expected,* and respondents felt they *lacked an understanding of the implementation requirements,* suggesting that the planning phase of the project was perhaps poorly understood or very superficial,

2. In a planning and operational sense the *information systems infrastructure was unable to support the BPR* project, confirms the above and further suggests that technology change (leverage) was not anticipated, despite some respondents commenting that *processes were designed to meet the requirements of a new software package,*

3. Operationally respondents found that the *implementation learning curve was very time consuming,* suggesting that BPR projects as whole are perhaps being under resourced.

When comparing the these findings with the Guimaraes and Bond (1996) study one finds that only the unanticipated size of the project (item 1 above) is in agreement, and confirms two elements of the KPMG (1996) study, in that skills shortfall and predetermined technology solutions, were factors that gave rise to project failure. Australian implementation problems can thus be viewed as predominantly planning in origin.

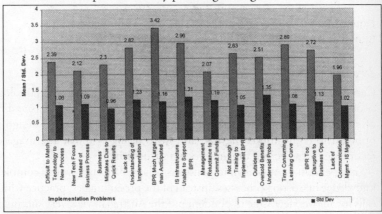

Figure 15a
Statistics of implementation problems experienced within BPR

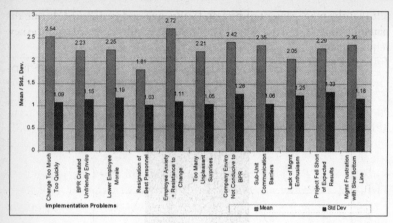

Figure 15b
Statistics of implementation problems experienced within BPR

Success of Training and Education

It is often tempting to think of BPR as merely a rethinking of the way work processes are performed by machines, and ignore the fact that work is performed by people pre and post machine interface. As such changing work processes requires an assessment of the impact these changes will have on people, and the implementation of a training plan to overcome the impact. Figure 16 shows that in general most respondents felt that the training provided successfully met their objectives.

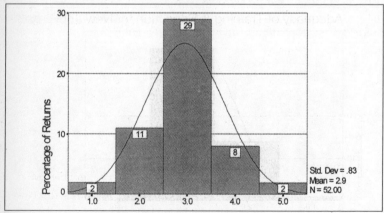

Figure 16
Histogram for success of training versus objective

Figure 17 shows that the quantity of employee training provided versus the plan tended to be skewed to *More than Plan*. This suggests that respondents felt that the management of human factors was underestimated during the planning process, and one would assume subsequently corrected with the new requirement.

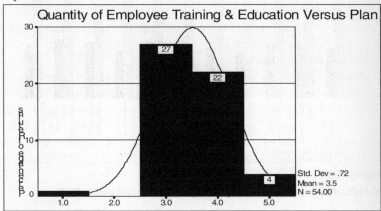

Figure 17
Histogram for training required during implementation versus plan

However Figure 18 shows that in general respondents felt that even though more training was provided, it was still slightly inadequate given an environment of changed job requirements. The data suggests that although respondents feel that the management of human factors (soft factors) were very important in their change planning, the focus still seems to be on reengineering the right processes right, and to a lesser extent training employees to perform the new processes right.

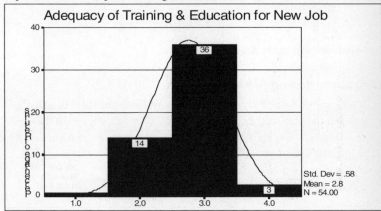

Figure 18
Histogram for adequacy of training given changes

Figure 19 shows that Australian respondents noted top management commitment as the primary contribution and top management leadership as the secondary contribution to their BPR efforts. The data supports the KPMG finding that strong sponsorship is an essential requirement for successful BPR, and confirms the experience of Carr and Johansson (1995), and Champy (1995), if one assumes that leadership overlaps with strategic focus and vision. As one typical respondent commented, top management provided 'total commitment to ensuring satisfactory outcomes including leadership, capital funds and resources necessary'.

However the data shows that 12 per cent of respondents did not list any contribution by their senior managers. This is an unusual finding and could be correlated with problems, benefits and outcomes to confirm its significance. It may indeed be as one respondent suggested, once 'top management initiate and establish a small group of dedicated resources, that includes all stakeholders, their role is reduced to monitoring.'

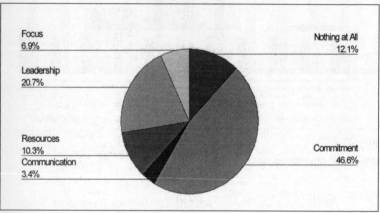

Figure 19
Top management contribution to BPR

Objectives Accomplished with BPR

Respondents were asked to rate the same list of *Goals and Objectives* that were included in the plan, as they relate to accomplishments. Figure 20 shows that companies which have implemented BPR projects have accomplished, at least to a moderate extent the following objectives:

1. remained focused on end results and objectives
2. built consensus on changes made
3. increased own competitiveness by reducing costs, and
4. redesigned end-to-end processes important to the company's success.

Those items underlined are in agreement with the Guimaraes and Bond (1996) study, while those bolded were rated highly as *goals* that were included in the BPR program. Despite the company-to-company variance, on average companies are accomplishing their enumerated goals to at least a moderate extent.

One can see from the data that reducing costs again features, this time as an accomplished goal. Significantly while the Guimaraes and Bond US data suggests an outward looking communication focus—operating effectively across organisational units, Australian organisations by comparison would have achieved an inward looking communication objective, that of consensus.

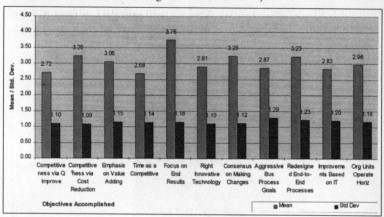

Figure 20
Statistics of objectives accomplished with BPR

Organisational Benefits from BPR

Respondents were asked to rate a list of eight potential benefits of BPR. The results presented in Figure 21 shows that the greatest benefits from Australian BPR, at least to a moderate extent, were:

1. productivity, decreased cycle time, inventory or cost
2. profitability, increased economic growth, and
3. quality, improved products or services and related information.

The only item in agreement with the Guimaraes and Bond(1996) study at the moderate extent level is productivity, though customer satisfaction and labour resources do feature at significant level. It is interesting to note that Australian respondents see more benefit from profit and quality than their counterparts in the USA and the UK (Guimaraes and Bond, 1996; Zairi and Sinclair,1995). This result again tends to confirm the internal focus of Australia BPR efforts, as opposed to the outward or customer focus of international BPR programs.

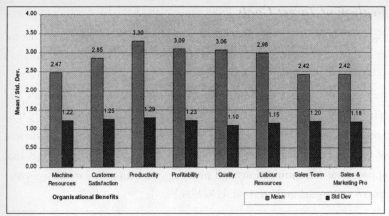

Figure 21
Statistics of organisational benefits from BPR

Satisfaction with Results of BPR Program

In this question respondents were asked to rate their overall level of satisfaction with the progress, or results, of the BPR effort so far, bearing in mind their original target goals. As stated previously one would expect to find a direct relationship between the realism of target goals and result satisfaction if BPR had been implemented with appropriate planning and communications.

Figure 22 shows that 80 per cent of respondents were at least modestly satisfied. This result compares well with Carr and Johansson's (1995) data where 95 per cent of respondents were at least modestly satisfied. However it is just as significant to note that almost 20 per cent of Australian respondents have found at least some level dissatisfaction with their BPR program.

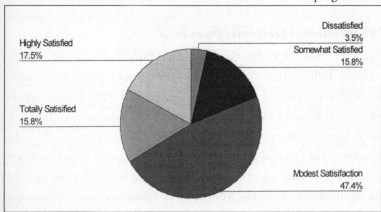

Figure 22
Satisfaction with results of BPR program

Realism of Target Goals

Figure 23 show that in the Australian environment BPR has been implemented in at least 50 per cent of cases with very realistic target goals, and resulted in at least total satisfaction in 32 per cent of cases. Intuitively one could anticipate that there is a direct relationship between the realism of target goals and result satisfaction with a mean of 3.4 versus a mean of 3.3 respectively. The Spearman correlation test confirms this with a rank correlation coefficient of 0.75 at a significance level less than 0.001. In general this suggests that appropriate communications and planning are being used to set *aggressive stretch target goals* and create stakeholder buy-in.

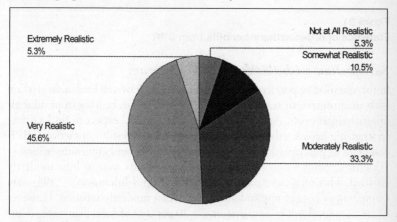

Figure 23 Realism of target goals

Organisational Outcomes from BPR

Figure 24 shows, as in the Guimaraes and Bond (1996) study, that the impact of BPR on Australian company performance is at best moderate on the three major financial fronts of, cost reduction, ROI and operating profit, with cost reduction being the only commonality. This result reaffirms the overall financial objective of Australian, but raises the question of whether this short term financial gain has any tangible long term corporate benefit attached e.g. product or service development. The early indications are that the organisational pain, staff reductions, and stress on company personnel is being driven by international cost best practice, while the real pain of product or service development is still to come.

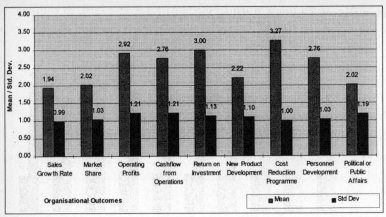

Figure 24
Organisational outcomes from BPR

Success Factors for BPR

Respondents were asked to rate the importance of 19 success factors to their BPR program. The results in Figure 25a and Figure 25b show that in Australian BPR projects:

1. customer demands are more motivating than surveys,
2. empowering the workers performing tasks, is more important than educating on BPR,
3. developing a defined project organisation and using resources effectively was considered very important,
4. continuous performance improvement was considered more important, and distinct from TQM programs
5. sharing and exchanging information willingly is very important,
6. communication of mission, vision, and project charter was seen to be only moderately important,
7. focus on outcomes (versus tasks) was preferable to market focus,
8. leadership from the top, as one would expect is considered very important.

When compared with the previous studies two major surprises emerge. Firstly while respondents considered continuous performance improvement a very important success factor, they seemed only moderately inclined towards a TQM culture. This supports the Carr and Johansson (1995) finding but as suggested by Zairi and Sinclair (1995) may mean that Australian organisations have yet to appreciate, that a Total Quality culture by its very nature can reduce implementation risk and costs—an all important factor to Australian organisations.

Secondly, it would seem that Australian BPR success is gauged distinctively on business outcomes and competitive pressures, and to a far lesser extent on a market or customer orientation. The data would seem to confirm the findings of the KPMG (1996) study, and again question the long term success of BPR in Australia.

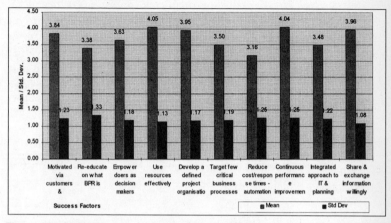

Figure 25a Statistics of success factors for BPR

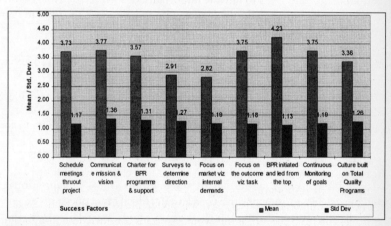

Figure 25b
Statistics of success factors for BPR (cont.)

Success of BPR in Australia Businesses

The aim of the survey was not only to quantify the use and success of business process reengineering in Australian organisations, but also to test the null hypothesis that: *Business Process Reengineering within Australian companies has not been successfully applied.*

The results of this hypothesis testing can also be benchmarked with the Guimaraes and Bond (1996) study to establish if there are lessons to be learned, 'gaps' in implementation, or opportunities for improvement.

To test the *Null Hypothesis* the Spearman rank correlation coefficients are calculated for each of the major constructs shown in Table 2. For the Null Hypothesis to be true the Spearman rank correlation coefficients for survey question G28—Organisational Outcomes—must be equal to or less than +0.25 at a significance level of 0.01. The hypothesis of interest is thus that: *Business Process Reengineering within Australian companies has been successfully applied,* where the Spearman rank correlation coefficients are actually NOT zero, BUT greater than +0.25 at a significance level of 0.01.

Table 2 Spearman correlation coefficients for Monash study

Question	Mean	Std. Dev.	A9	E19	A10	F24	G25	Variable Description
A9	2.96	0.83						Expect Change in Bus Proc
E19	2.44	0.66	+ NS					BPR Problems
A10	3.46	0.57	0.36	+ NS				Included Objectives
			< 0.01					
F24	3.06	0.69	0.33	- NS	0.50			Accomplished Objectives
			< 0.01		< 0.01			
G25	2.85	0.77	+ NS	- NS	0.35	0.63		Organisational Benefits
					< 0.01	< 0.01		
G28	2.55	0.71	0.47	- NS	0.46	0.66	0.72	Organisational Outcomes
			< 0.01		< 0.01	< 0.01	< 0.01	

Note: (51=>N<=58) (Coefficient/1-tailed Significance)

From Table 2 one can see that survey question G28—Organisational Outcomes—has a strong positive correlation with all other questions except E19—BPR Problems. Although there is no significant relationship, the indication, as one would expect, is that Organisational Outcomes are inversely related to BPR Problems. From the sample data it is thus possible to reject the Null Hypothesis and accept the Alternate Hypothesis that *Business Process Reengineering within Australian companies has been successfully applied.*

The finding that question E19—*Implementation Phase Problems*—could be uncorrelated with any other variable implies that the Australian experience with BPR has been very positive. This deviates markedly from the literature and could better be explained by either poorly defined problem alternative, or a sample size that is too small to gain any in-depth understanding of the problems experienced.

When benchmarked with Guimaraes and Bond's (1996) study it is noted that Organisational Outcomes are not as strongly correlated with Organisational Benefits and Accomplished Objectives as those for the current Australian study. This result would seem to confirm the fundamental difference in the usage or aims of BPR within the two data sets. As stated previously the Australian data suggests a narrow, short term, financial or cost focus to BPR, whereas the international data has a broader long term focus that includes financial objectives, but not at the expense of market, product, and personnel gains. It would thus seem that a broader perspective implies more pronounced implementation problems, weaker positive correlations between each project stage and Organisational Outcomes, and as such a lower success rate.

It might thus be said that Australian organisations have learnt from the experiences of their international counterparts and adopted a more focused, strategically oriented BPR program. From the data in question A8—Focus of Corporate Strategy—one would believe that the BPR program would be linked to a corporate strategy of customer service, and only as a secondary outcome, to cost reduction. However the common theme throughout the survey data are that the reverse is true, and that an apparent conflict exists. Despite this conclusion, one can see that the strategy has been used to assure BPR success via:

• business vision featuring highly as a success factor,
• a strong positive correlation between Included Objectives and Accomplished Objectives, and
• a very conscious effort made on skills development and education.

The cost reduction strategy of Australian business process reengineering is somewhat narrow and sterile. It implies that BPR in Australia has been reduced to another version of Neo-Taylorism, due in large to the international pressure on costs, and competition (Hammer and Champy (1993). However the future looks a little brighter, with 17 per cent of respondents realising that one off BPR catch up programs do not work, and instead adopting a continuous process redesign mode to forestall trouble, or take the opportunity to develop a lead.

Conclusion

The above survey findings confirms that, as well as confusion existing in the literature as to what exactly constitutes business process reengineering, different organisations and industrial sectors place differing emphasis on the many outcomes possible with BPR. Definitive outcomes of BPR are described by Davenport and Short (1990) and as the analysis and design of work flows and processes within and between organisations, and by Hammer and Champy (1993) as the fundamental rethinking and radical redesign of business processes to achieve dramatic improvements in critical measures of performance, such as cost, quality, service, and speed. The confusion over what reengineering actually is, was highlighted by respondents who commented that:

- we are targeting all business processes, not just a few cross-functional processes, or
- a major BPR goal is doing more in house.

We have little doubt that this confusion has had a major impact on the 20 per cent of organisations who reported that they were at best partially satisfied with their BPR program. However there was an overwhelming 80 per cent of organisations who reported that they were at least modestly satisfied with the results of their BPR program, and further the hypothesis that BPR has been successfully applied to Australian businesses was proven true. In summary the success of business process reengineering in Australia can thus be narrowed down to the following:

Strategic Alignment

In general organisations which adopt strong internal use of strategic planning and process management techniques place themselves in an ideal position to make maximum use of reengineering in their businesses for the longer term. Australian organisations have learnt from the experiences of their international counterparts and adopted, strategically oriented BPR program that is focused on cost reduction. Although somewhat narrow, and short term, the data suggests that approximately 20 per cent of respondents are adopting a continuous process redesign mode, in an effort to forestall future trouble, or create an opportunity to develop a lead. One can only hope that this trend will spread throughout the business community.

Senior management commitment

Almost fifty per cent of respondents noted commitment as the major contribution made by senior managers to the BPR project. This commitment is needed to reshape the culture, through such actions as proposing a challenging vision of the future or setting a major performance improvement targets, like cutting costs in half. Leadership also needs to be exercised through the strategy development process, to ensure broad participation, understanding, and acceptance of the chosen direction. This can only be achieved via face-to-face communications , and a committed approach to training and education. A strategic review of the company's sustainable competitive advantage at each BPR stage will also ensure that the redesign process is on-going.

Bottom-up redesign

The redesign effort requires forming teams that are responsible for the process outcome and appointing a process sponsor—typically the divisional general manager, and a process owner—typically the customer. At the same time the team is given more accountability, top managers must loosen their control by eliminating tight specifications of procedures and allow for clean slate redesign. This action makes it clear that the team is responsible for innovation while satisfying external and internal clients. These changes must be supported with investments in distributed information systems, and training so that members of the team know each other's role and can understand and use the information that is available. These bottom-up initiatives will not succeed on their own, because there still must be links between processes, and boundaries placed on behaviour so that energy is not diffused.

The enabling role of information technology

A process perspective on management problems, leading to the decentralisation of decisions, is the potential of information technology. It can enable organisations to do things they could not do before and thus develop new Core Competencies and skills. An integrated IT approach has many elements: shared databases, high-speed communication networks, decision-support systems, automatic product identification and tracking, and large-scale computing. However almost 75 per cent of respondents believe that Information Technology was an enabler for fundamental change rather than a driver of the process. It was also discovered that companies in Australia have been extremely slow or resistant to undergo radical change, suggesting that they are well behind world's Best Practice of linking the customer to suppliers via value added business processes.

BPR versus TQM

It would appear from the literature that the TQM improvement model and the BPR innovation model have appropriate places in the fundamental change of Business Processes. However while respondents considered continuous performance improvement a very important success factor, they seemed only moderately inclined towards a TQM culture. This suggests that Australian organisations have yet to appreciate, the potential of a Total Quality culture. It can produce a very efficient system encompassing competencies in change, teamwork and flexibility, which can mean the switch to a new business process via new Technology (possibly IT), can be made with manageable risk and lower costs—an all important factor to Australian organisations.

Recommendations

Based on the results, one is led to the conclusion that organisations are not emphasising some of the most important activities and tasks recommended in the literature as basic underpinnings for BPR, such as using time as a competitive reason, changes to customer-market-related business processes, the value-added element of every business activity, and applying the right innovative technology. Therefore, one may surmise that therein lies a major reason why many of the BPR project goals and objectives have been only modestly accomplished.

Thus, in general, before embarking on a BPR project executives should ensure that at least some of the success factors deemed very important by the respondents are present:

- the project is initiated and led from the top down by senior level managers,
- developing a defined project organisation
- continuous performance improvement,
- using resources effectively,
- sharing and exchanging information willingly,
- satisfying customer demands are more motivating than surveys,
- communication of mission, vision, and project charter, and
- focus on outcomes (versus tasks).

Accepting the alternate hypothesis that *Business Process Reengineering within Australian companies has been successfully applied* could suggest that on average companies broadening the scope of their BPR projects will not face any increase in implementation problems. This is clearly not the case, as indicated by the weak negative correlation between Organisational Outcomes and BPR problems. Top managers and project leaders alike need to be resistant to the temptation to expand BPR project goals and objectives without due consideration of the possible negative impact.

The extent to which BPR goals and objectives are accomplished is strongly related to the benefits the organisation derives from the BPR project, and also related to the extent the BPR project has an impact on company outcomes. The extent to which benefits are derived is also positively related to company outcomes. On average, the inclusion of goals and objectives in project plans has a implied project success, but the implication is that goals should be minimised to reduce the positive effect of implementation problems. Likewise, problem minimisation would also seem to have a weak positive effect on the extent to which project goals/objectives were accomplished, the derived company benefits from the project, and its favourable impact on company performance.

Based on the findings as a whole, top managers should not engage in BPR projects unless absolutely necessary to reposition the organisation strategically.

Otherwise, before using BPR to slash and burn, top managers should lead a crusade to improve organisational performance by:

- emphasising continuous improvement (TQM),
- team building,
- shortening communication channels,
- empowering doers with the authority and responsibility for decision making, and
- reducing bureaucracy.

The Future of BPR

The second generation of Australian reengineering should consist of enterprise-wide process constructs encompassing all four of the fundamental processes; cost, quality, service, and speed. Organisationally, the changes occurring will introduce seamless organisational, functional and inter-organisational boundaries, transforming the traditional organisational structure to a horizontal organisational architecture matching the flow of processes rather than functions. Leading international firms are reconfiguring their businesses to be virtual networks or resource-based, a configuration that is closely linked to a process-perspective, a hint at the possibilities for the future. Their Australian competitors will eventually have to match or exceed these capabilities to meet their customers' expectations of minimum acceptable performance. In the meantime Australian organisations must play catch up to provide a platform from which to apply the most innovative processes to new products and services.

References

Carr D., and H. Johansson, *Best Practices in Reengineering,* McGraw-Hill, New York, 1995.

Champy, J., *Reengineering Management,* London: Harper Collins, 1995.

Coulson-Thomas, C. (ed.), *Business Process Re-engineering: Myth and Reality,* Kogan Page, London, 1994.

Davenport, T. H., 'Need radical innovation and continuous improvement? Integrate process reengineering and TQM', *Planning Review,* Vol. 21 No. 3, May/June, 1993A, pp. 6-12.

Davenport, T. H. and J.E Short, 'The new industrial engineering: information technology and business process redesign', *Sloan Management Review,* Vol. 31, No. 4, Summer, 1990, pp. 11-27.

Dunn and Bradstreet, *Australia's Top 500 Companies 1996-97,* 10th edition, Dunn and Bradstreet (Australia) Pty. Ltd., Sydney, 1996.

Gadd, K. and J. Oakland, 'Chimera Or Culture? Business Process Re-engineering For Total Quality Management', *Quality Management Journal*, Vol. 3, No. 3, 1996, pp. 20-38.

Guimaraes T., and W. Bond, 'Empirically assessing the impact of BPR on Manufacturing firms', *International Journal of Operations &Production Management*, Vol. 16, No. 8, 1996, pp. 5-28.

Hammer, M. and J. Champy, *Reengineering the Corporation: A Manifesto for Business Revolution*, Harper Business, New York, 1993.

Kennedy, C., 'Re-engineering: the human costs and benefits', *Long Range Planning*, Vol. 27, No. 5, 1994, pp. 64-72.

Talwar, R., 'Business re-engineering—a strategy-driven approach', *Long Range Planning*, Vol. 26, No. 6, 1993, pp. 22-40.

Zairi M, and D. Sinclair, 'Business process re-engineering and process management A survey of current practice and future trends in integrated management', *Business Process Re-engineering & Management Journal*, Vol. 01 No. 1, 1995, pp. 8-30.

Zucco, N. (ed.), 'Re-engineering Australian Banks—Achieving a quantum leap in performance', Internal Study Paper, KPMG, 1996.

Section D
Strategy and
Performance

Encouraging strategic thinking at 'Communications Co.': Linking behavioural styles to creativity

Fiona Graetz,
Johanna Macneil and
John McWilliams

Abstract

The ability to 'think strategically' depends on the interaction between situational factors in the organisational setting and the characteristics of the individuals involved (Hurst, Rush & White, 1988; Eisenhardt, 1990; Peters, 1991: 18; Bahrami, 1992: 33; Limerick & Cunnington, 1993). This study considered two questions. Firstly, whether the decision style of middle managers at Communications Co. (as measured by Life Time Assessment Test) relates to their ability to think strategically. The latter was measured by quality of scenario planning. The second question was to investigate the effect of group dynamics as an intervening variable in the quality of scenario planning. While the results do not indicate a clear link between decision styles and level of creativity, group dynamics clearly acted as an intervening variable. The study also found that behavioural styles are strongly influenced by the prevailing workplace culture.

Introduction

Fostering strategic thinking in an organisation is a matter of the interaction between situational factors and the characteristics of the individuals involved.

Some situational factors may be necessary prerequisites to strategic innovation. According to one of the most prominent authors in the area, in order to develop an 'innovation-hungry' corporate culture (Peters, 1991: 18), organisational decision-makers must reform their traditional, top-down, linear approach to thinking and planning, and adopt systems and structures which support and reward 'novelty, innovation and change' (Bahrami, 1992: 33). This is supported by Burnside, Amabile and Gryskiewicz (1988: 170) who found that creativity was fundamentally dependent on the organisation's internal environment and whether it encouraged or hindered employee creativity. To be successful, it is argued that the new organisational mindset must incorporate flexibility, speed and adaptability (Hamel & Prahalad, 1994; Dunphy & Stace, 1993; Kanter *et al.,* 1992; Peters, 1988). Implicit in this is the requirement for a flatter 'boundaryless' organisational structure comprising smaller, autonomous business units run by highly trained, capable staff who are 'adept at exchanging ideas, processes and systems across borders' (Maruca, 1994).

Collins and Porras (1996: 66) argue that truly great companies have a deep sense of *yin* and *yang,* the rare ability to balance 'continuity and change'. For them, *yin* represents the unchanging core values and purpose of the company, its *raison d'être; yang,* on the other hand, represents the 'envisioned future', what the company 'aspires to become, to achieve, to create', the dreams, hopes and aspirations it plans to realise. Similarly, other studies suggest that organisations must be neither too rigid nor too bureaucratic. There needs to be 'loose/tight couplings': 'looseness' which allows individual freedom to follow through ideas, and 'tightness' which ensures deadlines are met and customer demands fulfilled (Peters & Waterman, 1982; Burnside *et al.,* 1988; Tichy & Devanna, 1991; Limerick & Cunnington, 1993).

A number of authors have focused on the individual correlates of strategic thinking. For example, strategic thinking has been described variously as:

- the ability to see external opportunities and integrate these back into the business (what Eisenhardt (1990: 41) refers to as the ability to integrate decisions and tactics);
- the ability to think laterally and intuitively; a person who demonstrates exceptional 'quality of understanding', 'an immense instinctive feel' and a 'superior grasp of the business' (Eisenhardt, 1990: 45; see also Agor, 1988);
- the ability to deal with novelty and ambiguity; to interpret and evaluate events, data, and determine what action needs to be taken (Hurst, Rush & White, 1988); and
- the ability to *build multiple, simultaneous alternatives,* working with a greater range of options than their more cautious, slow-response counterparts would think feasible (Eisenhardt, 1990: 46; Schoemaker, 1995: 27).

An examination of these definitions reveals a number of characteristics at play, all vested in the individual, including behaviour, attitudes, emotional maturity, knowledge, and intelligence. None, however, are common to all definitions, reflecting the developmental nature of this concept of strategic thinking.

The Study

The present study is the consequence of a naturally occurring field experiment (*cf.* Dunette, 1966). The communications company, for the purposes of this chapter named 'Communications Co.', is currently attempting to devolve capacity for strategic thinking from senior to middle managers and engaged the researchers to conduct workshops in developing strategic thinking skills. One emergent model of individual strategic thinking ability is provided in the literature on brain styles (Herrmann, 1989, 1996; Leonard & Straus, 1997). Collins and Porras's (1996) argument fits very closely with this stream of work, which uses hemispherical and cerebro-limbic dominance in the brain as a metaphor for thinking styles (Mintzberg, 1976; Herrmann, 1996; Davies, 1984; McAdam, 1995, in press). While strategic thinking may be influenced by environmental factors, it is also interesting to consider individual predisposition as a variable and, further, as a mode of diagnosis of organisational culture.

Life-Time Assessment Test

Mintzberg (1976) argued that management is a left-brain activity while planning is located in the right brain. The idea of a link between brain activity and personal preference has support from studies of the brain's architecture (Orstein, 1973; Herrmann, 1989; McLean, 1981). It has also been used as a metaphor by Herrmann (1996) with his Brain Dominance Instrument (BDI). Much of our discussion will draw on Herrmann's work. However, a limitation of his instrument is that it is likely to be influenced by the context in which it is completed. For example, McAdam (1996, in press) has demonstrated with an international sample of 1800 respondents that there is a consistent shift from right to left brain activity as a consequence of pressure. He obtained this data using the Life-Time Analysis Test (LTAT) (Davies, 1984) which measures the same underlying constructs as the Herrmann Instrument but elicits scores for behaviour in relaxed as well as under pressure states. For the present study, the LTAT was selected as it was felt that the groups would be working under pressure in the completion of the exercise assigned to them.

In the LTAT, behavioural styles are grouped into four quadrants (see Figure 1). Characteristics illustrative of the upper left quadrant, the *Producer,* are logical, critical, rational, linear thinking and analysis of facts. Profiles in which the lower left quadrant, the *Analyst,* dominate, exhibit an orderly, fastidious approach, an eye for detail, a practical approach to problem solving, a concern for procedures, and 'to get the job done' in a timely manner.

The right quadrants are said to be more reflective of eastern culture where the emphasis is on space rather than time. The upper right quadrant, the *Imaginist,* reflects the creative self, characterised by a holistic, intuitive, innovative, risk-taking behavioural style which tolerates ambiguity and sees the 'big picture'. The lower right quadrant, the *Teamist,* is the feeling, sensing, sharing, emotional self.

Strategic thinking operates in two domains. The first is the organisational domain of operational planning. The second is the creative element of event anticipation, demonstrated through activities such as scenario planning. A good planning capability would encompass both domains. In Herrmann's terms, then, one would expect effective strategy formulation to arise from a combination of Imaginist and Analyst styles.

Scenario Planning

Schoemaker (1991: 551) describes scenario planning as a 'thinking tool and communication device that aids the managerial mind rather than replacing it.' It is particularly valuable in times of high uncertainty and complexity as it serves to challenge the status quo. By identifying trends and uncertainties in an organisation's macro environment, scenario planning:

- provides a tool for sketching possible futures;
- attempts to capture a range of options;
- stimulates thinking about alternatives which might otherwise be ignored; and
- challenges the prevailing mindset. (Schoemaker, 1995)

Scenario planning was chosen as the method through which to assess strategic thinking ability.

The LTAT is a measure of individual brain styles, but the experiment was conducted at the level of the group. It was necessary to note the possible effect of group dynamics. Impartial observers were therefore used to provide evidence of the effect of this interaction.

Research Questions

The study was driven by two questions.
1. Do dominant brain styles relate to people's ability to think strategically, as measured by quality of scenario planning?
2. Are group dynamics an intervening variable in effective scenario planning?

Method

Participants in the study were selected from a pool of around 80 employees at middle management level identified by Communications Co. senior management as having leadership potential. Forty-six were invited to participate in one of two 'Strategic Thinking' Workshops and 25 accepted. Fifteen (3 females and 12 males) attended Workshop 1 and ten (2 females and 8 males) attended Workshop 2. The workshops were conducted by the authors.

Overall, there were five female and 20 male participants. Age groups represented were: 25 to 29 years (2); 30 to 34 years (6); 35 to 39 years (10); and 40+ years (7). The professions nominated as most characteristic of background and experience were: Engineering/Production (18); Computing (3); General Management (2); Finance/Accounting (1); and Marketing (1).

Participants were informed that the objectives of the workshops were to:

1. train Communications Co. employees in the management technique of scenario planning and test their skills in applying this technique;
2. test Communications Co. employees' strategic decision-making styles through the use of a decision styles survey; and
3. provide recommendations to Communications Co. on enhancing strategic thinking ability.

The researchers were primarily concerned with Objective 2.

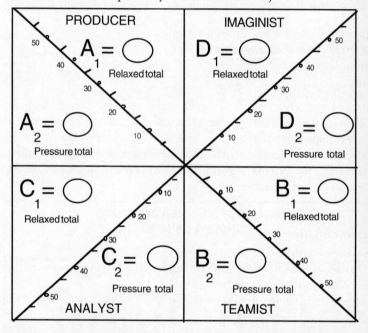

Figure 1
LTAT quadrants

Workshop Format

During each five-hour workshop program, participants:

1. were asked to complete the LTAT. The test was administered by a qualified psychologist who briefed participants on its purpose and relevance to the study. Participants completed the test individually.
2. were given training in scenario planning. Training was conducted by the authors, Graetz and Macneil.

3. took part in a scenario planning exercise. Each participant collaborated with four to five other colleagues in developing scenarios for a specified situation (the Sydney Olympics). Information on their role, tasks, and background material in the form of tables, news items and photographs of past Olympics, were provided in a five-page handout (See Appendixes 1 and 2). A passive, impartial observer from Deakin University sat with each group, observing the group process and taking notes of the discussion. Each group had 2 hours to build its scenario.

A follow-up session of 2 hours involving all participants was conducted two weeks after the final workshop to explain the results of the tests; to share scenario planning experiences; and draw out key learning outcomes.

Results and Discussion

Behavioural Styles Testing

Individual scores from the LTAT were recorded and then charted on a group-by-group basis (see Table 1). Figures 2 and 3 record the LTAT scores for each group member in Groups 1 and 2 relaxed and under pressure. Individual group members were allocated a unique letter against their group number (e.g. 1C, 2X, 3M etc.) to ensure confidentiality of results. *A score greater than or equal to 25 was considered significant.*

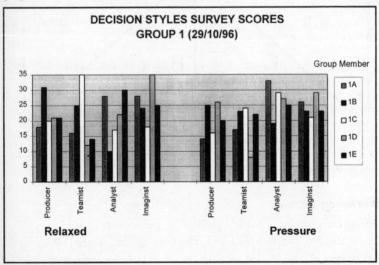

Figure 2
LTAT scores—Group 1
Note: Scores ≥ 25 were considered significant

DECISION STYLES SURVEY SCORES
GROUP 2 (29/10/96)

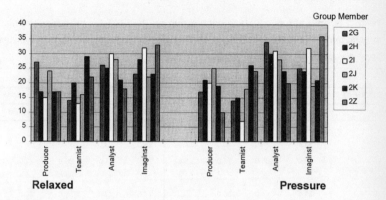

Figure 3
LTAT scores—Group 2

Figure 2 shows Group 1 LTAT scores in relaxed mode and under pressure mode. Person 1A scored relatively highly in the *Analyst* and *Imaginist* quadrant in a relaxed situation. Under pressure, however, Person 1A's score increased markedly in the *Analyst* quadrant and decreased slightly in the *Imaginist* quadrant.

Person 1C's scores were also interesting, scoring highly in the *Teamist* quadrant, with scores under 25 in all other quadrants. Under pressure 1C's teamist approach was overtaken by a marked increase in the *Analyst* quadrant. Scores for the rest of the people in Group 1 (Figure 2) and all of the members of Group 2 (Figure 3) can be read in the same way.

The predominant behavioural style exhibited across all groups **when relaxed** was *Imaginist;* and the predominant behavioural style exhibited across all groups **under pressure** was *Analyst.* The former indicates that a reasonably high level of creative potential exists within Communications Co., but when confronted by crisis or stressful situations, the Imaginist quadrant is abandoned in favour of the Analyst quadrant. In this quadrant, the emphasis is on structure, organisation, 'getting the job done', and playing safe by sticking to established procedures and routines.

The tendency for the Analyst quadrant to take precedence over the Imaginist quadrant under pressure may be reinforced in a team-based workgroup where the brain style of the dominant members of the group is Analyst.

It should be noted that the predominant style refers to the most preferred style within the group, not the style of the dominant person in the group. Clearly, group dynamics will have a substantial impact on the creativity demonstrated by the groups in constructing their scenarios. The dominant quadrants for each groups, as demonstrated in Table 2, emerged as Imaginist when *relaxed* and Analyst when *under pressure*. The effect of group dynamics is discussed under *Impact of group dynamics.*

Table 1 Scores of individuals in each group on the LTAT for producer, teamist, analyst and imaginist under relaxed and pressure conditions with group average scores shown

	LIFE-TIME ASSESSMENT TEST							
GROUP ID	**RELAXED**				**PRESSURE**			
	Producer	**Teamist**	**Analyst**	**Imaginist**	**Producer**	**Teamist**	**Analyst**	**Imaginist**
1A	18.0	16.0	28.0	28.0	14.0	17.0	33.0	26.0
1B	31.0	25.0	10.0	24.0	25.0	23.0	19.0	23.0
1C	20.0	35.0	17.0	18.0	16.0	24.0	29.0	21.0
1D	21.0	12.0	22.0	35.0	26.0	8.0	27.0	29.0
1E	21.0	14.0	30.0	25.0	20.0	22.0	25.0	23.0
Gp1 Avge	**22.2**	**20.4**	**21.4**	**26.0**	**20.2**	**18.8**	**26.6**	**24.4**
2G	27.0	14.0	26.0	23.0	17.0	14.0	34.0	25.0
2H	17.0	20.0	25.0	28.0	21.0	15.0	30.0	24.0
2I	15.0	13.0	30.0	32.0	20.0	7.0	31.0	32.0
2J	24.0	16.0	28.0	22.0	25.0	18.0	28.0	19.0
2K	17.0	29.0	21.0	23.0	19.0	26.0	24.0	21.0
2Z	17.0	22.0	18.0	33.0	10.0	24.0	20.0	36.0
Gp2 Avge	**19.5**	**19.0**	**24.7**	**26.8**	**18.7**	**17.3**	**27.8**	**26.2**
3M	17.0	35.0	13.0	25.0	23.0	16.0	28.0	23.0
3N	14.0	29.0	26.0	21.0	22.0	12.0	32.0	24.0
3O	20.0	18.0	26.0	26.0	17.0	24.0	30.0	19.0
3P	24.0	16.0	19.0	31.0	27.0	26.0	19.0	18.0
Gp3 Avge	**18.8**	**24.5**	**21.0**	**25.8**	**22.3**	**19.5**	**27.3**	**21.0**
4Q	18.0	21.0	24.0	27.0	15.0	15.0	32.0	28.0
4R	21.0	18.0	24.0	22.0	19.0	22.0	25.0	24.0
4S	26.0	16.0	34.0	14.0	19.0	15.0	33.0	23.0
4T	15.0	23.0	24.0	28.0	26.0	13.0	18.0	33.0
4U	19.0	22.0	17.0	32.0	23.0	26.0	19.0	22.0
Gp4 Avge	**19.8**	**20.0**	**24.6**	**24.6**	**20.4**	**18.2**	**25.4**	**26.0**
5A	25.0	22.0	20.0	23.0	28.0	25.0	18.0	19.0
5V	26.0	30.0	8.0	26.0	22.0	23.0	19.0	26.0
5W	10.0	19.0	30.0	31.0	13.0	25.0	25.0	27.0
5X	19.0	10.0	37.0	24.0	17.0	25.0	27.0	21.0
5Y	22.0	20.0	29.0	19.0	17.0	29.0	21.0	23.0
Gp5 Avge	**20.4**	**20.2**	**24.8**	**24.6**	**19.4**	**25.4**	**22.0**	**23.2**
Overall Average	**20.2**	**20.6**	**23.4**	**25.6**	**20.0**	**19.8**	**25.8**	**24.4**

GROUP ID	Relaxed Dominant	Relaxed Backup	Pressure Dominant	Pressure Backup
	DECISION STYLES SURVEY Comparative Dominant and Backup Styles			
Gp1 Mode	Imaginist + Analyst	Producer	Analyst	Imaginist
Gp2 Mode	Imaginist	Analyst	Analyst	Imaginist
Gp3 Mode	Imaginist + Teamist	Analyst + Producer	Analyst + Teamist	Imaginist
Gp4 Mode	Imaginist	Analyst	Analyst	Imaginist
Gp5 Mode	Analyst	Imaginist	Analyst	Teamist
OVERALL MODE	IMAGINIST	ANALYST	ANALYST	IMAGINIST

Table 2 Comparative dominant and backup decision styles

Scenario Assessment

Quality of scenarios was assessed by independent academic judges with knowledge of the technique of scenario planning. Participant groups were asked to construct a 'best' case and a 'worst' case scenario. Ratings of these by the judges were averaged to provide inter-rater reliability. Each assessor was given briefing notes and asked to record comparative rankings from 1 to 5 (where 1 was *least* like the description and 5 was *most* like the description) for the 'best-case' scenarios and the 'worst-case' scenarios.

The five descriptors with which the assessors judged the best-case and worst-case scenarios against were developed to assess the level of creativity (unique insights and breadth of thought), plausibility (credible, soundly argued story) and consistency (analysis and synthesis). Appendix 3 shows the actual criteria against which the two scenarios for each group were assessed. Items 1 and 2 assessed creativity; item 3 assessed plausibility; and items 4 and 5 assessed consistency. As strategic thinking has been defined as the ability to think laterally and intuitively and to integrate and interpret a range of ideas, it was seen as essential to assess group creativity and innovativeness in constructing scenarios. The plausibility and consistency factors, demonstrating a clear understanding of interrelationships within and between stakeholder groups, trends and uncertainties, were also emphasised by Schoemaker for the scenario to be considered relevant and effective (1995: 30).

In collating the assessment results, the researchers considered all results greater than and equal to 3.5 (with a maximum score of 5) as above average.

Figure 4 sets out comparative 'best-case' average assessment scores for the five groups. Group 4 performed very well against the first two questions which assessed the scenarios for creativity (unique insights and breadth of thought), although Group 3 almost matched Group 4's creativity score for unique insights. All groups ranked fairly poorly against question 3 which assessed plausibility, with scores ranging between 2 and 3 points.

Questions 4 and 5 assessed the scenarios for consistency. Group 1 performed relatively well for question 4 (clear use of analysis), scoring 3.5 points while groups 2 to 5 only scored 1.5 points; and Groups 3 and 4 both scored over 4 for Question 5 (synthesis of ideas), with Group 1 on 3 points.

In summary, Group 4 performed best overall scoring 4+ for both dimensions of creativity (questions 1 and 2) and for one dimension of consistency (synthesis of ideas). However, none of the best-case scenarios scored highly on the plausibility criteria. This is because assessors disagreed on which was the most plausible relative to other scenarios. When inter-assessor reliability is low, this might mean none of the scenarios was clearly more plausible than the others.

As can be seen from comparison of Table 1 and Figures 4 and 5, there is no clear linkage between group average scores on the LTAT and assessed quality of their scenarios. On the face of it, the evidence does not support the proposition that brain styles influence strategic thinking capacity. However, strong effects of group dynamics were observed during the scenario planning process and these are discussed below.

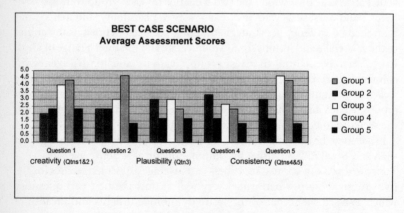

Figure 4

Best case scenario—Comparative average assessment scores

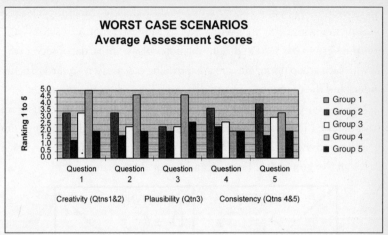

Figure 5
Worst case scenario—Comparative average assessment scores

Figure 5 sets out comparative 'worst-case' average assessment scores for the five groups. Group 4 performed well against each creativity question (unique insights and breadth of thought) and also on plausibility (Question 3). Group 1 scored just under 3.5 for both creativity questions and outperformed all other groups on both consistency criteria (clear use of analysis and synthesis of ideas). Assessor ratings for Group 1 on the two creativity criteria differed markedly. Two gave above average ratings, but these were 'neutralised' by poor ratings from the other assessor. The remaining three groups performed below average (under 3.5) on all criteria.

Impact of Group Dynamics
This section focuses on Groups 1 and 2.

It is important to note that the LTAT is an assessment of individual style while the scenario planning exercise, using the creativity, plausibility, consistency criteria, is an assessment of the group. Consequently, in the latter situation, group dynamics intervene between the creativity of the individual and the creativity of the group.

For this reason, we need to understand the profiles of individuals in a group in the context of how the group operates and, in particular, the profile of the dominant person or people in the group.

It is also necessary to differentiate between the dominant quadrant of the group (the mode) and the dominant quadrant of the dominant person or people in the group. For example, the most frequent dominant quadrant in a group might have been Imaginist, but if the dominant individual was Analyst, this might have intervened in any assessment of overall group creativity.

Therefore, before any conclusions could be drawn, the group scenario assessments were compared with the Decision Styles Survey scores on a group-by-group basis. In addition, the notes of the impartial observer who sat with each group during the scenario planning exercise were studied to better understand the group process and dynamics for each case.

Drawing on the impartial observers' notes, a decision styles diagram mapping the LTAT profiles *under pressure* for one or two dominant group members and the average score for the remaining group members was drawn up for all five groups (see Figure 6 and Figure 7 for examples).

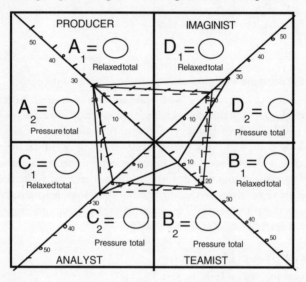

Figure 6 Group 1—Dominant and group average profiles under pressure

Legend: Dominant 1 ——————
        Dominant 2 ++++++++++
        Remaining Average - - - - - - - -

This enabled the study to consider whether there was an observable correlation between the dominant quadrant of a particular group member and the creativity of the group scenarios. For example, if the dominant group member's preferred quadrant under pressure was Imaginist, the scenarios might be expected to be assessed highly on creativity.

On the other hand, if the dominant quadrant in the group was Analyst, the scenarios might be expected to score more for consistency or plausibility as the Analyst behaviour would ensure that the story was at least 'sensible'.

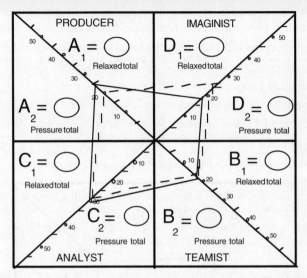

Figure 7 Group 2—Dominant and group average profiles under pressure

Legend: Dominant 1 —————
          Remaining Average - - - - - - - -

The profiles of each group were compared against the assessment of their performance in constructing the 'Worst Case' and 'Best Case' scenarios. While it is not possible to draw any definitive conclusions from such a small sample, the following observations were made in comparing the dominant profiles of Groups 1 and 2 with their results for the "Worst Case" scenario. (The 'Best Case' and 'Worst Case' scenarios prepared by Groups 1 and 2 are set out in Appendix 4.)

As noted previously in the section on scenario assessment results, Group 1 performed best overall in relation to all creativity and consistency criteria. It is suggested that these scores were at least partly a function of the intragroup dynamics, and the LTAT scores of the dominant members of the group.

Group 1 had five members, with two of these members dominating intragroup dynamics. Figure 6 shows the LTAT profiles under pressure of the two dominant members—called Dominant 1 and Dominant 2—and the average scores of the remaining three members.

Dominant member 1 (represented as 1A in Figure 2) scored equally highly on analyst and imaginist styles in the relaxed mode (28 for each), but under pressure his analyst score rose (to 33) and the imaginist score fell (to 26). Dominant member 2 (represented as 1D in Figure 2) scored extremely highly (35) on the imaginist scale in relaxed mode, with analyst as a distant backup (22). Under pressure, his preferred style remained imaginist (29) although the difference between this and his other scores reduced. It should also be noted that Dominant member 2 received a very low score (12) on the teamist style in relaxed mode, and this dropped even further (to 8) under pressure. Indeed, only one other person in the entire group of 25 participants received a lower teamist score under pressure (see Table 1).

The LTAT scores received by these two dominant group members was consistent with their behaviour in the group over the period of the scenario planning exercise.

Dominant Member 1 took the initial chairing role, dominating the discussion and the early decisions. For the first 30 minutes of the 1.5 hour exercise, Dominant Member 2 played very little part in the discussions except to remind the group that time was passing, and to make comments which the rest of the group seemed to regard as flippant, and which were ignored. Also during this early period, the other group members began to contribute ideas, although their suggestions were somewhat tentatively put to Dominant Member 1. In this period, one of the other group members made a suggestion which was ignored. Dominant Member 1 reiterated the idea a few minutes later, at which time it was accepted by the group.

At the end of the first 30 minutes, the group again took note of the time at the suggestion of Dominant Member 2. Part of the exercise was narrowed down at his suggestion, and he reminded the group that they could work through dinner (that is, take 2 hours for the exercise instead of 1.5 hours) if the extra time was required. At this time, Dominant Member 2 began to play a much more active role in discussion.

Dominant Member 1 began overriding the contributions of the other group members (with the exception of Dominant Member 2) with comments such as "That's what I was mentioning before" and "I've got a better idea". At 1 hour into the exercise, Dominant Member 1 assumed the position of notetaker from one of the other group members, whilst continuing in his role as chair. Subsequent discussion still included the other group members. Increasingly, though, Dominant Member 1, in his joint role as chair and notetaker, ignored their contributions in favour of the 'devil's advocate' advice being offered by Dominant Member 2. When Dominant Member 2 suggested, and the other group members agreed, that there was insufficient time remaining to work as a group to complete both scenarios, Dominant Member 2 further suggested that the group split into two, and complete one scenario each. The two dominant members formed one sub-group, with the three remaining members forming the second.

It was noted by the observer that as pressure on the group increased with the passage of time in the exercise, the two dominant members became more and more focused on 'getting the job done in a timely manner'; that is, they exhibited a retreat to analyst behaviour. This was ameliorated somewhat by the creative, or 'imaginist' suggestions made by Dominant Member 2. While these suggestions seemed to be regarded by other team members as 'out of left field' (hence the devil's advocate position), they were much more likely to be incorporated by Dominant Member 1 into the formal records of the exercise than the more apparently rational or factual ('producer') analyses presented by other group members. Further evidence of the domination of these two group members can be seen in the lack of teamist (i.e. feeling, sharing) behaviour in the group. Despite the fact that other group members scored quite highly on the teamist style under pressure (22, 23 and 24), as has been previously noted the teamist score for Dominant Member 2 was only 8, and for Dominant Member 1 it was 17.

In relation to performance on the scenarios, then, it is important to note that the worst case scenario for Group 1, while based on group analysis, was written only by the two dominant members of the group. This scenario scored well on consistency, reasonably well on creativity, but poorly on plausibility. The best case scenario, completed by the other three group members, scored equal first but not highly on plausibility, only average on consistency and poorly on creativity. However, in the other groups where the two scenarios were constructed by all group members, scores across best and worst case scenarios were more consistent; for example, Group 5 scored poorly on all three criteria for both scenarios; Group 4 scored most highly on creativity for both scenarios.

Group 2 performed very poorly on all aspects of creativity, plausibility and consistency in the worst-case scenario. The group profile (see Table 1) provides some clues for this poor performance. The one dominant group member (2J in Table 1) scored highly in the Analyst (lower left) quadrant and also in the Producer (upper left) quadrant, while the remaining group average fell equally between the Imaginist and Analyst quadrants.

Group 2 members themselves commented that too much time was spent in the 'analyst' quadrant so that the emphasis was on procedure, gathering facts and working through issues logically and systematically. They reported that the dominant group member also often overrode ideas. As a result, there was little opportunity or encouragement of new possibilities or unique insights.

In addition the strong anti-teamist stance (very low scores in the lower right 'Teamist' quadrant) characteristic of all members of Group 2 meant that there was little interest in overcoming interpersonal difficulties, or trying to 'cooperate, conciliate and persuade' to reach a satisfactory outcome.

It seems clear, then, that in the case of this sample of Communications Co. employees, group dynamics have acted as an intervening variable in effective strategic thinking. While Group 1 consisted of members who theoretically would be able to construct highly creative, consistent and plausible scenarios, in practice the way in which this group operated meant that not all of the skills and ideas of the group were properly tapped. Group 2 also had three members who were strong Imaginists (see Table 1), but their creative abilities were thwarted by the practical, problem-solving approach of Dominant Member 2J, the Analyst, who was focused on 'getting the job done' in an orderly, timely fashion rather than on exploring novel alternatives which might lead the group 'off the beaten track'.

Conclusion

In relation to the first research question, that is, whether dominant brain styles relate to a person's ability to think strategically, the answer is uncertain. The relaxed dominant profile across all groups is *Imaginist*. However, under pressure, the majority evacuated to the *Analyst* quadrant.

Evidence from participants, provided at the follow-up workshop, suggests that the traditional workplace culture at Communications Co. reflects an Analyst style. It was agreed that the prevailing mindset of the organisation is production driven with an emphasis on stability, detailed planning and review, efficiency, organisation, timeliness and following established procedures. This workplace culture is reinforced by the predominant engineering or production background of participants (18 of the 25). Although this is only a small sample of the Communications Co. workforce, these individuals were nominated by senior managers as potential future leaders of the company.

In relation to the second question, regarding the impact of group dynamics on strategic creativity, these preliminary findings seem to suggest a significant impact on the creativity, plausibility and consistency of scenario construction. The contrasting results for Groups 1 and 2 suggest that, when determining group composition, it is essential that Imaginist brain style behaviour, reflecting strategic creativity, not be overwhelmed by the more linear and concrete Analyst style if creative ideas are to be generated and come to fruition.

In addition the teamworking skills of the lower right quadrant (Teamist) may be critical in engendering cooperation between group members and in ensuring every voice is heard and respected. The logical, analytical skills of the upper left quadrant (Producer) may also help in ensuring ideas 'make sense' and can be realised.

The prevailing view amongst participants, ascertained at the follow-up session, is that little organisational recognition or encouragement is given to those with new ideas. This may help to explain why, when under pressure, dominant styles shifted. An Imaginist style may not be sustainable under pressure if it is not recognised or supported in the pressure work environment.

From participants' viewpoint, rewards in the organisation come for 'producing a report' and being results-oriented; the emphasis in the company was still on the short-term, here and now, problem-solving approach. One individual commented that, despite this new international push in Communications Co. for increased creativity, the company Appraisal Form was still results-oriented rather than concerned with developing individual creativity.

These findings indicate that the fostering of strategic creativity requires attention to situational factors as well as to appropriate encouragement of individual creativity; it may be dysfunctional for the organisation to consider one without the other. Further research, in a more extensive and controlled study, should be undertaken on how the two may be balanced to optimal effect on strategic creativity.

References

Agor, W. H. 1988. 'The logic of intuition: how top executives make important decisions'. In J. Henry (ed.). *Creative Management*. London: Sage Publications: 163-176.

Amabile, T. M., Conti, R. Coon, H., Lazenby, J., & Herron, M. 1996 'Assessing the Work Environment for Creativity'. *The Academy of Management*, 39(5): 1154-1184.

Bahrami, H. 1992. 'The Emerging Flexible Organisation: Perspectives from Silicon Valley'. *California Management Review*, 34(4), 33-52.

Burnside, R. M., Amabile, T. M., & Gryskiewicz, S. S. 1988. 'Assessing Organisational Climates for Creativity and Innovation: Methodological Review of Large Company Audits'. In Y. Ijiri and R. L. Kuhn (eds.). *New Directions in Creative and Innovative Management*, Massachusetts: Ballinger Publishing Company: 169-185.

Collins, J. C. & Porras, J. I. 1995 'Building a Visionary Company'. *California Management Review*, 37(2), Winter: 80-100.

Davies, J. E. 1984. *The Interpretation Manual of the Life-Time Assessment Test*. San Francisco: Identity Dimensions Inc.

Dunette, M. D. 1966. *Handbook of Industrial and Organisational Psychology*. New York: Wiley.

Dunphy, D. & Stace, D. 1993. *Under New Management: Australian Organisations in Transition*. Sydney: McGraw-Hill Book Company.

Eisenhardt, K. M. 1990. 'Speed and Strategic Choice: How Managers Accelerate Decision Making'. *California Management Review*, Spring 39-54.

Hamel, G. & Prahalad, C. K. 1994. *Competing for the Future*. Boston: Harvard Business School Press.

Herrmann, N. 1996. *The Whole Brain Business Book*. New York: McGraw-Hill.

Herrmann, N. 1989. *The Creative Brain*. Lake Lure, N.C.: Brain Books.

Hurst, D. K., Rush, J. C., & White, R. E. 1988. 'Top Management Teams and Organisational Renewal'. In J. Henry (ed.). *Creative Management*. London: Sage Publications: 232-253.

Kanter, R. M., Stein, B. A., & Jick, T. D. 1992. *The Challenge of Organisational Change*. New York: The Free Press.

Leonard, D. & Straus, S. 1997 'Putting Your Company's Whole Brain to Work'. *Harvard Business Review,* July-August, 111-121.

Limerick, D. & Cunnington, B. 1993. *Managing The New Organisation.* Sydney: Business & Professional Publishing.

McAdam, N. 1996. *Brain Styles and Strategic Management.* in press.

McAdam, N. 1994. 'On the Balance between Preserving and Creating: Brain Styles and Change: A Cross Cultural Reflection'. Paper presented at seminar of Organisational Models-Cultural Reflections, City University Business School, London.

McLean, P. D. 1981. 'The triune brain and the epistemics of the knowledge process'. Paper presented at 101st annual meeting of the American Association for the Advancement of Science, Toronto, Canada.

Maruca, R. F. 1994. 'The Right Way to Go Global: An Interview with Whirlpool CEO David Whitwam'. *Harvard Business Review,* March-April, 135-145.

Mintzberg, H. 1976. *Planning on the Left Side and Managing on the Right.* Englewood Cliffs, N. J.: Prentice Hall.

Orstein, R. 1973. *Psychology of Consciousness.* New York: W. H. Freeman and Co.

Peters, T. 1988. 'Facing Up to the Need for a Management Revolution'. *California Management Review,* Winter, 30(2), 7-37.

Peters, T. J. & Waterman Jr., R. H. 1982. *In Search of Excellence.* New York: Harper and Row.

Schoemaker, Paul J. H. 1991. 'When and How to Use Scenario Planning: A Heuristic Approach with Illustration'. *Journal of Forecasting* 10, 549-564.

Schoemaker, Paul J. H. 1992. 'Multiple Scenario Development: Its Conceptual and Behavioural Foundation'. *Strategic Management Journal* 14, 193-213.

Schoemaker, Paul J. H. 1995. 'Scenario Planning: A Tool for Strategic Thinking'. *Sloan Management Review,* Winter, 25-39.

Tichy, N. M. & Devanna, M. A. 1990. *The Transformational Leader.* New York: John Wiley & Sons.

Appendix 1
Scenario Planning
Your Role

You are the Chief Executive Officer of the Sydney Organising Committee for the Olympic Games (SOCOG). Your job is to plan for a successful Olympics in the year 2000.

Task[1]

We have *defined the issues* (task one in the Schoemaker scenario construction model) for you. You are asked to complete tasks 2 to 5. You should not feel limited by the issues we have identified in step 1. You may think of others which are equally important. These are just to help stimulate thought within each group.

1. *Define the Issues:* Your key concerns are with the Games budget (no blow-out); transport for the public and athletes to and from the Games; security for the public, media and athletes; and communications.

2. *Stakeholders:* Identify the major stakeholders who would have an interest in these issues, both those who may be affected by the Games and the pre-Games activities and those who could influence matters appreciably. Identify their current roles, interests and power positions.

3. *Trends:* Identify current trends and predetermined elements that will affect the issues of interest to you. A trend is something which is *likely to happen* "as perceived by industry experts, managers and knowledgeable outsiders". Justify trends (everyone must agree) and explain the impact of each on issues under consideration (positive, negative, uncertain).

4. *Uncertainties:* Identify key uncertainties—what events, whose outcomes are uncertain, will significantly affect the issues you are concerned with? Briefly explain why these uncertainties matter. Determine possible outcomes (just a few). Examine how they interrelate.

5. *Construct two forced scenarios:* Using steps 2 to 5, construct a 'worst-case' and a 'best-case' scenario. To do this:
   - put all positive outcomes of key uncertainties together and all negative outcomes together
   - check each scenario for internal consistency
   - add *consistent* trends and stakeholder analysis
   - write the two scenarios as a short story.

Preparing for the Sydney Olympics[2]

The Sydney Organising Committee for the Olympic Games (SOCOG) is the body responsible for staging the Games of the XXVII Olympiad in 2000. SOCOG is managed and controlled by a Board of Directors (15 in total) who are appointed by the Governor of NSW on the recommendation of the Premier and in consultation with John Coates, Executive President of the Australian Olympic Committee (AOC), and the Prime Minister..

In early September 1996, the NSW Minister for Sport, Michael Knight, assumed the role of President of SOCOG. He succeeded Mr John Iliffe, a prominent Sydney businessman, who stepped down after only six months in the position.

Note: 1. Task material is sourced from Paul J.H. Schoemaker (1991) "When and How to Use Scenario Planning: A Heuristic Approach with Illustration", *Journal of Forecasting,* 10: 549-564.
Note: 2. Material for this scenario was compiled from SOCOG Fact Sheets available on the Internet and from published journal articles.

Iliffe succeeded Gary Pemberton, the founding President,in March 1996. Mal Hemmerling took over the role of Chief Executive of SOCOG in September 1995. Both John Iliffe and Mal Hemmerling are members of the Board of Directors.

Economic Impact

An Economic Impact Statement prepared by KPMG Peat Marwick concluded that the net addition to Australia's GDP during the period 1994–2004 would be:

- Australia—A$7.336 billion
- NSW—A$4.587 billion
- Sydney—A$3.560 billion

Contributing factors included:

- Construction of facilities—33 different projects
- Cost of staging Games—A$1.7 billion
- Total tourism revenue—A$3.5 billion (1.5 million people expected to visit Sydney)
- Creation of 150,000 full and part-time jobs
- Anticipated increases in government tax revenue
  Federal—A$1.934 billion
  NSW—A$0.376 billion
  Local—A$0.073 billion

Games Budget

See Tables 1 and 2 for a summary of the Games Budget as presented to the IOC as part of Sydney's Olympic Bid in 1992.

Table 1 Revenue budget

Revenue	US$M 1992	US$M Nominal[†]	A$M* Nominal[†]
PROJECTED TOTAL REVENUE	975	1,312	1,873
Examples:			
Television Rights Fees	488	664	948
TOP Sponsorship	90	117	167
Local Sponsorship	207	276	394
Tickets	139	187	267

Table 2 Expenditure budget

Expenditure	US$M 1992	US$M Nominal†	A$M* Nominal†
PROJECTED TOTAL EXPENDITURE	960	1,292	1,847
Examples:			
Events, Ceremonies and Programs	301	413	590
Construction Reimbursements	127	156	223
Media	187	255	364
Transport	46	64	92
Security	30	41	59

Notes: * @US$0.78 = A$1.00. † Nominal figures are based on timing and escalation rate assumptions applied during the Games Budget preparation

The Atlanta Olympics

The following information provides you with a snapshot of some of the issues which organisers had to deal with at the Atlanta Olympics. The purpose of this information is to give you ideas to stimulate your thinking on issues you must consider as CEO of SOCOG.

> *Memories of Munich*
> "When I heard last night, I thought after 24 years, nothing has changed. Today, in the 20th century, the new reality in world sporting events like the Olympic and the World Cup is that they go hand in hand with terrorist acts."

> *Lessons for Sydney*
> Security plans for the Sydney Olympics will be reviewed following the bomb blast at Atlanta's Centennial Park. The review will cover the security of venues; whether Homebush Bay and Darling Harbor should have perimeter security; and problems for areas such as The Rocks which could be expected to attract large numbers of visitors during the Games.

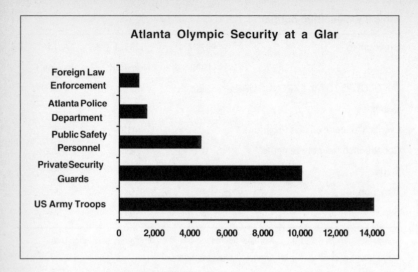

Atlanta Olympic Security at a Glar

Foreign Law Enforcement	
Atlanta Police Department	
Public Safety Personnel	
Private Security Guards	
US Army Troops	

0 2,000 4,000 6,000 8,000 10,000 12,000 14,000

Not awl right on the night

A packed, chaotic and sometimes non-existent transport system and glitches in a much-vaunted information system that left IBM looking more like Big Blues than Big Blue led to damning reports in international papers. "Shambles at the Olympics", screamed England's Daily Express.

France-Soir noted that African nations had never hosted a Games because of the "pretext that African countries don't have the necessary infrastructure. After Atlanta, any country in the world can apply to host the Games."

Atlantic Olympic Chaos Grows

Australia's men's basketball team had to wait just under three hours for transport back from a training session.

An Australian judo heavyweight who badly injured his back in a bout spent an hour waiting for a ride to hospital. The first ambulance to arrive had a dud battery and wouldn't start again.

A group of British, Polish and Ukrainian rowers waited and waited for a bus to take them 100 kms to the Lake Lanier venue. A bus for the field hockey venue arrived. The rowers clambered aboard and ordered the driver to go to Gainsville, and to ignore police trying to stop it.

Big Blues

Atlanta's much-hyped high-tech system, Info'96, had a rough first week. A joint project of ACOG and IBM, the touch-screen computer terminals were meant to be the latest in information services.

But the system was slower out of the blocks than a weightlifter attempting a sprint. Competitors' biographies simply went missing or the information provided was decidedly eccentric. Two athletes were listed as being aged in their 90s and a boxer was described as two feet tall. Broadcasters muttered about wanting their money back.

For IBM, the final indignity came when the IOC insisted on a back-up system being installed at the main stadium to ensure a consistent flow of information during the athletics.

Scapegoats

Among the many victims of Games chaos were bus-drivers, most of whom are people trying to do their bit to make the Olympics happen. They have been given a motley range of buses and insufficient training in how to get to the various venues (though they still tend to be better informed than local taxi drivers.)

Saddest case was the driver in charge of a media bus heading out to the rowing. She had a panic-attack on reaching one of Georgia's freeways and had to turn back. With passengers.

Note: Photographs were included to illustrate these vignettes.

Appendix 2
Scenario Planning Process

Each group nominated a chairperson, a timekeeper and a notetaker. The notetaker had to record all key ideas and decisions for each step. Proforma sheets were provided to all groups as one method of record keeping, or they could use the butcher's paper also provided. The notes compiled by each group were submitted to the Deakin University researchers for independent assessment at the end of the workshop session.

Issues

While participants in scenario construction would normally have to define the issues for themselves, it was decided, because of time constraints, to give participants four issues to consider (budget, transport, security and communications), with a timeframe to the year 2000. They were allowed to consider all four issues, focus on some, or introduce new ones. However, they were required to designate which issues they chose to consider.

Stakeholders

Participants were asked to identify the major stakeholders who would have an interest in the issues they had selected, both those who may be affected by the Sydney Olympic Games and the pre-Games activities and those who could influence matters appreciably. They had to identify the stakeholders' current roles, interests, power positions, and consider interrelationships between the different.

Trends

Participants were asked to identify current trends and predetermined elements that would affect the issues of interest to them. A trend was defined as something that was *likely to happen* "as perceived by industry experts, managers and knowledgeable outsiders" (Schoemaker, 1995).

Uncertainties

Participants were asked to identify key uncertainties, i.e. what events, the outcomes of which were uncertain, would significantly affect the chosen issues. They also needed to determine possible outcomes of each uncertainty, e.g. one positive and one negative outcome; and to examine how they might interrelate.

Scenarios

Using the ideas they had set down for the previous three steps, participants were asked to construct a 'worst-case' and a 'best-case' scenario. To do this, it was suggested participants:

1. put all positive outcomes of key uncertainties together and all negative outcomes together;
2. check each scenario for internal consistency (e.g. couldn't have low inflation, low unemployment and low interest happening simultaneously);
3. add consistent trends and stakeholder analysis to build the best-case/worst-case pictures; and
4. write up the two scenarios as a short story, a narrative—not a list.

Appendix 3
Criteria for Scenario Planing Assessment

ASSESSMENT SHEET

ASSESSOR'S NAME: _____

DESCRIPTION	'BEST-CASE' SCENARIO					'WORST-CASE' SCENARIO				
	Use ONLY Ranks 1 to 5 where 1 is *least* like the description, and 5 is *most* like the description									
	Gp1	Gp2	Gp3	Gp4	Gp5	Gp1	Gp2	Gp3	Gp4	Gp5
1. Unique insights? (original, exciting)										
2. Breadth of thought? (number of ideas)										
3. Story justified? (credible, soundly argued)										
4. Clear use of analysis? (story clearly drawn from selected issues, and stakeholders, trends, and uncertainties identified earlier)										
5. Synthesis of ideas? (story identifies links within and between steps; demonstrates a clear understanding of interrelationships within and between stakeholder groups, trends and uncertainties)										

Appendix 4
Best Case and Worst Case Scenarios, Groups 1 and 2

Best-case scenario: Group 1

Olympics in year 2000 will be running on budget with all projects completed on time. It is expected that interest rates will go down due to favourable economic conditions.

We anticipate a stable political environment with Pauline Hanson to resign and open the market for more experiences to come and she will manage her own Chinese take-away chain. We plan that she will cater for the Olympics team and hence increasing business revenue.

We expect all industrial reforms to have been passed and favourable accepted by all parties concerned resulting in successful completion ahead of project deadlines and in favourable budget expenditure levels.

Deregulation of telecommunications industry will produce an extremely competitive environment which will reduce usage cost and provide world best practice services to all local and international users.

We expect to have a very high level of safety during all Olympic activities which should increase interest in tourism in Australia.

We expect that Australia will host the best Olympics games and that it will win the bid for year 2004.

Worst Case Scenario: Group 1

"It ain't half hot!"

Industrial unrest is rampant, the Government's industrial relations package was not well received causing much strike action, many delays to project deadlines and stretching budgeted expenditure.

Pauline Hanson continues to push strong anti Asian views in federal politics causing unrest in local communities, and drawing adverse attention from regional neighbours. AKK Asian countries have boycotted the Olympics, and Asian companies have withdrawn investment in Australia. This has forced interest rates to rise which has increased the cost of our borrowings outside of original budget estimates, causing a shortage of funds for project completions.

Major Asian telecommunications giants refuse to do business with Australia resulting in substandard, high cost equipment which fails to meet stated needs and impacts on the quality of games management and efficiency.

The unrest in local Asian communities turns to violence resulting in the need for higher levels of security related expenditure. Asian tourism is non existent causing a further loss of budgeted revenue.

World opinion is that Australia has completely stuffed up and all confidence in our ability has been lost Investment drops away…

Best Case Scenario: Group 2

We will have stable political environment.

The IT and communication technology will be advanced and stable enabling a wider coverage of the Games.

Improved world economy will result in high disposable incomes and increased tourism.

Organisers, participants and spectators cooperate in a positive manner, resulting in the most successful Games ever.

Worst Case Scenario: Group 2

There are disagreements within the Olympic Committee, resulting in traffic chaos, incomplete infrastructure due to labour disputes.

Terrorist activities result in boycotts from large number of countries, resulting in financial disaster and irreparable damage to the Australian image.

Moving to a new era in international strategic management: Identifying export success factors of Australian entrepreneurial record companies

Alexander J.
Alexopoulos and
Max Coulthard

Abstract

This exploratory research utilised the Lumpkin and Dess (1996) Entrepreneurial Orientation (EO) construct as a means of characterising the extent to which Australian firms are entrepreneurial. The five dimensions (innovativeness, proactiveness, competitive aggressiveness, risk taking, and autonomy) were used to develop an entrepreneurship profile of 20 Victorian-based record companies. The study found those record companies who had an 'entrepreneurial orientation' were higher export performers than conservative-orientated companies. Various 'best practice' firms were identified and a profile of key export success factors developed. Overall, this study provides a sound starting point for business practitioners exploring strategic opportunities overseas.

Introduction

According to Covin & Slevin (1991), entrepreneurship is essential to improving firm-level performance, as it leads to greater understanding of organisational forces that impact on business success. This study explored entrepreneurship and its relevance to the export performance of the Victorian Sound Recording Industry (VSRI).

Entrepreneurship in Strategic Management

Entrepreneurship has been cited as a vital element for a nation's economic and social prosperity (Morris & Lewis, 1991). Numerous authors have attempted to link entrepreneurship with other disciplines. The most common has been with strategic management, where 'entrepreneurship choice is at the heart of the concept of strategy' (Schendel & Hofer, 1979: 6). According to the Industry Task Force (1995), entrepreneurship is a critical characteristic of good and effective strategic management, hence 'Entrepreneurship should not be thought of as absent or present in organisations...[it should be viewed] as a strategic dimension on which all firms can be plotted' (Covin & Slevin, 1991: 20).

The Sound Recording Industry

Successful entrepreneurship has been linked to business environments characterised as highly turbulent (Covin & Slevin, 1989). The Australian Sound Recording Industry[1] is an emerging export industry competing in a turbulent international environment dominated by multinational companies (PSA Report, 1990).

Even though substantial opportunities have been identified for export markets, in particular Asia (LEK Report, 1994), the sound recording industry has historically suffered from a trade deficit (PSA Report, 1990). To overcome this imbalance, research on export strategies to enhance and effectively capitalise on Australia's pool of musical talent appears timely.

Research Aims

- To determine the extent that Victorian record companies are entrepreneurial.
- To determine the impact entrepreneurship has on Victorian record companies' export performance.
- To develop a profile of key export success factors from 'best practice' record companies.

Literature Review

There is no recognised definition of 'entrepreneurship' (Brockhaus, 1993). A common definition of entrepreneurship is 'people following up on opportunities for creating new wealth' (Stewart, 1989: 11). The problem with this popularised definition is that it focuses on the 'entrepreneur'. The more current entrepreneurship paradigm is that 'any attempt to profile the typical entrepreneur is inherently futile' (Low & MacMillan, 1988: 20). Entrepreneurship has also been vaguely defined as the *creation of new business enterprises* (Low & MacMillan, 1988). However, according to Covin and Slevin (1991), entrepreneurship research does not restrict itself in a conceptual sense to the new venture creation process.

Recently, 'the focus of entrepreneurship research has progressed to become more contextual and process-orientated' (Low & MacMillan, 1988: 22). A major development in the literature has been to focus on entrepreneurial

---

1. The industry's total output is estimated at $1.4 billion, and employment at over 50,000 people for 1992 (LEK Report, 1994). Australian consumers of sound recordings rank as the eleventh largest in the world in 1992, and in 1993, Australia was ranked as ninth, contributing a 1.8% share of the world market (Baskerville, 1995).

processes at the firm-level (Miller, 1983). 'Entrepreneurial organisations...are those in which particular behavioural patterns are recurring. These patterns pervade the organisation at all levels and reflect the top manager's overall strategic philosophy on effective management practice' (Covin & Slevin, 1991: 7). Covin & Slevin (1993) refer to these firms as having an 'entrepreneurial posture' and which views entrepreneurship as a strong commitment to three key elements: *risk-taking, innovative and proactive* practices. Lumpkin & Dess (1996) build on these three predominant characteristics by adding two more, namely *autonomy* and *competitive aggressiveness* to develop their entrepreneurial orientation (EO) construct.

This study utilises the EO construct as a means of characterising the extent to which Victorian record companies are entrepreneurial. Findings from various studies indicate that exporting firms can be differentiated in terms of their entrepreneurial orientation, and, there is strong support for the applicability of the entrepreneurship construct to the exporting context (Yeoh & Jeong, 1995). However, no explicit research has been undertaken to incorporate the EO construct postulated by Lumpkin & Dess (1996) with export performance.

Methodology

Research Design

Hofer & Bygrave (1992) strongly encourage the use of qualitative analysis techniques in entrepreneurship research. Hence, this study design invited an in-depth, qualitative, investigation at an organisation's processes, and contexts in which entrepreneurship occurs (Savage & Black, 1995).

Hofer & Bygrave (1992) present nine typical 'archetypes' of research designs. Those that are pertinent to this study are:

- *Study of Representative Exemplars:* Primarily used to identify basic issues, processes, characteristics of the phenomena under investigation.
- *Study of Best Exemplars:* Used to identify the characteristics of best practice.

Case Study Method

A case study is particularly useful for exploring new processes or behaviours that are hard to define (Hartley, 1994). Herriott & Firestone (1983) argue that, the evidence from *multiple cases* is often considered more compelling, and the overall study is therefore regarded as being more robust (cited in Yin, 1994). This research study therefore, involved developing multiple-case studies, 'profiling' the entrepreneurial orientation and exporting performance of Victorian record companies.

Research Process

Survey data was collected through in-depth, face-to-face and telephone interviews. Interviews are particularly useful in the music industry which suffers from, being 'over surveyed' (LEK Report, 1994: 68) and like other small businesses, poor response rates (Bailey, 1985).

To minimise the inherent limitations of telephone interviews, the data was recorded using both note-taking and tape recorder. All interviews followed a semi-structured format based on a questionnaire schedule. Standardised questions were used to elicit comparable data. This is considered necessary in multiple-case studies or when many participants are interviewed (Marshall & Rossman, 1995).

There was an open-ended sequence of questions and a focused set of questions designed to elicit specific responses. As a result, the theory developed was grounded in the experiences and terminology of the study's participants.

The questionnaire had two sections. One section involved questions about demographic details. These questions, for example include the respondent's position in the business venture and questions about the organisation's performance and growth. This section of the schedule was consistent with that postulated by Katz *et al.* (1993).

The second section of the schedule focused on the dimensions of the firm's entrepreneurial orientation (EO). A separate question was allocated to each of the five dimensions. In order to assure realism, scenario type questions were developed (Fredrickson, 1986). Scenario or 'vignette' type questions provided a standardised stimulus to generate the respondent's interest and 'involvement' (Fredrickson, 1986: 481). Vignettes tend to elicit a higher quality of data from respondents than is possible from simple questions (Alexander & Becker, 1978). The content of each question employed industry-specific terminology as recommended by Fredrickson (1986).

The draft questionnaire was modified based on suggestions from prominent individuals in the VSRI. In addition, feedback from various academics was sought and a pilot study of four, randomly selected companies, conducted. Their advice was factored into the final questionnaire.

The Sample

The scope of this study focuses on all 'Victorian-based' record companies. The July 1996 *Australasian Music Industry Directory* identified 30 Victorian-based record companies from a total 163 Australia-wide. From the 30 firms listed in the directory, 27 served as the study's sample frame. Of the other three, one record company had ceased to exist and two record companies had moved into other music related businesses (i.e. publishing).

From the sample frame of 27, twenty firms were used in the analysis of data. The reasons seven companies were not analysed; four record companies were excluded as used to pilot-test the interview schedule; two were identified as non-exporting firms and one firm was unwilling to participate in the study.

The person undertaking the Artist and Repertoire (A&R) Manager function was interviewed because this was identified as the entrepreneurial function of the sound recording industry (Peterson & Berger, 1971).

Data Analysis

The data analysis process for the three research aims is depicted in the following flow chart.

Table 1 The study's data analysis process

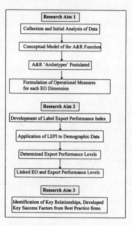

The *first research aim*, determined the extent that Victorian record companies were entrepreneurial. An initial analysis was performed on each case study to determine key themes that had emerged. As a result, a conceptual model of the A&R function was postulated. The aim of the conceptual framework was to help relate theory with the data and vice versa (Hartley, 1994). Essentially, the A&R role was seen as the strategic interface between the business and the artist.

The exploratory nature of the study gave rise to various 'archetypes' of the A&R role. The term archetype, refers to a series of different, though typical decision making processes associated with the A&R function (Miller & Friesen, 1978). Developing categories in which to place these underlying patterns of behaviour is suggested by Yin (1994). Hence, the VSRI behaviour patterns were systematically placed into the context of the previously postulated A&R framework. In turn, these A&R archetypes were utilised to operationalise the EO construct relevant to the VSRI. The A&R archetypes were translated into typologies and served as measuring standards for each EO dimension (Ragin, 1987). As suggested by Woo, et al. (1991) the A&R related typologies were derived from the data and from music industry literature. The EO levels for each dimension were determined, and an overall level of entrepreneurship was identified for each case.

The *second research aim,* examined the impact entrepreneurship had on the export performance of Victorian record companies. For the second research aim to be completed, an export performance indicator was used. The Label Export Performance Index (LEPI) incorporated both factual and subjective data (Cavusgil & Zou, 1994). It utilised common measures from the export performance literature (Moini, 1995) and was structured similar to that of Bailey (1985). The LEPI incorporates the following five variables:

• Age of firm
• Size of firm
• Percentage of Australian artists exported relative to the number of Australian artists 'signed' to the firm
• Percentage of export sales to overall sales for the previous financial year, and
• Perception of export growth in the last five years (or since inception).

The next step was to overlay the entrepreneurial orientation data with the export performance data so that direct comparisons and conclusions could be drawn for each case.

The *third research aim* was to develop a profile of key export success factors from 'best practice' firms. Those companies identified as high export performers and exhibited a high level of entrepreneurship were examined. The knowledge gained from these companies of their processes underlying the behaviour and its context can help to specify the conditions under which high export performance can be expected to occur (Hartley, 1994). From this in-depth analysis, certain key themes and organisational practices were derived which may serve as success factors for exporting firms within the music industry.

Results
Demographic Data
The following profile of the survey participants was established:

• Ninety five percent of the respondents were Australian owned and small to medium sized firms.
• The average number of years worked in the sound recording industry was 13.5 years. In addition, informants averaged 6.5 years with their current employer.
• Those interviewed consisted of seven specialist A&R managers, whilst the remaining where either label managers (4), owners (5), or, directors (4) of the company.

- The average number of employees within the twenty companies was 13 people, and the average age of the surveyed firms was 10 years in operation.
- The average number of total artists 'signed' to a record company was 25. The average number of artists who are Australian was 21. Furthermore, on average, 16 of those 21 Australian artists were being exported.
- The major forms of exporting identified were licensing agreements, and distribution deals with foreign intermediaries. The respondents who identified exporting physical product as their primary export strategy, were all found to be record companies who manufacture in Australia.
- On average, the percentage of sales attributed to exports was 22% (however, some were calculated guesses).

Research Aim One: To determine the extent that Victorian record companies are entrepreneurial.

A tentative framework was proposed depicting the A&R role within its two major interfaces, the artistic and business interface, as seen in Table 2.

Table 2 A conceptual model of the A & R function

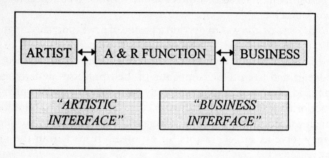

The entrepreneurial orientation construct utilised a contingency framework in order to fit the three key variables of strategy (strategic), structure (internal) and environment (external) (Covin & Slevin, 1991). The artistic and business interfaces were analysed using these three key constructs. This allowed the A&R role of the music industry's entrepreneurial function to be more accurately categorised.

The next step of the data analysis process was to determine what were the specific A&R 'archetypes'. The underlying patterns and themes discovered during the initial data analysis were adapted to each of the three constructs of the firm-level model. Tables 3.1 and 3.2 show for each interface, the nature of these A&R function archetypes.

The critical behavioural forces of the A&R function were put into context of the firm-level constructs. The next step was to apply these categorisations to each of the five EO dimensions. This process involved revisiting relevant theory illustrated in Lumpkin & Dess (1996). Tables 4.1 to 4.5 depict which archetypes relate more to each dimension. All archetypes can be applied for each dimension, however, only those more pertinent were selected as operational measures for the EO construct.

The level of each EO dimension for every firm was determined. This process was achieved by revisiting the data and applying the relevant archetypes as a standard qualitative measure to each case. Each firm's entrepreneurial level was subjectively deciphered by utilising a High-Moderate-Low scale. Table 5 summarises for every case, their level for each dimension.

The next step of the analysis was to determine the overall EO for each case. This stage required more than just a simple addition of each dimension, hence an additional procedure was used. According to Lumpkin & Dess, (1996) the extent each EO dimension is useful for predicting the nature and success of a company is contingent on the industry context. Therefore a unique combination that characterised the music industry was developed and used as a measuring standard to determine the overall EO level. Table 6 shows the Low-Moderate-High frequencies for each element. The EO dimensions collectively, formed a combination pertinent for the music industry (Gartner, 1985, cited in Lumpkin & Dess, 1996). The proactiveness, risk taking and autonomy dimensions show that a moderate level is the most widely practiced. The dimension of innovativeness shows that low and moderate levels are common.

Table 3.1 Artistic interface archetypes

STRATEGY	STRUCTURE	ENVIRONMENT
• *Input into Artistic Process*	• *Resource Commitments*	• *Accessibility of Artist*
Artistic Freedom vs. Label Control	(Long-term vs. Short-term orientation:)	(Market potential of Artist)
• *Artist Sourcing*	'Develop' Artist vs. 'Consolidate' Artist	Highly Unique vs. Mildly Unique
Eclectic (diverse) vs. Defined Genre	'New' 'Established Artist' Artist vs.	Artistic 'Purity' vs. 'Market' Appeal

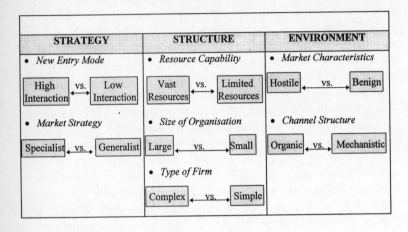

Table 4.1 Autonomy dimension archetype

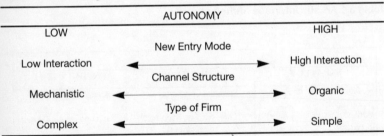

Table 4.2 Innovativeness dimension archetypes

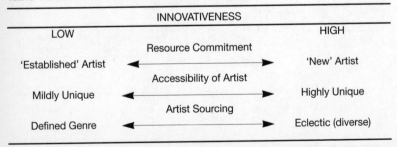

Table 4.3 Risk taking dimension archetypes

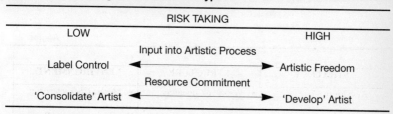

Table 4.4 Proactiveness dimension archetypes

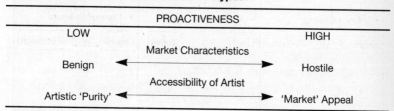

Table 4.5 Competitive aggressiveness dimension archetypes

Table 5 The EO dimensions for each case

| Record Company | THE ENTREPRENEURIAL ORIENTATION DIMENSIONS | | | | |
	Autonomy	Innovative	Risk Taking	Proactive	Competitive Aggressive
label 1	low	low	moderate	moderate	low
label 2	high	low	moderate	moderate	low
label 3	moderate	moderate	low	moderate	low
label 4	high	high	moderate	moderate	low
label 5	low	low	low	moderate	low
label 6	moderate	high	moderate	low	low
label 7	low	low	moderate	moderate	low
label 8	high	moderate	high	moderate	low
label 9	high	moderate	moderate	moderate	low
label 10	moderate	moderate	moderate	moderate	moderate
label 11	moderate	high	moderate	high	low
label 12	moderate	high	moderate	moderate	low
label 13	high	moderate	moderate	moderate	low
label 14	high	moderate	moderate	high	low
label 15	low	low	high	low	low
label 16	moderate	low	moderate	low	low
label 17	low	low	moderate	low	moderate
label 18	moderate	moderate	high	moderate	low
label 19	moderate	moderate	low	low	low
label 20	moderate	low	low	low	low

Table 6 Relevance of each 'level' type

| | FREQUENCY FOR EACH 'LEVEL' TYPE | | | | |
	Autonomy	Innovative	Taking Risk	Proactive	Competitive Aggressive
LOW	5	8	4	6	18
MOD	9	8	13	12	2
HIGH	6	4	3	2	0
Common Industry Type	Moderate	Low/Moderate	Moderate	Moderate	Low

The competitive aggressive dimension shows that nearly all firms practice a low level of competitive and responsive behaviour against other Australian firms in international markets. Lumpkin & Dess (1996) stipulate that various dimensions may not be useful or relevant in certain contexts. To avoid elevating most firms into a higher overall EO level the competitive aggressiveness dimension was excluded from determining the overall EO level.

The final step that determined the extent to which record companies were entrepreneurial, was to compare each case's type levels to those of the industry's standard type levels. To complete this task, the components for each dimension were weighted based on a value rating of the common industry type (refer Table 6) for the music industry. Table 7 depicts the results for each case's EO level.

Table 7 The entrepreneurial orientation

Record Company	Entrepreneurial Orientation
label 1	moderate
label 2	moderate
label 3	high
label 4	high
label 5	low
label 6	moderate
label 7	moderate
label 8	moderate
label 9	high
label 10	high
label 11	moderate
label 12	high
label 13	high
label 14	high
label 15	low
label 16	moderate
label 17	low
label 18	high
label 19	moderate
label 20	low

Research Aim Two: To determine the impact entrepreneurship has on Victorian record companies' export performance.

The next step was to utilise the Label Export Performance Index (LEPI) to determine each firm's export performance level. Each of the five variable scores were added together and translated into a qualitative measure of Low-Moderate-High. The final stage was to overlay the results from research aim one and the corresponding export performance level for each firm. The results are shown in Table 8.

The comparison of the EO and export performance constructs revealed two important findings. Firstly, there is a relatively strong relationship between those firms identified with a high level of entrepreneurship and a high export performance. Secondly, those firms identified as high export performers, nearly all exhibited a high level of entrepreneurship. *Label 17* was identified as a high export performer, however, the LEPI is biased towards large and well established companies (Bailey, 1985). As a result, the study focused on cases which were high export performers, and exhibited a high level of entrepreneurship.

Table 8 The label's EO and export performance

Record Company	Entrepreneurial Orientation	Export Performance
label 1	moderate	moderate
label 2	moderate	low
label 3	high	moderate
label 4	high	high
label 5	low	low
label 6	moderate	moderate
label 7	moderate	low
label 8	moderate	moderate
label 9	high	moderate
label 10	high	high
label 11	moderate	low
label 12	high	high
label 13	high	moderate
label 14	high	high
label 15	low	low
label 16	moderate	low
label 17	low	high
label 18	high	moderate
label 19	moderate	moderate
label 20	low	moderate

Research Aim Three: To develop a profile of key export success factors from 'best practice' record companies.

Four cases were identified as 'best practice' firms within the data set. These were identified by soliciting opinions from respondents as to what constituted best practice and who were considered its best proponents, then matching these responses to the results from the EO and LEPI constructs. The key proponents were found to have above industry average EO and export results.

A critical evaluation of the four firms, revealed a common set of organisational behaviours conducive to high export performance. These recurring themes were identified in two small sized firms, as well as two medium sized companies. The export success factors described below may apply for all size type companies, and can be adapted to each company's context. It is important to note these factors are relative to the study's sample, however some generalisation to the whole sound recording industry, may be possible. It is recognised that this profile is not exhaustive or definitive for the music industry, but it does help gain an insight into successful entrepreneurial practices which lead to high export performance.

Export Success Factors for the Sound Recording Industry

Intimate Knowledge of Market

All four firms were identified as having an intimate knowledge of their marketplace, particularly their respective overseas markets. Essentially, this involved having the ability to know which foreign market was 'best fit' for their artists' products. All these firms conducting good market research, that is were 'in touch' with market trends and patterns. They had a reputation of responding quickly to market interest, by building a 'vibe' for their acts. This process was achieved by having in place a rapid feedback system enabling the latest and most accurate market information to be collected and analysed.

Comprehensive Network of Contacts

The successful record companies had an extensive range of industry contacts domestically and internationally. These contacts were built up over many years of hard work and persistence. Each label had the demonstrated ability to choose which contact was more appropriate for a particular need by sourcing market information, or successfully releasing new product. Firms participating in these arrangements for information and knowledge had a competitive advantage over record companies which did not enter co-operative arrangements. The advantages of co-operation for record companies include lower costs, quicker reactions to market changes and a greater capacity to innovate. Therefore, it appears overseas success requires developing a wide range of overseas contacts and fostering long-term relationships with them.

Exceptional Product Quality and Innovation

What constitutes quality in music is very subjective. Consumers' tastes and preferences are diverse and often unpredictable. A high 'quality' product is relative to what the company's target market perceives as high quality, and also dependent on what the A&R manager believes. The successful record companies understood what constituted quality in their target markets, whether it be the mainstream, or a specific genre market.

Successful, innovative products, were found to be highly differentiated from most other contemporary music, that is, viewed as unique and different in the eyes of the consumer. Small successful labels, in particular, invested in music which was purely experimental and is not necessarily conducive to mass market appeal. Successful exporting labels tended to favour hard working acts, i.e. artists who were willing to do concert tours of foreign countries that coincided with their music releases.

Globally Orientated Strategy

Successful record companies adopted an international orientation. These record companies recognised that their music is produced for an international audience, not just for domestic consumption. The label's new market entry strategy was both proactive and reactive to environmental forces and foreign industry structures. Their strategy focused on penetrating specific markets and taking calculated risks, by pursuing the right marketing 'angle' relative to each record release.

Label Recognition

Building a strong reputation as an innovative, progressive record company was considered a critical success factor when venturing into foreign markets. Respondents considered a positive image by industry participants and artists inevitably translated into more opportunities for business growth. This recognition was gained by working in collaboration with artists and other record companies, distributors, publishers, and so on, with the view of long-term, fruitful relationships. Successful record companies were found to continuously re-invest funds back into their businesses.

Conclusions

The VSRI is operating in a turbulent environment. According to Peterson & Berger (1971), record companies use entrepreneurship as a means to cope with extremely turbulent environments This may account for the majority of record companies surveyed exhibiting entrepreneurial characteristics as opposed to a conservative orientation.

The study's major finding was that record companies (except for one) with a high export level of performance exhibit high levels of entrepreneurship.

This supports Yeoh & Jeong's (1995) proposition that entrepreneurial exporting firms can expect to have higher export performance levels than conservative exporting firms. This finding implies that firms adopting a high level of entrepreneurship may enhance their export performance.

This study identified successful entrepreneurial practices for exporting new music into foreign territories. Those firms identified as providing 'best practice' were further analysed, and a set of typical organisational export behaviours and practices arose. The study of best exemplars resulted in a profile of five key success factors. They were, having an intimate knowledge of the external marketplace, having a comprehensive network of overseas contacts, producing an exceptional and innovative product, having a globally orientated strategy plus gaining and sustaining a favourable company image.

A greater understanding of the organisational forces and processes that lead to enhanced entrepreneurship should be determined (Covin & Slevin, 1991). The results of this study suggest record companies should view entrepreneurship as an important management strategy. Hence, a profile depicting key exporting practices from successful entrepreneurial firms, provides a sound starting point for practitioners. Those cases identified as low and moderate entrepreneurial firms have the ability to 'renew themselves and their markets' by adopting a high entrepreneurial orientation (Miller, 1983: 770).

Research Limitations

The study's greatest limitation was the lack of quantitative data. From the outset, it was recognised that to elicit confidential information, such as a firm's financial and sales performance would be difficult within an industry that has traditionally been very secretive (Breen, 1992), even if the study assured confidentiality (see PSA Report, 1990).

The exploratory nature of this study also limits the conclusions that can be drawn. The link between entrepreneurship and export performance though compelling, needs to be further investigated to ensure validity within the VSRI.

Implications for Future Research

This study contributes to the field of entrepreneurship theory by using the entrepreneurship model by Covin & Slevin (1991) within an industry framework. Research into the strength of the modified Lumpkin & Dess's (1996) EO dimensions as definitive constructs needs further testing. Empirical research initiatives need to also focus on further understanding the relationship between the entrepreneurial orientation and the exporting context.

The export success factors identified in four high export performing organisations within the VSRI need to be tested to ensure validity and relative importance.

References

Alexander, C. & Becker, H. (1978) 'The Use of Vignettes in Survey Research,' *Public Opinion Quarterly,* Vol. 42, pp. 93-104.

Australasian Music Industry Directory (July, 1996), 17th edition, Immedia!.

Bailey, J. (1985) *The Small Business Owner/Manager in Australia: Characteristics, Performance and Development,* Unpublished Ph.D. Thesis, University of Melbourne.

Baskerville, D. (1995) *Music Business Handbook,* 6th edition, SAGE Publications Inc.

Breen, M. (1992) 'Copyright, Regulation and Power in the Australian Recorded Music Industry: A Model,' *Cultural Policy Studies, Occasional Paper,* No. 13, Griffin University.

Brockhaus, R. (1993) 'Series Introduction,' In Katz, J. & Brockhaus, R. (eds.) *Advances in Entrepreneurship, Firm Emergence, and Growth,* JAI Press, Vol. 1, pp. 1-5.

Cavusgil, S. & Zou, S. (1994) 'Marketing Strategy-Performance Relationship: An Investigation of the Empirical Link in Export Market Ventures,' *Journal of Marketing,* Vol. 58, No. 1, pp. 1-21.

Covin, J. & Slevin, D. (1989) 'Strategic Management of Small Firms in Hostile and Benign Environments, *Strategic Management Journal,* Vol. 10, pp. 75-87.

Covin, J. & Slevin, D. (1991) 'A Conceptual Model of Entrepreneurship as Firm Behaviour,' *Entrepreneurship: Theory & Practice,* Vol. 16, No. 1, pp. 7-25.

Covin, J. & Slevin, D. (1993) 'A Response to Zahra's 'Critique and Extension' of the Covin-Slevin Entrepreneurship Model,' *Entrepreneurship: Theory & Practice,* Vol. 17, No. 4, pp. 23-28.

Fredrickson, J. (1986) 'An Exploratory Approach to Measuring Perceptions of Strategic Decision Process Constructs,' *Strategic Management Journal,* Vol. 7, pp. 473-483.

Hartley, J. (1994) 'Case Studies in Organisational Research,' In Cassell, C. & Symon, G. *Qualitative Methods in Organisational Research; A Practical Guide,* Sage Publications, pp. 208-229.

Hofer, C. & Bygrave, W. (1992) 'Researching Entrepreneurship,' *Entrepreneurship: Theory & Practice,* Vol. 16, No. 3, pp. 91-100.

Industry Task Force on Leadership and Management Skills (1995) *Enterprising Nation; Renewing Australia's Managers to Meet the Challenges of the Asia-Pacific Century,* Australian Government Publishing Service.

Katz, J., Brockhaus, R. & Hills, G. (1993) 'Demographic Variables in Entrepreneurship Research,' In Katz, J. & Brockhaus, R. (eds.) *Advances in Entrepreneurship, Firm Emergence, and Growth,* JAI Press, Vol. 1, pp. 197-236.

LEK Partnership Report to the Commonwealth Department of Communications and the Arts (1994) 'The Export of Performing Arts and Music,' 7 July, The LEK Partnership.

Low, M. & MacMillan, I. (1988) 'Entrepreneurship: Past Research and Future Challenges,' In Jennings, D. (1993) *Multiple Perspectives of Entrepreneurship: Text, Readings and Cases,* South-Western Publishing Co., pp. 14-31.

Lumpkin, G. & Dess, G. (1996) 'Clarifying the Entrepreneurial Orientation Construct and Linking it to Performance,' *Academy of Management Review,* Vol. 21, No. 1, pp. 135-172.

Marshall, C. & Rossman, G. (1994) *Designing Qualitative Research,* 2nd edition, Sage Publications.

Miller, D. (1983) 'The Correlates of Entrepreneurship in Three Types of Firms,' *Management Science,* Vol. 29, No. 7, pp. 770-791.

Miller, D. & Friesen, P. (1978) 'Archetypes of Strategy Formulation,' *Management Science,* Vol. 24, No. 9, pp. 921-933.

Moini, A. (1995) 'An Inquiry Into Successful Exporting: An Empirical Investigation Using a Three-Stage Model,' *Journal of Small Business Management,* Vol. ?, No. ?, pp. 9-25.

Morris, M. & Lewis, P. (1995) 'The Determinants of Entrepreneurial Activity: Implications for Marketing,' *European Journal of Marketing,* Vol. 29, No. 7, pp. 31-48.

Peterson, R. & Berger, D. (1971) 'Entrepreneurship in Organisations: Evidence From the Popular Music Industry,' *Administrative Science Quarterly,* Vol. 16, pp. 97-106.

Prices Surveillance Authority (1990) 'Inquiry into the Prices of Sound Recordings,' Report No. 35, 13 December, Prices Surveillance Authority.

Ragin, C. (1987) *The Comparative Method,* University of California Press, Ltd.

Savage, G. & Black, J. (1995) 'Firm-Level Entrepreneurship and Field Research: The Studies in Their Methodological Context,' *Entrepreneurship: Theory & Practice,* Vol. 19, No. 3, pp. 25-34.

Schendel, D. & Hofer, C. (eds) (1979) *Strategic Management,* Little, Brown Publishing

Stewart, A. (1989) *Team Entrepreneurship,* Sage Publications.

Woo, C., Cooper, A. & Dunkelberg, W. (1991) 'The Development and Interpretation of Entrepreneurial Typologies,' *Journal of Business Venturing,* No. 6, pp. 93-114.

Yeoh, P. & Jeong, I. (1995) 'Contingency Relationships Between Entrepreneurship, Export Channel Structure and Environment; A Proposed Conceptual Model of Export Performance,' *European Journal of Marketing,* Vol. 29, No. 8, pp. 95-115.

Yin, R. (1994) *Case Study Research, Design and Methods,* 2nd edition, Sage Publications.

The relationship between diversification and economic performance: The Australian experience

Geoffrey Lewis and Kevin Jarvie

Abstract

The pressure to increase the value created for shareholders has led many Australian companies to review their diversification strategies. This study, covering the period 1985 to 1994, has two principal objectives:

- *to examine the history and types of diversification of 63 of Australia's largest listed companies, using Rumelt's (1974) classification scheme, and*
- *to determine whether, in an Australian context, there is a relationship between the type of diversification and performance. Performance is measured using market, economic and accounting measures.*

The major conclusion of the study was that there was no consistent relationship between the degree of diversification and performance for the companies studied. An unrelated finding was that no correlation was found between the economic performance measure (EVA), and the market-based measure of performance (Total Shareholder Returns). This brings into question the argument that shareholder value can be maximised by maximising EVA.

Introduction

The key responsibility of the senior management of companies is to ensure that value is created for shareholders. In order to do this they must address the company's strategy at three levels (Lewis, 1993: 72):

- The corporate level, which is concerned with such questions as: What business or businesses are we in? How do we allocate resources among businesses? How do we add value at the corporate level?
- The business level, which involves the coordination of functional strategies and issues of vision, organisational commitment and capability building.

Business level strategy is concerned with issues such as: How do we compete? How do we develop and sustain competitive advantage?
• The functional level, which is concerned with ensuring that all the business' functions, or value-activities, support the business strategy in a mutually consistent way.

Although a high proportion of Australian companies are diversified, this aspect of corporate strategy has received little attention by researchers. This study focuses on the specific issue of whether there is a relationship between diversification and the creation of shareholder value.

Objectives of the Study

This study has two principal objectives:
1. To examine the history and types of diversification used by Australia's largest listed companies.
2. To determine whether, in the Australian context, the adoption of a particular degree of diversification results in enhanced economic performance and creation of value for shareholders.

Research Design

To achieve these objectives the study was broken into three components.

The first of these was the evaluation and classification of the type of diversification used by each company in the sample. There are a number of methods available to measure a company's level of diversification and of these Rumelt's (1974) methodology was chosen because it was considered important to be able to compare Rumelt's findings with the results of this study. The validity of Rumelt's methodology has been substantiated by Hall and St. John (1994) who found that Rumelt's categories successfully predicted difference in performance according to the extent and type of diversity.

The data used to determine each company's level of diversification were obtained from the segment reporting information included in annual reports. Based on these data and a subjective assessment, each company was classified into one of Rumelt's nine minor categories. These classifications were then reviewed by an informed and independent panel. As a result of this process, the original classification of some companies was revised.

The classification data were then analysed to examine if there was a systematic behaviour in how groups of companies exhibiting the same level of diversification changed their diversification through time. This analysis was repeated for to five year periods, 1985 to 1989 and 1990 to 1994 to ensure consistency.

The second component was the measurement of the historical performance of each company. Based on the inconsistency in the results of earlier studies, it was decided to adopt a range of accounting, economic, and market measures. The accounting measures of performance were included to allow comparison of results between this study and the results of Rumelt (1974) and McDougall and Round (1984). The economic measures were used to overcome the inadequacies of accounting measures in determining creation of shareholder value. To contrast these internal measures of performance, an external and independent market based performance measure was also used

A measurement of the economic performance of each company requires an estimate of the company's cost of capital. Because of the number of assumptions made in estimating a company's cost of capital, the company's cost of capital was calculated using six different sets of assumptions. The results were correlated to ensure that the economic performance measures were robust and were not introducing artefacts into the study results.

The use of three different types of performance measure also allowed the strength of correlations between the performance measures to be analysed using F-tests.

The final component of the study was the analysis of the relationship between the degree of diversification and performance. To determine the statistical validity of any relationships observed, F-tests were used to determine if, across the different strategic categories, there were statistically significant differences among the performance means. T-tests were used to compare the individual strategic category means with the mean of the rest of the sample.

The statistical analysis was conducted over two five year periods; 1985 to 1989 and 1990 to 1994. This approach was adopted to ensure that the results were not influenced by either the time period selected. The analysis was then repeated for the ten year period 1985 to 1994 to ensure that the results were consistent over a time frame which is similar to a company's planning horizon. By using these three different time periods, more robust conclusions can be drawn.

Sample

A sample of 63 companies was developed from the companies included in the Australian Stock Exchange's list of the 100 largest companies, based on market capitalisation, during the period 1990 to 1994. This approach was selected to avoid two potential problems. The first potential problem was bias resulting from the diversification behaviour of a particular industry. The second potential problem was to ensure that a range of diversification types would be present in the sample. The companies studied are listed in Appendix A.

Literature Review

Although limited research has been conducted in Australia, there have been a large number of international studies carried out to examine the relationship between diversification and performance. It should be noted that the despite the widespread belief that excellent companies (that is, companies with sustained superior financial performance) generally "stick to the knitting" (Peters and Waterman, 1982) or focus on "core competencies" (Prahalad and Hamel, 1990), the findings of studies investigating the effects of diversification on performance are inconclusive (Ramanujam and Varadarajan, 1989).

Summary of Previous Studies

The studies of US companies carried out by Rumelt (1974, 1982), Berry (1975) and others (for example Bettis, 1981; Palepu, 1985; Stubbart and Grant, 1983) show that there is a correlation between the level of firm diversification and firm performance. Subsequent studies, using multivariate analysis to separate the impact of diversification strategy from other influences on firm performance, show that the differences that Rumelt observed could be largely attributed to industry effects (Christensen and Montgomery, 1981; Bettis and Hall, 1982). Rumelt's later research confirmed that even after adjusting for industry effects, the Related-Constrained diversifiers earned the highest return on assets (1982).

Montgomery (1985) later found that profitability was unrelated to diversification when the effects of industry and market-share variables were considered

Other studies (Michel and Shaked, 1984; Dolan, 1985) have observed that firms that diversified into unrelated businesses outperformed, on the basis of either returns to stockholders or accounting measures, those that diversified into related businesses.

Rajagopalan and Harrigan (1986) found non-significant differences in stockholder returns or accounting performance measures between the Rumelt categories.

The results of the various studies show there is no clear relationship between diversification and profitability or economic performance. The results appear to be sensitive to research design parameters such as time period, performance measures, control variables and the method of analysis (Grant, Jammine and Thomas, 1988).

Studies conducted outside the United States have also been inconclusive. The Australian research by McDougall and Round defined diversification as manufacturing "new products and services using significantly different inputs from existing products and services, and/or selling to new industries" and allowed the companies to determine whether or not they had diversified between 1969 and 1978 (1984: 388). Of the 108 companies studied, 63 considered that they had diversified during this period. The most important finding of this study was that there was no significant difference in either return on total assets or return on equity of diversified and non-diversified companies (McDougall and Round, 1984: 390-91).

The other Australian study, by Gibbs, found only a tentative relationship between diversification and financial performance (1984: 101).

Discussion

How should these conflicting results be interpreted? Conflicting research findings may, and possibly should, be expected in the case of studies carried out in different countries at different times because the contexts in which the firms operate varies (Johnson and Thomas, 1987). The notion of context is fundamental to strategic management. Porter (1986), for example, argues that an understanding of the industry environment is critical to the development of a successful strategy and firm performance.

Robins and Wiersema (1995) make the observation that, although there has been a great deal of research on the corporate diversification, these studies usually have a weak relationship to resource-based theory (Teece, Pisano and Shuen, 1991). Their study indicates that there is a positive relationship between the ability to share strategic assets such as capabilities or know-how and the performance of a multi-business firm.

Although the methodology proposed by Robins and Wiersema (1995) may provide a better theoretical measurement of diversification, it was not adopted for this study because it relies on data about the technology flows between industries. These data could not be gathered for Australian industries, and so more traditional measures of diversification were employed.

Diversification Measures

The concept of diversification does not lend itself to easy measurement. A variety of measures have been developed:

* Categorical measures of diversification where a firm's pattern of diversification is classified or categorised into discrete types. The most commonly used methodology is that used by Rumelt (1974).
* Continuous measures of diversification which are based on the Standard Industrial Classification (SIC) system such as the weighted product count measure (Gorecki, 1980; Montgomery, 1982) or the entropy measure (Berry, 1975; Jacquemin and Berry, 1979).
* Combinations of both systems to produce a hybrid classification system (Baysinger and Hoskisson, 1989; Palepu, 1985; Varadajan, 1986).

A study by Hall and St. John (1994) has two important findings that are relevant to this study. First, both categorical and continuous measures of diversity capture the same underlying construct of portfolio diversity to some extent. Second, although Rumelt's categories successfully predicted difference in performance according to the extent and type of diversity, the continuous measures such as the weighted product count or the entropy measure did not predict a performance relationship when applied to the same sample of firms.

One area of diversification not considered by Rumelt is geographic diversification. Throughout this study it was observed that many Australian companies have diversified into international markets, while remaining in the same product or industry classification. This is probably due to companies needing to access larger markets because of limited growth opportunities in the domestic market.

Methodology

Rumelt's methodology uses three values to categorise a company's pattern of diversification;

* the Specialisation Ratio, which is the proportion of a firm's total revenue derived from its largest single business or industry to the total revenue,
* the Relatedness Ratio, which is the proportion of a firm's total revenue derived from its single largest group of related businesses or industries, and,
* the Vertical Ratio, which is the proportion of the firm's total revenue that arise from all by-products, intermediate products and end products of a vertically integrated sequence of processing activities.

For this study, the data used to calculate these ratios was gathered from the segment information in company reports. For most companies the external sales revenue of each industry segment was used without adjustment. Where external sales revenue was unavailable, the total sales revenue for each segment was used after the following adjustments:

* Calculating the proportion of total sales revenue that the segment contributed.
* Using the proportion of total sales revenue as the basis for allocating the intersegment sales to each business unit.
* Subtracting the allocated intersegment sales from the segment's total sales revenue.

Classification of Diversification Strategies

The classification methodology used was that developed by Rumelt (1974), which was adapted from that proposed by Wrigley (1970). Figure 1 shows the four major strategic categories can be defined in terms of the Specialisation Ratio and the Relatedness Ratio: Single Business, Dominant Business, Related

Business and Unrelated Business. These four major strategic categories can be further subdivided into nine minor strategic categories as shown in Table 1. The classification of the minor categories was aided by using the decision tree shown in Figure 2.

Table 1 Subdivision of the four major strategic categories into nine minor strategic categories

Major Strategic Categories	Minor Strategic Categories
Single Businesses	Single Businesses
Dominant Businesses	Dominant - Constrained
	Dominant - Linked
	Dominant - Vertical
	Dominant - Unrelated
Related Businesses	Related - Constrained
	Related - Related
Unrelated Businesses	Acquisitive Conglomerates
	Unrelated - Passive

The criteria for discriminating between the Constrained and the Linked classification is subjective. The distinction between the two categories is based on the history of diversification shown by the company. A Constrained company has only diversified into new businesses which are closely related to its 'core' business. In contrast, a Linked company has diversified further by entering new businesses which are closely related to existing peripheral or non-core businesses.

The criteria for discriminating between the Unrelated-Passive and Acquisitive Conglomerates was based on the company's history. Acquisitive Conglomerates are those companies that have over the preceding five years:

* An average growth rate in earnings per share of at least 10 per cent per year. Acquired five or more businesses, at least three of which, were unrelated to past activities.
* Issued new equity shares whose total value (based on prevailing market prices) was equal to or exceeded the total amount of common dividends paid during the same period.

Results of Classification

The percentages of the 63 companies allocated to each of the four major categories and nine subcategories are shown in Table 2. The same information is displayed graphically in Figure 3.

A more detailed analysis of the classifications has shown that the majority of Single, Dominant and Related Businesses will remain in their existing industries, while companies that have altered their diversification category have generally increased their degree of diversification. It can also be observed that it is usually the Unrelated Businesses that decrease their degree of diversification. Finally, the small percentage of companies that are classified as Dominant-Unrelated indicate that some companies adopt diversification strategies which do not appear to have an underlying strategic logic.

Discussion

The patterns of diversification observed in this study show strong similarities with the model proposed by Hubbard (1991). In summary, the model proposes four basic patterns of diversification.

1. Single or Dominant Businesses would acquire companies in their existing industry, and capitalise on its technical capabilities. Once these businesses perceive limited opportunities for further growth within their existing industries they would diversify into related industries.

2. Related Businesses would be expected to seek acquisition targets in their existing industries to use their existing cluster of capabilities. Eventually, these businesses would exhaust the opportunities for further growth in their existing businesses and would acquire new unrelated businesses.

3. Unrelated Businesses may either acquire businesses within their existing portfolio of industries or use their financial acumen to identify undervalued businesses, which could be restructured or broken up. It is possible that companies using the first option may eventually become Related or Dominant Businesses through prudent acquisition, while companies using the second option may become increasingly diversified.

There are some forms of acquisition which do not have a strategic logic; for example a Dominant Business pursuing an unrelated acquisition target.

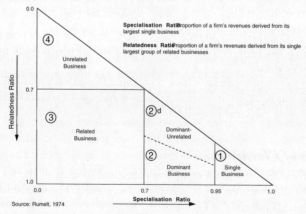

Source: Rumelt, 1974

Figure 1
Strategic categories defined in terms of the specialisation ratio and the relatedness ratio

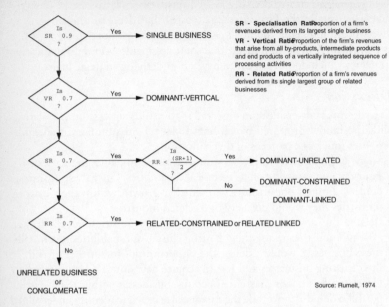

Figure 2
Decision tree for categorising companies

Measurement of Performance

This section describes how the performance of the 63 companies studied was measured. For the purposes of this paper, performance measures can be classified into three types: economic performance measures, accounting performance measures and market performance measures.

- *Economic Performance Measures:* A company's economic performance is measured by the economic profit generated. For the purposes of this paper, economic profit is the income remaining after all capital costs have been deducted from the operating profit (Stewart, 1991: 742).
- *Accounting Performance Measures:* Many authors have pointed out the failure of accounting-based measures to accurately measure the true economic performance of a company. Several accounting-based performance measures have been included in this study, however, to allow comparison with the work of Rumelt (1974) and McDougall and Round (1984).
- *Market Performance Measures:* Total Shareholder Returns was used as the market-based measure of performance, because it incorporates both capital gains and dividend payments. In contrast to the preceding measures, this is an external measure of firm performance.

These measures were calculated for the three periods covered by the study: 1985 to 1989, 1989 to 1994 and 1985 to 1994.

Economic Performance Measures

There are a number of techniques for measuring economic profit. The strength of these methods is that they are consistent with the discounted cash flow model (Stewart, 1991; Mills and Print, 1995). The Economic Value Added (EVA) technique described by Stewart (1991) was chosen as the means of measuring the economic performance of the companies for the following reasons:

* It is a widely accepted method, which is considered to be robust because it is conceptually simple and the calculations do not require significant assumptions to be made.
* It did not require the use of proprietary software as is the case with the BCG-Holt method.

Underlying the EVA method is the following simple expression: *EVA = operating profits - a capital charge.*

This expression shows that the economic profit created through a company's operations is the income remaining after the cost of the capital employed in creating that income has been deducted. An alternative way of expressing this is: *EVA = (r- c*) x capital.*

where:

r   is the rate of return on capital employed

c^* is the weighted average cost of capital

capital   is the economic book value of capital employed

The rate of return is a measure of the periodic, after-tax, cash-on-cash yield earned in the business. (Stewart, 1991: 742-3). It is calculated using the following expression:

$$r = \frac{NOPAT^*_1}{capital_0}$$

where:

$NOPAT^*_1$ is the adjusted Net Operating Profit After Tax at the end of the period

$capital_0$ is the economic book value of capital employed at the start of the period

From these two expressions it can be seen that the calculation of EVA is based on three variables:

1. The adjusted Net Operating Profit After Taxes, (NOPAT*).

2. The economic book value of the capital employed, (capital). For this study, the value of capital employed has been standardised to allow comparison of different companies.

3. The weighted average cost of capital, (c*). In this study the weighted average cost of capital has been calculated using six different sets of assumptions including the effect of Australia's imputation tax system. These assumptions are outlined in Appendix B.

The impact these assumptions was tested by developing a correlation matrix. The correlation for each period showed that the assumptions made in calculating the cost of capital were not significantly affecting the how standardised EVA measured each company's relative performance. This result also indicates that standardised EVA is a robust performance measure of relative performance provided that all companies being studied are being treated similarly.

One of the most important characteristics of the rate of return, as defined by Stewart, is that it is the rate of return based on the capital outstanding at the beginning of a period. This is because Stewart assumes that additions to capital during the period will not become productive and add to profits during the period (1991: 128). This assumption appears to be questionable for several reasons. First, where a company makes a significant acquisition during the year it will have a significantly increased NOPAT* without a corresponding increase in capital. This circumstance can result in an anomalously high EVA.

A good example of this is BTR-Nylex during the period 1985 to 1989. Second, there is a great deal of variation in the length of the investment-return cycle between industries. For example, soft drink or snack food manufacturers can have investment-return cycles less than a year, while mining or petroleum companies may have much longer investment-return cycles. In the case of long-lead time, capital intensive industries such as mining, petroleum, base metals and chemicals, etc. a low EVA is virtually unavoidable while they continue to grow.

Accounting-Based Measures of Performance

Six different accounting based measures of performance were included in the analysis:

- Average annual growth in sales (GSALES)
- Average annual growth in earnings (GEARN)
- Average annual growth in earnings per share (GEPS)
- Average annual return on equity (ROE)
- Average annual return on capital invested (ROC), and
- Average annual ratio of equity to capital (E/C).

	1985	1986	1987	1988	1989	1990	1991	1992	1993	1994
Major Classifications										
Single Business	28.1	22.4	22.0	23.0	23.8	25.4	25.4	27.0	28.6	28.6
Dominant Business	21.1	27.6	28.8	31.1	30.2	27.0	30.2	30.2	30.2	30.2
Related Business	19.3	20.7	22.0	19.7	22.2	23.8	23.8	25.4	23.8	23.8
Unrelated Business	31.6	29.3	27.1	26.2	23.8	23.8	20.6	17.5	17.5	17.5
Minor Classifications										
Single Business	28.1	22.4	22.0	23.0	23.8	25.4	25.4	27.0	28.6	28.6
Dominant-Vertical	8.8	12.1	11.9	11.5	11.1	9.5	11.1	11.1	11.1	11.1
Dominant-Unrelated	-	1.7	1.7	1.6	1.6	1.6	1.6	3.2	3.2	3.2
Dominant-Constrained	10.5	10.3	11.9	14.8	14.3	12.7	14.3	12.7	11.1	11.1
Dominant-Linked	1.8	3.4	3.4	3.3	3.2	3.2	3.2	3.2	4.8	4.8
Related-Constrained	7.0	8.6	8.5	6.6	6.3	7.9	7.9	7.9	7.9	7.9
Related-Linked	12.3	12.1	13.6	13.1	15.9	15.9	15.9	17.5	15.9	15.9
Unrelated -Passive	24.6	22.4	20.3	19.7	19.0	22.2	20.6	17.5	17.5	17.5
Acquisitive Conglomerate	7.0	6.9	6.8	6.6	4.8	1.6	-	-	-	-
No. of Companies	57	58	59	61	63	63	63	63	63	63

Table 2 Percentage of companies in each diversification category for the period 1985 to 1994

PERCENTAGE PROPORTION OF CLASSIFICATIONS BY YEAR

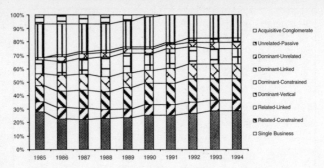

Figure 3
Percentage of companies in each diversification category.

Market-Based Measure of Performance

Compared with the other measures of performance, a market-based measure is an external, unbiased and more meaningful evaluation of a company's performance than either the economic or accounting-based measures of performance (Toomey, 1996). Total Shareholder Returns was used as the market-based measure of performance, because it incorporates both capital gains and dividend payments. This measure, calculated by the Australian Stock Exchange, is the 12 month compound rate of return over each of the periods studied. The following assumptions are used in the calculation:

- Bonus shares are held.
- Rights are sold on the first day of trading and are reinvested in the underlying security.
- Dividends are reinvested in the underlying security at the month end price following each ex-dividend date.
- No brokerage fees are incurred.

Correlation of the Various Performance Measures

To examine the relationship between the different types of performance measures, correlations were carried out. Of particular interest was the strength of the relationship between the economic measures and the market-based measures. Based on the work of Stewart (1991) it was expected that a strong correlation between the economic measures and the market-based measure would be observed. Surprisingly, the correlation between standardised EVA and Total Shareholder Returns was weak with an average correlation coefficient of approximately 0.19 (see Figure 4). F-tests showed that there was no statistically significant relationship between standardised EVA and Total Shareholder Returns in any of the three periods covered by the study.

The weak correlation between standardised EVA and TSR is surprising because, contrary to popular theory (Chenoweth, 1997), it indicates that EVA does not capture the full extent of value created for shareholders.

Relationship Between Diversification and Performance

The relationship between diversification strategy and economic performance was examined in two ways:

- Statistical analysis of the average performance of the four major categories used by Rumelt (1974).
- Statistical analysis of the average performance of the nine minor categories as defined by Rumelt (1974).

Analysis of Performance for the Major Classifications

This analysis was conducted to determine whether there were statistically significant differences in the average performance of the four major strategic classifications (Single Businesses, Dominant Businesses, Related Businesses and Unrelated Businesses).

To test the hypothesis that there were significant differences in performance between the major diversification categories two statistical techniques were used. The first was an F-test which was run using a 90 per cent confidence limit (a = 0.10). Christensen and Montgomery have suggested that more exactness cannot be expected from estimates extracted from publicly available information (1981: 333).

The second was a T-test which was used to assess the relative performance of each diversification category. The T-tests were run using three different confidence limits, 90, 95 and 99 per cent (a = 0.1, 0.05 and 0.01 respectively).

The results of the statistical analyses for each of the three periods of the study are summarised in Tables 3, 4 and 5.

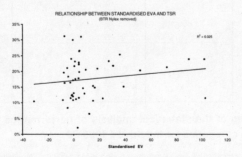

Figure 4
Relationship between EVA and TSR for the period 1990 to 1994

1985 - 1989

Category Means	Economic Measures							Accounting Based Measures						Market Based Measure
	Method 1	Method 2	Method 3	Method 4	Method 5	Method 6	Spread (%)	GSALES (%)	GEARN (%)	GEPS (%)	ROE (%)	ROC (%)	E/C (%)	TSR (%)
Single Businesses	12.98	12.80	14.86	14.63	14.72	14.36	8.47	26.17	87.38	0.67–	10.56	9.42	74.12†‡	11.68–
Dominant Businesses	15.00	14.13	15.26	14.60	14.56	13.74	9.31	47.60	87.75	72.45	12.46	9.52	50.88	15.14
Related Businesses	38.82	38.41	38.32	37.18	35.13	34.31	15.97	51.78	124.37	44.70	13.88	10.49	58.65	18.84
Unrelated Businesses	75.57	74.85	74.16	72.82	71.21	70.37	20.16	45.43	50.80	3.18–	16.85+	11.87	51.38	18.44
Overall Mean	36.89	36.28	36.82	35.95	35.09	34.36	13.60	43.69	83.80	33.84	13.71	10.37	56.91	16.18
F value	1.11	1.11	1.06	1.09	1.05	1.05	1.83	0.18	0.39	1.12	1.84	1.11	3.31+	0.83

Table 3 Results of the statistical analysis of performance for the major diversification categories for the period 1985-89

Note: The plus or minus sign following a category mean indicates that it differed significantly ("+" for a positive deviation, "-" for a negative deviation) from the mean of other categories at the 0.1 level. The † indicates a significant T-test at the 0.05 level and ‡ indicates a significant T-test at the 0.01 level. The plus sign following an F value indicates a significant difference at the 0.1 level.

1990 - 1994

Category Means	Economic Measures							Accounting Based Measures						Market Based Measure
	Method 1	Method 2	Method 3	Method 4	Method 5	Method 6	Spread (%)	GSALES (%)	GEARN (%)	GEPS (%)	ROE (%)	ROC (%)	E/C (%)	TSR (%)
Single Business	1.28	1.02	1.21	1.56	1.54	1.20	0.98	11.08	6.08	10.95	9.83	9.10	73.45+‡	9.25
Dominant Business	5.15	4.27	5.20	5.05	4.93	4.03	3.74	-1.31-†	13.52	8.61	9.23	8.57	52.16	13.75+†
Related Business	-0.70-†	-1.04-†	-0.73-†	-0.38-†	-0.49-†	-1.00-	-0.14-	2.56	0.36	0.67	9.93	8.69	62.53	7.52
Unrelated Business	3.93	3.51	3.87	4.26	4.03	3.38	2.67	3.23	8.51	-1.11-†	10.64	9.44	46.03-†	8.30
Overall Mean	2.56	2.05	2.54	2.73	2.62	2.00	1.93	3.55	7.62	5.62	9.79	8.89	58.96	10.19
F value	1.24	1.01	1.26	1.06	1.04	0.86	1.02	2.57+	0.67	1.40	0.20	0.25	4.75+	1.97

Table 4 Results of the statistical analysis of performance for the major diversification categories for the period 1990 to 1994. Refer to Table 3 for an explanation of the symbols.

1985 - 1994

Category Means	Economic Measures							Accounting Based Measures						Market Based Measure
	Method 1	Method 2	Method 3	Method 4	Method 5	Method 6	Spread (%)	GSALES (%)	GEARN (%)	GEPS (%)	ROE (%)	ROC (%)	E/C (%)	TSR (%)
Single Business	3.40–†	3.26–	4.08–	4.74–	5.07–	3.99–	4.26–	55.80	28.15	6.10	11.06	9.01	71.66+‡	13.92–†
Dominant Business	16.44	14.77	16.76	16.53	16.45	14.74	7.13	32.23	70.47+	6.33	12.92	9.11	53.23	18.21
Related Business	14.77	13.56	14.59	14.86	13.53	11.95	6.45	14.61–	10.69-‡	0.66	11.90	9.35	59.90	19.15
Unrelated Business	53.43	51.37	52.12	52.88	51.37	48.52	12.34	19.07	28.41	2.69	13.34	10.89+	48.57–	21.52
Overall Mean	22.27	20.93	22.15	22.46	21.82	20.00	7.63	29.68	37.13	4.03	12.41	9.58	57.53	18.33
F value	1.44	1.45	1.40	1.39	1.33	1.33	1.61	1.46	2.78+	0.60	0.56	1.14	3.13+	1.66

Table 5 Results of the statistical analysis of performance for the major diversification categories for the period 1985 to 1994. Refer to Table 3 for an explanation of the symbols.

Results for the Major Categories

The most important result of the analysis of the major categories was that none of the economic or market-based measures of performance revealed any consistent differences between diversification categories. The only conclusion that can be drawn from this result is that the degree and form of diversification had no systematic impact on a company's performance of these companies during the periods studied.

Reviewing the results of the statistical analyses for the major categories indicates that only one accounting-based measure of performance (the ratio of equity to capital) has statistically significant F-test results for the three periods studied. By incorporating this with the results of the T-tests it can be concluded that the Single Business category is contributing to this result. In each of the three periods, the majority of companies classified as Single Businesses were either gold mining companies, or property trusts.

Most of these companies have a very low level of debt and a corresponding high level of equity to capital. It was concluded from the analysis that this result was due to the nature of the industries represented in the Single Business category, rather than the diversification strategy itself.

Analysis of Performance for the Minor Classifications

This analysis was conducted to determine whether there were statistically significant differences in the average performance of the nine minor strategic classifications proposed by Rumelt (1974).

The methodology used to determine that there were statistically significant performance differences between the minor diversification categories was the same as that previously described for the major categories.

The results of the statistical analyses for the three periods covered by the study are summarised in Tables 6, 7 and 8.

Results for the Minor Categories

The most significant result from the analysis of the minor diversification categories was that there was no consistent relationship between the market-based and economic measures of performance and the degree of diversification. This lack of relationship can be explained by the variation in performance within each diversification category, compared with the variance between diversification categories.

Portraying the results as a frequency distribution (Figure 5) shows that while most of the companies had Total Shareholder Returns of between 5 and 25 per cent, there were a number of companies that had values of Total Shareholder Return that were either above or below this range within each diversification category. It is these companies that contributed to the large variance within each category.

The large variation in performance within each diversification category supports the conclusion that diversification strategy had no systematic relationship with a company's performance. This conclusion is reinforced by the observation that companies in the same diversification category, and participating in the same industry, can also have a large variation in economic performance.

In general, the accounting-based measures of performance did not show any relationship between diversification strategy and performance. The only category that was consistently highlighted is Dominant-Constrained. The results of the T-tests indicate that the Dominant-Constrained category was a consistently below-average performer in terms of average annual growth in sales, average return on capital and the ratio of equity to capital. While the F-test results indicate that only the equity to capital ratio was significant, it is necessary to determine whether there may be some other explanation for these results.

A review of the business activities of the companies classified as Dominant-Constrained revealed that more than fifty per cent of the companies were banks. Most of the banks were found to have low rates of growth in sales, low or average rates of return on capital, and low ratios of equity to capital. Based on this observation, it was considered that the below average performance of this category was more a reflection of the characteristics of the banking industry than the firms' diversification strategies.

Comparison of Results with Other Studies

The results of this study have been compared to the results of the studies by Rumelt (1974) and McDougall and Round (1984).

A comparison of the results of the T-tests from this study and those of Rumelt do not show any similarity in the relative performance of the major or minor categories. Rumelt's results indicate that of the major categories, the Related Businesses had a higher level of profitability than the other categories. This conclusion is not supported by the results of the T-tests for the major categories in any period in this study. The Dominant Businesses, which Rumelt regarded as having a low level of profitability, show average levels of profitability in all three periods in this study. It should be noted that while the Dominant Businesses had the lowest average return on capital invested in all three periods of this study, this result is not statistically significant.

The minor categories that Rumelt considered to have high profitability, Dominant-Constrained and Related-Constrained show average or below average profitability in this study. Similarly, the categories described by Rumelt as low-performance categories (Dominant-Vertical and Unrelated-Passive), have average levels of profitability in this study.

The other significant difference between the results of the T-tests conducted in this study and those of Rumelt is that there does not appear to be a clear association between the level of profitability for a particular degree of diversification and the rate of growth of a company.

1985 - 1989

Category Means	Economic Measures							Accounting Based Measures						Market Based Measure
	Method 1	Method 2	Method 3	Method 4	Method 5	Method 6	Spread (%)	GSALES (%)	GEARN (%)	GEPS (%)	ROE (%)	ROC (%)	E/C (%)	TSR (%)
Single Businesses	12.69	12.80	14.86	14.63	14.72	14.36	8.47	26.17	87.38	0.67–	10.56	9.42	74.12+‡	11.68–
Dominant-Vertical	19.58	19.14	19.58	18.99	19.18	18.76	11.90	34.71	173.76	132.18	12.97	11.09	62.37	13.51
Dominant-Constrained	13.29	11.76	14.07	13.54	13.56	12.22	8.64	22.88–	42.12	51.91	9.83–†	7.87–‡	35.81–†	16.56
Dominant-Linked	14.57	14.28	13.32	12.89	11.76	11.17	9.04	185.81	34.33–	15.80	19.11	8.99	51.70	10.76
Dominant-Unrelated	6.22–	5.95–	6.86–	5.20–†	5.14–†	4.88–†	3.14	53.42	22.71–†	2.21	14.59	11.12	70.11–†	19.56
Related-Constrained	20.94	19.77	20.77	21.05	21.08	20.63	10.82	17.87–	122.10	75.09	12.32	8.85	54.37	21.72+
Related-Linked	49.48	49.06	48.36	46.39	43.17	42.12	18.92	71.15	125.66	27.34	14.77	11.44	61.09	16.92
Unrelated-Passive	22.24	21.82	21.58	21.98	21.16	20.63	13.06	16.26–†	35.66–	6.81	13.70	11.01	53.85	17.28
Acq. Conglomerates	248.90	247.20	245.04	238.07	233.87	232.01	43.23	140.24	100.00	-8.61–	27.07	14.68	43.34	22.20
Overall Mean	36.89	36.28	36.82	35.95	35.09	34.36	13.60	43.69	83.80	33.84	13.71	10.37	56.91	16.18
F value	2.43+	2.43+	2.43+	2.41+	2.35+	2.34+	2.50+	1.85+	0.50	0.76	2.86+	1.12	2.52+	0.48

Table 6 Results of the statistical analysis of performance between the minor diversification categories for the period 1985 to 1989. Refer to Table 3 for an explanation of the symbols.

1990 - 1994

Category Means	Economic Measures							Accounting Based Measures						Market Based Measure
	Method 1	Method 2	Method 3	Method 4	Method 5	Method 6	Spread (%)	GSALES (%)	GEARN (%)	GEPS (%)	ROE (%)	ROC (%)	E/C (%)	TSR (%)
Single Businesses	1.60	1.02	1.21	1.56	1.54	1.20	0.98	11.08	6.08	10.95	9.83	9.10	73.45+‡	9.25
Dominant-Vertical	2.75	2.15	2.88	2.99	2.82	2.33	2.17	3.91	5.77	4.79	9.71	8.24	63.22	15.77+†
Dominant-Constrained	5.21	3.84	5.24	5.09	5.03	3.56	4.10	-5.37-‡	29.87+†	17.55+	9.59	7.63-	35.50-†	14.49
Dominant-Linked	13.39	12.85	13.36	12.89	12.61	12.08	8.27	3.32	-18.97	-3.43	6.40	11.13	68.73	15.48
Dominant-Unrelated	0.93	0.78	0.89	0.35	0.38	-0.02	0.74	-8.23	15.87	-0.21	10.18	10.16+†	63.49	0.74
Related-Constrained	-2.00	-1.53	-1.14	-1.03	-1.10	-1.63	-0.57	1.68	-6.82	-6.71	8.82	7.22	54.18	6.13
Related-Linked	-0.56-†	-0.79-	-0.53-†	-0.06-	-0.19-	-0.69-	0.08	3.00	3.95	4.36	10.49.	9.43	66.71+†	8.22
Unrelated-Passive	3.93	3.51	3.87	4.26	4.03	3.38	2.67	3.23	8.51	-1.11-†	10.64	9.44	46.03-†	8.30
Acq. Conglomerates	-	-	-	-	-	-	-	-	-	-	-	-	-	-
Overall Mean	2.56	2.05	2.54	2.73	2.62	2.00	1.93	3.55	7.62	5.62	9.79	8.89	58.96	10.19
F value	0.96	0.80	0.91	0.78	0.77	0.69	0.70	1.53	1.62	1.40	0.47	0.88	3.92+	1.81

Table 7 Results of the statistical analysis of performance between the minor diversification categories for the period 1990 to 1994. Refer to Table 3 for an explanation of the symbols.

1985 - 1994

Category Means	Economic Measures							Accounting Based Measures						Market Based Measure
	Method 1	Method 2	Method 3	Method 4	Method 5	Method 6	Spread (%)	GSALES (%)	GEARN (%)	GEPS (%)	ROE (%)	ROC (%)	E/C (%)	TSR (%)
Single Businesses	3.40–†	2.82–†	4.08–	4.74–	5.07–	3.99–	4.26–	55.80	28.15	6.10	11.06	9.01	71.66+‡	13.92–†
Dominant-Vertical	19.62	18.65	20.10	20.05	20.20	19.38	7.85	23.13	61.81	1.85	13.94	10.38	64.86	18.14
Dominant-Constrained	16.05	13.05	16.51	16.30	16.22	13.19	7.34	7.84–‡	82.56	5.90	10.42–	7.64–†	35.87–	18.80
Dominant-Linked	8.09	7.64	7.25–	7.21–	6.25–	5.06–	4.65	167.28	82.57	25.16	17.44	8.15	54.45	12.95
Dominant-Unrelated	10.40	10.07	10.89	8.55	8.37	7.92	4.89	5.69	30.94	7.51	13.32	11.03	79.19	20.56
Related-Constrained	7.13	6.22	7.25	7.19	7.20	6.44	3.98	12.50–†	11.04–†	6.06	10.91	7.97	53.32	15.14
Related-Linked	19.01	18.23	18.67	19.11	17.05	15.01	7.82	15.79	10.49–‡	-2.35–‡	12.46	10.11	63.56	21.66
Unrelated-Passive	53.43	51.37	52.12	52.88	51.37	48.52	12.34	19.07	28.41	2.69	13.34	10.89+	48.57–	21.52
Acq. Conglomerates														
Overall Mean	22.27	20.93	22.15	22.46	21.82	20.00	7.63	29.68	37.13	4.03	12.41	9.58	57.53	18.33
F value	0.60	0.60	0.58	0.58	0.55	0.55	0.74	3.31+	1.24	1.16	0.84	1.22	3.16+	1.05

Table 8 Results of the statistical analysis of performance between the minor diversification categories for the period 1985 to 1994. Refer to Table 3 for an explanation of the symbols.

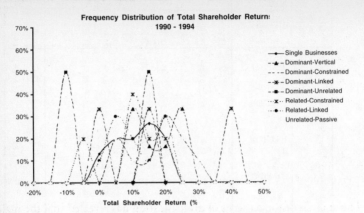

Figure 5
Results of a frequency analysis of Total Shareholder Returns for each minor diversification category. 1990–1994

The results of the F-tests performed on the average ratio of equity to capital indicate that there were significant differences between both the major and minor categories in any period. Rumelt's findings were not supported by the results of F-tests performed on other measures of performance. In his study, Rumelt concludes that there were significant differences between the means of both major and minor diversification categories. This study has found that, in general, there is no significant difference between the performance of either the major or minor strategic classifications (1974).

A direct comparison with the study by McDougall and Round (1984) is not possible because of the different approaches taken in measuring diversification. Despite this, three general comparisons can be made:

- McDougall and Round concluded that there was no significant relationship between a company's degree of diversification and its profitability. This study has also concluded that there is no clear relationship between the degree of diversification and accounting-based measures of profitability.
- McDougall and Round observed that the relative profitability of diversified and non-diversified firms was not consistent when measured in different periods. A similar observation was made in this study.
- McDougall and Round observed that diversified companies had consistently achieved higher rates of growth in earnings after tax than non-diversified companies. In contrast, this study did not find that there was such a clear relationship between the degree of diversification and the rate of growth in earnings.

Overall, it is reasonable to conclude there is consistency of findings between this study and that of McDougall and Round (1984).

Conclusions and Implications

This study has used the methodology proposed by Rumelt (1974) to investigate two aspects of the corporate strategy of Australian companies:

- The history and types of diversification used by 63 of Australia's largest listed companies between 1985 and 1994.
- Whether a relationship exists between diversification strategy and the creation of shareholder value in Australian firms.

The analysis of the patterns of diversification has revealed that the majority of Single, Dominant and Related Businesses will remain in their existing industries. Companies that move from these categories have generally increased their degree of diversification. It was also observed, between 1990 and 1994, that a large percentage of Unrelated Businesses decreased their degree of diversification. These results support the model proposed by Hubbard (1991) to explain the takeover and, by inference, the diversification behaviour of companies in strategic terms.

The relationship between the type of diversification strategy and economic performance has been investigated for three intervals: 1985 to 1989, 1990 to 1994 and 1985 to 1994. Based on the results of the statistical analyses three conclusions can be drawn:

1. There is no discernible relationship between the type of diversification and a company's financial performance. This result is inconsistent with Rumelt's original findings (1974). However, this result is consistent with the findings of McDougall and Round (1984).
2. There is greater difference in performance within any diversification category than between the diversification categories.
3. The relative performance of the different diversification categories is not consistent in different periods.

Another important result from the study is that while standardised EVA is a robust measure of economic performance, it does not necessarily reflect the value created for shareholders. This can be explained by economic performance measures (including EVA) do not incorporate either the present value of future cash flows or the value of the options implicit in a firm's strategy. Both of these factors are reflected in the share price and, therefore, are incorporated into the Total Shareholder Return measure. It seems likely that the extent to which these factors cause EVA to diverge from TSR will vary between industries Further analysis is being conducted to test this hypothesis. For example, it would be expected that industries with long investment cycles would show a greater difference between EVA and TSR than those with short investment cycles. Attempts to establish a stronger correlation between economic and market performance measures by elaborate adjustments to the basis EVA approach are probably misguided. More practical methods for valuing tangible and intangible options promise more useful benefits.

Implications from the study for Australian senior management are fourfold:

* First, and most importantly, diversification is not a simple solution to the question of how to create greater value for shareholders. Greater value for shareholders may be created by focussing on other elements of strategy such as developing corporate and business capabilities.
* Second, the range of performance within any diversification category highlights the difficulty of managing diversified businesses to consistent create shareholder value. It also suggests that not all companies have the skills, knowledge, resources or capabilities required at the corporate level to manage a diversified business.
* Third, the corporate strategy of a company should not be unchanging over time. The lack of consistency in relative performance of the different diversification categories between 1985 to 1989 and 1990 to 1994 highlights that a company's corporate strategy needs to be continuously and critically monitored to ensure that value is being, and will continue to be, created.
* Finally, the adoption of economic performance measures, such as EVA, needs to be considered carefully. Without a good understanding of the underlying assumptions of such measures, and adjustment of these assumptions to fit specific industries it is possible that management may make sub-optimal decisions leading to long-term value destruction rather than value creation.

Acknowledgement

The authors would like to thank National Australia Bank for their financial assistance in conducting this research.

The authors would also like to extend their appreciation to the two anonymous reviewers for their helpful comments and encouragement during the revision of this paper.

References

Baysinger, B. and Hoskisson, R.E. 1989. Diversification Strategy and R&D Intensity in Multiproduct Firms, *Academy of Management Journal,* 32:310-332

Berry, C.H. 1975. *Corporate Growth and Diversification.* Princeton: Princeton University Press

Bettis, R.A. 1981. Performance Differences in Related and Unrelated Diversified Firms, *Strategic Management Journal,* 2:379-393

Bettis, R.A. and Hall, W.K. 1982. Diversification Strategy, Accounting Determined Risk and, Accounting Determined Return, *Academy of Management Journal,* 25:254-264

Chenoweth, Neil 1997. 50pc of companies failing their shareholders, *Australian Financial Review,* June 10, 1997:1.

Christensen, H.K. and Montgomery, C.A. 1981. Corporate Economic Performance: Diversification Strategy versus Market Structure, *Strategic Management Journal,* 2:327-343

Dolan, M.J. 1985. The Case for the New Conglomerate, unpublished paper, Booz, Allen and Hamilton, New York in Grant, R.M., Jammine, A.P. and Thomas, H. 1988. Diversity, Diversification, and Profitability Among British Manufacturing Companies, 1972-84, *Academy of Management Journal,* 31:771-801

Hall, E.H. jr and St. John, C.H 1994. A Methodological Note on Diversity Measurement, *Strategic Management Journal,* 15:153-168

Hubbard, G. 1991. When do Takeovers Make Sense? *The Practising Manager,* June:14-21

Gibbs, S. 1984. Corporate Diversification in Australia, Honours thesis, University of Western Australia, Perth WA

Gorecki, K. 1980. A Problem of Measurement from Plants to Enterprise in the Analysis of Diversification: A Note, *Journal of Industrial Economics,* 28:327-334

Grant, R.M., Jammine, A.P. and Thomas, H. 1988. Diversity, Diversification, and Profitability Among British Manufacturing Companies, 1972-84, *Academy of Management Journal,* 31:771-801

Jacquemin, A.P. and Berry, C.H. 1979. Entropy measure of diversification and corporate growth, *Journal of Industrial Economics,* 27:359-369

Johnson, G. and Thomas, H. 1987. The Industry Context of Strategy, Structure and Performance: The U.K. Brewing Industry, *Strategic Management Journal,* 8:343-361

Lewis, G. 1993. The Fundamentals of Strategic Analysis, In G. Lewis, A. Morkel. and G. Hubbard, *Australian Strategic Management: Concepts, Context and Cases:* 51-90. Prentice Hall

McDougall, F.M. and Round, D.K. 1984. A Comparison of Diversifying and Nondiversifying Australian Industrial Firms, *Academy of Management Journal,* 27:384-398

Michel, A. and Shaked, I. 1984. Does Business Diversification Affect Performance? *Financial Management,* 13:4:18-24.

Mills, R. and Print, C. 1995. Strategic Value Analysis, *Management Accounting - London,* 73:2:35-37

Montgomery, C.A. 1982. The Measurement of Firm Diversification: Some New Empirical Evidence, *Academy of Management Journal,* 25:299-307

Montgomery, C.A. 1985. Product-market Diversification and Market Power, *Academy of Management Journal,* 28:789-798

Palepu, K. 1985. Diversification Strategy, Profit Performance and the Entropy Measure, *Strategic Management Journal,* 6:239-255

Peters, T.J. and Waterman, R.H. 1982. *In Search of Excellence: Lessons from America's Best-Run Companies.* New York: Harper and Row

Porter, M.E. 1980. *Competitive Strategy.* New York: Free Press

Prahalad, C.K. and Hamel, G. 1990. The Core Competence of the Corporation, *Harvard Business Review,* 90:79-91

Rajagopalan, S and Harrigan, K.R. 1986. Diversification and Market Performance: In Defence of the Unrelated Diversification Strategy, paper presented at the 46th meeting of the Academy of Management, Chicago

Ramanujam, V. and Varadarajan, P. 1989. Research on Corporate Diversification: A Synthesis, *Strategic Management Journal,* 10:523-551

Robins, J. and Wiersema, M.F. 1995. A Resource-based Approach to the Multi-Business Firm: Empirical Analysis of Portfolio Interrelationships and Corporate Financial Performance, *Strategic Management Journal,* 16:277-279

Rumelt, R.P. 1974. *Strategy, Structure and Economic Performance.* Boston: Harvard Business School Press

Rumelt, R.P. 1982. Diversification Strategy and Profitability, *Strategic Management Journal,* 3:359-369

Stewart, G.B. 1991. *The Quest for Value: A Guide for Senior Managers.* Harper Collins

Stubbart, C.L. and Grant, J.H. 1983. Diversification Strategy, Decentralization and Corporate Performance, Paper presented at the Strategic Management Society Conference, Paris

Teece, D.J., Pisano, G. and Shuen, A. 1991. Firm Capabilities, Resources and the Concept of Strategy: Four Paradigms of Strategic Management, Working Paper

Toomey, G. 1996. The Role of Value Management in Steering Qantas Airways, *Journal of Applied Finance and Investment,* 1:2:8-14

Wrigley, L., 1970. Division, Autonomy and Diversification, Doctoral dissertation, Harvard Business School, Boston MA

Appendix 1 Companies Included in the Study

Advance Bank
Amcor
Ampolex
Arnotts
Ashton Mining
Australia & New Zealand Banking Group
Australian Foundation Investment
Australian Gas Light Company
Australian National Industries
Bank of Melbourne
Boral
Brambles Industries
Brierley Investments
Broken Hill Proprietary Company
BTR-Nylex
Burns, Philip & Company
Burswood Property Trust
C R A
C S R
Caltex Australia
Coal & Allied Industries
Coca-Cola Amatil
Coles Myer
Comalco
Email
F.H. Faulding and Company
Fletcher Challenge
Foster's Brewing Group
General Property Trust
Gold Mines of Kalgoolie
Goodman Fielder
Highlands Gold

Homestake Gold of Australia
Howard Smith
ICI Australia
James Hardie Industries
Jupiters
Lend Lease Corporation
Mayne Nickless
Metal Manufacturers
MIM Holdings
National Australia Bank
News Corporation
North Limited
Pacific Dunlop
Pasminco
Pioneer International
Placer Pacific
Q.B.E. Insurance Group
QCT Resources
Renison Goldfields Consolidated
Rothmans Holdings
Santos
Schroders Property Fund
Stockland Trust Group
TNT
Tubemakers of Australia
Wesfarmers
Western Mining Corporation Holdings
Westfield Holdings
Westfield Trust
Westpac Banking Corporation
Woodside Petroleum

Appendix 2 Assumptions Made in Calculating the Cost of Capital

The cost of capital is an important factor in determining economic performance. To test the effect of different assumptions on the relative economic performance of the sample companies, six different sets of assumptions or methods were developed.

The assumptions underlying the six methods are described below.
Method 1 calculates the after tax cost of debt assuming a classical tax system and each company's annual effective tax rate. The cost of equity was calculated using the company's annual beta values reported by the Centre for Research in Finance, Australian Graduate School of Management. These values were then weighted using annual proportions of debt and equity.

Method 2 calculates the after tax cost of debt assuming an imputation tax system and each company's annual effective tax rate. The cost of equity was calculated using the company's annual beta values as reported. These values were then weighted using annual proportions of debt and equity.

Method 3 calculates the after tax cost of debt assuming a classical tax system and each company's annual effective tax rate. The cost of equity was calculated using the company's average beta values for the period. These values were then weighted using annual proportions of debt and equity.

Method 4 calculates the after tax cost of debt assuming an imputation tax system and each company's annual effective tax rate. The cost of equity was calculated using the company's average beta values for the period. These values were then weighted using annual proportions of debt and equity.

Method 5 calculates the after tax cost of debt assuming a classical tax system and an effective tax rate of 36 per cent. The cost of equity was calculated using the company's average beta values for the period. These values were then weighted using average proportion of debt and equity for the period.

Method 6 calculates the after tax cost of debt assuming an imputation tax system and an effective tax rate of 36 per cent. The cost of equity was calculated using the company's average beta values for the period. These values were then weighted using average proportion of debt and equity for the period.

15

Best predictors of high performance quality organisations: Evidence from Australia and New Zealand

Milé Terziovski

Abstract

This paper is based on a doctoral research study which analysed a large data base consisting of 962 responses from Australian manufacturing firms and 379 responses from New Zealand manufacturing firms. Multiple discriminant analysis was used to explore the differences between manufacturing firms grouped according to their level of organisational peformance. The study concluded that high peforming organisations focus on the 'softer' quality practices such as breaking down barriers between departments and continuous improvement, while low performing organisations tended to focus on the 'harder' quality practices such as ISO 9000 certification, and benchmarking.

Literature Review

There is a great deal of literature on TQM which falls into two groups:
1. Prescriptive literature.
2. Empirical literature.

Both groups fail to articulate the critical practices associated with high organisational performance. The prescriptive literature describes in detail various quality management practices and examines various approaches of single organisations in detail. Although these types of articles are useful to practitioners in learning about the implementation of various quality management practices, they fail to scientifically link these practices to quality performance. The second group of studies mainly compare quality management practices implemented in the United States and Japan. Both groups fail to articulate the relationship between the use of specific quality management practices and quality performance.

Rigorous research to establish the relationship between TQM practice and organisational performance is scarce. This is partly because TQM initiatives have not been running for long enough to give the TQM philosophy and methods a full test. This is demonstrated by the limited research which complies with generally-accepted standards of methodological rigour. For example, Sluti (1992); Powell (1995); Flynn. *et al.* (1995); Forker (1996) conducted empirical studies in order to test the relationship between quality management practice and organisational performance. The empirical evidence from these studies suggests that TQM brings increased quality and productivity, along with improved customer and employee satisfaction. Moreover, Sluti (1992) found significant structural equation model links among the following performance outcomes: employee satisfaction, product quality, productivity, customer satisfaction, and cooperation.

Flynn, *et al.* (1995) utilised multiple discriminant analysis to examine the differences between plants grouped according to their level of quality performance, and to separate out the critical success factors that high performing firms use. Flynn, *et al.* (1995) examined the differences in quality management practices between plants that achieve high, intermediate, and low levels of quality performance. Empirical data were obtained from US plants in the machinery, transportation components, and electronics industries. The study identified the following critical practices: concurrent engineering, new-product quality, employee involvement, feedback, maintenance, labour skill level, selection for teamwork potential, process control, and supplier relationships. An interesting result that emerged from the study was that best and poorest levels of quality performance firms used similar (strong) levels of quality management practices. On the other hand, firms that achieved intermediate levels of quality performance used inferior quality management practices. The authors speculated that the intermediate-quality plants may have been complacent, while the low-quality plants were striving to catch up and the high-quality plants were seeking continuous improvement.

Research Questions

Two questions emerged from the literature review which are addressed in this study:

1. What is it about high-quality organisations that makes them different from other organisations?
2. Which quality management practices are most critical in achieving high-quality performance?

These questions were addressed by applying the Multiple Discriminant Analysis (MDA) technique. This statistical technique allows researchers to examine the differences between organisations grouped according to their level of organisational performance (Hair, *et al.,* 1992). MDA also allows the identification of the critical practices focussed on by high performance organisations, and by those with low organisational performance.

Theoretical Framework and Hypotheses

Principles of TQM

Based on the work of leading experts such as Deming (1982); Crosby (1979, 1985); Juran and Gryna (1988); and Tribus (1988), Samson (1991) articulated eight principles that were associated with moving to a total quality culture.

Principle 1: People work in a system

- Managers must work on the system to improve it.
- Managers should be able to identify and describe systems.
- Employees should be taught how to observe and improve systems.
- Managers should lead improvement efforts and lead improvement teams.
- Managers should be able to reason with statistics.

Principle 2: All systems exhibit variability, and variability must be controlled

From the pioneering work of Deming (1982) it is evident that good practice in quality management involves an understanding and measurement of variability so that process control can be achieved. Once processes are in control, then process capability can be systematically addressed, and products and services can be designed in a robust manner to satisfy customer requirements. TQM tools and techniques such as seven Quality Control tools, and Ishikawa diagrams are applied for collecting and analysing data for problem solving and decision making.

Principle 3: Most problems result from poorly designed systems

Wide experience such as that reported by Juran and Gryna (1988) shows that 80 per cent of problems are due to system related problems, and fewer than 20 per cent are due to operator errors. It is therefore more effective to improve the quality by improving the system.

Principle 4: The answer to many problems involves instilling quality in the process

Problem solving means removing the constraints and limiting factors that act as barriers to doing an excellent job. This involves an assessment of process capability, with the desired outcome of matching design specifications to machine and operator capacity. Quality awareness should aim to raise the level of personal concern felt by employees towards the quality reputation of the company. Training, motivation and involvement are essential in this endeavour.

Principle 5: *The relevant definition of quality is that of the customer*

The goal of satisfying customers is fundamental to TQM and is expressed by the organisation's attempt to design and deliver products and services that fulfil customer needs. The rationale for this principle is the belief that customer satisfaction is the most important requirement for long-term organisational performance. This requires that the entire organisation be focused on customers' needs. Practices exemplifying customer focus include promoting direct contact with customers, collecting information about customers' expectations, and disseminating this information within the organisation. These practices and techniques can also be applied to internal customers (ie. those whose work depends on prior work by others in the organisation).

Principle 6: *All members of an organisation should contribute to the quality culture*

Schein (1985) identified three levels of organisational culture:

1. *Artefacts:* Observable activities, behaviours, events, rituals.
2. *Values:* Statements about what is good or bad. Often used to explain an artefact.
3. *Basic assumptions:* Commonly held views of the world that are taken for granted and usually drive much of the organisation's behaviour.

Many organisations find it relatively easy to make changes in artefacts and values, but fail to challenge their deeply held beliefs about customers, organisation's mission, the means of achieving performance goals, people, motivation, and what level of quality is achievable. Beliefs are the most critical elements of any organisation, as they determine where executives and managers place their priorities and what options they consider.

Principle 7: *Improvement must be planned and must be continuous*

Continuous improvement can be considered at two levels. The first level is the improvement of the quality culture and overall integrity of all aspects of the organisation. The second is improvement of systems, processes, products, and services that are offered to customers. Spontaneous change is rare in organisations. Change must be planned, with people being encouraged to change their mindset of work from 'near enough is good enough' to 'improvement is a way of life' (Kanter, 1987; Blackburn & Rosen, 1993; Conger & Kanungo, 1988; Creech, 1994).

The TQM philosophy and methods are underpinned by the continuous improvement concept driven by the Deming Cycle (Evans & Lindsay, 1995) and the KAIZEN concept (Imai, 1986). This is a methodology for continuous improvement, composed of four stages: Plan, Do, Check, and Act. The Plan stage consists of studying the current situation, gathering data and planning for improvement. In the Do stage, the plan is implemented on a trial basis.

The Check stage is designed to determine if the trial plan is working correctly and if any further problems or opportunities are found (Imai, 1986; Dean & Bowen, 1994; Dean & Evans, 1994). The last stage, Act, is the implementation of the final plan to ensure that the improvements will be standardised and practiced continuously. This leads back to the Plan stage for further diagnosis and improvement. It is during the Act stage where an ISO 9000 quality certification system can play a role. According to Binney (1992), the role of a quality system acts as a 'wedge' to sustain the achievement of the PDCA cycle, thus preventing performance from sliding backwards.

The concepts and principles of TQM discussed above are encompassed by the Malcolm Baldrige National Quality Award Criteria (MBNQA Criteria, 1995). The seven categories of the criteria: leadership, people, customer focus, strategic planning, process management, information and analysis, and organisational performance have been adopted as the TQM model for the discriminant analysis. For a complete exposition of the TQM model see Terziovski (1997).

Principle 8: Quality pays

The TQM philosophy and methods, when successfully implemented in an organisation can lead to improvement in organisational performance, such as: improved process yields, motivated employees, satisfied customers, improved quality, productivity and profitability.

Organisational Performance

Organisational Performance is a recurrent theme in most branches of management, including strategic management, and is of interest to academics and practitioners (Venkatraman & Ramanujam, 1986). Although the importance of the performance concept (and the broader area, organisational effectiveness) is widely recognised, some researchers have expressed considerable frustration with the concept. (Venkatraman & Ramanujam, 1986).

The organisational performance construct is made up of four key measurable areas of a company's operations in accordance with the GAO Study (Ritter, 1991). These areas are:

• Operating Performance
• Financial Performance
• Customer Satisfaction
• Employee Relations

Hypotheses

Based on the research questions and the theoretical framework discussed above, the following hypotheses were articulated for testing:

H1: High performing firms differentiate themselves by emphasising the 'softer' dimensions of the MBNQA: leadership, people management and customer focus, than the medium, and low performing firms which place emphasis on the 'harder' categories of the MBNQA: strategic planning, information & analysis, and process management.

H2: The TQM practices that are most significant in differentiating between high, medium, and low performing companies are: elimination of barriers by management; pursuit of continuous improvement; all employees believing that quality is their responsibility; effective 'top-down' and 'bottom-up' communication; and shop floor ideas used by management.

Methodology

The aim of the study was to separate the key TQM practices that high, medium, and low performing organisations use in their pursuit of a total quality culture. This type of analysis allows us to develop group profiles which would help us to understand why TQM works in some organisations and not in others.

The MDA function available on the SPSS for Windows program was used to generate the discriminant functions and test hypotheses H1 and H2. The MDA procedure involves the computation of a single composite discriminant score for each firm in the analysis. The discriminant scores are then averaged for all firms within a group to derive the *group mean*. This group mean is referred to as the *centroid*. The group centroids show how far apart the groups are along the dimension being tested. Therefore, MDA is the appropriate statistical technique for testing the hypothesis that the group means for two or more groups are equal.

Variable Selection

The procedure for computing discriminant functions began with the selection of the independent variables from the Surrogate—MBNQA (Terziovski, 1997). These variables were included in the analysis of each of the two hypotheses being tested, H1 and H2. Discriminant functions were computed by using the direct simultaneous method on SPSS for Windows, MDA function (Hair, *et al.,* 1992: 99). Two discriminant functions were generated for each hypothesis, since there were three a *priori* groups. These functions were used to test hypothesis H1.

Consequent to the above analysis, the organisational performance construct was transformed to a non-metric 'dummy categorical variable' by using the 'transform variable' function on SPSS. The normal distribution curve for the organisational performance construct was plotted using the descriptive statistic function on SPSS. The sample was divided into approximately three equal categories: high performance, medium performance, and low performance. The Z scores on the horizontal axis of the distribution curve were used to define the range for each group:

- *Low Performing Group:* (Category Code: 0) Range - 3.25 < Z < - 0.75
- *Medium Performing Group:* (Category Code: 1) Range - 0.75 < Z < + 0.75
- *High Performing Group:* (Category Code: 2) Range +0.75 < Z < +3.25

Therefore, a new categorical variable for organisational performance was created (ALLCAT). After the selection of the independent variables and the creation of the new categorical dependent variable ALLCAT, the next step was to compute the discriminant functions for hypotheses, H1 and H2.

Results
Statistical Significance of Discriminant Functions

The Chi-square statistic was computed to describe the discriminant functions' ability to discriminate between groups. This statistic was the overall measure of the statistical significance of the discriminant functions. Table 1 provides information related to the statistical significance of the discriminant functions H1(A) and H1(B) for hypothesis H1.

Similarly, Table 2 provides information related to the statistical significance of the discriminant functions H2(C) and H2(D) for hypothesis H2. The Chi-square for discriminant function H1 (A) was calculated at 204.8, and for H1 (B) the Chi-square was calculated at 2.55. As a secondary check, the statistical significance of the discriminant functions was confirmed by using the conventional criterion level of significance, p=0.05. Therefore, H1(A) was found to have a significance level of p=0.00, while H1 (B) was found to have a significance level of p=0.77. These results indicate that the discriminant function H1(A) was statistically significant, while H1 (B) was statistically non-significant.

The same procedure was repeated for hypothesis H2. The Chi-square for discriminant function H2 (C) was calculated at 338.7, and for H2 (D) the Chi-square was calculated at 26.99. As a secondary check, the statistical significance of the discriminant functions was confirmed by using the conventional criterion level of significance, p=0.05. Therefore, H2(C) was found to have a significance level of p=0.00, while H2(D) was found to have a significance level of p=0.89. These results indicate that the discriminant function H2(C) was statistically significant, while H2 (D) was statistically non-significant. Therefore, for hypotheses H1 and H2, the statistically significant functions H1 (A) and H2 (C) explain the largest amount of difference between the three groups. The statistically non-significant discriminant functions H1 (B), and H2 (D) explain the largest amount of residual variance, after the variance for the first discriminant function was removed. The canonical correlation coefficients indicate each discriminant function's importance. Squared, they indicate the per cent of variance explained.

Table 1 shows that the discriminant function H1 (A) accounts for 18.05 per cent of the variance in the dependent categorical variable. On the other hand, H1(B) accounts for almost zero (0.003) per cent of the variance in the dependent categorical variable. Similarly, Table 2 shows that the discriminant function H2 (C) accounts for 27 per cent of the variance in the dependent variable. On the other hand, H2 (D) accounts for only (0.03) per cent of the variance in the dependent variable. The Wilks' lambda statistic was used to check how well the discriminating functions differentiated among the three groups: high, medium, and low performance firms. Smaller values of Wilks' lambda for each independent variable indicate greater differences among the three groups. Table 1 shows that H1 (A) and H1(B) have a Wilk's lambda of 0.82 and 0.99 respectively. Table 2 shows that H2 (C) and H2 (D) have a Wilk's lambda of 0.71 and 0.97 respectively. Considering these results, it is evident that the discriminant function H2(C) was the greatest discriminator among the three groups, followed by H1(A) and H2(D). The weakest discriminating function among the three groups was found to be H1(B).

To characterise each of the groups, the value of the means of each of the independent variables was checked. Higher group mean values correspond to 'better' TQM practices as defined by the TQM model and the literature review (Flynn, *et al.*, 1995, p.21). Table 3 lists the means, F values and the statistical significance of the F value for high, medium and low performance firms. Table 3 shows that the high performing groups typically used the better TQM practices, as indicated by the high group means. The medium performing firms used the second most effective TQM practices and the low performing firms used the least effective TQM practices.

For example, the people category scored the highest mean with the high performing companies (0.50), while information and analysis scored the highest mean with the low performing companies (0.01). The people category had the smallest Wilk's lambda. This was followed by the leadership, customer focus strategic planning and process management. The information & analysis category had the largest lambda value, indicating that the differentiating power of this category was the weakest.

Group Centroids

Group centroids are the mean of the discriminant function scores for observations in each discriminating group. Group centroids were computed (Table 4) to determine where the significant differences lie. Comparisons were made between the different combinations of high, medium, and low performing groups.

The two discriminating functions, H1(A) and H2(C) provide the most significant differences between the high performance group and a combination of medium and low performance groups.

Validation of Discriminant Functions

To determine the predictive ability (validity) of the discriminant functions, the analysis involved the development of classification matrices. The Hit Ratios (percentage correctly classified) for the significant discriminant functions H1(A) and H2(C) were 44.42 per cent and 53.42 per cent respectively.

Classification Accuracy Relative to Chance

According to Hair, *et al.* (1992: 105) '...the question of classification accuracy is crucial.' If the percentage of correct classification is significantly larger than would be expected by chance, an attempt can be made to interpret the discriminant functions in the hope of developing group profiles. Hair, *et al.* (1992) suggest that the classification accuracy should be at least 25 per cent greater than that achieved by chance. For example, if chance accuracy is 50 per cent (two-group equal sample sizes) the classification accuracy should be 62.5 per cent. If chance accuracy is 30 per cent, the classification accuracy should be 37.5 per cent. In our analysis we have three group sizes of approximately equal size, therefore, chance accuracy is 33.33 per cent. Therefore the classification accuracy should be 25 per cent greater than the chance accuracy, i.e. 41.58 per cent. Examining the hit ratio results for both significant discriminant functions we find that the hit ratio for H1(A)= 44.42 per cent, and the hit ratio for H2(C)=53.42 per cent. For both discriminant functions, the hit ratios were greater than the chance accuracy of 41.58 per cent.

Press' Q

Press' Q statistic was used to provide a check on the discriminating power of the classification matrix when compared to chance (Hair, et al., 1992: 105). This measure compares the number of correct classifications with the total sample size and the number of groups. The calculated value is then compared with a critical value (the Chi-square value for 1 degree of freedom at the desired confidence level). If it exceeds this critical value, then the classification matrix can be deemed statistically better than chance.

Hair, *et al.* (1992: 106) recommend a critical value of 6.63 at a significance level of 0.01. The formula for Press' Q (Hair, *et al.,* 1992: 106) was used to compute the Press' Q value for the statistically significant discriminating function, H1 (A). The calculated value is 56.55. Since this value exceeds the critical value of 6.63, the classification matrix for the discriminating function H1 (A) was deemed statistically better than chance. Similarly, Press' Q value was calculated for the second statistically significant discriminant function, H2 (C). The calculated value is 187.46. Since this value exceeds the critical value of 6.63, the classification matrix for the discriminating function H2 (C) was deemed statistically better than chance.

Interpretation of the Discriminant Functions

To check the linear correlation between each independent variable and the statistically significant discriminant functions, H1(A) and H2(C), the independent variables were analysed using rotated discriminant loadings (structure correlations). The structure correlations reflect the variance that each independent variable share with the discriminant function. Hair, *et al.* (1992: 119) state that 'In simultaneous discriminant analysis...variables exhibiting loadings +/- 0.3 or higher are considered significant.' Considering this rule, hypotheses H1 and H2 were tested in the following section by interpreting the results obtained for each independent variable.

Test of Hypothesis H1—Discriminant Loadings

The following independent variables (rank ordered according to the discriminant loading) were found to contribute significantly to the discriminant function H1(A):

- People (0.874).
- Leadership (0.775).
- Customer focus (0.633).
- Strategic planning (0.610).

Furthermore, the discriminant function H1(A) was found to be statistically significant at the 0.05 level of significance and had a Chi-square value of 204.8. Considering these findings, *hypothesis H1 is supported.* The discriminant function H1(B) was found to be statistically non-significant, and explains only a minor percentage of the variance in the dependent variable. However, the process management category had a discriminant loading of 0.83 (>0.3) and therefore contributed significantly to the discriminant function, H1(B). Information & analysis had a discriminant loading of 0.091 and therefore did not contribute significantly to the discriminant function H1(B).

Test of Hypothesis H2—Discriminant Loadings

The following independent TQM variables (rank ordered according to their discriminant loading) were found to contribute significantly to the discriminant functions H2(C) and H2(D):

le2 (0.617): Unity of purpose and eliminated barriers between individuals and/or departments.

le4 (0.591): Pursuit of continuous improvement rather than 'fire-fighting.'

pe3 (0.539): Effective 'top-down' and 'bottom-up' communication.

le5 (0.512): Ideas from production operators used in assisting management.

qp8 (0.511): All employees believe that quality is their responsibility.

pe6 (0.445): Employee flexibility, multi-skilling and training are actively used to support improved performance.

cf2 (0.424): Customer requirements are effectively disseminated and understood
throughout the workforce.

pl6 (0.411): Manufacturing operations are effectively aligned with the central business mission.

pl4 (0.410): Customer requirements, supplier capabilities, and needs of other stakeholders, including the community are incorporated when plans, policies, and objectives are developed.

pe5 (0.409): Occupational health and safety practices are excellent.

pe4 (0.377): Employee satisfaction is formally and regularly measured.

cf5 (0.367): Effective process is in place for resolving external customer complaints.

pe2 (0.357): Organisation-wide training and development process, including career path planning, for all employees.

qp5 (0.356): Established methods to measure the quality of products and services.

pl1 (0.351): Mission statement which has been communicated throughout the company and is supported by our employees.

pe1 (0.347): The concept of the internal customer is well supported.

cf7 (0.346): External customer satisfaction is systematically and regularly measured.

pl3 (0.344): Plans focus on achievement of 'best practice'

pl2 (0.317): Comprehensive and structured planning process which regularly sets and reviews short and long term goals.

le3 (0.313): 'Champions of change' are used to drive 'best practice.'

Hypothesis H2, stated the TQM practices that were most significant differentiators between high, medium, and low performing firms were:

- Elimination of barriers by management.
- Pursuit of continuous improvement.
- All employees believing that quality is their responsibility.
- Effective 'top-down' and 'bottom-up' communication.
- Shopfloor ideas used by management.

The independent variables listed above have discriminant loadings greater than 0.30, therefore, they were considered to contribute significantly to the discriminant function H2(C). Furthermore, the discriminant function H2(C) was found to be statistically significant at the 0.05 level of significance and had a Chi-square value of 338.7. Considering these findings, hypothesis H2 is supported. The discriminant function H2(D) was found to be statistically non-significant, and explains only a minor percentage of the variance in the dependent variable. However, there was one independent TQM variable that had a discriminant loading greater than 0.3, and therefore contributed significantly to the discriminating function H2(D). This variable was qp6.

qp6 (0.326): Site-wide standardised and documented operating procedures.

Discussion of Discriminant Analysis Results

This section provides a non-technical discussion of the results, and the implications of the findings. The results of the MDA indicate which TQM practices best differentiate between high, medium, and low performing firms. The people management category was the best contributor to the statistically significant discriminant functions, H1(A) and H2(C). This category was followed (in order) by leadership, customer focus, and strategic planning. The TQM categories that were relatively poor contributors to the discriminant functions were process management and information & analysis. Hypotheses H1 and H2 were, therefore, supported.

The most significant discriminant function in the test of hypothesis H1, was found to be H1(A). This function reflects the distinction between the firms that achieved high levels of performance, and the combination of the firms that achieved both medium and low levels of performance. Table 3 indicates the nature of the differences between the groups according to their relative means. The high performing groups typically used the better TQM practices, as indicated by the high group means. The medium performing firms used the second most effective TQM practices and the low performing firms used the least effective TQM practices. These results show strong support for the importance of the 'soft' categories of the TQM model: people management, leadership, and customer focus.

TQM Practices as Independent Variables

The second hypothesis, H2, shows that the 'softer' TQM practices do indeed contribute to differences in organisational performance. The five independent TQM variables that contributed significantly to these differences include:

- Unity of purpose and barriers eliminated between individuals and/or departments (leadership category)
- Pursuit of continuous improvement (leadership category)
- Effective 'top-down' and 'bottom-up' communication (people category)
- Ideas from production operators used in assisting management (leadership category)
- All employees believe that quality is their responsibility (people category)

The second discriminant function, H2(D) was found to be statistically non-significant. These results indicate that medium and low performing firms tend to differentiate themselves on 'hard' TQM practices as compared to high performing firms which tend to differentiate themselves on the 'soft' TQM practices. The hit ratio (per cent of firms correctly classified) was calculated to be 53.52 per cent for discriminant function, H2(C) and H2(D) as compared to 44.42 per cent for the discriminant functions H1(A) and H1(B). In both cases the two statistically significant discriminant functions discriminated better than chance.

Implications for Managers

Many organisations have found it difficult to implement an effective TQM policy. One of the prime reasons for this is that organisations do not have credible evidence in terms of which TQM practices contribute to organisational performance, and why and how they contribute to this performance. This generally causes misunderstanding and disagreement on the expected benefits of TQM. Therefore, confirmation of Hypotheses H1, and H2, has significant implications for managers at all levels of the organisation for the implementation of TQM philosophy and methods.

Hypothesis H1 confirmed that the 'softer' dimensions of the MBNQA leadership, people management and customer focus are better predictors of organisational performance than the 'harder' dimensions of strategic planning, information & analysis, and process management. This finding would alert managers that priority should be placed on the 'softer' dimensions of TQM rather than the 'harder' dimensions. There is a clear message for managers that leadership, people management issues and customer focus are characteristic of high performing, best practice organisations.

Hypothesis H2 has implications for middle and supervisory managers. The research identified five significant TQM practices that differentiate between high, medium, and low performing companies. These practices are listed below in order of discriminating power between the three groups:

• Unity of purpose and elimination of barriers between departments
• Pursuit of continuous improvement
• Shopfloor ideas used by management
• Effective top-down and bottom-up communication
• All employees believe that quality is their responsibility

Conclusion

Based on Multiple Discriminant Analysis of manufacturing firms that were categorically grouped according to their level of performance (high, medium, low), the study concludes that high performing firms differentiate themselves by placing more emphasis on the 'softer' dimensions of the TQM model.

On the other hand, low performing firms were found to place more emphasis on the 'harder' categories of the TQM model: information & analysis, and process management. Medium performing firms were found to place emphasis on both 'soft' and 'hard' practices. Therefore, it is reasonable to speculate that the medium performing firms were going through a 'transitional' phase and would eventually place more emphasis on the 'soft' TQM practices and become high performing firms. The most surprising finding of the study was that the process management and information & analysis categories were poor discriminators between high, medium, and low performing groups.

Considering the support for hypotheses H1 and H2, it is reasonable to conclude that a high performing quality organisation would have a strong leader who believes in unity of purpose and breaks down barriers between departments and individuals. The leader achieves this by constantly communicating the vision and mission of the organisation from the 'top-down' and constantly seeks feedback from the 'bottom-up.' This encourages all employees in the organisation to believe that quality is their responsibility.

References

Binney, G., Making Quality Work: Lessons from Europe's Leading Companies, The Economist Intelligence Unit, Special Report No.P655 Ashridge, 1992.

Blackburn, R., & Rosen, B. Total Quality and Human Resources Management: Lessons Learned from Baldrige Award-winning Companies. Academy of Management Executive, 7(3): 49-66, 1993.

Conger, J. A., & Kanungo, R., The Empowerment Process: Integrating Theory and Practice, Academy of Management Review, 13: 471-482, 1988.

Creech, B., The Five Pillars of TQM: How to Make Total Quality Management Work For You, Truman Talley Books/Dutton, New York, 1994.

Crosby, P. B., Quality is Free: The Art of Making Quality Certain, New York: New American Library, 1979.

Dean, J. W., Jr., & Evans, J. R., Total Quality: Management, Organisation. and Strategy. St. Paul, MN: West, 1994.

Dean, J.W., Jr. & Bowen, D.E., Managing Theory and Total Quality: Improving Research and Practice Through Theory Development, Academy of Management Review, Vol. 19, No. 3, pp. 392-418, 1994.

Deming, W. E. Out of the Crisis, Cambridge: Massachusetts Institute of Technology Press, 1986.

Deming, W.E., Quality Productivity and Competitive Position, MIT, Mass, 1982.

Evans, J. R., & Lindsay, W. M., The Management and Control of Quality, West Publishing Company, 3rd edition, 1995.

Flynn, B.B., Schroeder, R., and Sakakibara, S., Determinants of Quality Performance in High - and Low - Quality Plants, Quality Management Journal, Vol. 2, No. 2, pp. 8- 25, Winter, 1995.

Forker, L., The Contribution of Quality to Business Performance, International Journal of Operations and Production Management, Vol 16, No. 8, pp 44-62, 1996.

Hair, J.F. Jr., Anderson, R.E., and Tatham, R.L., Multivariate Data Analysis, Macmillan Publishing Company: New York, Third Edition, 1992.

Imai, M., Kaizen: The Key to Japan's Competitive Success. New York: McGraw-Hill, 1986.

Juran, J.M. and Gryna, F.M. Juran's Quality Control Handbook. 4th edition. McGraw-Hill, New York,1988.

Kanter, R., Quality Leadership and Change, Quality Progress, pp.45-51, February, 1987.

Malcolm Baldrige National Quality Award Criteria, Washington, DC: United States Department of Commerce, National Institute of Standards and Technology, 1995.

Powell, T.C., Total Quality Management as Competitive Advantage: A Review and Empirical Study, Strategic Management Journal, Vol.16, No.1, pp.15 -37, January 1995.

Prahalad, C. K., & Hamel, G., The Core Competence of the Corporation. Harvard Business Review, Vol. 68, No.3, 79-89, 1990.

Ritter, D., Report to the House of Representatives on Management Practices, US Companies Improve Performance Through Quality Efforts, United States General Accounting Office, Washington, D.C., 1991.

Samson, D.A., Manufacturing and Operations Strategy, Prentice - Hall, New York, 1991.

Schein, E.H., Organisational Culture and Leadership: A Dynamic View, San Francisco: Jossey - Bass, 1985.

Sluti, D.G. Linking Process Quality with Performance: An Empirical Study of New Zealand Manufacturing Plants, PhD Dissertation, The University of Auckland, Auckland, N.Z. 1992.

Terziovski, M., The Relationship Between Quality Management Strategies and Organisational Performance in Manufacturing Firms, Unpublished PhD Thesis, Melbourne Business School, The University of Melbourne, February, 1997.

Tribus, M., Total Quality Management, Notes on a Lecture Series, BHP The Tribus Lectures, 1988.

Venkatraman, N., and Ramanujam, V., Measurement of Business Performance in Strategy Research: A Comparison of Approaches, Academy of Management Review, Vol.11, No.4, pp.801-814, 1986.

Appendix

Statistic \ Hypothesis	Discr. Funct	Canon. Correl.	% Variance Explained	Wilk's Lambda	Chi-square	Degree of freed df	Signif. Level
H1 High performing firms differentiate themselves by focusing on the 'softer' dimensions of the MBNQA: leadership, human resources development and customer focus	H1 (A)	0.43	18.05	0.82	204.8	12	0.00
than the medium, and low performing firms which tend to focus on the 'harder' dimensions of the MBNQA: strategic planning, info. & analysis and process management.	H1 (B)	0.05	0.003	0.99	2.55	5	0.77

Table 1 Canonical discriminant functions characteristics

Statistic \ Hypothesis	Discr. Funct	Canon. Correl.	% Variance Explained	Wilk's Lambda	Chi-square	Degree of freed df	Signif. Level
H2 The TQM practices which are the most significant differentiators between high, medium, and low performing firms are: elimination of barriers by management, pursuit of continuous improvement, all	H2 (C)	0.52	27	0.71	339.16	78	0.00
employees believing that quality is their responsibility, effective 'top-down' and 'bottom-up' communication and shop floor ideas used by management.	H2 (D)	0.16	0.03	0.97	27.36	38	0.89

Table 2 Canonical discriminant functions characteristics—TQM practices

Table 3 Group means of the TQM categories

Independent Variable	High Perf. Mean	Medium Perf. Mean	Low Perf. Mean	F Value	Sigf Off	Wilks Lamba
People	0.50	0.05	-0.62	85.65	0.00	0.856
Leadership	0.48	0.03	-0.55	67.47	0.00	0.883
Cust. Focus	0.38	0.04	-0.47	44.97	0.00	0.919
Strategic Planning	0.37	0.03	-0.45	41.69	0.00	0.924
Process Mgmt.	0.20	0.05	-0.35	20.08	0.00	0.962
Info. & An.	-0.02	0.00	0.01	0.07	0.94	0.999

TABLE 4 Centroids for discriminant analysis by categories and TQM practices

Categorical Group	Discriminant Function	High Performance	Medium Performance	Low Performance
High vs Medium and Low	1A (Category)	0.63	0.05	-0.76
Medium vs High and Low	1A (Category)	-0.07	0.04	-0.05
High vs Medium and Low	2B (TQM pract)	0.83	0.06	-0.97
Medium vs High and Low	2B (TQM Pract)	-0.21	0.15	-0.16

16

Do cultural differences explain the problems faced by Western firms in China?

Edward Vaughan

Abstract

The troubled record of Sino-Western joint ventures in China has been widely attributed to cultural differences and the failure of Western managements to adapt to Chinese ways of thinking and acting. This is only partly correct. Cultural conflict is as much a problem within China as it is a problem between China and the West, and it therefore cannot be resolved by Western adaptation to Chinese ways of thinking and acting.

Introduction

The uneven performance record of international joint ventures in China has undoubtedly contributed to China's reputation as 'Asia's epicentre of both opportunity and risk' (Asia Yearbook, 1996: 7). There can equally be no doubt from studies and surveys that frustration, tension and acrimony have soured relations in many of these partnerships, and that negotiations and human resource management have been the primary areas in which disputes have erupted, particularly in Sino-Western joint ventures (Aiello, 1991; Tsang, 1994; Bjorkman & Schaap, 1994; Huo and Von Glinow, 1995). Many analysts claim that differences between Chinese and Western management are especially pronounced and problematic in these areas, and their advice to Western companies has been to make a thorough study of Chinese management practices before entering into a joint venture with a Chinese enterprise (Kirkbride & Tang, 1994; Zhao, 1994; Xing, 1995).

Reports which observe that Chinese and Western management practices differ are not incorrect, nor are those which claim that differences between Chinese and Western cultures can lead to misunderstandings and tensions in jointly managed projects. However, those which add that Western companies have been mainly to blame for the problems should certainly be disputed. While it shall not be denied that opposing values have played a large part in causing problems, these conflicts are as much reflective of internal cultural conflicts in China as they are indicative of cultural conflicts between China and Western nations. In addition, adaptation has proceeded the opposite way from that suggested in much of the literature: traditional culture and customs in developing nations have given way to modern 'rationalist' values and practices.

Before outlining these arguments, the 'cultural differences hypothesis' (as it shall be termed) will be discussed in some detail so that it, and the objections to it, will be more clearly understood.

The Cultural Differences Hypothesis

Ferraro (1990: 7) summed up the cultural differences hypothesis clearly when, after noting the poor record of international joint ventures in China and other developing nations, he concluded that problems have usually arisen more from 'an inability to understand and adapt to foreign ways of thinking and acting, rather than from technical or professional incompetence'.

Claims about the differences between Chinese (or, more generally, Asian) culture and Western culture owe much to the research of Hofstede (1984), who found, among other differences, a wide difference on an Individualism-Collectivism cultural dimension. In brief, a nation's position on this shows the extent to which it encourages self-interest to be put above group or community interests, or *vice versa*. According to Hofstede, Western nations, particularly English-speaking nations, favour the former and encourage people to assert their independence and to compete for recognition and reward. Similarly, Kornhauser (1954) had much earlier theorised on how these values supply a strong motive to view conflict as a legitimate means of asserting one's rights and achieving one's ends.

Surveys of Asian nations reveal the opposite cultural disposition, encouraging subordination of self-interest to the collective interest. The roots of this collectivism are said to lie in traditional Asian culture, particularly in Confucianism, which emphasises the desirability of social harmony and consensus and requires that respect be shown to persons with authority and status, and also respect generally for the 'face' (or dignity) of others. Business relationships, management practice, and other official dealings and communications are said to be influenced by the same traditional values (Lockett, 1987; Pheng, 1994; Satow & Wang, 1994; Zhao, 1994), and are therefore similarly expected to reflect mutual personal respect and demonstration of good faith. Unfortunately, the behaviours that result from these values can easily be misinterpreted when viewed from a Western cultural perspective. Problems are naturally likely to develop when Western managers have no knowledge of these cultural values, and view the behaviour of their Chinese partners as time-wasting, evasive, and inefficient.

The clear implication in much of the advice emanating from the cultural differences hypothesis is that companies abroad bear the greater responsibility to understand and adapt to the other culture. The gist of the advice, as Weiss (1996) remarked, has been to 'do as Romans do'.

The latter is value-free advice in the sense that it regards foreign cultures neutrally. As Perlitz (1994) observed, it is not the culture that is judged to be good or bad, but rather the fit between management practice and cultural demands. The advice is therefore consistent with the broad contingency approach that attempts to match organisation and management to environmental demands, and is also utterly pragmatic, in the manner of *Realpolitik,* in implying that there is no realistic alternative but to adapt to culture if the company is survive and prosper. The advice acknowledges what some have termed the 'cultural imperative' (Schuler, Dowling and DeCieri, 1993), and others the 'political imperative' (Doz, 1987). In either case it asserts that if it is good for business to adapt to local culture and customs, then management has no choice but to adapt. There have been doubters, such as Hardman (1996), who warn that cultural adaptation might make it appear that unethical practices are being condoned, but the reply to this would be that cultural relativism (the belief that there are no absolute grounds for judging one culture to be better or worse than any other) is no more morally questionable than the cultural elitism implied in criticising practices that are condoned abroad.

There is a separate and distinct argument for cultural adaptation that has carried less weight, but which should also be included here. It contradicts the cultural neutrality of the previous argument by claiming that Asian cultural values offer a positive example for Western managers to follow. The argument is therefore basically an extension of that favoured in the 1980s, when influential writers, such as Ouchi (1981) and Peters and Waterman (1982), had urged Western managers to imitate Japanese culture and management practices—especially human resource management practices—in their own organisations, since it was believed that these had given Japan an advantage over the West.

'Japanisation' has thus been broadened to 'Asianisation', and this has also been at least partly due to the influence of Hofstede. Hofstede and Bond (1988) found that South East Asian nations with high rates of economic growth, including Korea, Taiwan, Singapore, and Hong Kong, share the same philosophical-cultural tradition of Confucianism. They theorised that this could explain their strong economic growth, because, as well as valuing harmony and balance in everyday life, Confucianism also emphasises the virtues of persistence, thrift, and working collectively for future prosperity. The result, Hofstede and Bond claimed, is a 'Confucian dynamism' that illustrates the opposite of Western values, such as individualism and emphasis on short term gain.

Perhaps China, with its large, costly, and inefficient state-enterprise sector, might not provide a good example of Confucian dynamism, but some writers argue that there might be a sufficiently strong cultural similarity between China and other South East Asian nations to suggest some useful lessons for Western managers in China's culture, particularly its lessons on negotiation and leadership style (Kirkbride & Tang, 1994; Pheng, 1994).

In summary, the cultural differences hypothesis has attributed the poor performance record of Sino-Western joint ventures to problems arising from national cultural differences and, more especially, the inability or refusal of Western companies to understand and adapt to Chinese ways of thinking and acting. Western companies have been urged to remedy this failing, either because the cultural imperative leaves them no choice or because there are some useful lessons in the Chinese approach to management that can be learned and applied. Either way, the advice to Western management assumes that Chinese ways of thinking and acting can be easily identified, understood and applied. As it happens, this is a questionable assumption.

Some Questions Raised

Generalised cultural comparisons of this kind give only a partial glimpse of Chinese and Western cultures and the differences between them. To be fair to Hofstede and others, their research has usually only attempted to identify work-related values in national culture, rather than to give a complete picture. Nevertheless, even here the resulting picture of values affecting attitudes toward work, management, and industrial enterprise in China and Western nations, and their consequent effects on organisational practice and performance, has been over-simplified and rendered static.

The poet and literary critic T. S. Eliot once wrote on the 'baffling problem' of defining culture (Eliot, 1975). He had raised the point that industrialisation and modernisation have been accompanied by cultural disintegration. While it may be possible to speak of culture being expressed through the values of religion, tradition, literature, politics, and work, for example, these do not describe an integrated value system. In effect, he argued, they describe different cultures.

Asian nations might be less multi-cultural than Western nations, but it remains misleading to suggest that 'Asian culture' is dominated by a traditional, unitary, and stable set of values. Although references to a shared Confucian cultural tradition have led to that impression, Engardio (1995) expressed scepticism, pointing out that it may seem remarkable that Asian leaders with widely differing political, social, and economic convictions should profess commitment to the same traditional values. Statements such as these might resemble, he surmised, Western leaders' professed commitment to 'family values': politically expedient, but hardly a true indication of social, economic, and political life. A further note of scepticism about Asian values was sounded by Chan (1995), who remarked that the regular Chinese criticism of Western values and management styles has been highly selective and seemingly blind to the fact that China's Asian joint venture partners have often shown Chinese employees much less respect and sensitive consideration than their Western partners have done. This has belied the general image of Asian-style management as being more socially skilful, consultative, and respectful of feelings than Western-style management.

Emphasis on the importance of traditional values in China and other Asian nations has likewise implied that Asian culture is resistant to modern influences. This must also be doubted. The former Singaporian political leader, Lee Kuan Yew, voiced his own doubt about this when speaking of the need to preserve Confucian values against increasing Western cultural influence (Zakaria, 1994). He admitted that Asian nations cannot easily become more modern without also becoming more Western, because many modern technologies and useful ideas have emanated from the West. (It should perhaps be added that traditional Western cultural values have been no less susceptible to challenge from new technologies and ideas.)

The relationship between culture, management, and economic performance is actually more open and dynamic than some of the literature on culture and cultural differences has assumed. The assumption of a one-way causal connection between national culture and national economic performance raises a basic question, Yeh and Lawrence (1995) pointed out. Why would the economic fortunes of nations fluctuate while their cultures are presumed to have remained stable? They concluded that traditional Asian culture does not give a complete explanation for the economic performance of Asian nations, and added that Hofstede and Bond (1988) had in any case presented a false contrast between Asian and Western cultures because the underlying values of Confucian dynamism and Western individualism are in fact much alike.

There is always a risk in assuming that any particular set of values or style of management gives a permanent guarantee of good business or economic performance. One need only think of Blumberg's (1968) enthusiasm for the Yugoslav system of worker self-management—which he believed had demonstrated the powerfully unifying effects and economic advantages of democratic management—to be reminded of the risk. Yugoslavia no longer exists, and 'industrial democracy' now belongs in an old and out-moded vocabulary of workforce management, pushed aside by rival enthusiasm for Japanese corporate culture and management. The fate of the latter should serve as an even more powerful reminder of the risk, since many Japanese companies have been forced by economic pressures to abandon the management policies and practices that Western companies had been urged to adopt. Benson (1996) reported, for example, that labour flexibility has now become an important strategic management objective in Japanese firms, and that casual and contract labour are being used increasingly as a way of exerting tighter control over costs. This conflicts with the assurance of employment for life that had previously been a distinctive feature of Japanese management and corporate culture. It seems scarcely necessary to note that internal labour market flexibility has been a common strategic goal among European and American companies for more than a decade.

Long-established values and customs combine uneasily with the type of thinking that welcomes modernisation and change, and the strains are presently nowhere more evident that in China's goal of 'reform with Chinese characteristics'. China's current Five-Year Plan, announced in September 1995, contains a conflicting mixture of conservative and reformist thinking (Asia Yearbook, 1996). It declares government intention to strengthen control over the economy, including regulation to reduce the gap between high and low incomes, and rejects privatisation as an option for the inefficient and hugely costly state-owned sector. While these goals accord with socialist political and economic orthodoxy, and are therefore to be expected, they appear incompatible with the promise of modernisation and continuing market-oriented reforms that the Plan also announces.

The goals and values of Chinese enterprises, not surprisingly, appear muddled and confusing to foreign observers. Aufrecht and Bun (1995) identified three competing sets of values—tradition, socialism, and economic development—and they remarked on how the importance of each vacillates continually as priorities shift. Similarly, Ding (1994) spoke of a sense of ambiguity and 'institutional amphibiousness' in China. Unlike the clearly delineated conflict in the old Soviet Union before the collapse of communism, there is no sharp sense of ideological conflict in China, but rather an impression of intermingling and mutual infiltration of competing values. This is confusing to foreign joint venture managers who would prefer to have more certainty, and their confusion is compounded by Chinese laws on joint ventures that are themselves ambiguous (Roehrig, 1994). It is difficult to see how this situation can persist indefinitely.

Cultural and Economic Imperatives

It is usually assumed that compliance with the 'cultural imperative' is necessary if Western firms in China are to prosper. This is not always the case, and will depend on the strategic objective of entering into a joint venture in China. In some situations, compliance with the cultural imperative will threaten the strategic objective and the viability of the business project.

Doz (1987) had described how multi-national corporations often face a conflict between a cultural (or 'political') imperative, which demands adaptation to local culture and customs, and an economic imperative which demands a high level of organisational efficiency. Internationalisation of operations has come increasingly to require central planning and co-ordination of processes, and this extends to decisions on product design, production processes, and even human resource management policy (Schuler, *et al.*, 1993).

This centralisation of control is necessary in order to achieve maximum economies of scale, but it obviously limits the degree to which regional management can respond to local cultural expectations about 'good corporate citizenship'.

The cultural imperative only has equivalent force if the host nation market is large enough (and perhaps also protected enough) to guarantee a good profit from management compliance with local culture and customs. This has been the situation for many Western firms in China, but not all. Companies have been attracted to joint ventures in China for one or other of two reasons, according to Mills and Chen (1996). Firstly, with one-fifth of the world's population, China has enormous potential as a consumer market in which to produce and sell. Secondly, it offers a low-cost production base from which to export to other markets.

If Western companies have formed joint venture partnerships with Chinese enterprises for the first reason, then it might indeed have profited them to comply with local culture and customs, even if compliance threatens the efficiency of operations. An *Economist* article reported this to have been the situation that had faced Volkswagen in its joint venture with four Chinese state enterprises ('Inscrutable', 1990). The price of vehicles turned out to be *six times* higher than Volkswagen management had estimated, and, in large part, this resulted from the government employment bureau appointing 2,300 employees to do the work of the 800 employees that Volkswagen management had calculated to be sufficient. Volkswagen still made a good profit, however, because it was able to sell components to the joint venture company under the terms of the contract, and because the government placed large purchase orders and restricted competition. A similar situation existed in the Beijing Jeep Corporation joint venture, involving Chrysler. Aiello (1991: 58) reported how inefficient organisation and poor quality hardly mattered because 'most of BJC's customers have been state units who rarely refuse a vehicle, regardless of its quality'.

If companies have embarked on joint ventures for the second reason, then they have faced an entirely different situation. Inefficient organisation and management will clearly threaten their aim to export. Zhu and Dowling (1995) reported one such case, involving a Sino-Western joint venture to grow, process, and export asparagus. The prospects had looked good for exporting the product to Japan, but arrangements for growing and supplying asparagus for the processing factory were changed after the contract was signed, leading to much higher costs than had been calculated. Inefficient and unhygienic work practices in the factory only made matters worse. The Western companies in the venture had no control over these factors, and their complaints only created tensions in their relations with Chinese managers and local government officials. The Chinese felt that the Western managers had not shown them sufficient respect, and so had caused them to lose face. The venture collapsed amid mutual recriminations when, after an inspection of the factory, the prospective Japanese buyer refused to buy.

Modernisation and Tradition: A Concluding Note

References to the conflict between economic and cultural imperatives might make it appear that economic organisation and culture are opposed and unconnected. This is not the case. The conflict might alternatively be described as one between economic rationalist values, on the one side, and long-established orthodoxy and custom, on the other. Culture will be affected no matter which prevails.

Modernisation entails substitution of old with new, and the assumption underlying it is that new knowledge, methods, and solutions are superior to the old. This is what China's modernisation policy must assume, at least in part. Modernisation is therefore essentially the outcome of a process that seeks newer, better, and more efficient ways of doing things. The latter broadly summarises the rationalisation process which sociologists describe as the major force for change in industrial society, and the source of many social problems as well (Eisenstadt, 1966; Faunce, 1968; Giddens, 1990; Ritzer, 1993). The effects of this rationalisation process are most clearly seen in the evolving structure and processes of economic organisation, but are also generally visible in the type of thinking that distinguishes what Max Weber had termed 'the rationalist way of life' (Gerth & Mills, 1995). This is characterised by a pragmatic, self-interested, and calculative 'matter of factness' that pays little heed to traditional values and customs unless they happen to be useful. An example exists in university education. Weber observed, long before universities had dedicated themselves so thoroughly to serving the needs of industry, that the old ideal of education for the 'cultivated personality' had been overtaken by demand for specialised vocational training of the 'useful' type, for the professional or technical expert. This is hardly now remarkable, which perhaps illustrates a further point he made about the inconceivability of challenging rationalist values once they are firmly entrenched.

Weber had explained that the rationalisation process in Western society had been assisted by a number of historical developments, foremost the growth of the market economy, the 'spirit of capitalism', and the Reformation. Brubaker (1984: 24) described the latter, particularly, as having prompted 'a radical breakthrough in the domain of attitudes and dispositions' by liberating education, science, and individual conscience from the traditional and restrictive authority of the Catholic church. Hard work, worldly ambition, and material wealth attained a virtue under the 'Protestant ethic' that had previously been denied, and this stimulated economic activity and self-interested rationality.

The rationalisation process is not universally embraced, however, even when the social and economic conditions for it are established. Indeed,

Brubaker (1984: 66) had added that rationalisation, 'far from rendering insignificant the clash of value orientations, in fact sharpens the clash'. Redundancy and unemployment, increasing separation between social and work roles, and (as T. S. Eliot observed) the disintegration of major elements of culture that had previously given meaning to social experience, contribute to the loss of meaning and insecurity that accompany rationalist life and the passing of traditional society (Lerner, 1958; Ritzer, 1993). This is precisely what the Chinese government fears will result from unchecked economic reform, and the recent death of Deng will have added to its anxiety about future instability and unrest.

China has opened its economy to the world, nevertheless, and is committed to a policy of modernisation. It cannot ignore the press for rationalisation and change without retarding economic development. As mentioned earlier, it is difficult to see how reform with Chinese characteristics can succeed for long in balancing the competing values of tradition, socialism, and economic development without serious strains developing. Warner (1996: 41) concluded the same, declaring, among other things, that China 'faces a trade-off between modernisation and full employment ...[and] the political fall-out could be considerable'.

There are some signs that the rationalisation of economic organisation is gaining momentum in China and changing previous ways of thinking and acting. There are indications, for example, that young Chinese managers are being converted to 'Western ways of thinking' (Ralston, Gustafson, Terpstra & Holt, 1995), and there are signs also of a more modern management culture being shaped by joint ventures that have proved successful. The Beijing Stone Group Corporation (a Sino-Japanese joint venture in electronics and diversified products) has been cited as a case in point, with its emphasis on staff training and customer service being likened to that of IBM (Kennedy, 1995). Finally, a recent IMF survey (World Economic Outlook, 1996), and another by Warner (1996), noted important reforms within state enterprises, including changes that give management greater decision making authority and more control over hiring and employment contracts.

It is too soon to predict how conflicting social, political, and economic goals will be resolved in China. In the meantime, Western companies will continue to find Chinese culture, as one frustrated Western partner complained, 'almost too hard to come to terms with' (Warner, 1991: 73). It is a mistake, though, to think that Western insensitivity to cultural differences are mainly to blame for this. This is not to condone insensitivity to cultural differences or to overlook the cultural conflicts that it can cause. Rather, the intention here has been to show that the cultural differences hypothesis that has formed the basis of so much analysis of cross-cultural management offers only a partial explanation of problems affecting Sino-Western joint ventures in China. Cultural conflicts are certainly at the root of many problems, but they are largely internal to China and Western companies are only peripherally involved in them. The problems that have beset the management of Sino-Western business partnerships in China will not disappear if Western companies train their managers to understand adapt to Chinese ways of thinking and acting. This is a sensible thing to do, but it can be only partially effective while the internal conflicts persist.

References

Aiello, P. 1991. Building a joint venture in China: the case of Chrysler and the Beijing Jeep Corporation. *Journal of General Management,* 19: 47 - 64

Asia Yearbook. 1996. *Far Eastern Economic Review,* 37th ed.

Aufrecht, S. E. & Bun, L. S. 1995. Reform with Chinese characteristics: the context of Chinese civil service reform. *Public Administration Review,* 55: 175 - 182

Benson, J. 1996. Management strategy and labour flexibility in Japanese manufacturing enterprises. *Human Resource Management Journal,* 6: 44 - 57

Bjorkman, I. & Schaap. A. 1994. Outsiders in the middle kingdom: expatriate managers in Chinese-Western joint ventures. *European Management Journal,* 12: 147 - 153

Blumberg, P. 1968. *Industrial democracy: the sociology of participation.* London: Constable

Brubaker, R. 1984. *The Limits of Rationality.* London: Allen & Unwin

Chan, A. 1995. The emerging patters of industrial relations in China, and the rise of two new labour movements. *China Information,* 9: 36 - 59

Ding, X. L. 1994. Institutional amphibiousness and the transition from communism: the case of China. *British Journal of Political Science,* 24: 293 - 318

Doz, Y. L. 1987. Strategic management in multinational companies. In A. C. Hax (Ed.), *Planning strategies that work:* 212 - 238. New York: Oxford University Press

Eisenstadt, S. N. 1966. *Modernization: Protest and change.* Englewood Cliffs, N.J.: Prentice-Hall

Eliot, T. S. 1975. Notes towards the definition of culture. In F. Kermode (Ed.), *Selected prose of T. S. Eliot:* 292 -305. London: Faber & Faber

Engardio, P. 1995. The Confucius confusion. *Economist,* February 24 - March 1, p. 34

Faunce, W. A. 1968. *Problems of an industrial society.* New York: McGraw-Hill

Ferraro, G. P. 1990. *The cultural dimension of international business.* Englewood Cliffs, N.J.: Prentice-Hall

Gerth, H. H. & Mills, C. W. (Eds). 1995. *From Max Weber: Essays in Sociology.* London: Routledge & Kegan Paul

Giddens, A. 1990. *The consequences of modernity.* Cambridge: Polity

Hardman, W. 1996. When sexual harassment is a foreign affair. *Personnel Journal,* 75: 91 - 97

Hofstede, G. 1984. Culture's consequences: *International differences in work-related values.* Beverly Hills, California: Sage

Hofstede, G. & Bond, M. H. 1988. The Confucius connection: From cultural roots to economic growth. *Organizational Dynamics,* 16: 4 - 21

Huo, Y. P. & Von Glinow, M. A. 1995. On transplanting human resource practices to China: a culture-driven approach. *International Journal of Manpower,* 16: 3 - 15

Inscrutable. 1990. *Economist* March 17, p.70

Kennedy, S. 1995. *China Business Review,* 22: 41 - 44

Kirkbride, P. S. & Tang S. F. 1994. Negotiation: lessons from behind the bamboo curtain. *Journal of General Management,* 12: 60 - 75

Kornhauser, A. 1954. Human motivations underlying industrial conflict. In A. Kornhauser, R. Dubin & A. M. Ross (Eds.), *Industrial conflict:* 62 - 85. New York: McGraw-Hill

Lerner, D. 1958. *The Passing of Traditional Society.* New York: The Free Press

Lockett, M. 1987. China's special economic zones: the cultural and managerial challenges. *Journal of General Management,* 12: 21 - 31

Mills, R. & Chen, G. 1996. Evaluating Chinese joint venture opportunities using strategic value analysis. *Journal of General Management,* 24: 31 - 44

Ouchi, W. J. 1981. *How American business can meet the Japanese challenge.* Boston: Addison-Wesley

Perlitz, M. 1994. The impact of cultural differences on strategy innovations. *European Business Journal* 6: 55 - 61

Peters, T. J. & Waterman Jnr J. B. 1982. *In search of excellence.* New York: Harper & Row

Pheng, L. S. 1994. Lessons from Lao Tzu's Tao Te Ching for the facilities manager. *Facilities* 12: 6 - 14

Raltson, D., Gustafson, D., Terpstra, R. & Holt, D. 1995. Pre-post Tiananmen Square: changing values of Chinese managers. *Asia-Pacific Journal of Management,* 12: 1 - 20

Ritzer, G. 1993. *The McDonalization of Society.* Thousand Oaks, Cal.: Pine Forge.

Roehrig, M. 1994. The right time and place. *China Business Review,* 21: 8 - 9

Satow, T. & Wang Z. M. 1994. Cultural and organizational factors in human resource management in China and Japan. *Journal of Managerial Psychology,* 9: 3 - 11

Schuler, R., Dowling, P. J. & DeCieri, H. 1993. An integrative framework of strategic international human resource management. *International Journal of Human Resource Management* 4: 717 - 764

Tsang, E. W. K. 1994. Human resource management problems in Sino-foreign joint ventures. *International Journal of Manpower,* 15: 4 - 21

Warner, M. 1991. How Chinese managers learn. *Journal of General Management,* 16: 66 - 84

Warner, M. 1996. Human resources in the People's Republic of China. the 'three systems' reforms. *Human Resource Management Journal,* 6: 32 - 43

Weiss, S. E. 1996. Negotiating with 'Romans'. In S. M. Puffer (Ed.), *Management across cultures:* 385 - 407. Cambridge, Mass.: Blackwell

World Economic Outlook. 1996. Washington, DC: IMF Publishing Service

Xing, F. 1995. The Chinese cultural system: implications for cross-cultural management. *Advanced Management Journal,* 60: 14 - 20

Yeh, R. & Lawrence, J. 1995. Individualism and Confucian dynamism: a note on Hofstede's cultural root to economic growth. *Journal of International Business Studies,* 26: 655 - 669

Zakaria, F. 1994. A conversation with Lee Kuan Yew. *Foreign Affairs,* 73: 109 - 126

Zhao, S. 1994. Human resource management in China. *Asia Pacific Journal of Human Resources,* 32: 3 - 12

Zhu, C. & Dowling, P. J. 1995. An unsuccessful international joint venture in China: case and analysis. *Proceedings of Annual Conference of the Academy of International Business,* Seoul, South Korea, November 15 - 18

Section E
Ownership, power and advancement

Takeover defence decisions: A study of the impact of management and large shareholder ownership

Helen Lange, Ian Ramsay and Li-Anne Woo

I Introduction [1]

This paper seeks to establish what form of management structure, ownership structure and financial characteristics are exhibited by firms that propose and subsequently adopt anti-takeover charter amendments (ATCAs) in Australia over the period June 1986 to 1990. An ATCA is essentially a restriction of partial takeover activity implemented though shareholder approval to changes in a firm's articles of association. Approval for such changes is obtained through majority agreement from a plebiscite of shareholders.

The method adopts a control sample design to analyse if characteristics differ statistically from adopting ATCA firms and those which do not adopt ATCAs during the sample period. Following this, a logistic regression analysis establishes the importance of variables considered to have a role in distinguishing between ATCA adoptees and firms without ATCAs. This research is motivated by the fact that little is known about the reasons for alternative corporate governance structures in Australia and is a natural extension to Armstrong, Lange and Woo (1994) which determined that firms adopting ATCAs were likely to experience increases in firm value around the announcement date of the ATCA.

As the implementation of the ATCA proposal is not costless (in terms of the initial set up costs and the costs of post-adoption monitoring), the very existence of an ATCA recommendation by a board suggests that there must be some economic, political or hybrid factors underlying the decision to adopt. While this research does not reveal why ATCAs are adopted, it is possible to establish factors associated with the ATCA adoption, and provides the groundwork for further research. These factors yield key insights as a detailed study of adopting firms may signal inefficiencies in other corporate governance mechanisms, both direct and indirect.

The Australian data provided a unique opportunity to address the following research questions[2]: What type of firms adopt anti-takeover amendments in Australia? What financial and organisational structure do they have ? Do firms that adopt ATCAs possess similar or different characteristics ? If characteristics do vary, then how are they different? Answers to these questions allow researchers and practitioners alike to understand the inter-connectivity between various forms of corporate governance and under what circumstances particular features may prove to be most useful.

The paper is structured as follows. Sections II and III provide a detailed background on the institutional features and legal framework that existed in Australia over the sample period. Section IV discusses previous literature and Section V relates justification as to the method employed and introduces the variables adopted in the paper. Section VI reports results of the study, while the final section contains concluding remarks.

II Corporate Governance and the Law

Corporate governance is concerned with the way corporations are governed, as distinct from the way businesses within corporations are managed (Tricker, 1994). At its heart is the relationship between the various stakeholders in a corporation and those who direct its affairs—the board of directors (Prentice, 1993). A significant part of corporate governance concerns identifying ways in which agency costs that may exist between various stakeholders within the corporation are reduced.

There are a number of ways such agency costs may be reduced. First, various market forces may operate to reduce them (Fama, 1980). These market forces include the product market, capital market, market for corporate control and the labour market for managers. Second, firms may adopt various governance structures designed to reduce agency costs. For example, the proportion of independent to executive directors in particular corporations may reflect an attempt to balance the interests of managers and shareholders as independent directors are considered by some to be an effective means of ensuring management accountability to shareholders. Remuneration packages of corporate executives may be designed to reduce agency costs. Third, regulators may play a significant role in reducing agency costs by enforcing laws that have the objective of reducing agency costs.

The role of legal regulation in corporate governance and its effect upon agency costs is complex. The effect of legal regulation upon agency costs may be either direct or indirect. Two prominent examples of the way in which legal regulation may have a direct impact on agency costs are (i) directors' duties, and (ii) mandatory disclosure requirements. A significant part of corporate law comprises the imposition of mandatory legal duties upon directors and other corporate officers. Under Australian law, these duties include duties to act honestly and in the best interests of the corporation, to exercise care and diligence, not to make improper use of information acquired by virtue of being an officer of the corporation, and not to make improper use of position as an officer of the corporation (Corporations Law, s. 232). Such laws are designed to achieve managerial accountability.

A second aspect of managerial accountability is achieved through the imposition of mandatory disclosure obligations upon corporate managers. These disclosure obligations apply both generally, such as where a director has a personal interest in a matter that is before the board of directors (Corporations Law, ss. 231 and 232A), and in specific contexts such as where the corporation is raising capital from investors. Such mandatory disclosure requirements may be justified upon a number of grounds, one such ground being that disclosure requirements assist in the monitoring of managers by shareholders (Blair and Ramsay, 1997).

Legal regulation may also play an indirect role with respect to reduction of agency costs. We have already noted how market forces may operate to reduce agency costs. The extent to which these market forces do actually achieve this objective depends upon the competitiveness of the markets. In this respect, legal regulation can aim to ensure that markets are competitive (for example, by way of anti-trust and trade practices legislation) and therefore indirectly reduce agency costs.

III Australian Anti-takeover Charter Amendments: Background and Operation

We noted in Section II how legal regulation may affect corporate governance and, in particular, operate to reduce agency costs resulting from a divergence of interests between shareholders and managers. The market for corporate control is often viewed as an important market for reducing such agency costs (Manne, 1965; Easterbrook and Fischel, 1991). Legal regulation may play a significant role in determining how effective the market for corporate control is in achieving this objective. An illustration is provided by the 1986 amendments to the Australian takeovers legislation. In brief, these amendments did two things:

1   they restricted the way in which an offeror could conduct a partial takeover; and
2   they allowed target companies to implement ATCAs to make hostile partial takeovers more difficult.

Each of these is discussed in the following two sections.

Types of Partial Takeover

Prior to 1986, an offeror could conduct a partial takeover in Australia in one of two ways (Ramsay, 1992). First, under s. 16(2)(a)(i) of the Companies

(Acquisition of Shares) Act (as it then was) an offeror could pro-rata the shares from each shareholder who accepted the offer to ensure that the desired objective was achieved. For example, if an offeror with no shareholding in the target company bid for 60 per cent of the target's shares then, assuming that some shareholders declined the offer, the offeror could take a greater percentage of shares from each of the accepting shareholders in order to ensure that the objective of 60 per cent was achieved.

The alternative method of conducting a partial takeover was to proceed via section 16(2)(a)(ii). In this case, the offeror would bid for a proportion of the shares held by each shareholder in the target company. The offeror could not pro-rata the shares from the accepting shareholders. Assume, once again, that an offeror with no shareholding in the target company desires 60 per cent of the target's shares. A bid under section 16(2)(a)(ii) for 60 per cent of each shareholder's holding would fail to achieve the desired objective if only one shareholder decided not to accept. Because pro-ratoring of shares is not permitted under this option, an offeror would, in order to achieve a holding of 60 per cent of the target's shares, need to bid for a higher proportion of each shareholder's holding in order to take account of the possibility that some shareholders will not accept the offer.

It is clear that the first alternative provides the greater certainty to the offeror. At the same time, this alternative provides the least certainty to the target company shareholders. This is because the shares may be pro-rated, and therefore a target company shareholder will not know the number of shares that he or she will be selling to the offeror until the offer period closes. The 1985 report of the Federal Government's Companies and Securities Law Review Committee (CSLRC) recommended that the second alternative (proportional bids) be the sole method for conducting a partial takeover. This recommendation was enacted in 1986, and is now contained in section 635(b) of the Corporations Law. The basis of the CSLRC recommendation was that pro-rata partial bids place coercive pressures on target company shareholders. This sentiment is outlined in the following paragraph from the CSLRC report:

> A partial bid where pro-rating will apply presents a powerful psychology for acceptance (described by some as 'coercion') in that offeree shareholders must compete among themselves. Each accepting shareholder hopes that as many as possible of his co-investors will not accept so that his own returns may be maximised, and no shareholder hoping to maximise current returns can afford to reject the offer. Failure to accept may result in permanent loss by reason of transfer of the control premium otherwise inherent in all voting shares to the shares acquired from those who do tender. (CSLRC, 1985a, para. 12)

Anti-takeover Charter Amendments (ATCAs)

The second legal change was to allow potential target companies to implement ATCAs in their articles of association. A typical article provides that if a partial bid is made, the directors will convene a general meeting of shareholders to consider a resolution to approve the bid. The offeror and persons associated with the offeror are not entitled to vote on the resolution. If the resolution is carried, the partial bid proceeds in the normal way. However, if the resolution is rejected by shareholders, all takeover offers are withdrawn and any contracts arising from acceptances are rescinded (Corporations Law, s. 671; Renard and Santamaria, 1990). The basis of this CSLRC recommendation to allow corporations to adopt ATCAs was that it would 'allow shareholders to separate out considerations of the desirability of the bid and whether to participate in it' (CSLRC, 1985b, para. 86).

The insertion of an ATCA into a corporation's articles of association requires the approval of 75 per cent of shareholders who actually vote[3] on the resolution. Once inserted, an ATCA cannot remain operative for more than three years unless renewed by a further resolution of shareholders.

Effect of legal amendments

The effect of the 1986 amendments was dramatic. Prior to the introduction of the Companies (Acquisition of Shares) Act, partial takeovers constituted approximately 17 per cent of all takeovers undertaken in Australia (Gross, 1983). By late 1982, this percentage had increased to 40 per cent according to Gross[4]. However, the period since the 1986 amendments has witnessed the demise of partial takeovers in Australia as Table 1 illustrates.

In 1987, partial takeovers constituted 6 per cent of all takeovers of that year. By 1988, the percentage declined to 5 per cent, and 1989 saw a further decline to less than 2 per cent. In the early 1990s (from 1991 to 1993) we see that the percentage of partial takeovers has remained very low, and has varied between only 1 per cent and 4 per cent of all takeovers.

IV Previous Literature

The agency framework in which the ATCA proposals takes place is no longer a simple two party setting traditionally described in the classic agency framework. In the early agency literature, the separation of ownership and control results from the size of the firm becoming larger than the wealth of any single individual, in addition to the need for diversification for risk management purposes.

The fact that owners and managers may no longer comprise the same group means that management incentives are not naturally and perfectly aligned with those of shareholders. This view was principally fortified by Jensen & Meckling (1976).

Table 1: Bid Type and Bid Outcome 1988-1993[5]

Panel A: 1991 to 1993

Bid Method	Successful			Unsuccessful			Total		
	1993	1992	1991	1993	1992	1991	1993	1992	1991
Full	37	30	52	22	24	33	59	54	85
Partial	2	0	1	0	1	0	2	1	1
Total	39	30	53	22	25	33	61	55	86

Panel B: 1988 to 1990

Bid Method	Successful			Unsuccessful			Total		
	1990	1989	1988	1990	1989	1988	1990	1989	1988
Full	67	113	169	26	63	105	93	176	274
Partial	1	-	5	3	3	10	4	3	15
Total	68	113	174	29	66	115	97	179	289

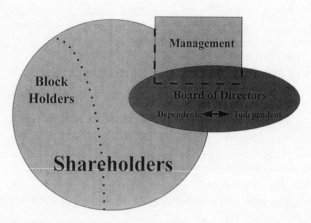

Figure 1: A Schematic of the Inter-connectivity of Agency Relationships

To ensure that management undertook the shareholders' bidding, the resolution of inherent conflicts of interests was frequently assumed away in the early literature. An easy solution often being that management was provided with shares or options on the shares of the company, effectively linking management's utility as closely as possible to expected shareholder returns[6].

In more recent investigations, the corporate governance literature has been interested in exploring a richer set of relationships between shareholders on the one hand and management and appointed boards of directors on the other. It is the latter relationship, namely that between shareholders and the board, which is particularly interesting. The board of directors may have members which partly belong/align themselves to either the shareholders or the management group. Moreover, directors may be appointed to represent any other group of stakeholders, such as either a major creditor or the employees of the company. These more complex structures bring the potential for greater conflicts amongst the various constituencies. John and Senbet (1997) argue that 'left alone, each class of stakeholders pursues its own interest which may be at the expense of other stakeholders'.

The current corporate governance relationships have evolved over time as a result of both formal and informal stakeholder interactions. This is hardly surprising as, for example, Jensen and Meckling (1976), Fama (1980) and Williamson (1990), considered that the firm is a nexus of contracts between various parties, and Tirole (1989, 16) considers that the firm fulfils three distinct roles, technological, operational, and contractual. How these arrangements are introduced, monitored and evaluated are indirectly related to the mode of corporate governance adopted by the firm.

The inter-connectivity of contractual relationships can be seen in Figure 1 below. In the following sections, the various elements of this figure are discussed.

The Role of the Board of Directors

The board of directors is regarded as the ultimate authority in the organisational structure of the modern corporation. In one of the best-known Australian legal judgments regarding the duties of company directors (AWA Ltd v Daniels (1992) 7 Australian Corporations and Securities Reports 759), Justice Rogers stated that the functions of a board of directors are to:

i. set goals for the corporation;
ii. appoint the corporation's chief executive;
iii. oversee the plans of managers for the acquisition and organisation of financial;
iv. and human resources towards attainment of the corporation's goals, and
v. review, at reasonable intervals, the corporation's progress towards attaining its goals.

The particular role of directors exists because diverse shareholdings make it difficult for atomistic shareholders to adequately monitor and bond firm management either individually or as a coalition. This limits the shareholders' opportunity to reduce agency costs. The board of directors, is theoretically expected to watch over management and assist in the global decision making of the firm on behalf of shareholders. Quite frequently, the agency contract literature has ignored the importance of the board of directors per se, and looked solely at managerial agency costs. In this sense, the literature assumes away the potential agency costs implicit in the board of directors. This assumption is often used to simplify the modelling, but in doing so removes a potentially important reflection of the real world relationships. It is important to consider the role of the board independently as board members are also utility maximisers, who act autonomously and are likely to have objective functions that are different from management or shareholders. It makes sense to characterise them as a separate group from management, capable of influencing the firm's decisions.

Warther (1994) considers the relationship of the board of directors to management and shareholders. Warther models the board selection, structure and compensation and represents one of the first papers to critically examine the assumption that board members are perfectly aligned with either management or shareholder. While from a legal perspective the board is responsible for the decision making within the firm, the board is not always independently and objectively formed. Warther acknowledges a circularity in the selection of the members of the board of directors. As noted by Whisler (1984), Mace (1981), Rosenstein and Wyatt (1990) and Lorsch (1989), the board is frequently chosen by the firm's management7. Further, it is argued that the tenure of the any particular director is a function of their ability to successfully interact with management and other board members and to achieve 'global objectives', rather than to achieve 'shareholder objectives'.

How directors behave and whether they align themselves with managers have a direct bearing on the ease with which the board formulates agendas, resolves uncertainties and makes decisions. It also has a bearing on whether the 'independence' checks and balances, which presumably exist to protect shareholders' interests actually work. Unlike previous research cited in this paper, our focus is not to examine how board composition and structure affects firm performance, but rather considers a distinct board decision affecting all stakeholders in the firm. This decision is a significant one in terms of corporate governance, as the observed anti-takeover proposal has to first pass through the board, and then be subjected to a plebiscite of shareholders, before it can be promulgated. One can consider this particular anti-takeover proposal as an ultimate consensus decision by the firm8, as most other firm decisions are dispensed with at the board level or below.

The absolute number of directors may substantially affect the likelihood of and ATCA decision. The direction of the influence, however, depends greatly on the extent to which full consensus among the constituencies of the board of directors is achieved. This can occur as the result of the following.

It is more likely for small numbers of individuals to agree on a particular outcome. In such cases, the board of directors may be able to make value maximising decisions through investment in positive NPV projects. This will also be the case for large boards in which members are like minded/preferenced individuals. However, this type of large board is more likely to be the exception rather than the rule. See Figure 2, below. In these cases, optimising the value of the firm through positive NPV investment decisions will reduce the possibility of a takeover threat and will also lessen the firm's need for an ATCA.

However, in cases where consensus is not readily achieved, the adoption of an ATCA may be an objective way of protecting atomistic shareholder interests. This is more likely for large boards, as a large group of individuals is less likely to reach a decision than a small group. This implies that rather than reach a positive corporate governance decision at board level, the large board is more likely to resort to the adoption of an ATCA. By proposing an ATCA the large board of directors is recommending that defensive mechanisms be structured in such a way to 'force a bidder to either pay a higher price for a firm's shares or to offer the same terms to shareholders' (Megginson, 1997: 6).

We claim that large boards are particularly susceptible to ATCA adoption because:

(i) difficulty in board decision making may result in the adoption of a simple board decision rule, where board members support all management proposals;

(ii) difficulty or failure to implement value maximising investments, may make the firm a more likely takeover target, and more in need of anti-takeover defences to protect the board members and management, and/or

(iii) failure or difficulty to agree at the board level may lead to the adoption of a formal and costly alternative defence mechanism previously adopted by other firms, such as an anti-takeover device.

Consequently, we would expect that firms with large boards are more likely to propose ATCAs than those with smaller boards, because decision making in general is more difficult, consensus on value maximising investment decisions is less likely, and the threat of takeover is greater. Hence the relationship betweens board size and an ATCA proposal is likely to be positive.

Directors of the firm can be classified as dependent or independent. Dependent directors are those directly involved in the day-to-day operation and management of the firm, such as the Chief Executive Officer. In contrast, independent directors are not involved in firm operations[9]. Their role, theoretically, is to act as monitors of shareholder interests at the board level. Whether they complete this task to the satisfaction of shareholders is both controversial and difficult to determine.

The theoretical analysis of Noe and Rebello (1995) suggests that independent directors with the ability to block management sponsored policies increases efficiency (effective capital allocation) which may lead to optimal firm decisions. However, they show that this is only true when directors' bonuses are a function of the firm achieving pre-set hurdle rates of return.

At the time of the ATCA adoption analysed in this study, few Australian firms paid performance related remuneration packages for boards members. Typically directors' fees were set as a fixed amount and approved by shareholders at the annual general meeting. As practice in Australia differs from the Noe and Rebello's framework, it would be of interest to determine whether board of director composition has any impact on ATCA adoption.

The proportion of dependent directors will also affect the extent to which consensus is likely. The higher the proportion of inside or dependent directors, the higher the probability that management dominated proposals will be accepted, all other things being equal. Noe and Rebello (1995: 9) suggest that whenever the dependent directors belong to the same faction, and if the CEO is strong, then the effectiveness of outside directors is reduced.

In light of this, we expect that the proportion of dependent directors will be positively related to the probability of an ATCA proposal, on the assumption that the ATCA is favoured by management as a means of entrenching their position. We would expect that independent directors act more like outside large shareholder groupings, who prefer market forces to protect the interests of shareholders.

There is nothing to prevent directors from holding equity in the firm, and in terms of basic agency issues, it may be desirable to grant directors equity to align their interests with those of shareholders. Quite frequently, the shares they hold have the same voting rights of ordinary shareholders. However, it is possible for separate classes of shares to be made available to management/directors which have more restrictive rules governing their marketability[10]. As a result, the proportion of shares held in the hands of the directors establishes the extent to which directors can affect or perhaps offset the voting power of other investors. As the shareholdings of each of the directors is tied to their personal wealth levels, we would anticipate in a general sense, that directors' holdings of shares are, on average, a smaller fraction of the firm than those of large institutional investors.

The relationship between the directors' holdings and the likelihood of an ATCA proposal is predicted to be of a similar direction to large shareholdings. This is because the directors with shareholdings are more likely to act in best the interests of shareholders, and moreover, are more likely to vote than most atomistic shareholders. However, due to the relative small size of any individual shareholding, this relationship is likely to be relatively weak compared to that of large shareholders. The empirical results of Morck, Schleifer and Vishny (1988) tend to support this reduced influence of directors holdings, finding that firms with insider ownership of between 5 and 25 percent had significantly lower Tobin's Q.

The Role of Shareholders

Shareholders supply equity capital to the firm. They can influence the decision making of a firm in terms of the issues brought to a vote at Annual General or Extraordinary meetings. Shareholders influence is heterogeneous, whereby some shareholders are afforded greater influence than others. This view of shareholders is far more realistic than the notion that shareholders are homogeneous in both interests and influence. This is because shareholders hold varying numbers of shares, each of which has a right to one vote. This means that the role of large shareholders is important, as they can wield greater voting power and are more likely to influence the structure of what the board and subsequent decision making of the firm.

The two ownership groups most likely to impact the corporate governance of the firm by virtue of the size of their share holding, and the attached voting rights, are institutional shareholders and large block holders. Hence, these groups are likely to exercise the most power and control over management.

SIZE OF THE BOARD OF DIRECTORS

	SMALL	LARGE	POTENTIAL TAKEOVER THREAT
HIGH	• small groups are more likely to produce consensus in corporate activity, needing less reliance on ATCAs	• large groups are less likely to agree, but possible if constituents are like minded, requiring a lower reliance on ATCAs.	• consensus means that the firm can maximise firm value, requiring a lower reliance on ATCAs.
Probability of Consensus	• more likely to agree, but maybe the result of small but powerful factions may lead to a reliance on ATCAs.	• large groups are more likely to disagree causing a greater reliance on implementing an external and simple decision rule which will alleviate board of directors' tension.	• compromised decisions may not be value maximising, leading to more disagreement, and a greater need to adopt ATCAs
LOW			

Figure 2: Influence of the Size of the Board on the Likelihood of ATCA Adoption

The density of share ownership may also affect the likelihood of potential takeover. On the one hand, block holders are capable of delivering a large parcel of shares in one transaction, thereby reducing search costs of any potential takeover offerer, but at the same time block holders may only divest their large shareholding for a premium[11]. On the other hand, a diversely held ownership structure may be indicative of high takeover potential and correspondingly high search costs.

The more concentrated the ownership, the higher the potential that these large block holders privately instigate informal corporate governance mechanisms. Low levels of ownership concentration may result in a firm being an easier takeover target, and this is more likely to be associated with an ATCA adoption at management and board level.

In addition, institutional investors are less likely to desire ATCA adoptions, as it reduces their ability to profit from any potential takeover and may lead to expensive entrenchment in the firm's share register. This view is consistent with evidence provided by Brickley, Lease and Smith (1988) and Agrawal and Mandelker (1990). A contrary view is given by the Pound (1988) empirical analysis which implies that management may 'capture' votes from institutional investors as institutions align themselves to the strategies of incumbent management.

Consequently, we would expect that both the concentration of shareholdings and the proportion of institutional ownership are negatively related to any anti-takeover proposal.

Growth

Firms which have a large set of investment opportunities, and which are exploiting the opportunities with positive net present values, will be less likely to be takeover targets. There are two main reasons for this.

Firstly, when firm growth is high, firms have less opportunity to depart from value maximising paths, and the costs associated with agency issues will be lower (refer to Lange and Sharpe (1995) and Garvey (1987) in particular). Firms with high levels of growth demonstrate that they are exploiting these opportunities. Consequently, both growth and future growth opportunities are highly valued by the market. The first, because the opportunities are being exploited, and the second because further growth opportunities exist. Such firms will be less attractive takeover target, than either firms which are not growing, or firms which have no future growth potential.

Secondly, when a firm is exploiting its growth opportunities, information asymmetries between shareholders and management and between the management and the board will be reduced. Lower information asymmetries will lower agency costs and consequently, the need for any anti takeover provisions is alleviated (see, for example, Hirshleifer and Thakor, 1992; Bizjak, Brickley and Coles, 1993; Stein, 1988).

So, in summary, by taking advantage of growth opportunities a firm is more likely to be characterised by a higher franchise value on the one hand, and by lower information asymmetries on the other, making the directors' need to introduce anti-takeover amendments less necessary. Consequently, we would expect to find an inverse relationship between the proposal of an ATCA and the exploitation of a firm's growth opportunities.

Firm Size Effects [12]

Firm size is commonly used in most empirical studies of anti-takeover activity. This is because firms size acts as a control variable. Firm size may also indicate the extent to which any costs incurred in providing any defensive mechanism can be absorbed by the firm. There is also theoretical argument for examination of the firm size in relation to anti-takeover mechanisms. The cash flows of large firms are exposed to less costly contract adoption than smaller firms which are capacity constrained and less likely to adopt ATCAs on the basis of affordability.

If the costs of introducing an ATCA are relatively small, however, this issue would not impact the decision to introduce any amendment[13].

Another interpretation of the size variable is that large firms are more likely to have more widely disperse shareholdings, all other things held constant. This means that directors of large firms, both individually and collectively are less well monitored, and are less likely to be threatened by a takeover.

In addition, the very size of the larger firms limits takeover opportunities. This is due to the fact that a takeover (the purchase of a controlling proportion of ownership) of a large firm requires a larger sum than that required for a smaller firm. This reduces the number of potential raiders on the firm, lowering the probability of a takeover.

Consequently we would expect to find that the larger the firm, the less likely the proposal of an ATCA.

V. Methodology, Sample and Data
Methodology

To test the hypotheses outlined in Section IV, a logistic model is used to examine the corporate governance mechanisms in place at the time of the proposal to introduce a partial anti-takeover device. As the proposal to adopt an ATCA is in itself a defensive move on the part of management, it is interesting to analyse the relationship between this decision and the various alternative monitoring devices, both internal and external, in place at the time of ATCA consideration. The relationships existing at the time of such a defensive decision on the part of management provides some indication of the effectiveness of the corporate governance in situ, and whether certain firm types are likely to adopt ATCAs.

It is also interesting to note that in this study, there is one overriding monitoring device in play throughout. Namely, the shareholders must provide the final approval of the anti-takeover provision, by way of plebiscite. While theory would suggest that this final approval by shareholders should make a difference in that the directors' decision will be subject to the final scrutiny of shareholders, empirical testing may provide some insight into the strength and effectiveness of this final monitoring device.

The anti-takeover mechanism studied in this paper: (i) is the only anti-takeover device available to Australian firms which is specifically authorised under the Australian Corporations Law[14], and (ii) requires the approval of shareholders before adoption. This is in contrast to previous studies of anti-takeover mechanisms where a heterogeneous set of anti-takeover devices have been examined, only some of which require shareholder approval. Consequently, any bias resulting from the heterogeneity in previous work has been avoided in this study, enabling the conduct of a more controlled experiment.

The discussion in Section IV suggests that the probability of directors' proposing an anti-takeover device is related to the current performance of the firm, the growth potential of the firm, the size of the firm, as well as the various corporate governance mechanisms represented by

1 characteristics of the board itself including the number of directors, the composition of the board in terms of independent versus dependent directors, and holdings of shares by directors; and

2 groups with large shareholdings, such as institutional ownership and concentration of ownership by the largest shareholders.

Consequently, the model tested is:

Probability of ATCA proposal = Function (firm performance, growth potential, number of board members, the mix of dependent and independent directors, directors holdings, institutional ownership, concentration of ownership, company size) + Error term

The proxies chosen to test this model are discussed below under **Sample and Data.**

The event examined in this paper is the probability of a company board proposing an anti-takeover device. The particular device is the only anti-takeover device specifically authorised under Australian Corporations Law, and is the partial takeover blocking provision discussed in Section III. To examine this event we employ a logistic regression analysis[15], which is specified as:

$$P_i = F(\alpha + \beta X_i) = \frac{1}{1 + e^{-(\alpha + \beta X_i)}}$$

where P_i is the probability that a board will recommend adoption of an ACTA, β is the vector of slope coefficients and the X_i are the independent variables described in the model above. P_i takes on the value of one for firms which have introduced ATCAs, and zero otherwise.

Sample and Data

The sample of ATCA firms used was the same as that employed by Armstrong, Lange and Woo (1994). There were 37 firms in the top 150 companies each year[16] which implemented anti-takeover devices from the earliest possible date, June 1986, through to the end of 1990. These 37 firms form our ATCA group.

The firms introducing anti-takeover mechanisms were identified from the Australian Stock Exchange (ASX) Company Papers Files. These files are comprised of all correspondence that the stock exchange receives from publicly listed companies, including proposals for partial takeover restrictions. Based on the list of Top 150 firms ranked by market capitalisation each year, 37 firms chose to adopt ATCAs during the period June 1986 to1990. Because the top 150 firms change each year, a total of 289 companies over the five-year period were examined for anti-takeover proposals. Table 2 provides details of the introduction of the partial anti-takeover amendments by year of proxy signing. In all cases, the directors' proposal to introduce an ATCA was adopted by a plebiscite of members[17].

The sample of ATCA firms, despite being small when compared to studies in other countries, is however an almost complete group of all Australian firms proposing anti-takeover over the five years being examined[18].

Table 2: Distribution of Partial Anti-takeover Amendments by Year of Proposal

Year	Number
1986	10
1987	17
1988	4
1989	5
1990	1
Total	37

Source: Armstrong, Lange and Woo (1994)

Figure 3 shows the distribution of the number and value of takeovers in Australia in the period covered by this study. A comparison of Table 2 and Figure 3 reveals that the incidence of ATCA adoption did not appear to impact the number or value of takeovers in subsequent years. Most of the anti-takeover amendments were adopted in 1986 and 1987, in the years immediately following the changes to the corporations law. Any impact on takeovers would most likely to occur in the 1987 to 1989. However, Figure 3 shows that takeovers reached their maximum in both number and value in 1988, with only a small reduction in value in 1989.

To facilitate the logistic regression analysis, the companies announcing partial anti-takeover amendment proposals were matched with firms which did not implement such provisions. The matched sample used was that constructed by Armstrong, Lange and Woo (1994). The matching was made on the basis of market capitalisation[19]. Consequently, the control group was selected from those companies which had not introduced ATCA proposals to shareholders and whose market capitalisation most closely matched that of the ATCA company at the date on which the proxy statement detailing the anti takeover provision was signed. Similar data to that collected for the 37 ATCA companies was collected for the control group[20].

The collection of directors' numbers and shareholdings proved very difficult. When data was available, it was obtained manually from the company's annual reports. However, inconsistencies in corporate reporting meant that director's holdings data on some companies may not always be considered reliable. Consequently, the final sample size was reduced further to only those with complete reliable data, a total of 66 companies[21].

A summary of the proxies selected to test the theoretical considerations outlined in section IV is set out in Table 3. Earnings performance was proxied by both earnings per share and dividend per share, but only the results for earnings per share are reported. The company's size was measured by both the natural log of total assets and the natural log of market capitalisation. Both size proxies produced similar results and only the latter is reported. Data relating to earnings per share (EPS), dividends per share (DPS) and market capitalisation (SIZE)were obtained from the Australian Stock Exchange Statex Files[22].

Data relating to all of the board of director variables (DIRNUM, PROPDEP, DIRHLDGS) and the remaining ownership variables (INSTHLDGS, TOP20) were collected manually from the most recent company annual reports[23] prior to the ATCA proposal[24].

Institutional owners were identified using the approach used by Crough (1980), Lange and Sharpe (1995) and Armstrong, Lange and Woo (1994), whereby institutional investors are categorised as life and general insurance offices, superannuation funds, trustee investment companies, and state treasury corporations and financing authorities.

The exploitation of growth potential is a difficult concept to measure. As discussed in Section IV, growth has been measured in a number of ways in previous literature, and its formulation will influence the correlations of growth with other factors included in the study. Hence, the results of this analysis may be sensitive to how growth is measured in the study. Consequently, several measures of growth were adopted in the study. A static measure of growth (GROWTH1) was defined in terms of total fixed assets plus investments, standardised by total assets, whereas the percentage change in total assets and investments from one year to the next represented a flow measure of growth (GROWTH2)[25]. Data for each of these was also collected from the Australian Stock Exchange Statex Files.

Detailed descriptive statistics of data for both the ATCA and the control groups are shown in Table 4.

Figure 3: Number and Value of Takeovers in Australia, June 1986–1990

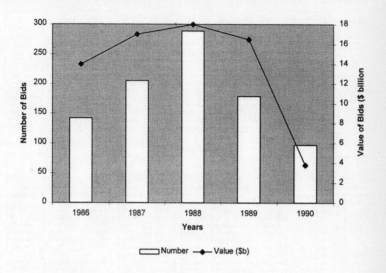

Source: Corporate Adviser, (1998 -1993) Analysis of Takeover Activity in Australia

Variable	Proxy[26]	Proxy Name	Source	Hypothesised Sign
ATCA	1 if in the ATCA group, and 0 otherwise	ATCA	ASX Company Papers' File	not applicable
Performance	1. Earnings per share 2. Dividend per share	EPS DPS	ASX Statex Files	negative
Growth Potential	3. Fixed Assets plus Investments relative to total assets 4. Proportional change in fixed assets plus investments[27]	GROWTH1 GROWTH2	ASX Statex Files	negative
Board characteristics[28]: 1. Number of Directors 2. Mix of Dependent and Independent Directors 3. Directors' shareholdings	1. Number of Directors 2. Proportion of Dependent directors 3. Proportion of shares held by directors	DIRNUM PROPDEP DIRHLDGS	Company Annual reports	1. positive 2. positive 3. negative
Institutional shareholdings	Proportion of shares held by institutions by the largest 20 shareholders	INSTHLDGS	Company annual reports	negative
Concentration of Ownership	Proportion of shares held by the largest 20 shareholders	TOP20	Company annual reports	negative
Size	Natural Logarithm of Market Capitalisation	SIZE	ASX Statex	negative

Table 3: Variables, Proxies and Hypothesises Sign

PANEL A: ATCA Group

| | N | | | | Std. | | | Percentiles | | |
	Valid	Missing*	Mean	Median	Deviation	Minimum	Maximum	25%	50%	75%
DEPDIR	36	1	2.58333	2.00000	1.592393	.00000	7.00000	1.0000000	2.0000000	4.0000000
DIRHLDGS	34	3	2.3E-02	2.8E-03	6.08E-02	.00016	.33455	7.728E-04	2.809E-03	2.072E-02
DIRNUM	36	1	8.88889	8.50000	2.670236	3.00000	15.00000	7.0000000	8.5000000	11.0000000
DPS	37	0	10.0924	9.7600	7.7770	.00	29.92	4.3050	9.7600	13.8350
EPS	37	0	19.3835	15.6800	16.6457	-6.63	58.75	6.8800	15.6800	26.0000
GROWTH1	37	0	.5336809	.5964647	.2016353	.15639	.91016	.3815747	.5964647	.6706255
GROWTH2	37	0	2.13517	9.7E-02	11.17143	-.19636	68.05721	5.946E-03	9.736E-02	.2981672
INSTHLDG	37	0	.3249476	.3255000	.1895669	.03599	.73040	.1449181	.3255000	.4917797
LNDIRHLD	37	0	5.6E-02	2.6E-03	.2194044	.00000	1.31817	5.099E-04	2.554E-03	2.091E-02
LNINST	37	0	.2714746	.2817897	.1425158	.03535	.54835	.1353105	.2817897	.3999672
LNMKCAP	37	0	5.88483	5.69434	1.331399	2.85755	9.23304	4.8054331	5.6943372	6.8138325
LNTOP20	36	1	.4961001	.4922122	9.31E-02	.27763	.63652	.4320890	.4922122	.5857492
SIZE $m	37	0	913.167	297.180	1771.510	17.41882	10229.56	122.172419	297.179753	913.057901
PROPDEP	36	1	.2903975	.2678571	.1616247	.00000	.66667	.1488095	.2678571	.3937500
TOP20	37	0	.6361838	.6210000	.1689613	.16850	.88990	.5353000	.6210000	.7923000

PANEL B: Control Group

| | N | | | | Std. | | | Percentiles | | |
	Valid	Missing*	Mean	Median	Deviation	Minimum	Maximum	25%	50%	75%
DEPDIR	35	1	2.77143	3.0000000	1.956674	.00000	10.00000	1.0000000	3.0000000	4.0000000
DIRHLDGS	32	4	6.8E-02	1.342739E-03	.1654707	.00000	.60929	1.481E-04	1.343E-03	1.088E-02
DIRNUM	35	1	8.54286	8.0000000	3.752198	2.00000	18.00000	6.0000000	8.0000000	11.0000000
DPS	36	0	12.3294	10.0050	16.1064	.00	88.24	2.9250	10.0050	14.7400
EPS	36	0	30.0761	23.4250	26.7222	-2.72	95.29	6.3200	23.4250	49.0075
GROWTH1	36	0	.4957683	.4923284	.2423534	.03073	.99494	.3369398	.4923284	.6454754
GROWTH2	36	0	315.264	.2733348	1878.211	-.56551	11271.44	7.284E-02	.2733348	.8933477
INSTHLDG	36	0	.3288423	.2759470	.2171830	.00000	.86898	.1873720	.2759470	.4409134
LNDIRHLD	36	0	5.0E-02	9.365585E-04	.1272061	.00000	.47579	7.393E-05	9.366E-04	9.643E-03
LNINST	36	0	.2721397	.2436847	.1559725	.00000	.62539	.1717404	.2436847	.3652591
LNMKCAP	36	0	5.98118	5.8391412	1.107080	3.51307	7.82189	5.2080184	5.8391412	6.8622473
LNTOP20	36	0	.5513548	.5578608	9.34E-02	.33368	.69175	.4953053	.5578608	.6253966
SIZE $m	36	0	669.771	343.6402063	679.4579	33.55099	2494.627	182.757968	343.640206	955.584467
PROPDEP	35	1	.3772298	.3000000	.2838891	.00000	1.00000	.1428571	.3000000	.5714286
TOP20 %	36	0	.7428500	.7469500	.1588705	.39610	.99720	.6410000	.7469500	.8690000

* Missing includes data not reported in the annual reports and data not available by other tractable means.

Table 4: Descriptive Statistics

VI Results

Table 5 reports a selection of the results of the various logistic regression analysis regressions. Examination of these results reveals that while the empirical analysis supports a number of the hypotheses outlined in Section IV, there are some surprises.

The predictive power of the model was reasonable with the percentage of correct predictions in each of the regressions shown at 77.27 and 78.79 percent.

The strongest relationships found were those for both concentrated shareholdings and directors' shareholdings. These were the only variables which consistently showed significant relationships.

The Role of Directors

In all regressions, directors' holdings always showed a negative relationship, but this was not always significant. These results, both the sign and the relatively low significance of directors' holdings, are in line with our expectations following examination of the literature. Here, the result provides some support for the notion that when directors' holdings are high, then the directors' interests are more aligned to shareholders and less aligned to management, making the probability of an ATCA proposal less likely.

The other director variables, however, were not found to be significant, and their signs were not always consistent with expectations. For example, the proxies for the number of directors were the actual directors numbers and the natural log of the number of directors. These produced different signs across the various regressions.

In addition, the proportion of dependent directors (measured by both the actual proportion as well as the natural log of one plus this proportion) was not significant and was consistently negative, the opposite sign to that expected. Consequently, in contrast to our expectations, our results suggest that board structure is not important in the corporate governance decision analysed.

The Role of Shareholders

In all models tested, the top 20 shareholdings was highly significant and negative, as predicted by our discussion in Section IV. This provides evidence that the concentration of shareholdings is an effective means of monitoring the board of directors, by aligning the board's interests with those of the shareholders. Consequently, the board is less likely to introduce any anti takeover proposal when block shareholders own a relatively large proportion of the firm's shares. This result may also indicate some degree of active monitoring by the block shareholders.

However, the other shareholder variable, institutional holdings, was neither significant nor of the expected sign. One of the concerns with the measurement of this variable was the impact of nominee holdings. In general, nominee holdings were excluded except where they could be clearly identified as an institution (as defined in Section V above). Consequently errors in the correct identification of institutional holdings, because of the elimination of some relevant nominee shareholders, may have produced this unexpected result[29]. However, the insignificance of institutional holdings is consistent with the findings of Armstrong, Lange and Woo (1994), with respect to ATCA proposals.

Growth, Size and EPS

Of the other variables tested in this analysis, only the performance variable gained any significance. The proxy for performance, EPS, was found to be negative, as expected and weakly significant. The negative sign was consistent with the expectation that poor performing firms are most likely to introduce anti-takeover devices.

Both the growth and the size proxies were of the expected negative sign. However, neither were significant. The insignificance of the growth proxy would indicate that growth potential itself is not regarded by directors as a sufficient constraint on takeover activity, although the results do show that the probability of an ATCA proposal is less likely when there is high growth. All size proxies produced a negative relationship as expected, although none was significant.

The performance variable, EPS, was always negative and was weakly significant, indicating that only poorer performing firms were likely to introduce an ATCA.

VII Conclusions

The objective of this analysis was to test the conjectures in the literature about the role of the board of directors in corporate governance. While both in theory and in law, the board has a responsibility to act in the best interests of the shareholder, the extent to which this has happened is an empirical question.

Our analysis has captured a relatively unique event covering a relatively short period of time, in which firms engaged in changing their articles of association to incorporate anti-takeover amendments. The events examined in this study are homogeneous, and represent one example of an ultimate decision making process in a firm, where owners' representatives and owners both get the opportunity to vote.

The results of the analysis are mixed. (Table 5.)

In general, however, the results tend to indicate that the structure of the board of directors is not relevant to the corporate governance decision to adopt an ATCA. Yet, the shareholdings of both directors and the block shareholdings are important in the corporate governance decisions of firms. So the collective proportion of shareholdings of directors is of greater significance than the actual structure of the board itself.

The results also suggest that external monitoring through large proportions of ownership is useful to ensure fair and proper decisions on the part of the board of directors. This is consistent with the view of previous findings that the composition of the board of directors may not be independently or objectively formed. Because of this, the board of directors may not have exclusive rights and authority to act completely independently. In this sense, the role of large shareholders is significant as an active and real alternative monitor of managerial and board actions.

This is particularly important as the indication is that poor performing firms are more likely to introduce antitakeover devices, and without the monitoring of large investors, there is more likely to be both management and board entrenchment.

Table 5: Results of logistic regression analysis: Probability of ATCA proposal (t statistics in brackets)

VARIABLE NAME	Regression A ESTIMATED COEFFICIENT	Regression B ESTIMATED COEFFICIENT	Regression C ESTIMATED COEFFICIENT
EPS	-0.02461*	-0.02405	-0.02472*
	(-1.6878)	(-1.6532)	(-1.6999)
GROWTH2	-0.00070	-0.00070	-0.00060
	(-0.5717)	(-0.5736)	(-0.8211)
LNINSTHLDGS	1.38250	1.28700	1.38170
	(0.6800)	(0.6261)	(0.6784)
LNTP20	-7.86780**	-7.90180**	-8.25000**
	(-2.2729)	(-2.2893)	(-2.4969)
DIRNUM		-0.00394	
		(-0.0401)	
LNDIRNUM	0.16726		0.27733
	(0.2047)		(0.3462)
PROPDEP	-1.73210	-1.87290	
	(-1.1585)	(-1.2950)	
LNPROPDEP			-1.96510
			(-0.9684)
LNDIRHLDGS	-6.84040*	-6.82990*	-7.01760*
	(-1.6986)	(-1.6784)	(-1.7485)
LNSIZE	-0.50035	-0.48168	-0.51030*
	(-1.6566)	(-1.5903)	(-1.6874)
CONSTANT	7.91080**	8.26120**	7.92410**
	(2.2823)	(2.6245)	(2.3096)
Number of observations	66	66	66
Log-Likelihood Function =	-36.077	-36.097	-45.717
Percentage of right predictions	77.27%	77.27%	78.79%

**, * significant at the 5% and 10% levels respectively

Notes

1   The authors gratefully acknowledge the financial support provided from research grants awarded by Macquarie University and the University of Melbourne. The use of data provided by the Australian Stock Exchange is also acknowledged.

2   Data on adopting and control firms relating to directors' ownership, institutional ownership and various growth variables was painstakingly collected from annual reports to compile an unique micro-level data set.

3   As opposed to shareholders who are eligible to vote.

4   There is some dispute concerning the exact proportion of takeovers occurring during the 1980s in Australia which were partial takeovers. There is no doubt that the percentage of partial takeovers increased significantly during the first half of the 1980s as the following statistics indicate, although they may never have counted for as high as 40 per cent of all takeovers.

Year	Partial takeovers as % of all takeovers
1980	5%
1981	8%
1982	23%
1983	13%
1984	20%
1985 (2 year)	18%

Source: Bishop, Dodd and Officer (1987, 69).

5   Source: Corporate Adviser (1989-1993) Analysis of Takeover Activity.

6   Thereby aligning financial incentives of management (agents) to wealth changes of shareholder (principals). In practice, it is unusual for all management to hold shares. Information on CEO holdings of ordinary shares is not readily available, however, a study of the largest 100 companies in 1990 (Defina, Harris and Ramsay, 1994) found that the median proportion of CEO holdings was only 0.02 percent of all shares on issue, representing a value of $146,000. Of the CEO's of the top 100 companies, 46 percent held shares with a total value of less than $100,000.

7   This essentially 'captures' the directors. There is some disagreement about who really wears the pants in this arrangement, is real power held in the directors or the management group, which party is the stronger coalition ? This question is difficult to answer and remains a much sort after research issue.

8   A decision to amend an articles of association to incorporate an ATCA is one example of an 'ultimate consensus decision' under Australian corporations law. Another example is the decision to vary a company's share capital (such as capital reduction) which requires both a resolution of the board and a resolution of the shareholders. It is also commonly the case that dividends require both a recommendation of the board and final approval of shareholders.

9   We note that this definition of independent directors differs from that of the Australian Investment Manager's Association. Under the Association's guidelines, to be an independent director, a director must not have any significant financial dealings with the company in addition to being a non-executive.

10 In Australia, listed corporations cannot issue ordinary shares with differential voting rights. Section 249(1) of the Corporations Law provides that every member (shareholder) of a company has one vote for every share held unless the articles (constitution) of the company provide otherwise. Consequently, s249 represents a default rule but one which is frequently contracted out of by private companies or (less frequently) unlisted public companies. As to the structure of these differential voting right shares, it is possible to have shares with 'super' voting rights or shares with no voting rights. The situation is different for listed companies. Australian Stock Exchange Listing Rule 6.9 provides that on a poll (as opposed to a resolution decided on a show of hands) each holder of an ordinary share has one vote for each fully paid share held (and a fraction of a vote for each partly paid share held based upon the proportion paid up on the share). This is of course a mandatory rule.

11 However, it is worth noting that under Australian takeovers law, this would only be permissible if the blockholder held less than 20 percent of the shares. An attempt by someone to buy more than 20 percent of a target corporation requires either a full takeover or a proportional partial takeover.

12 Author note: For some firms, capital raisings may result in distortions from year to year.

13 The costs of introducing an ATCA can be high if the company calls an extraordinary meeting of shareholders to discuss and vote on the issue. These costs are alleviated somewhat if the matter is discussed and voted on at an annual general meeting. In our sample of 37 firms introducing ATCAs 26 introduced their ATCA at their annual general meeting, and only 11 called extraordinary meetings of shareholders. Consequently, we would not expect this effect to be subdued in our analysis.

14 However, there are other defensive tactics and strategies available to companies. These include share placements to friendly shareholders and capital reconstructions.

15 This model is appropriate as it relates probabilistically, observed choices, such as an ATCA decision, to the observed characteristics of the company. It is preferred to the linear probability model which can lead to probability estimates outside the [0,1] range. Refer Griffiths, et al (1993, p. 753).

16 Top 150 companies, ranked by market capitalisation.

17 Section II describes the process required to be undertaken by a company to adopt a partial anti-takeover mechanism.

18 This was examined by Armstrong, Lange and Woo (1994), which found that majority of anti-takeover amendments occurred subsequent to the revision of the Companies (Acquisition of Shares) Act in June 1986. North Broken Hill Holdings was the only company to propose partial takeover restrictions prior to 24 June 1986, and was able to do this as the uncertainty surrounding the revisions to the corporations legislation had been largely resolved by this time. Armstrong, Lange and Woo state that a discussion with the legal staff at the Australian Stock Exchange revealed that it was only large firms which had introduced ATCA proposals to shareholders. Consequently, the authors limited their investigations to the top 150 firms in each of the years examined.

19 While matching on the basis of both industry and size would have been the most preferable approach, as noted in Armstrong, Lange and Woo (1994), the smallness of the Australian market made this approach intractable. Consequently, as the firms in the ATCA group were a part of the largest 150 companies by market capitalisation, the control group was also formed from the top 150 companies.

20 Armstrong, Lange and Woo (1994) found on inspection of the control group data revealed that one of the firms showed an excessive decline in its stock price during the estimation period, believed to be caused by unusual firm specific issues, and as such was dropped from the control sample. Consequently, the number of control group companies is 36.

21 Of the seven cases which were eliminated because of missing director's shareholdings, three were from the ATCA sample, and four were from the control group.

22 Earnings per share and dividends per share have been adjusted for any capital readjustments.

23 As a part of the Australian Stock Exchange listing rules, companies are required to report directors shareholdings, director numbers and details of the largest twenty shareholders in their annual reports.

24 In all cases the annual report dates were relatively close to the ATCA proposal date, and in 26 cases the annual report dates coincided with the ATCA proposal acceptance date.

25 Research and development expenditure is another measure often used as a proxy for growth potential, however, this is not available for the sample firms as R & D expenditure was not itemised in the annual reports of Australian firms in the period examined.

26 To mitigate the effect of outliers and to ensure that the proxies were not bounded variables, the natural logarithm of many of the variables was used. For example, all of the shareholding variables are limited to the range (0,1). In these cases, the variable tested was the natural log of (1 + proportion of shareholding). This transformation retains both the sign and size relativity. Without these transformations, there is the possibility that the use of bounded variables will cause the significance levels to be estimated with error.

27 Two measures of market value to book value were also used to proxy growth potential. However, while the results for all were similar, the growth variables listed in Table 2, based on those used by Garvey (1987) and Lange and Sharpe (1995), were the best performers in the empirical analysis. In addition, the proxies used are better indicators of the exploitation of growth opportunities, as opposed to growth opportunities per se.

28 In all cases, the final proxies for all ownership and directors proportional variables used in the analysis were natural logs of one plus the proportion of the ownership. This was done to overcome inaccurate significance tests in the case of bounded variables.

29 It is important for readers to understand that it is virtually impossible to obtain reliable information on the extent of institutional investment in Australian companies. There are two reasons for this. Firstly, listed companies are only required to disclose the holdings of their largest 20 registered ordinary shareholders. Secondly, institutional shareholders often use nominee companies to hold their

investments, and it is impossible to identify the ownership of shares held by nominee companies.

References

Armstrong S., H. P. Lange, and L.E. Woo, 1994 Can Antitakeover Activity Really Create Wealth, *Asia Pacific Journal of Management,* Vol 11, No. 2, pp.327-343, October.

Agrawal, A and G. N. Mandelker, 1990 Large shareholders and the monitoring of managers: The case of antitakeover charter amendments, *Journal of Financial and Quantitative Analysis,* 25/2, 143-161.

Bethel, J.E., Porter-Liebeskind, J., & Opler, T., 1996 Block Share Purchases and Corporate Performance, Fisher College of Business, *Ohio University Working Paper,* October

Bishop, S., Dodd, P. and Officer, R., 1987, *Australian Takeovers: The Evidence* 1972-1985, Centre for Independent Studies, Sydney.

Bizjak, J. M., J. A. Brickley and J. L. Coles 1993, Stock-based incentive compensation and investment behavior, *Journal of Accounting and Economics,* 16, pp. 349-372.

Blair, M. and Ramsay, I., Mandatory Corporate Disclosure Rules and Securities Regulation in Walker, G., Ramsay, I. and Fisse, B. (eds), 1997, *Securities Regulation in Australia and New Zealand,* 2nd edition, Oxford University Press.

Brickley, J. A., R. C. Lease and C. W. Smith , 1988, Ownership structure and voting on antitakeover amendments, *Journal of Financial Economics,* 20, 267-291.

Companies and Securities Law Review Committee, 1985a, *Discussion Paper on Partial Takeover Bids.*

Companies and Securities Law Review Committee, 1985b, *Report to the Ministerial Council on Partial Takeover Bids.*

Corporate Adviser, 1989-1993, *Analysis of Takeover Activity.*

Crough, G. J., 1980, Financial institutions and share ownership: A case study in money, work and social responsibility, G. J. Crough (Ed), *Transnational Corporations Research Project,* University of Sydney, 185-202.

Defina, A., T. Harris and I. Ramsay (1994) What is Reasonable Remuneration for Corporate Officers? An Empirical Investigation into the Relationship between Pay and Performance in the Largest Australian Companies, *Company and Securities Law Journal,* 12, 341.

Easterbrook, F. and Fischel, D., 1991, *The Economic Structure of Corporate Law,* Harvard University Press, Cambridge.

Fama, E., 1980, Agency Problems and the Theory of the Firm, *Journal of Political Economy,* 88, 288.

Garvey, G. 1987, Corporate agency conflicts and the presence of large shareholders, *Australian Graduate School of Management Working Paper:* 87-029.

Gross, D., 1983, Partial Takeovers—A Critique of the Provisions in the Companies (Acquisition of Shares) Act and Codes, *Company and Securities Law Journal,* 1, 251.

Griffiths, W., R. Carter Hill and G. Judge, 1993, *Learning and Practicing Econometrics,* John Wiley & Sons.

Hirshleifer, D. and A. Thakor, 1992, Managerial conservatism, project choice and debt, *Review of Financial Studies,* 5, pp. 437-470.

Hirshleifer, D. and A. V. Thakor, 1994, Managerial Performance, Boards of Directors and Takeover Bidding, *Journal of Corporate Finance,* 1, 63-90.

John, K., and L. W. Senbet, 1997, Corporate Governance and Organisation Design, Stern School of Business, *New York University Working Paper.*

Lange, H. P. and I.G. Sharpe, 1995, Monitoring Costs and Ownership Concentration: Australian Evidence, *Applied Financial Economics,* 5, pp 441-447.

Lorsch, J., 1989, *Pawns or Potentates: The Reality of America's Corporate Boards,* Harvard Business School Press, Boston.

Manne, H., 1965, Mergers and the Market for Corporate Control, *Journal of Political Economy,* 73, 110.

Megginson, W. L. 1997, *Corporate Finance Theory,* Addison-Wesley Educational Publishers, Reading, MA, USA.

Morck, R., A. Schleifer and R. Vishny, 1988, Management Ownership and Market Valuation: An Empirical Analysis, *Journal of Financial Economics,* 20, 293

Noe, T. H. and M. J. Rebello 1995, The Design of Corporate Boards: Composition, Compensation, Factions and Turnover, *Georgia State University Department of Finance Working Paper.*

Pound, J., 1988, Proxy contests and the efficiency of shareholder oversight, *Journal of Financial Economics,* 20, 237-265.

Prentice, D., 1993,Some Aspects of the Corporate Governance Debate in Prentice, D. and Holland, P. (eds), *Contemporary Issues in Corporate Governance,* Clarendon Press, Oxford.

Ramsay, I., 1992, Balancing Law and Economics: The Case of Partial Takeovers, *Journal of Business Law,* 369.

Renard, I. and Santamaria, J., 1990, *Takeovers and Reconstructions in Australia,* Butterworths, Sydney.

Reve, T. 1990 The firm as a nexus of internal and external contracts, in M. Aoki, B. Gastafsson and O. E. Williamson (eds) *The firm as a nexus of contracts,* Chapter 7, Saga Publications.

Rosenstein, S. and J. G. Wyatt, 1990, Outside Directors, Board Independence, and Shareholder Wealth, *Journal of Financial Economics,* 26, 175-191.

Stein, J. C. 1988, Takeover threats and managerial myopia, *Journal of Political Economy*, 96, 61-80.

Tricker, R., 1994, *International Corporate Governance*, Prentice Hall, Singapore.

Warther, V. A., 1994, Board Effectiveness and Board Dissent: A Model of the Board's Relationship to Management and Shareholders, *USC Working Paper*.

Williamson, O. E. 1990, The firm as a nexus of treaties: an introduction, in M. Aoki, B. Gastafsson and O. E. Williamson (eds) *The firm as a nexus of contracts,* , Chapter 1, Saga Publications.

An investigation of the relationship of power and cognition of organisational elites, using computer-aided content analysis of annual reports

Paul L Nesbit and Boris Kabanoff

Abstract

Kipnis' (1976) metamorphic theory of power suggests that power can impact the cognitions of the powerful. We apply this theory to the study of organisational elites, specifically the CEO and the board of directors. Two CEO power factors and three board power factors were developed as measures of CEO and board power. Using computer-aided content analysis of annual reports hypothesised relationships of elite power and cognition were explored.

Introduction

Studies of elite cognitions and their impact on organisations, have mainly been interested in studying how leaders' thinking influence their behaviour and subsequently organisational outcomes (Calori, Johnson, & Sarnin, 1994; Fiol & Huff, 1992). The reciprocal impact of the organisational environment on the behaviour and cognitions of elites is generally ignored. The question is rarely asked, how does the experience of being a member of the organisational elite influence an elite's cognitions? One factor that is expected to play an important role in shaping their cognitions is power.

Theoretical Background
Metamorphic Theory of Power

An empirical approach to researching the impact of power on the cognitions of the powerful is the work of Kipnis (1976; 1990) who suggests that the successful use of power leads to changes in the perceptions and attitudes of the powerholder. Kipnis argues that, to the extent the powerholder perceives that he or she controls the actions of the target of influence, the powerholder feels there is less need to give the target full credit for his or her actions. Thus powerholders attribute the target's behaviour to the influence mechanisms they control rather than the internal motivations of targets.

The perception of being able to influence others leads to the powerholder's belief that his or her ideas and views are superior. Reinforcing this perception is the flattery and deference powerholders receive from the less powerful (Kipnis, 1990). Associated with this raised-worth and attribution of control is the devaluation of the target of influence. Kipnis (1976) notes that the value of autonomy in western society is highly prized and suggests that the lack of perceived target autonomy can contribute to devaluation of the target.

Kipnis also proposes that the powerholder's devaluation of the target is associated with the powerholder's preference to increase social and psychological distance from the target. Other researchers (Hofsteade, 1980) have also noted that high power differentiation is associated with social distancing between the powerful and the less powerful. The process of perceptual change associated with the use of power is represented in figure 1, as Kipnis' Metamorphic Model of Power.

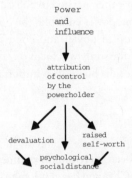

Figure 1: Kipnis' metamorphic model

Kipnis' model suggests that power can influence the powerholder's self-perceptions and the perceptions of those the powerholder has power over. Given the centrality of power within the experience of organisational leaders (Pettigrew, 1992; Pfef, 1981), the study of power and its association with cognitions seem overdue. additionally, since organisations channel a great deal of power into senior roles, the question of whether the experience of power impacts the way leaders' think has practical relevance since costs associated with poor decisions can be high.

Organisational elites and power effects

Organisational elites occupy formally defined positions of authority (Pettigrew, 1992). They are comprised of the board of directors and the senior members of the corporate executive team, headed by the CEO. According to metamorphic theory, both the executive and the board will be susceptible to metamorphic effects. That is, as members of the organisational elite, the executive and board may have similar perspectives about the less powerful, and these perspectives are related to their experience of power.

In contrast, corporate governance literature assumes that power may have differential impacts on the executive and the board. Strengthening the power of the board is commonly suggested to counter managerial domination of boards (Molz, 1988; Pearce & Zahara, 1991). Powerful boards are assumed to more adequately carry out their function to protect the interests of shareholders against self-interested actions of powerful CEOs and executives. Thus underlying corporate governance literature is an assumption that power 'ennobles' the board but negatively impacts on the executive.

Thus the literature exhibits two contradictory perspectives of the effects of power on organisational elites' cognitions. One, based on Kipnis' metamorphic theory of power, suggests that both the executive and the board may be negatively impacted. The other perspective, assumed within corporate governance literature, is that power ennobles the board. This study aims to investigate the relationship of power and cognitions of organisational powerholders. Specifically, the study will focus on the power and cognitions of the CEO and members of the board, two important loci of power within organisations.

Measuring Power

In recent years there has been increasing use of demographic variables as proxies for the power of the CEO and board (Ocasio, 1994; Westphal & Zajac, 1994; Singh & Harianto, 1989; Finkelstein & D'Aveni, 1994; Molz, 1988). The present study used a variety of demographic variables as proxy measures of CEO and board power, in recognition of the complex and multi-dimensional nature of power (Finkelstein, 1992). In all, ten indices of power were selected from the literature, five for the CEO and five for the board. The five proxy measures of CEO power were: proportion of total company shares owned; length of tenure as CEO; duality, ie., CEO was also chair; proportion of non-executive board members appointed during CEO reign; number of non-affiliated boards sat on. The five proxy measures of board1 power were: proportion of total company shares owned by board members; average length of board member's tenure; proportion of outsiders on board; average number of non-affiliated boards sat on; length of chair tenure. All the variables selected have been used in previous research on CEO and board power.

Measuring Metamorphic Effects

Computer-aided content analysis of elite communication was used to search for evidence of metamorphic effects. Concern for issues is determined by the relative frequency of words associated with a theme of interest (Huff, 1990; Weber, 1990). The greater the frequency the more 'cognitively central' or important that theme is held to be to the author/s of the communication.

In computer-aided content analysis a theme is entered into a search command to represent all the words under that theme. The computer program highlights each word related to the theme and determines the frequency of each word within a document. Text associated with 'hits' or frequency counts of each theme are extracted and visually inspected for appropriateness of semantic meaning and to aid in refinement of computer coding rules. The 'hits' or frequency counts are then divided by the total number of words in a document in order to normalise for document size. The normalised score represents an intensity value for a theme.

An important source of elite communication about organisationally relevant concerns is the annual report. The content of annual reports can be considered as important indicators of what elites are attending to, focusing on and seeking to communicate to external and internal audiences, and so are generally closely monitored by organisational leaders (Fiol, 1995; D'Aveni & MacMillan, 1990). Text analysis of annual reports has been utilised by a number of researchers interested in identifying aspects of the cognitive structures of organisational leaders (Barr, Stimpert & Huff, 1992; Bettman & Weitz, 1983; Clapham & Schwenk, 1991; Salancik & Meindl, 1984). Barr et al. (1992) noted that 'few rival data sources exist that can provide insight into the changing mental methods of top managers over time' (p.21).

Thus annual reports were content analysed for themes seen as representing metamorphic effects. The following section discusses the relationship of themes to metamorphic effects and suggests hypotheses regarding these relationships.

Hypotheses

Metamorphic theory argues that elites, as powerholders who influence others in the organisation, are susceptible to metamorphic effects. Thus, the CEO and members of the board all experience high levels of power and in principle would be subject to the same metamorphic effects. This view that both powerful CEOs and boards are susceptible to metamorphic effects is termed the 'elite perspective'.

However, as noted earlier, corporate governance literature raises the prospect that power may have a differential impact on the executive and the board. Thus proposed associations relating to the 'governance perspective' are presented below as alternate hypotheses. Hypotheses are grouped under the four cognitive effects proposed by the metamorphic model. A summary of hypotheses is given in figure 2.

Devaluation of those with less power

According to the metamorphic model powerful CEOs and boards are expected to attribute control over the actions of employees to themselves. One consequence of this attribution is that elites will devalue the worth of those they have control over. The targets of influence of elites are the employees and managers of the organisation. These groups are not expected to be of central importance in the minds of elites nor in their communications. Thus powerful CEOs and boards are hypothesised to have negative associations with reference to employee themes.

In contrast, 'ennobled' boards are proposed to be less likely to attribute outcomes only to themselves and other elites but to recognise the contributions made by managers and employees. Thus their communications will seek to give these groups greater credit in discussion of organisational outcomes. These different perspectives give rise to alternate hypotheses.

- *Elite perspective hypothesis 1:* The greater the power of the CEO and board the fewer references to 'employees' and 'management' themes within annual reports.
- *Governance perspective hypothesis 1a:* The greater the power of the board the more frequent the reference to 'employees' and 'management' themes within annual reports.

Raised self-esteem and self-worth

Metamorphic theory suggests that the self-attribution of control by powerful CEOs and board members will be accompanied by an inflated sense of self-worth and self-regard. In other words, elites consider themselves to be important people in the organisation. Thus the communications of elites will tend to focus on their actions and roles.

In contrast, 'ennobled' boards will recognise the contribution of employees and managers, and downplay the attention given to themselves in their communications. Thus alternate hypotheses are presented.

Elite perspective hypothesis 2: The greater the power of the CEO and board the more frequent the references to 'elite' themes within annual reports.

Governance perspective hypothesis 2a: The greater the power of the board the fewer references to 'elite' themes within annual reports.

Attributions of control

Fundamental to metamorphic theory is the argument that attribution of control by powerful elites results in overestimation of their influence. As a result of this metamorphic effect, powerful elites are likely to consider their own role and actions as highly important in influencing organisational outcomes. Thus, in their communications, elites will give emphasis to their leadership responsibilities and duties, such as providing direction to others through the setting of goals. Elites are also likely to give substantial attention to organisational performance, since the results are seen as a direct outcome of their leadership role and actions. Thus themes of leadership, goals, and performance are hypothesised to figure prominently in their communications. In contrast, elites will be less attentive to themes that reflect worker commitment, participation and teamwork, since these suggest control of workers over their efforts and performance.

A different pattern of themes is expected from the 'governance perspective'. It is argued that boards do not attribute control to themselves but recognise the contributions of employees. Therefore board communications are likely to emphasise the importance of participatory work practices that involve employees and give recognition to the contribution of employees. Thus, 'ennobled' boards are likely to refer to participation, commitment and teamwork themes in their communications. In terms of the themes of goals and performance it is unclear that a powerful board will be as focused on these two themes as a metamorphosed CEO. However, it is unlikely that an 'ennobled' board would actually de-emphasise these themes, given their value to shareholders.

- *Elite perspective hypothesis 3:* The greater the power of the CEO and board the more reference to 'leadership', 'goals' and 'performance' themes in annual reports.
- *Governance perspective hypothesis 3a:* The greater the power of boards the less reference to 'leadership' themes in annual reports.
- *Elite perspective hypothesis 4.* The greater the power of the CEO and board the less reference to 'participation ', 'commitment' and 'teamwork' themes in annual reports.
- *Governance perspective hypothesis 4a:* The greater the power of boards the more frequent the reference to 'participation', 'commitment' and 'teamwork' themes in annual reports.

Social and psychological distance

Since employees and other non-elites would not figure in the organisational communications of metamorphosed elites their communication would be exclusive rather than inclusive in nature. Thus, metamorphosed elites' communications would not contain many references to affiliative themes.

The governance perspective, in contrast, suggests that management and employees make substantial contribution to the organisation. Recognition of these contributions would create an orientation of inclusion and so it is proposed that the organisational culture will reflect an affiliative nature.

- *Elite perspective hypothesis 5:* The greater the power of the CEO and board the less affiliative the annual report.
- *Governance perspective hypothesis 5a:* The greater the power of the board the more affiliative the annual report.

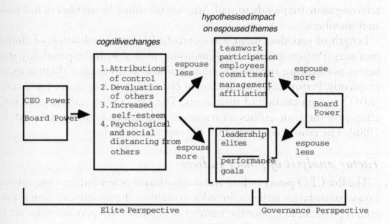

Figure 2: Summary of hypotheses.

Method
Sample

The sample is made up of 142 large Australian organisations from a variety of industries. They were selected on the basis of availability of demographic data for the CEO and all board members. The average market capitalisation of the sample in 1993 = A$1.2 billion (SD = A$1.9 billion) and average staff numbers over the two years was 6,630 (SD = 15,856).

Text data

Similar to the majority of studies that use annual reports to assess managerial cognitions (Barr et al., 1992; D'Aveni & MacMillan, 1990) the focus was on those sections that can be specifically attributed to the CEO or board — the CEO's letter to shareholders and the Chair's[2] statement. The text data was collected for 1993 and 1994, and totalled 522,151 words. The two year period allowed for lag effects between power estimates of demographic data (collected for 1993) and subsequent thematic patterns in the annual report. Average number of words per organisation was 3677 (SD = 2629).

Control Variables

Since Australian organisations typically separate the positions of CEO and Chair, the format of the annual report can be quite diverse. The variety of letters complicates the content analysis process as different themes may be related to letter format. To control for annual report format, dummy variables for type of letters appearing in the annual report were used in the analysis.

Larger organisations may have thematic 'biases' in their text, such as referring more frequently to staff. Size was measured by number of full-time staff members.

Length of text document was controlled by standardisation of theme measures. Performance was also controlled to deal with the possibility that better performing organisations mentioned performance themes more frequently. Performance was measured by earnings before interest and taxes (EBIT) as a proportion of total assets. The EBIT/assets ratio assesses how efficiently the firm utilises its resources to produce a gross profit (Molz, 1988). The ratio was averaged for the two year period.

Factor analysis of power indices

The five CEO power indices and the five board power indices were entered into separate factor analyses, in order to examine the underlying dimensions and, if possible, to reduce the number of variables to a parsimonious set of power factors.

Principal component analysis of the CEO variables using varimax rotation resulted in the extraction of two factors with eigenvalues greater than 1 and together accounted for 66.6 per cent of variance. The first factor, was termed 'CEO-Dominance' and represented an established and institutionalised CEO. The second factor was termed 'CEO-Network' reflecting the network connections, among other organisational elites, obtained by membership of other boards. Table 1 summarises the results of the factor analysis of the CEO variables.

Demographic indices	CEO-Dom	CEO-Network
1. CEO shares	.77	-.28
2. CEO tenure	.87	.20
3. Duality	.62	-.06
4. Proportion of Bd Appts	.70	.16
5. No. of Bds	.03	.96

Table 1. Summary of factor analysis for CEO indices of power.

Principal component analysis of the board variables using varimax rotation resulted in the extraction of three factors which together accounted for 73 per cent of variance. The first factor was termed 'board-expertise', reflecting experience gained from length of service on the board. The second factor was termed 'board-focus', reflecting the attention given by board members with a high financial stake in the company and the necessarily reduced attention given by board members when they are on a large number of boards. The number of outsiders on the board loaded on the third factor. This factor was termed 'board-independence', reflecting the independence typically ascribed to boards comprised predominantly by outsiders (Westphal & Zajac, 1994). Table 2 summarises the results of the factor analysis of the board indices.

Demographic indices	Expertise	Focus	Independence
1. Bd shares	.00	.81	.15
2. Average No. of Bds sat on	.12	-.73	.16
3. Proportion of outsiders on Bd	-.01	-.00	.98
4. Average Bd tenure	.86	-.06	-.03
5. Chair tenure	.79	.21	.00

Table 2. Summary of factor analysis for board indices of power.

Analysis of themes

Given the topical nature of human resources in organisational literature and greater calls for participation and involvement of workers, it was surprising to find that the themes of 'participation', 'commitment', 'leadership' and 'teamwork' were poorly represented in the text data. There was a large percentage of elites' letters with little or no mention of these themes.

Two approaches were taken to analyse these poorly represented themes. The themes of 'participation', 'commitment' and 'teamwork', which were all hypothesised to be negatively associated with elite power, were combined into a single overall score titled 'employee-attributions'. Results were then treated the same as other themes. For the leadership theme frequency counts were rescaled as a dichotomous variable (0 = no mention at all and 1 = mentioning).

Other variables' distributions were examined and log transformations were used to normalise the distribution and control for heteroscedasticity. Thematic data were analysed using multiple regression, except for the theme of 'leadership' which was analysed using logistic regression.

For both logistic and multiple regressions a hierarchical regression procedure was employed. Control variables were entered first as a block into the regression to control for their effect on the themes. Next, power variables were entered. Separate models were developed for CEO and board power. Given the exploratory nature of the research and the fact that hypotheses included direction of associations, p-values of less than .10 were used to measure significance in the analysis of regressions.

Results

Table 3 presents means, standard deviations and correlations among variables including the individual variables that made up the power factor scores for the board and the CEO. Average CEO tenure was 5.79 years (SD = 4.67 years) and average board tenure was 6.48 years (SD = 3.73 years). Tenure for CEOs and boards were significantly associated (r = .23) and the tenure of the CEO as a board member was also highly related to board tenure (r = .34). These correlations suggest that elites tend to form relatively stable relationships at the top of organisations.

The results of the regressions carried out are presented in table 4. The 'employee' theme is significantly related to board expertise (p<.05). CEO dominance (p<.10) and board expertise (p<.10) are significant and positively associated with the 'management' theme.

For the 'elite' theme there are no significant CEO power variables but board independence is significant (p<.05).

The power factor of CEO-network is negatively associated with 'employee attribution' (p<.05) and 'performance' themes (p<.05). No CEO power factors are significantly associated with the theme of goals. There are no significant associations between board power factors and the themes of employee attribution, goals or performance. CEO-network power factor is positively associated (p<.05) with reference to the theme of leadership.

Board power factors of expertise (p=.01) and focus (p=.06) were positively associated with affiliation. There were no significant findings for CEO power factors.

Variable	Mean	SD	1	2	3	4	5	6	7	8	9	10	11	12	13	14	15	16	17	18	19	20	21	22	23	24	25	26	27	28
1. EBIT/Assets	7.69	5.64																													
2. Staff No.	6630	15836	-.02																												
3. Chair letter	.12	.33	-.08	-.09																											
4. CEO letter	.23	.42	.04	.06	-.20*																										
5. Joint letter	.11	.32	.06	.22**	-.13	-.19*																									
6. Both letters	.54	.50	-.02	-.13	-.40**	-.58**	-.38**																								
7. CEO-dominance	.00	1.00	.17**	-.16	.02	.36**	-.12	-.24**																							
8. CEO-network	.00	1.00	-.10	.09	-.03	-.12	.14	.02	.01																						
9. Bd-expertise	.00	1.00	.03	-.05	.13	.12	-.03	-.16	.18*	-.20*																					
10. Bd-focus	.00	1.00	.09	-.25**	.16	-.01	-.07	-.03	.19*	.14	.00																				
11. Bd-independenc	.00	1.00	.16	.09	-.00	-.23**	.12	.12	-.35**	.08	.00	.00																			
12. Emp-attribution	.48	.40	.12	-.03	-.19*	.09	-.04	.07	.19*	-.16	-.13	.09	-.16																		
13. Affiliation	2.21	.75	.06	.22**	.03	.07	-.17*	.04	.07	-.06	.19*	.10	-.07	.26**																	
14. Elites	2.02	.60	-.00	.06	.29**	-.13	.09	-.13	.02	-.03	-.08	.10	-.13	-.04	-.10																
15. Employees	1.36	.51	.05	.19*	.04	-.02	-.06	.01	-.05	-.03	.17*	.02	.12	.15	.23**	.16															
16. Goals	.58	.36	.03	.13	-.06	.06	-.03	.17*	-.18*	.03	.14	-.11	.13	.25**	.06	-.07	.00														
17. Management	1.15	.46	.07	.14	-.04	.10	-.12	.04	.15	-.02	.14	-.00	.02	.03	.27**	.16	.25**	.05													
18. Performance	2.47	.33	.04**	.00	-.12	-.04	.07	.03	-.06	-.18*	.05	-.09	-.05	.03	.06	.08	.28**	.00	.16												
19. Leadership	.45	.50	-.02	.21*	-.12	-.12	-.05	.22**	-.02	.19*	-.17*	-.00	-.09	-.05	-.13	.02	.08	-.06	.12	-.01											
20. CEO Own	.04	.11	.11*	-.13	.01	-.12	.11	-.19*	-.02	.23**	-.01	.02	-.24**	-.05	-.01	.02	.00	-.18	.24**	.06	-.05										
21. CEO Tenure	5.79	4.67	.15	-.14	.18*	.14	-.00	-.18*	.37**	.28**	.17*	.12	-.39**	.16	-.04	.01	-.03	-.03	-.01	-.11	-.03	.58**									
22. Duality	.18	.39	.12	-.03	-.12	-.58**	-.17*	-.29**	.65**	.17*	-.06	.15	.00	.16	.10	.08	.00	-.12	.13	-.11	-.03	.43**	.26**								
23. Loyalty	.50	.34	.06	-.17*	-.03	.17*	-.07	-.07	.79**	.07	.11	.11	-.22**	.05	-.02	-.06	-.17*	-.07	-.01	-.13	.04	.26**	.61**	.36**							
24. CEO-bd-No	.92	1.37	-.08	.10	-.02	-.05	.12	-.02	.03	.96**	.07	-.19*	.12	-.16	-.05	-.02	-.01	.01	.05	-.16	.19*	-.11	.16	.05	-.11						
25. Bd Own	.05	.14	-.10	-.10	.13	-.05	.10	-.03	-.11	.81**	.16	.05	.06	.05	.08	-.08	.02	.06	.08	.04	-.06	.14	.16	.05	.06	.02					
26. Bd-bd-No	2.42	1.72	-.12	.28**	-.17*	-.05	.10	.08	-.24**	-.13	.73**	-.00	.16	-.06	-.01	-.09	.13	-.04	-.08	-.04	.10	-.15	-.18*	.05	-.08	-.00	-.09				
27. % Outsider	.70	.16	-.15	.07	.01	-.25**	.11	.12	-.34**	-.01	-.13	-.00	.98**	-.15	-.10	-.12	.13	.12	-.01	.00	-.05	-.23**	-.22**	-.00	-.12	-.20*	-.15	.20*			
28. Bd-av-ten	6.48	3.73	.04	.03	.18*	.10	.04	-.22**	.10	.86**	-.01	-.06	-.03	-.16	.04	.21**	.21**	-.16	.04	.05	-.15	.13	.23**	.23**	-.20**	-.25**	.05	.04	-.12		
29. Chr Tenure	5.99	5.36	.01	-.15	.05	.10	-.10	-.05	.24**	.79**	.21**	.21*	.00	-.04	.13	-.04	.05	-.07	.20*	.04	-.14	.31**	.26**	-.01	.03	.08	-.01	-.12	-.14	.39**	

+p<.10, *p<.05, **p<.01

Table 3: Means, Standard Deviations and Correlations

Power factors	Employee theme	M'ment theme	Elite theme	Employee attribution	Perform theme	Goal theme	Affiliation theme	Leadership theme
CEO-Dominance	-.02 a	.17*	.06	.01	-.09	-.13	.10	.19
CEO-Network	-.04	-.01	-.02	-.17**	-.17**	.03	-.05	.38**
Bd-Expertise	.18**	.15*	-.10	-.13	.06	-.11	.21***	-.29
Bd-Focus	.05	.06	.08	.05	-.02	-.09	.16*	.01
Bd-Independence	.10	.03	-.17**	-.06	.04	.11	-.08	-.23
Adj Rsq after entering control variables	.01	.02*	.07*	.03	.03*	.03	.07***	ns
Adj Rsq after entering CEO power factors	.00	.03	.06	.04	.05*	.02	.07	Sign *
Adj Rsq after entering Board power factors	.03*	.03	.10*	.03	.01	.03	.12**	ns

aFigures are standardised beta scores except for 'leadership' which is in actual beta scores.
* $p < .10$; ** $p < .05$; ***$p < .01$

Table 4: Regression results for themes.

Curvilinear associations were also examined to further explore the relationship between themes and the two time-based power factors (tenure loads heavily on CEO dominance and board expertise in the factor analysis). Two themes showed significant results (table 5). CEO dominance (squared) was significantly associated ($p < .05$) with reference to the theme of 'management'. There was also a significant result for board-expertise (squared) with employee attribution theme ($p < .05$).

Finally, reduced models (table 5) using only the significant squared power variables and significant power factors were tested. For the 'management' theme, CEO-dominance (squared) and board-expertise were entered as a block after partialling out the effect of control variables. The overall change in R-square from a control model was significant ($p < .05$). For the 'employee attribution' theme, Board-expertise squared and CEO-network resulted in a significant change from the control model ($p < .05$).

Power factors	Management theme		Employee attribution theme	
	Model 1	Model 2	Model 1	Model 2
CEO-dom Sq	.21** a	.20**		
CEO-network	.04			-.17**
Bd-exptise Sq		.14*	-.19**	-.19**
Bd-expertise				
Bd-focus			.07	
Bd_independ			.07	
Adj R sq	.05*	.06**	.05*	.08*

a Figures are standardised beta scores.
* $p < .10$; ** $p < .05$; ***$p < .01$

Table 5: Curvilinear and Reduced Models for management and employee attribution themes.

Discussion
Devaluation of the less powerful

Hypotheses for this metamorphic effect received mixed support. 'Employee' and 'management' themes were positively related to powerful boards which supports the governance perspective. However, CEO power factors were not significantly related to employee themes which limits the support for the governance perspective.

Curvilinear results suggests that references to management increase for a time but begin to decrease as CEO tenure increases. One explanation for this result could be that powerful CEOs recognise management as an important mechanism of control over others but with increasing institutionalisation of their dominance and comfort in their role, they begin, as predicted by the metamorphic theory of power, to devalue and limit their recognition of managers. Board-expertise power, however, suggests a positive relationship with this theme.

Thus taken overall, the pattern of results for the 'management' theme is supportive of metamorphic effects of devaluation of the less powerful by the CEO, while board power tends to counter these effects. In other words, a governance perspective is reflected for the metamorphic effect of devaluation of the less powerful.

Raised self-esteem and self-worth.

The hypothesis derived from the elite metamorphic model was not supported. There were no statistically significant results for CEO factors in the regression of the 'elite' theme. However, the factor board-independence was negatively associated and significant ($p<.05$) with the theme of 'elites', suggesting that board members are less inclined to refer to 'elites'. Overall these results give some support for the governance metamorphic model.

Social and psychological distance

The elite metamorphic perspective hypothesis for this metamorphic effect was not supported. Regression results for the theme of 'affiliation' were not significant for CEO factors. Board factors (expertise $p<.01$ and focus $p<.10$), however, were significantly and positively related to references to the theme of 'affiliation'. This result lends support to the governance perspective that powerful boards influence corporate communications towards non-metamorphic theme patterns.

Attribution of control

Hypotheses derived from the elite metamorphic model for this effect received mixed support. CEO power was positively associated with reference to the 'leadership' theme (CEO-network p<.05), and negatively associated with the 'employee attribution' theme (CEO-network p<.05) as predicted.

There were no significant associations between board power and themes reflecting this metamorphic effect. However, the results of the curvilinear and reduced regression support the elite metamorphic model. Overall, the results show that, whereas powerful CEOs tend to decrease their reference to 'employee attribution' themes, board power counters this pattern for a time but at high levels of board expertise there is a decrease in reference to "employee attribution themes'. The result for employee attribution' theme is supportive of the elite metamorphic perspective.

It had been hypothesised that 'metamorphosed elites' would be more likely to discuss 'performance' themes since they attribute these outcomes to their control. However, the results were contrary to expectations. CEO power was negatively associated with performance themes (CEO-networking p<.05). This finding is consistent with research that shows that the more powerful the organisation's top-dyad (the CEO and chair) the less references to 'performance' is made in the annual report (Kabanoff & Nesbit, 1997). One explanation could be that elites who focus most on elite roles within the organisation are less concerned with communicating about organisational performance to other stakeholders because they believe it is an issue best left to them. That is, while power might create a sense of psychological distancing from those they have power over, it might also create a sense of psychological distancing from and decreased concern about external stakeholders —in essence a reduced sense of accountability.

Having discussed the results in terms of the four metamorphic effects, the following discussion relates the findings to the two metamorphic perspectives of the study.

Elite Perspective

The proposition that powerful CEOs and boards would both be associated with a similar metamorphic pattern of themes within the letters of the CEO and Chair was supported by the results for 'employee attribution' themes but only when a curvilinear association for board- expertise was involved. In most other themes, significant results for the board tended to support hypotheses based on the governance perspective. Results concerning CEO power factors were broadly supportive of metamorphic theory. There were significant findings in hypothesised directions for 'leadership' and 'employee attribution' themes, and curvilinear association with 'management' and 'employee attribution' themes.

Governance Perspective

The hypotheses that board power would have contrasting associations but that the overall pattern of association of CEOs would correspond to metamorphic theory received encouraging support. Significant associations of board power with 'affiliation', 'employee', 'management' and 'elite' themes supported the governance perspective. Board-expertise and board-focus factors were positively associated with 'affiliation'; board-expertise was positively associated with 'employee' and 'management' themes; and board-independence was negatively associated with the theme of 'elites'.

While the results are supportive of the 'governance perspective' hypotheses, these conclusions would be strengthened by significant but opposite associations between the CEO and these themes. Unfortunately there were no regressions where both CEO and board power factors were significant in opposite directions for the same theme. However, leadership showed support for the 'governance perspective' being positively associated with CEO power and close to significance and negative for board power (p=.12). In addition, hypotheses predicting directions of associations were supported for both positive and negative associations increasing the validity of results.

Summary

In summary, the results of this study showed encouraging support for a governance perspective of the association of power and thematic content. That is, power is associated with the content of annual report but this association differs for powerful CEOs and powerful boards. However, limited and mixed statistical findings prevent any definitive affirmations about the association of power and metamorphic effects within the themes of the annual report.

Notes.

1. Only non-executive board member data were used in development of proxy measures of power for the board.
2. The gender neutral term 'Chair' is used, although 'Chairs' in the sample were male.

References

Barr, P. S., Stimpert, J. L., & Huff, A. S. (1992). Cognitive change, strategic action, and organizational renewal. *Strategic Management Journal,* 13, 13-36.

Bettman, J. R., & Weitz, B. A. (1983). Attributions in the board room: Causal reasoning in corporate annual reports. *Administrative Science Quarterly,* 28, 165-183.

Clapham, S. E., & Schwenk, C. R. (1991). Self-serving attributions, managerial cognition, and company performance. *Strategic Management Journal,* 12, 219-229.

Calori, R. Johnson, G., & Sarnin, P., (1994). CEO's cognitive maps and the scope of the organisation. Strategic Management Journal, 15(6), 437-457.

D'Aveni, R. A., & MacMillan, I. C. (1990). Crisis and the content of managerial communications: A study of the focus of attention of top managers in surviving and failing firms. *Administrative Science Quarterly*, 35, 634-657.

Finkelstein, S. (1992). Power in top management teams: dimensions, measurement, and validation. *Academy of Management Journal*, 35(3), 505-538.

Finkelstein, S., & D'Aveni, R. A. (1994). CEO duality as a double-edged sword: How boards of directors balance entrenchment avoidance and unity of command. Academy of Management Journal, 37(5), 1079-1108.

Fiol, C. M. (1995). Corporate communications: Comparing executives' private and public statements. *Academy of Management Journal*, 38(2), 522-536.

Fiol, C. M., & Huff, A. S. (1992). Maps for managers: Where are we? Where do we go from here? *Journal of Management Studies*, 29, 267-285.

Hofsteade, G, (1980) *Culture's Consequences: International Differences in Work-related Values*, Beverly Hills:Sage.

Huff, A. S. (1990). *Mapping Strategic Thought*. Chichester: Wiley.

Kabanoff, B., & Nesbit, P.L., (1997). Metamorphic effects of power as reflected in espoused organisational values: Implications for Corporate Governance, Australian Psychologist, 32 (1), 62-70.

Kipnis, D. (1976). *The Powerholders*, University of Chicago Press, Chicago.

Kipnis, D. (1990). *Technology and Power*. New York: Springer-Verlag.

Molz, R. (1988). Managerial domination of Boards of Directors and financial performance. *Journal of Business Research*, 16, 235-249.

Ocasio, W. (1994). Political dynamics and the circulation of power: CEO succession in U.S. industrial corporations, 1960-1990. *Administrative Science Quarterly*, 39, 285-312.

Pearce, J., III., & Zahra, S. A. (1991.). The relative power of CEOs and Boards of directors: Associations with corporate performance. *Strategic Management Journal*, 12, 135-153.

Pettigrew, A. M. (1992). On studying elites. *Strategic Management Journal*, 13, 163-182.

Pfeffer, J. (1981). *Power in Organizations*. Massachusetts: Pitman Publishing Inc.

Salancik, G. R., & Meindl, J. R. (1984). Corporate attributions as strategic illusions of management control. *Administrative Science Quarterly*, 29, 238-254.

Singh, H., & Harianto, F. (1989). Management-Board relationships, takeover risk, and the adoption of golden parachutes. *Academy of Management Journal*, 32(1), 7-24.

Weber, R. P. (1990). *Basic Content Analysis*. London: Sage Publications.

Westphal, J. D., & Zajac, E. J. (1994). Substance and Symbolism in CEOs' Long-term Incentive Plans. *Administrative Science Quarterly*, 39,

Predictors of Advancing in Management: Advancers Versus Nonadvancers

Phyllis Tharenou

Abstract

The aim of the study was to explain advancement in management. Using longitudinal samples of three cohort pairs, consisting of those who had advanced versus not advanced in management, predictors of advancement were examined at three increasingly higher transition points. Entry to management was explained by career tournament wins, individuals' managerial traits, and gender-linked social factors. Advancement from initial to middle management continued to be explained by traits and gender-linked social factors, and also by promotion opportunities and investments in human capital. Advancement from mid to upper levels was explained by returns on earlier challenging work assignments, but also by gender-linked effects in relation to promotion and job moves, and male managerial hierarchies.

Introduction

Much research has been published in the last decade to explain advancement in management, including women's underrepresentation (see Tharenou's, 1997, review). Recently, large organisations have been restructuring by downsizing and outsourcing (Filipowski, 1993). Restructuring may affect the traditional managerial career path, although its effects are not clear. The overall number and proportions of managers has increased (Gordon, 1996), but managers may need to change organisations to advance (consistent with outsourcing), or their roles may change, especially those of middle managers (Floyd & Wooldridge, 1994). Restructuring has occurred worldwide. From 1993 to 1995, 57 percent of Australian organisations downsized; 25 percent of those removed one layer, nine percent two layers, and 50 percent no layers (Littler, Dunford, Bramble, & Hede, 1997).Careers may thus no longer be largely vertical within firms. The aim of the present study is to explain how advancement in management arises for employees in early and mid career in the period of restructuring.

Ragins and Sundstrom (1989) proposed that individual, interpersonal, and organizational level factors, operating as embedded systems, are the immediate causes of managerial advancement. Individuals must be motivated to advance in management, and must have the knowledge, skills and abilities to do so. They need selection and promotion opportunities to allow advancement (Ragins & Sundstrom, 1989), including wins in career tournaments and internal labor markets and promotion opportunities. Interpersonal processes in terms of career support and similarity to the hierarchy are also important to advancing in management (Ragins & Sundstrom, 1989).

The aim of the present study is to explain advancing in management from individual traits and human capital, selection and promotion opportunities, and social processes. Most of the previous studies have not been longitudinal (see Tharenou's, 1997, review), and are thus not predictive. Theories relevant to managerial advancement (traits, career tournaments, human capital, similarity-attraction) suggest certain factors are most explanatory at particular stages. Unlike previous longitudinal studies, the present study compares predictors at transition points for managerial advancement (entry to management; lower manager to middle manager transition; middle manager to upper manager transition) to explain men's and women's advancement.

Individuals' Traits and Human Capital

Managerial traits

Traits of masculinity, dominance, motivation to manage, and advancement motives have been consistently related to advancement in management (Tharenou, 1997) and to perceptions of leaders (Lord, De Vader, & Alliger, 1986). Individuals' motive drive, direct and select their behaviours in order to achieve desired goals (McClelland, 1985). Employees with high managerial aspirations should seek managerial positions to achieve their desired goal. In addition, traits allow individuals to implement their self-concepts when choosing occupations (Super, 1957). Masculinity is an instrumental, task-oriented focus on getting the job done or problem solved (Bem, 1981). Subordinates with masculine gender roles fit the task demands of managerial roles, as well as the stereotypes of successful leaders (e.g., Schein, Mueller, Lituchy, & Liu, 1996). Hence, traits provide drive and person-job fit. However, traits do not necessarily predict managerial advancement consistently across career stages. Some appear especially important early; for example, motivation to manage influences students' intentions to gain a managerial job, as well as advancement in early and mid career (Miner, 1993). Advancement motives and ambition predicted managerial advancement most in early career, maintained importance in late early career, but reduced to little impact in late career for advancing to upper manager (Howard & Bray, 1990).

Hypothesis 1 proposes that traits of managerial aspirations and masculinity predict initial and middle level managerial advancement (to lower or middle manager), reducing to little impact later (advancement to upper manager).

Human capital.

Human capital theory proposes that employees who invest in education, training, and work experience increase their knowledge and skill, increasing pay and job status later in their careers, because of increased productivity (Becker, 1993). Education increases knowledge, skills, and ways of solving problems; on-the-job training results in learning and perfecting skills that, as work experience increases, makes employees more productive. Human capital does not increase immediate rewards, but ensures future productivity, thus providing later increases in pay and job status (Becker, 1993).

Hypothesis 2 proposes that human capital investments of education, training and development, and challenging work assignments predict managerial advancement at mid- and later levels (to middle or upper manager) rather than early (to lower manager).

Selection and Promotion Opportunities

Starting opportunities

Motivated and talented individuals need to gain starting opportunities to initially enter management. Individuals enter career tournaments on organizational entry (Rosenbaum, 1984). If they win early (i.e., younger), they can progress to compete in increasingly more selective rounds. If they do not, they are restricted in play to consolation rounds or are eliminated completely from competition (Rosenbaum, 1984). Early loss, as shown by older age and more company tenure than other subordinates, has prevented subordinate advancement into management (e.g., Nicholson, 1993). Sponsorship of protçgçs by mentors in early career is an important starting opportunity for their winning initial career tournaments (Rosenbaum, 1984).

Hypothesis 3 proposes that favourable starting opportunities through career tournament wins (younger age, less company tenure) and mentor support predict early advancement (to lower manager) rather than mid or later.

Later opportunities: Promotion opportunities.

Once initial managerial advancement has occurred, further advancement should occur through promotion opportunities. Occupation type is important. Higher level 'primary' jobs (i.e., managerial and administrative occupations) provide promotion ladders through skill development and career paths/higher ceilings more than lower level, 'secondary' jobs do (e.g., clerical; Markham, Harlan, & Hackett, 1987). Most employees do not become managers on entry to the labor force, and thus do not enter the managerial and administrative occupation type. Occupational labor markets are thus most likely to facilitate middle and later advancement, rather than early.

Advancement beyond initial management to higher levels can arise internally to the organisation or externally. To advance further, employees can be promoted in their organisations or move jobs through changing employers/organisations or relocating, including for their employers (e.g., Brett, Stroh, & Reilly, 1992; Department of Finance, 1993-1994; Herriot, Gibson, Pemberton, & Pinder, 1993). Job moves through relocation and changing companies may be needed to advance beyond initial management levels when downsizing and outsourcing are occurring.

> Hypothesis 4 proposes that promotion opportunities (occupation type, managerial promotions, job moves) predict mid (to middle manager) and later (to upper manager) advancement rather than earlier (to lower manager).

Because the proportion of women managers is low beyond first-level management, women are likely to need particular selection and promotion opportunities to advance to middle- and later levels. Relocation has been found especially important for women's managerial advancement (Brett et al., 1992); changing organisations may be similarly important. Equal employment opportunity (EEO) and affirmative action (AA) may also be especially needed for women to advance past initial management. Hence,

> Hypothesis 5 proposes that women's advancement is predicted especially by job moves and EEO/AA, more for mid- and upper level (to middle or upper manager) than early (to lower manager) managerial advancement.

Social Processes

Social contacts are found especially important to advance to high management levels, providing support, options, and information (Burt, 1992). At high management levels, candidates need to fit with the organisation's values and culture and be compatible with senior others (Forbes & Piercy, 1991). Similarity to the managerial hierarchy is therefore important to advance in management, especially to top jobs (Baron & Pfeffer, 1994). The attraction-similarity thesis says that individuals are attracted to (Byrne, 1971), and prefer to work with (Baron & Pfeffer, 1994), similar others, partly because communication and development of trust are easier. Because managerial hierarchies are comprised chiefly of males, women are dissimilar to, and thus less preferred than, men. In studies of chiefly middle managers to CEOs, more female managerial hierarchies have been found to increase women's advancement in management (Konrad & Pfeffer, 1991; Pfeffer, Davis-Blake, & Julius, 1995; Tharenou, 1995; Tharenou & Conroy, 1994). As found for more female managerial hierarchies, career encouragement was especially related to women's advancing in management, including to high levels (Tharenou, 1995; Tharenou & Conroy, 1994), perhaps because it increases persistence when barriers exist (Tharenou, Latimer, & Conroy, 1994).

> Hypothesis 6 proposes that male managerial hierarchies reduce, and career encouragement increases, women's managerial advancement, especially for later (middle and upper manager) than earlier (lower manager) advancement.

In summary, some factors are most likely to predict initial advancement into management (e.g., starting factors); some to most predict initial and mid-level advancement (e.g., managerial traits); and others to especially predict mid- and upper-level advancement (human capital, selection and promotion processes, social processes), including gender-linked influences.

Method

Respondents and Data Collection

Questionnaire data were gathered from administrative, professional and clerical employees of the Commonwealth Public Service and private sector companies (e.g., banks). Fulltime employees below executive levels, where advancement could occur, were sought. Women form about 25% of Australian managers (Australian Bureau of Statistics, 1993); hence, a stratified sampling procedure was used where possible (e.g., through computerised personnel records) to mail to selected men and women using their grade levels and occupation streams. Data from the Commonwealth public sector and the banks (which had downsized since 1990-1991) showed that the percentage of management jobs had slightly increased at all major levels since 1990-1991 (including middle managers), whereas subordinate jobs decreased (Affirmative Action Agency, 1987-1996; Department of Finance, 1995-1996).

Survey data were collected at three times a year apart, using reply-paid post. The first and third repeated data collections only were used, to allow sufficient numbers of persons to have advanced to the next major level for analysis, and because managers have been shown to change jobs about every two years (Nicholson, 1990). On the first mail-out, the respondents (who were anonymous to the researcher) were able to volunteer by providing their addresses for a longitudinal study. The Time 1 return rate was 52% (5627: 2614 women, 3013 men); 83% volunteered for the longitudinal study. The Time 2 response was 79% (3434: 1593 women, 1841 men). The Time 3 response was 84% (2884; 1337 women, 1547 men). On the second and third mail-outs, about 9% of respondents were lost through incorrect addresses, death, or leaving fulltime employment. Part-time employees and owner managers were removed from the Time 3 sample, reducing it to 2547: 1167 women and 1380 men. At Time 1, the nonrespondents at Time 3 were different to the Time 3 respondents (chi-square analyses are available from the author upon request). At Time 1, compared to respondents, Time 3 nonrespondents were younger, less likely to have a spouse, had fewer children, were less educated, more likely clerks and sales and service workers and less likely managers, professionals and paraprofessionals, and more likely to work in smaller organisations and in the private sector.

Respondents provided their managerial level at Times 1, 2 and 3 on a 1 to 8 point-scale from 1, nonsupervisor/nonmanager to 8, chief executive officer (see Table 1). For the public sector and most private companies, their own classification system was inserted next to the eight levels to allow employees to place themselves accurately. In order to determine predictors of advancement at transition points for managerial advancement, the samples of interest were those who stayed at their Time 1 level versus those who advanced from that level to the next major management level two years later, at transition points. The upper manager/executive transition sample was removed as it was not of interest and very small. First-line supervisors and lower managers were combined into 'lower managers' because they may not have a major difference in level. Since Time 1, 56% of the Time 3 sample stayed at the same level, 32% went up in level (27% one major level, 5% more than one), and 11% moved down in level. With the restrictions imposed, 28% (712) of the Time 3 sample were excluded. The three cohort pairs for analysis were thus: (a) subordinate nonadvancers (586; 291 women, 295 men) versus subordinates who advanced to lower managers (272; 136 women, 136 men); (b) lower manager nonadvancers (377; 154 women, 223 men) versus lower managers who advanced to middle manager (184; 74 women, 110 men); and (c) middle manager nonadvancers (327; 146 women, 181 men) versus middle managers who advanced to upper manager (89; 39 women, 50 men). There were other items in the survey that allowed checks of whether changes in managerial levels had occurred: respondent position, occupation, number of subordinates, salary, time since last promotion, and gaining an internal promotion or external higher level job in the last year. Where a discrepancy existed, a decision was made by two independent raters (postgraduate students) based on answers to all questions to decide the managerial level.

The three cohort samples at Time 1 are described in Table 1. At Time 1, the subordinates (858) were chiefly in early career (44% were 20 to 29 years

Table 1 Description of samples of three cohorts at time 1 by percentage frequencies on demographic items[a]

Item	Subordinates	Lower managers	Middle managers	Item	Subordinates	Lower managers	Middle managers
Age[b]				Salary			
20 - 24	23	6	0	$15,001-25,000	24	3	0
25 - 29	21	23	6	$25,001-35,000	54	53	9
30 - 34	18	21	19	$35,001-45,000	19	27	39
35 - 39	13	21	26	$45,001-55,000	3	15	36
40 - 44	12	15	23	$55,001-65,000	0	2	10
45 - 49	8	9	16	$65,001-75,000	0	0	4
50 - 54	3	3	7	$75,001-85,000	0	0	1
55 - 59	2	2	2	$85,001-95,000	0	0	0
60 - 64	0	1	0	Over $95,000	0	0	1
Fulltime work tenure				Number subordinates			
< 5 years	25	9	2	None	97	5	4
5 up to 10 years	28	22	12	1 to 5	3	71	57
10 up to 15 years	18	24	21	6 to 10	0	21	
15 up to 20 years	12	18	22	11 to 15	0	4	9
20 up to 25 years	8	14	19	16 to 20	0	2	3
25 up to 30 years	5	7	14	21 to 25	0	1	3
30 up to 35 years	3	5	7	26 to 30	0	1	0
>35 years	2	2	4	Over 30	0	1	2
Organization tenure				Education level			
< 5 years	54	33	33	Some secondary			
				school 3	3	1	
5 up to 10 years	27	29	21	10 years completed	13	17	12
10 up to 15 years	11	16	15	12 years completed	28	32	27
15 up to 20 years	5	10	10	Technical college			
				course 11	11	6	
20 up to 25 years	2	7	9	Associate diploma	4	4	4
25 up to 30 years	1	3	7	Diploma	3	2	4
30 up to 35 years	0	2	2	Undergraduate			
				degree	28	19	25
>35 years	0	0	2	Honours/graduate			
				diploma	8	8	15
Gender				Masters' degree	2	3	4
Women	50	41	44	PhD 1	1	2	
Men	50	59	56				
				Organization size			
Spouse				Up to 1000	31	28	36
Spouse	52	70	78	1001-2000	8	5	8
No spouse	48	30	22	2001-4000	13	13	13
				4001-8000	9	8	10
Dependent children				>8000 38	46	32	
None	71	56	43				
One or more	11	15	15	Industry			
Two	13	20	28	Finance, property			
Three	4	6	11	& business services	24	34	25
Four	1	3	2	Public administration	64	53	59
Five	0	0	0	Community services	9	8	10
Six or more	0	0	0	Other	3	5	6
Occupation type				Employer			
Managers	0	20	50	Public sector	69	60	66
Professionals	38	31	32	Private sector	31	40	34
Paraprofessionals	20	17	9				
Clerks	39	29	8				
Other	3	3	1				

[a]Each cohort combines those who stayed at that level and those who advanced from that level to the next major management level two years later.
[b]No employees were 19 or fewer years.

old; 53% had fewer than 10 years fulltime employment; 52% no spouse; 71% no children); the lower managers (561) were in early to mid career (44% were 25 to 34; 46% had 5 to 15 years fulltime employment; 70% had a spouse; 44% had at least one child); and the middle managers (416) were in mid career (49% were 35 to 44 years; 43% had 10 to 20 years fulltime employment; 78% had a spouse; 57% had at least one child). The relativities on other items were consistent with the three management levels: (a) 78% of subordinates earned $15,000 to $25,000 (Australian), almost none had subordinates, and their occupations and positions were coded as professionals, paraprofessionals, and clerks; (b) 80% of lower managers earned $25,000 to $45,000, 95% had subordinates (71% had 1 to 5, 22% had more than 5), and most were coded as managers, professionals, paraprofessionals, and clerks; (c) 75% of middle managers earned $45,000 to $65,000, 96% had subordinates (57% 1 to 5, 38% had more than 5), and most were coded as managers and professionals. Most respondents were from public administration, finance, and community services, and were public servants.

Measures

Managerial traits and human capital.

Masculinity was the average of the 10, 7-point items of the short form of the Bem (1981) Sex-Role Inventory. Managerial aspirations were the average of the 13, 5-point items of Tharenou and Terry's scale (in press; a = .94, test-retest reliability = .77), measuring the extent to which the respondent desires and intends to advance to a (higher) managerial level. The education item is given in Table 1. Training and development was the average of the 6, 7-point items of Tharenou and Conroy's (1994; a = .81) scale measuring participation in training and development courses and on-the-job development activities. Challenging work assignments in the first 3 months on the job and since then were the average of 2, 7-point items (Tharenou and Conroy, 1994; a = .77).

Starting factors.

Age and company tenure items are given in Table 1. Mentor career support was the average of the 9, 7-point items that emerged as the first factor (sponsoring, coaching, and challenging work) from Ragins and McFarlin's (1990) mentor support scale with the present sample. Respondents (9%) who did not answer the scale because they reported not having had a mentor were given scores of zero.

Promotion opportunities.

Occupation type was the average of codes assigned to the respondents' occupations and positions using the Australian Classification of Occupations (Department of Employment and Industrial Relations, 1987), decreasing from

1, managers and administrators to 6, sales and service (Table 1). Managerial promotions (total number) were from 1, none to 6, 9 or more. Job moves were 2, 5-point items of the number of times employees had relocated or changed organisations for advancement (Tharenou & Conroy, 1994). EEO was the number of years the organisation had had an EEO policy, from 1, none to 6, 11 or more years. Affirmative action averaged 2, 7-point items of the extent to which the organisation provides special employment and training programs for women and minority groups.

Social processes.

Male hierarchy was the average of 3, 5-point items measuring the extent to which the managerial hierarchy was male (Tharenou & Conroy, 1994; Tharenou et al., 1994; a = .64). Career encouragement was the average of 3, 7-point items of the extent to which employees reported encouragement from colleagues and more senior organizational staff for career development and promotion (Tharenou & Conroy, 1994; Tharenou et al., 1994; a = .80).

Demographic variables.

Organizational and individual demographic variables (given in Table 1) were taken into account in the multivariate analysis: Employer sector, organizational size, gender, marital status, and number of dependent children.

Method of Analysis

The aim of the study was to explain advancing in management level. Hence, predictors of advancement versus nonadvancement were examined. To do this, three contrasting pairs of cohorts were analysed separately by discriminant analyses (DA). Employees were contrasted on their Time 1 measures (demographics, traits, human capital, starting opportunities, promotion opportunities, social processes) to discriminate those at Time 3 who stayed at their Time 1 management level (nonadvancers) from those who advanced to the next major management level two years later (advancers). The DAs were conducted on the three cohorts of nonadvancers versus advancers previously described. For all three DAs, the nonadvancers were a larger sample than the advancers, especially for the upper managers. In DA, unequal group sizes have been shown acceptable for analysis (Tabachnick & Fiddell, 1989). However, to ensure this was so, the DAs were also performed drawing a random sample of the larger group similar in size to the smaller group. Because the same pattern of results emerged with equal sized groups, the full samples are presented here. Missing data reduced the sample sizes by 3%.

Results

Table 2 provides the correlation matrix and alpha coefficients for the variables, showing there were not problems with lack of reliability or with multicolinearity (intercorrelations of greater than .70, Tabachnick & Fidell, 1989). Tables 3 (total samples), 4 (women), and 5 (men) present the results of the discriminant analyses.

The three DAs comparing advancers with nonadvancers each yielded one significant function (p =. 00). The variance explained (squared canonical correlations) was: (a) 27.44% for subordinates versus those who advanced to lower manager, (b) 40.07% for lower managers versus those who advanced to middle manager, and (c) 30.25% for middle managers versus those who advanced to upper manager. The groups were correctly classified 61.23%, 67.40%, and 67.57% of the time, respectively, exceeding the 50% by chance. The structural loadings combined with the lower group mean centroids (Table 3) supported Hypothesis 1. Managerial aspirations and masculinity predicted initial advancement into management (to lower manager) and mid-level advancement, but not later advancement (to upper manger).

Partially supporting Hypothesis 2, education, training and development, and challenging work assignments predicted mid and later advancement more than earlier (Table 3); none predicted earlier advancement (to lower level manager). They did predict middle level managerial advancement, apart from challenging work. Only challenging work predicted later, upper level advancement.

Supporting Hypothesis 3, favourable starting opportunities through being younger than older, having fewer than more years' company tenure, and having mentor support predicted initial managerial advancement but not mid or upper advancement. The effects were less consistent for women than men on age and tenure (Tables 4, 5).

Partially supporting Hypothesis 4, promotion opportunities of high occupation type, managerial promotions, and job moves predicted mid- and later, upper-level advancement (not occupation type or organisation change for upper advancement) than early advancement (only relocation predicted). Consistent with Hypothesis 5 (Table 4), job moves predicted advancement for women (relocation, organisation change) more than men (Table 5), for whom they were not significant. However, not supporting Hypothesis 5, job moves for women were not especially predictive later than earlier; relocation predicted advancement at all stages, whereas organisation changes predicted only mid-level advancement. Not supporting Hypothesis 5, women's advancement was not predicted by EEO and AA more than men's; more years of organizational EEO reduced men's mid-level advancement.

Supporting Hypothesis 6, overall, managerial hierarchies reduced, and career encouragement increased, women's advancement, but not especially for later than earlier advancement. In support, more male hierarchies increased

Correlations

Variables	1	2	3	4	5	6	7	8	9	10	11	12	13	14	15	16	17	18	19	20	21	22	23
1. Employer sector	-																						
2. Organization size	19	-																					
3. Education	-18	-18	-																				
4. Age	-12	-11	-09	-																			
5. Company tenure	15	17	-27	46	-																		
6. Mentor	12	04	-03	-15	-10	85																	
7. Occupation type	13	12	-28	-15	-09	-04	93																
8. Masculinity	10	03	-04	03	-02	12	-08	88															
9. Aspirations	16	03	08	-22	-16	15	-04	38	95														
10. Training	-24	08	09	36	19	10	-41	15	-01	79													
11. Challenging work	01	02	09	02	09	21	-28	12	02	35	72												
12. Spouse	-05	00	05	-30	-19	02	16	-06	04	-21	-10	-											
13. Children	-05	-01	-05	-35	-24	05	15	-03	00	-25	-08	45	-										
14. Gender	11	10	-05	11	25	-08	-08	-03	08	08	04	-13	-22	-									
15. EEO	-13	19	-08	00	09	04	09	-06	-06	-00	01	02	-00	03	-								
16. AA	-55	03	01	03	-10	03	-04	-03	-10	20	02	05	03	-08	20	94							
17. Promotions	13	07	13	42	37	06	-30	19	04	50	21	-27	-29	18	-01	-05	-						
18. Relocated	27	09	-05	21	25	-04	-13	12	08	12	07	-13	-19	21	-03	-15	38	-					
19. Changed orgs	-11	-23	13	24	-24	-01	-18	11	05	31	03	-09	-12	-04	-18	04	04	24	-				
20. Encouragement	-14	10	-07	-04	00	32	-05	08	03	26	30	00	01	-03	13	21	07	16	-05	79			
21. Male hierarchy	62	23	-15	-09	19	10	11	07	13	-20	02	-08	-08	23	-09	-48	14	31	-13	-11	66		
22. Managerial level Time 1	08	-03	07	30	30	08	-48	21	10	54	31	-23	-25	07	-07	-07	57	26	22	05	08	-	
23. Managerial level Time 3	11	-01	09	24	24	11	-45	23	15	51	29	-21	-23	07	-08	-08	53	26	22	07.	09	88	-

Note. Decimal points have been omitted from correlations. Correlations greater than .05 are significant at p<.05, at .07 are significant at p<.01, and at .08 are significant at p<.001. Alpha coefficients are in the diagonal. Dashes indicate where alphas could not be calculated; N=1835; orgs= organisations.

Table 2 Correlations and Alpha Coefficients for All Variables for the Total Time 1 Sample

Predictor variables	Structural loadings: S LM	Subordinates M	Subordinates SD	Lower manager M	Lower manager SD	Structural loadings: LM MM	Lower manager M	Lower manager SD	Middle manager M	Middle manager SD	Structural loadings: MM UM	Middle manager M	Middle manager SD	Upper manager M	Upper manager SD
Sector	.53 ***	1.17	0.38	1.31	0.46	.02	1.34	0.48	1.35	0.48	.48 **	1.25	0.43	1.41	0.50
Org size	.36 **	3.04	1.73	3.41	1.64	-.08	3.43	1.71	3.30	1.71	.19	2.92	1.70	3.17	1.70
Spouse	.16	1.47	0.50	1.52	0.50	-.09	1.31	0.46	1.27	0.44	-.33 *	1.24	0.43	1.14	0.35
Children	-.00	1.71	0.45	1.71	0.45	-.22 *	1.60	0.50	1.49	0.49	.05	1.43	0.50	1.45	0.50
Gender	-.04	1.51	0.50	1.50	0.50	.03	1.58	0.49	1.60	0.49	.04	1.56	0.81	1.57	0.50
Masculinity	.30 *	4.58	0.93	4.76	0.95	.27 **	4.84	0.82	5.04	0.80	.30	5.06	0.87	5.25	0.78
Aspirations	.51 ***	3.49	0.92	3.77	0.85	.40 ***	3.59	0.91	3.92	0.82	.20	3.74	1.51	3.87	0.87
Age	-.41 ***	4.29	1.92	3.82	1.66	-.04	4.63	1.77	4.70	1.49	.24	5.49	1.84	5.77	1.56
Tenure	-.41 ***	1.87	1.20	1.59	0.97	-.10	2.52	1.54	2.38	1.56	.08	2.83	1.65	2.94	2.00
Mentor	.50 ***	3.99	1.87	4.53	1.54	.04	4.37	1.70	4.44	1.64	.08	4.49	2.45	4.59	1.47
Education	-.13	4.80	2.26	4.62	2.19	.39 ***	4.16	2.19	4.98	2.44	-.03	5.27	1.27	5.22	2.38
T&D	.02	3.18	1.34	3.19	1.36	.41 ***	3.89	1.25	4.36	1.26	-.04	5.29	1.67	5.24	1.14
Challenge	.12	3.73	2.08	3.89	1.95	.15	4.54	1.90	4.79	1.76	.47 **	5.13	1.02	5.72	1.44
Occ type	.15	3.42	1.40	3.55	1.38	-.47 ***	3.02	1.43	2.38	1.45	-.08	1.76	1.07	1.70	0.98
Promotion	.04	1.54	0.81	1.56	0.77	.43 ***	2.32	0.78	2.66	0.99	.41 **	2.98	1.42	3.32	1.20
Relocated	.33 **	1.50	0.90	1.69	1.04	-.23 *	1.94	1.39	2.25	1.52	.36 *	2.19	1.41	2.60	1.62
Changed org	-.02	1.64	1.10	1.63	0.91	.34 ***	1.67	1.08	2.04	1.32	.01	2.33	1.26	2.33	1.43
EEO	-.10	4.40	1.24	4.32	1.32	-.17	4.44	1.16	4.27	1.15	-.10	4.18	2.20	4.08	1.39
AA	-.14	4.29	1.98	4.11	2.14	-.08	3.93	2.04	3.78	2.16	-.25	4.01	1.72	3.61	2.01
Encouragement	.37 **	3.09	1.65	3.48	1.87	-.10	3.48	1.60	3.33	1.83	.12	3.40	1.72	3.56	1.87
Male hierarchy	.50 ***	3.71	0.16	3.77	0.21	.02	3.78	0.22	3.79	0.20	.43 **	3.74	0.20	3.81	0.24
Canonical R²	27.44 ***					40.07 **					30.25 **				
	Group centroids					Group centroids					Group centroids				
	S -.20					LM -.31					MM -.17				
	LM .42					MM .61					UM .61				
N	564,264					361,182					320,87				

Note. S=subordinates; LM=lower managers; MM=middle managers; UM=upper managers; org=organization; T&D=training and development; Occ= occupation.
*p<.05. **p<.01. ***p<.001.

Table 3 Results of three discriminant analyses for total sample

Predictor variables	Structural loadings: S LM	Subordinates M	Subordinates SD	Lower manager M	Lower manager SD	Structural loadings: LM MM	Lower manager M	Lower manager SD	Middle manager M	Middle manager SD	Structural loadings: MM UM	Middle manager M	Middle manager SD	Upper manager M	Upper manager SD
Sector	.53 ***	1.17	0.38	1.31	0.46	.02	1.34	0.48	1.35	0.48	.48 **	1.25	0.43	1.41	0.50
Org size	.36 **	3.04	1.73	3.41	1.64	-.08	3.43	1.71	3.30	1.71	.19	2.92	1.70	3.17	1.70
Spouse	.16	1.47	0.50	1.52	0.50	-.09	1.31	0.46	1.27	0.44	-.33 *	1.24	0.43	1.14	0.35
Children	-.00	1.71	0.45	1.71	0.45	-.22 *	1.60	0.50	1.49	0.49	.05	1.43	0.50	1.45	0.50
Gender	-.04	1.51	0.50	1.50	0.50	.03	1.58	0.49	1.60	0.49	.04	1.56	0.50	1.57	0.50
Masculinity	.30 *	4.58	0.93	4.76	0.95	.27 **	4.84	0.82	5.04	0.80	.30	5.06	0.81	5.25	0.78
Aspirations	.51 ***	3.49	0.92	3.77	0.85	.40 ***	3.59	0.91	3.92	0.82	.20	3.74	0.87	3.87	0.87
Age	-.41 ***	4.29	1.92	3.82	1.66	-.04	4.63	1.77	4.70	1.49	.24	5.49	1.51	5.77	1.56
Tenure	-.41 ***	1.87	1.20	1.59	0.97	-.10	2.52	1.54	2.38	1.56	.08	2.83	1.84	2.94	2.00
Mentor	.50 ***	3.99	1.87	4.53	1.54	.04	4.37	1.70	4.44	1.64	.08	4.49	1.65	4.59	1.47
Education	-.13	4.80	2.26	4.62	2.19	.39 ***	4.16	2.19	4.98	2.44	-.03	5.27	2.45	5.22	2.38
T&D	.02	3.18	1.34	3.19	1.36	.41 ***	3.89	1.25	4.36	1.26	-.04	5.29	1.27	5.24	1.14
Challenge	.12	3.73	2.08	3.89	1.95	.15	4.54	1.90	4.79	1.76	.47 **	5.13	1.67	5.72	1.44
Occ type	.15	3.42	1.40	3.55	1.38	-.47 ***	3.02	1.43	2.38	1.45	-.08	1.76	1.02	1.70	0.98
Promotion	.04	1.54	0.81	1.56	0.77	.43 ***	2.32	0.78	2.66	0.99	.41 **	2.98	1.07	3.32	1.20
Relocated	.33 **	1.50	0.90	1.69	1.04	.23 *	1.94	1.39	2.25	1.52	.36 *	2.19	1.42	2.60	1.62
Changed org	-.02	1.64	1.10	1.63	0.91	.34 ***	1.67	1.08	2.04	1.32	.01	2.33	1.41	2.33	1.43
EEO	-.10	4.40	1.24	4.32	1.32	-.17	4.44	1.16	4.27	1.15	-.10	4.18	1.26	4.08	1.39
AA	-.14	4.29	1.98	4.11	2.14	-.08	3.93	2.04	3.78	2.16	-.25	4.01	2.20	3.61	2.01
Encouragement	.37 **	3.09	1.65	3.48	1.87	-.10	3.48	1.60	3.33	1.83	.12	3.40	1.72	3.56	1.87
Male hierarchy	.50 ***	3.71	0.16	3.77	0.21	.02	3.78	0.22	3.79	0.20	.43 **	3.74	0.20	3.81	0.24
Canonical R²	30.59 ***					51.62 **					38.83				
Group centroids	S -.22					LM -.42					MM -.21				
	LM .46					MM .86					UM .82				
N	277,133					150,73					141,37				

Note. S=subordinates; LM=lower managers; MM=middle managers; UM=upper managers; org=organization; T&D=training and development; Occ= occupation.
*p<.05. **p<.01. ***p<.001.

Table 4 Results of three discriminant analyses for women

Predictor variables	Structural loadings: S LM	Subordinates M	SD	Lower manager M	SD	Structural loadings: LM MM	Lower manager M	SD	Middle manager M	SD	Structural loadings: MM UM	Middle manager M	SD	Upper manager M	SD
Sector	.60 ***	1.14	0.35	1.31	0.47	.19	1.39	0.49	1.46	0.50	.53 **	1.36	0.48	1.58	0.50
Org size	.35 *	3.47	1.71	3.03	1.59	-.03	3.62	1.64	3.58	1.67	.29	3.14	1.73	3.56	1.64
Spouse	.05	1.46	0.50	1.47	0.50	-.23	1.27	0.44	1.19	0.40	-.16	1.12	0.33	1.08	0.27
Children	-.04	1.69	0.46	1.67	0.47	-.30	1.48	0.50	1.37	0.48	.08	1.27	0.44	1.30	0.46
Masculinity	.31 *	4.52	0.96	4.75	0.93	.28	4.80	0.81	4.97	0.80	.18	5.07	0.84	5.20	0.81
Aspirations	.42 **	3.52	0.95	3.81	0.86	.37 *	3.75	0.83	3.98	0.78	.11	3.76	0.91	3.85	0.89
Age	-.46 ***	4.47	1.91	3.84	1.69	.00	4.85	1.63	4.85	1.54	.17	5.73	1.44	5.94	1.42
Tenure	-.36 *	1.66	1.36	2.01	1.15	-.01	2.84	1.68	2.83	1.74	.15	3.49	2.01	3.74	2.17
Mentor	.50 ***	3.81	1.89	4.48	1.53	.13	4.23	1.70	4.40	1.60	.11	4.39	1.59	4.54	1.32
Education	-.17	4.73	2.20	5.01	2.12	.24	4.14	2.15	4.54	2.35	-.12	4.73	2.38	4.48	2.37
T&D	-.10	3.38	1.35	3.27	1.35	.41 **	3.96	1.27	4.35	1.26	-.07	5.22	1.38	5.15	1.11
Challenge	-.06	3.81	2.15	3.90	1.87	.17	4.54	1.93	4.77	1.19	.41 *	5.19	1.72	5.76	1.42
Occ type	.09	3.30	1.33	3.39	1.40	-.44 **	2.88	1.44	2.40	1.40	-.05	1.78	1.07	1.74	1.00
Promotion	.08	1.69	0.88	1.63	0.91	.45 **	2.48	0.89	2.80	1.06	.43 *	3.20	1.19	3.64	1.27
Relocated	.18	1.57	0.98	1.70	1.10	.25	2.31	1.56	2.61	1.66	.29	2.56	1.58	2.96	1.70
Changed org	-.05	1.65	1.14	1.69	0.93	.17	1.68	1.12	1.83	1.22	.00	2.14	1.35	2.14	1.43
EEO	.02	4.36	1.26	4.38	1.37	-.32 *	4.52	1.20	4.24	1.13	.08	4.22	1.30	4.31	1.40
AA	-.11	4.10	1.91	4.26	2.06	-.19	3.76	1.99	3.48	2.08	-.36	3.75	2.06	3.12	2.08
Encouragement	.18	3.15	1.69	3.39	1.92	-.02	3.36	1.59	3.34	1.88	.03	3.32	1.78	3.37	1.77
Male hierarchy	.55 ***	3.71	0.17	3.79	0.22	.20	3.82	0.22	3.86	0.23	.40 *	3.84	0.22	3.33	0.23
Canonical R^2	33.03 ***					33.77 **					33.16				

Group centroids		Group centroids		Group centroids	
S	-.24	LM	-.26	MM	-.18
LM	.52	MM	.50	UM	.66
N	287,131		211,109		179,50

Note. S=subordinates; LM=lower managers; MM=middle managers; UM=upper managers; org=organization; T&D=training and development; Occ= occupation.

*p<.05. **p<.01. ***p<.001.

Table 5 Results of three discriminant analyses for men

men's early advancement and reduced women's middle level advancement. Not supporting Hypothesis 6, male managerial hierarchies predicted later advancement both for men and women. Career encouragement predicted women's early managerial advancement but not men's (but not women's later advancement, contrary to Hypothesis 6).

Discussion

The results of the study suggest that managerial advancement is explained by individual, interpersonal and organisational factors that vary in importance at transitions to initial, mid, and upper level advancement. Advancement into management arises from favourable starting circumstances in terms of early career tournament wins and from individuals' managerial traits through motives and person-job fit. Middle level advancement continues to arise from managerial traits, combined with knowledge and skill from earlier human capital investments, and promotion opportunities through managerial promotions and job moves. Later, upper level managerial advancement arises from returns on earlier challenging work assignments and from male hierarchies. As expected, there were gender-linked effects at different transitions. Similarity to the male managerial hierarchy assists advancement, thus reducing women's advancement (middle level) and increasing men's (early). Career encouragement was needed by women early to advance, and not men. However, the effects for social processes were earlier rather than later for advancement. Women also needed to use job moves to advance at all levels more than men, rather than simply at mid and later levels.

This study is rare in assessing predictors of advancement by comparing cohorts who actually advanced with those who did not, on earlier measures of the predictors, at increasingly higher transition points (initial, mid, upper stages). It thus allows inferences to be drawn about the process of advancement.

The Process of Managerial Advancement

To gain entry to management, the results support the view that subordinates need to win early career tournaments (Rosenbaum, 1990). Early winning (in terms of being younger than older, fewer than more years in the organisation) predicts entry to management, as found (Nicholson, 1993). Mentor support through sponsoring, coaching, and providing challenging work also helps protÇgÇs' win in early competitions for management jobs, as proposed (Rosenbaum, 1984). In a different vein, career tournaments also operate for mid-level advancement. To gain middle level managerial advancement, the results suggest managers need to gain promotion. Managerial promotions allow lower managers to remain in career tournaments and thus be able to compete, and provide ability signals of career velocity and job status that increase chances in the next competition (Rosenbaum, 1990) — to middle manager.

To gain entry to management, the results suggest that motives for, and fit to, the managerial role help. Subordinates with high aspirations to gain a managerial position satisfy their goal by advancement. As found (Howard & Bray, 1990), the strongest effects of advancement motives are on managerial advancement in early career. Also important, but to a lesser degree, was the fit to the managerial role. Subordinates with masculine gender roles fit the task demands of managerial roles, and can implement their self-concepts through gaining managerial roles (Super, 1957). The managerial traits need to be sustained to advance to mid levels, as found (e.g., Howard & Bray, 1990).

For middle level advancement, knowledge and skills — factors linked to future productivity — are predictive. Advancement is competitive because there are fewer middle management positions than lower management, and middle management is a difficult role (Floyd & Wooldridge, 1994). Consistent with human capital theory, highly educated managers who have been trained and developed gain middle-level advancement, because they provide employers with greater productivity through increased knowledge and skills (Becker, 1993). Becker proposed that human capital returns are lagged; mid-level advancement is the most likely period when returns from education and training and development are realised. As well, education and training and development signal potential productivity to employers (Spence, 1993, 1994). Employers especially need signals in uncertain selection situations to recognise suitable individuals (Spence, 1973, 1974); middle manager positions provide more uncertain selection situations (more competitive, more difficult) than lower management.

For middle level advancement, the results suggest that lower managers need promotion opportunities. Lower managers in lower occupation types (e.g., clerical) rather than higher (e.g., managerial and administrative) advance less in this sample, because of shorter promotion ladders and lower ceilings (Markham et al., 1987).

To advance to upper level management, the results suggest that human capital as challenging work assignments is needed. Challenging work assignments develop the credibility and familiarity and trust that is important for senior others to feel comfortable with candidates (Forbes & Piercy, 1991). Retrospective, qualitative studies also indicate that late career advancement is linked to earlier challenging work assignments, and that these were key factors for both men (Forbes & Piercy, 1991) and women (Mainiero, 1994) to advance to high levels in later career.

Gender Differences

For initial and middle level advancement, the results suggest that similarity by gender to the managerial hierarchy predicts advancement, rather than, as expected, for mid and later advancement. Male hierarchies helped men subordinates gain management jobs, thus setting them on a career path. It appears that, because men are similar to the male hierarchy and women are not, men are preferred for entry to the management hierarchy. Homosocial reproduction results (Kanter, 1977). It was unexpected that male hierarchies would not reduce women's advancement to upper levels, and that effects for male hierarchies would be earlier. Previous studies of effects on women's advancement of male hierarchies have been chiefly of middle managers through to executive levels (Konrad & Pfeffer, 1991; Pfeffer, Davis-Blake, & Julius, 1995; Tharenou, 1995; Tharenou & Conroy, 1994), and thus can only assess effects on mid to later, upper advancement. The present study suggests the effect is also for early and middle advancement.

To gain initial managerial advancement, the results suggest that women subordinates have to use their own initiative (relocation) and others' assistance (through career encouragement) to advance. Because male managerial hierarchies favour men in this sample for early advancement, women would need encouragement from superiors and colleagues to persist in seeking initial managerial roles (Tharenou et al., 1994), and may relocate to provide a way to advance.

To gain middle level advancement, men advance through traditional promotion opportunities (occupation type, promotions). By contrast, women managers need additional promotion factors. Women continue to need to move jobs through relocation, as for early advancement, unlike men. Women also need to change organisations to advance to middle levels. This is likely to be because there are more barriers to women's advancement beyond initial levels than men's. The male hierarchy reduces women's middle-level advancement in this sample, presumably because women are dissimilar and therefore preferred less than men. Women managers also report greater discrimination than men for advancement at mid (and early) career (Murrell, Olson, & Frieze, 1995; Schneer & Reitman, 1995). Perhaps job moves through changing organisations and relocating must be used by women managers to overcome discrimination and advance. EEO did not help the women managers of this sample to advance in mid-career, but reduced men's. More years of EEO may result in men being advanced less automatically than when it has been introduced fewer years.

For later, upper level advancement in management, the results suggest promotion opportunities continue to be important, but differently for women and men. Men in this sample continue to advance later in their careers through promotion, suggesting career tournaments continue to operate for them (e.g., Herriot et al., 1993). By contrast, women need to relocate - suggesting barriers continue to operate for them, or family needs (Brett et al., 1992). It is reasonable to assume that women managers will perceive their male hierarchies as detrimental to their advancement, because male hierarchies favoured the men in early career and disadvantaged women in mid-career. Relocation is thus a solution to barriers. It was unexpected that male hierarchies would not reduce women's advancement to upper levels. The present results indicate that organisations with male hierarchies increase later, upper level advancement both for women and men. The result suggests that similarity, with its attendance effects on preference, does not cause advancement at this level. The impact of male hierarchies is consistent with male occupations and 'organisations' having greater rewards than female.

Limitations and Future Research

Limitations of the present study render findings less convincing than desirable. These include small sample sizes, the limited sample (chiefly public servants), self-report data, the classification of nonadvancers and advancers, and the low variance suggesting omitted predictors. To overcome the low variance, future research needs to assess the impact of other variables found important to advancement, including informal social networks (Burt, 1992), politics (Ferris & Judge, 1991), and managerial skills and job performance. Inferences have been drawn about the process of advancement from predictors at the three transition points. However, future research needs to better explain the process by assessing predictors for the same cohorts as they advance through increasing transitions.

The present results help explain problems with the effectiveness of, and gender representation in, management. In this study, managerial advancement arises from both meritorious (education, training and development) and nonmeritorious (age, managerial aspirations, managerial hierarchies) factors, as well as gender-linked factors (managerial hierarchies, occupation type). The nonmeritorious and gender-linked factors affect initial advancement into management, perhaps contributing to the lack of effectiveness found for managers (e.g., Hogan, Curphy, & Hogan, 1994) and the underrepresentation of women in management. Hence, structured objective procedures should be implemented for selection and promotion of managers (especially early) and identification of individuals for training and development. Organisations should help employees increase their human capital from access to training and development, education, and challenging work assignments. Programs should enable interpersonal support (mentors, career encouragement). The first women should be appointed to particular managerial positions to reduce the male managerial hierarchy (Pfeffer et al., 1995).

References

Affirmative Action Agency. 1987-1996. *Affirmative action data*. Canberra: Affirmative Action Agency.

Australian Bureau of Statistics. 1993. *The labour force Australia* (Catalogue no. 6203.0). Canberra: Australian Government Publishing Service.

Department of Finance. 1993-1994. *Australian public service statistical Bulletin.* Canberra: CPN Publications.

Department of Finance. 1995-1996. *APS statistical bulletin* 1995-1996. Canberra.

Baron, J.N., & Pfeffer, J. 1994. The social psychology of organizations and inequality. *Social Psychology Quarterly,* 57: 190-209.

Becker, G.S. 1993. *Human capital.* Chicago: University of Chicago Press.

Bem, S.L. 1981. *Bem Sex-Role Inventory.* New York: Consulting Psychologists Press, Inc.

Brett, J.M., Stroh, L.K., & Reilly, A.H. 1992. Job transfer. In C.L. Cooper and I.T. Robertson (Eds.), *International Review of Industrial and Organizational Psychology:* 323-362. New York: Wiley.

Burt, R.S. 1992. *Structural holes.* Cambridge, MA: Harvard University Press.

Byrne, D. 1971. *The attraction paradigm.* New York: Academic Press.

Department of Employment and Industrial Relations. 1987. *Australian standard classification of occupations.* Canberra: Australian Government Publishing Service.

Ferris, G.R., & Judge, T.A. 1991. Personnel/human resources management: A political perspective. *Journal of Management,* 17: 447-488.

Filipowski, D. 1993. Downsizing isn't always rightsizing. *Personnel Journal,* November, 71.

Floyd, S.W., & Wooldridge, B. 1994. Dinosaurs and dynamos? Recognizing middle management's strategic role. *Academy of Management Executive,* 8: 47-57.

Forbes, J.B., & Piercy, J.E. 1991. *Corporate mobility and paths to the top.* NY: Quorum Books.

Gordon, D.M. 1996. *Fat and mean: The corporate squeeze of working Americans and the myth of managerial downsizing.* New York: The Free Press.

Herriot, P., Gibson, G., Pemberton, C., & Pinder, R. 1993. Dashed hopes. *Journal of Occupational and Organizational Psychology,* 66: 115-123.

Hogan, R., Curphy, G.J., & Hogan, J. 1994. What do we know about leadership. *American Psychologist,* 49: 493-504.

Howard, A., & Bray, D.W. 1990. Predictions of managerial success over long periods of time. In K.E. Clark, & M.B. Clark (Eds.), *Measures of leadership:* 113-130. West Orange, NJ: Leadership Library of America.

Kanter, R.M. 1977. *Men and women of the corporation.* New York: Basic Books.

Konrad, A.M., & Pfeffer, J. 1991. Understanding the hiring of women and minorities in educational institutions. *Sociology of Education,* 64: 141-157.

Littler, C.R., Dunford, R., Bramble, T., & Hede, A. 1997. The dynamics of downsizing in Australia and New Zealand. *Asia Pacific Journal of Human Resources,* 35: 65-79.

Lord, R.G., De Vader, C.L., & Alliger, G.M. 1986. A meta-analysis of the relationship between personality traits and leadership perceptions. *Journal of Applied Psychology,* 71: 402-410.

Mainiero, L.A. 1994. Getting anointed for advancement: The case of executive women. *Academy of Management Executive,* 8: 53-67.

Markham, W.T., Harlan, S.L., & Hackett, E.J. 1987. Promotion opportunity in organizations. *Research in Personnel and Human Resources Management:* 223-287. New York: JAI Press.

McClelland, D.C. 1985. *Human motivation.* Glenview, IL: Scott, Foresman.

Miner, J.B. 1993. *Role motivation theories.* Routledge: London.

Murrell, A.J., Olson, J., & Hanson Frieze, I. 1995. Sexual harassment and gender discrimination. *Journal of Social Issues,* 51: 139-149.

Nicholson, N. 1990. The transition cycle. In S. Fisher and C.L. Cooper (Eds.), *The psychology of change and transitions:* 83-108. New York: Wiley.

Nicholson, N. 1993. Purgatory or place of safety? *Human Relations,* 46: 1369-1389.

Pfeffer, J., Davis-Blake, A., & Julius, D.J. 1995. The effect of affirmative action officer salary changes on managerial diversity. *Industrial Relations,* 34: 73-94.

Ragins, B.R., & McFarlin, D.B. 1990. Perceptions of gender roles in cross-gender mentoring relationships. *Journal of Vocational Behavior,* 37: 321-339.

Ragins, B.R., & Sundstrom, E. 1989. Gender and power in organizations. *Psychological Bulletin,* 105: 51-88.

Rosenbaum, J.E. 1984. *Career mobility in a corporate hierarchy.* New York: Academic Press.

Rosenbaum, J.E. 1990. Structural models of organizational careers. In R.L. Breiger (Ed.), *Social mobility and social structure:* 272-397. Cambridge: Cambridge University Press.

Schein, V.E., Mueller, R., Lituchy, T., & Liu, J. 1996. Think manager-think male. *Journal of Organizational Behavior,* 17: 33-41.

Schneer, J.A., & Reitman, F. 1995. The impact of gender as managerial careers unfold. *Journal of Vocational Behavior,* 47: 290-315.

Spence, A.M. 1973. Job market signaling. *Quarterly Journal of Economics,* 87, 355-375.

Spence, A.M. 1974. *Market signaling.* Cambridge, MA: Harvard University Press.

Super, D.E. 1957. *The psychology of careers.* New York: Harper.

Tabachnick, B., & Fidell, L.S. 1989. *Using multivariate statistics.* New York: Harper and Row.

Tharenou, P. 1995. Correlates of women's chief executive status. *Journal of Career Development,* 21: 201-212.

Tharenou, P. 1997. Managerial career advancement. In C.L. Cooper and I.T. Robertson (Eds.), *International Review of Industrial and Organizational Psychology:* 39-94. New York: Wiley.

Tharenou, P., & Conroy, D.K. 1994. Men and women managers' advancement. *Applied Psychology: An International Review,* 43: 5-31.

Tharenou, P., Latimer, S., & Conroy, D.K. 1994. How do you make it to the top? *Academy of Management Journal,* 37: 899-931.

Tharenou, P., & Terry, D.J. in press. Reliability and validity of scales to measure managerial aspirations. *Educational and Psychological Measurement.*

GAYLORD S